CREATIVE ARTS IN INTERDISCIPLINARY PRACTICE

Inquiries for Hope & Change

Editor: **Cheryl McLean**
Associate Editor: **Robert Kelly**

Creative Arts in Interdisciplinary Practice:
Inquiries for Hope and Change © 2010
Cheryl McLean

Library and Archives Canada Cataloguing in
Publication

Creative arts in interdisciplinary
practice / Cheryl McLean, editor.

Includes bibliographical references.
ISBN 978-1-55059-385-3

1. Arts medicine. 2. Arts--Therapeutic use.
3. Arts and society. I. McLean, Cheryl L.
(Cheryl Lee), 1953-

R702.5.C74 2010   610
C2010-902932-1

We recognize the support of the government
of Canada through the Canada Books Program
for our publishing program.

We also acknowledge the support of the
Alberta Foundation of the Arts for our
publishing program.

SAN 113-0234
ISBN 978-1-55059-385-3
Printed in Canada.
Cover design by James Dangerou

Detselig Enterprises Ltd.

210 1220 Kensington Rd NW
Calgary, Alberta   T2N 3P5
www.temerondetselig.com
temeron@telusplanet.net
p. 403-283-0900   f. 403-283-6947

The business of art is rather to understand Nature and to reveal her meanings to those unable to understand.
It is to convey the soul of a tree rather than to produce a fruitful likeness of a tree.
It is to reveal the conscience of the sea, not to portray so many foaming waves or so much blue water.
The mission of art is to bring out the unfamiliar from the most familiar.
–Kahlil Gibran

Acknowledgements

I WOULD LIKE TO THANK OUR MANY CONTRIBUTORS for sharing their research and stories with us in this book. It has been a privilege throughout this project to work with so many outstanding individuals who are creative leaders in their respective disciplines.

Special thanks to Ted Giles of Detselig Enterprises Ltd. for his support as our publisher and to Shane Riczu for his input and enthusiasm at the outset of this project as well as James Dangerous[†], artist and designer, for his innovative contemporary design for our cover and exacting attention to the typography and layout for this book.

I would also like to extend special thanks to Associate Editor, Robert Kelly, and to express my appreciation for his encouragement, guidance and unfailing optimism throughout this project as "the journey of this idea" has finally come to fruition. I would also like to thank my husband Don for his support on this journey as many a field and many an idea has been planted and sown.

—Cheryl McLean

† See blog post "Dangerously good design for Creative Arts in Interdisciplinary Practice
http://creativeartpractice.blogspot.com/2010/04/dangerously-good-desiging-for-creative.html

TABLE OF CONTENTS

PART 2
Performance in Health,
Embodied Understandings

PART 3
Creative Arts In Action And Practice, Special Populations
Self Expression, Identity, Community

PART 4
Narrative and Story

PART 5
Interdisciplinary Art Practice
for Personal and Community Healing

Shaping the Field

Cheryl McLean

Beginnings

THE SEEDS FOR THIS BOOK were planted in the spring of 2006. At that time I had envisioned a global community linked around the creative arts and its broader applications in practice, a network that would extend well beyond any single modality, methodology or exclusive field of study drawn from across disciplinary borders in health, education and training.

To achieve this goal, and to provide the necessary communication channels for research and information, individuals were identified and organizations interested in arts in health, training and education were contacted personally to ask if they might like to access a web based newsletter that featured articles about the creative arts as applied across disciplines. The response to this inquiry was overwhelmingly positive. The Canadian Creative Arts in Health, Training and Education e/newsjournal (CCAHTE) was launched in September 2006 as an open access (OA) internet news/journal, *the interdisciplinary journal of the creative arts in health, training and education*. The Canadian Creative Arts in Health, Training and Education (CCAHTE) advisory board was established with representation from leading universities and institutions across North America and diverse disciplines in education, healthcare (nursing, public health, medicine) fine arts and design.

CCAHTE Journal operated on a free subscription basis and welcomed articles from contributors worldwide. Three years later, in consultation with the journal advisory board and to reflect the publication's broadening scope and international status as the open access peer reviewed academic journal in the field, the journal was renamed *The International Journal of The Creative Arts in Interdisciplinary Practice IJCAIP*.

The International Journal of The Creative Arts in Interdisciplinary Practice IJCAIP, has a large international subscriber base and is accessible to researchers, educators and students in over 15 000 libraries in sixty countries around the world, including developing nations.

The publication also sponsors a number of interconnected IJCAIP websites as well as a monthly newsletter and several blogs. The Creative Arts in Interdisciplinary Practice Series (CAIP) book blog at HTTP://CREATIVEARTPRACTICE.BLOGSPOT.COM was created to introduce information and news about the CAIP text series and to preview our contributors and new research. The Creative Arts in Interdisciplinary Practice (CAIP) research series includes three volumes, *Creative Arts in Interdisciplinary Practice, Inquiries for Hope and Change, Creative Arts in Research for Community and Cultural Change,* and *Story Technology and Transformation.*

Publishing activities at the International Journal of the Creative Arts in Interdisciplinary Practice over the last four years have contributed significantly to propagating a new and fertile knowledge base for research and information in the field. The IJCAIP journal has published articles which feature a broad range of the creative arts in action and practice from new research about readers' theatre in healthcare and caregiver training to articles featuring physicians from across Canada and the U.S. reporting on new developments in the arts in medical education. There is a viable network across disciplines eager for research and information about the creative arts in interdisciplinary practice and a critical mass of leading researchers and others seeking to share their projects and knowledge with a growing worldwide readership.

About the book

CONCEPTUALLY, THE BOOK *Creative Arts in Interdisciplinary Practice, Inquiries for Hope and Change* was created with three primary goals. The collection was envisioned as a gathering place for knowledge and experience, a circle of connection where individuals and groups currently active in the creative arts in research in its many forms could share and witness a variety of approaches in action. Secondly, this book would carry accounts of the creative arts in research and practice further afield crossing disciplinary borders reaching new audiences while inspiring other explorations and laying the groundwork for research and/or alternative approaches to programming. And finally it was hoped the book would foster further innovation and development in creative arts research strengthening the knowledge base in the field and potentially leading to new research methodologies suited to the distinctive and expressive nature of the creative arts as applied in practice.

It was our intention to show, by way of example, the considerable breadth and scope of the research. First hand topical accounts are featured from leading academics, health researchers, nurse educators, physicians, educators, environmentalists, artists and others who actively use the creative arts in interdisciplinary practice in cutting edged research and in methodologies for health, hope and change The accounts traverse methodological borders while addressing multiple challenges and serving diverse populations in practice. That being said most of the articles share a common interest in action for hope and change and this thematically grounded our content . . . thus the reference in our subtitle "*Inquiries for Hope and Change*".

We worked to bring to form a contemporary text which would not only teach but tell, becoming a catalyst for dialogue while *creating its own conversations*. For example, in one article an artist researcher seeks to articulate what it is to write about homelessness. In another a theatre artist proposes how we might actively seek to identify with the condition of homelessness and persons who are homeless through deep listening and theatre based processes, and later on an interdisciplinary artist shares how collaborative live art practices can help transform experiences of displacement. One story calls for narrative and a place for the caregiver's story, and another offers a path to understanding and honouring caregivers through arts based research.

> A performance can raise awareness educating well beyond the podium conveying lived experience in action with elements visual, emotional, physical and spiritual. In this field process we are told and we tell stories engaging in one of the most primal, meaningful and universal of human connections
> *Cheryl McLean play notes, ethnodrama "Remember Me for Birds"* {xv}

Creative Arts in Interdisciplinary Practice, Inquiries for Hope and Change is a contemporary research collection that features methods that are participative, communal, active and experiential. It speaks of approaches that actively re-illuminate lived experiences and foster and encourage deep and multi-sensory communication and embodied forms of expression with elements visual, emotional, physical and spiritual. In this book, we bring together a field that stresses the vital importance of creativity and the human story, a body of work that seeks to help give voice to the silenced, the oppressed and the marginalized, narrative accounts of personal transformation that honour creative expression as fundamental and at the very source of human meaning and purpose. We invite you to journey through these articles and share in accounts of the creative arts in interdisciplinary practice for hope and change.

Suggested reading:

CHARON, R., *Narrative medicine: Honouring the Stories of Illness*, New York: Oxford University Press, Inc., 2006.

DENZIN, N.K., *Performance Ethnography, Critical Pedagogy and the Politics of Culture,* Sage Publications, Thousand Oaks, London, 2003.

GOLD, M., *Therapy Through Drama: The Fictional Family*, Charles C. Thomas Publisher, Ltd., Springfield, Illinois, 2000.

KELLY, R., LEGGO C., (eds), *Creative Expression, Creative Education, Creativity as a Primary Rationale for Education*, Detselig Enterprises Ltd., Calgary, 2008.

LEWIS, P., JOHNSON, D.R. (eds), *Current Approaches in Drama Therapy*, Charles C. Thomas, Publisher, Ltd., Springfield, Illinois, 2000.

MCLEAN, C., KELLY, R. (eds), *Creative Arts in Interdisciplinary Practice, Inquiries for Hope and Change*, Detselig Enterprises Ltd., Calgary, 2010.

MCLEAN, C., KELLY, R. (eds), *Creative Arts in Research for Community and Cultural Change* Detselig Enterprises Ltd., Calgary, 2010.

SALDANA, J. (ED.), *Ethnodrama: An Anthology of Reality Theatre*, Walnut Creek, CA: AltaMira Press., 2005.

Other resources:

The International Journal of The Creative Arts in Interdisciplinary Practice IJCAIP
IJCAIP Journal website: HTTP://WWW.IJCAIP.COM

Creative Arts in Interdisciplinary Practice CAIP Research Series BLOG
contributor profiles, articles, video, supplementary info., recent news
ordering info.
HTTP://CREATIVEARTPRACTICE.BLOGSPOT.COM/

Creative Arts in Interdisciplinary Practice, Inquiries for Hope and Change
editor profiles: Cheryl McLean, Robert Kelly
HTTP://CREATIVEARTPRACTICE.BLOGSPOT.COM/2010/03/INTRODUCING-OUR-EDITORS-CAIP-RESEARCH.HTML

email address: Cheryl McLean, Editor CAIP Research Series CHERYLMCLEAN@IJCAIP.COM

Participatory methodologies make more fluid
and congruent the coexistence of art, activism
and research, their bottom-up approach to
knowledge production suggests a social democracy.
In designing a research method, we might need
to start from childlike freshness: unfettering our
imagination and propelling research
beyond the ordinary.

-Kyung-Hwa Yang, student,
Department of Integrated Studies in Education,
Faculty of Education, McGill University

Creative Arts in
Research and Action
for Community
Change

Community Based Research, Collaborating for Change

Collaborating to Tell the Stories of Homelessness in Toronto

Izumi Sakamoto, Matthew Chin, & Cyndy Baskin

If a picture is worth a thousand words, how many pictures does it take to understand just one word: homelessness?

–Jim Meeks, peer researcher
& Collaborative Team member

Introduction

Homelessness in Toronto, Canada

OMELESSNESS[1] IS A SERIOUS and pervasive issue that affects many people in Canada, as well as in Toronto[2] (Khandor & Mason, 2007) the largest city in Canada[3]. Statistics indicate that 32 000 different people slept in shelters in 2002, and approximately 6500 individuals stayed in shelters on any given night in 2006[4] (Khandor & Mason, 2007). People who experience homelessness are negatively affected by intersecting oppressions such as poverty, lack of access to housing, sexism, racism, homophobia, and violence (Rafael, 2008). However, there is a scarcity of literature with respect to the diverse experiences of individuals who are homeless and face multiple forms of oppressions. Further, despite the fact that numerous research studies have documented the rapid increase of homelessness to date, few effective interventions have been pursued. There is a pressing need to reach out to the public to raise awareness of the issue and to change social policies.

Arts-Informed Research and Community-Based Research

WHEN CONDUCTING RESEARCH WITH marginalized communities, it is important for researchers (especially for those without the lived experience of the particular social issue under study) to ask how best to capture and represent peoples' experiences without misrepresenting their realities. One response to this question is to conduct research collaboratively with people who are directly affected by the issue, as promoted by principles of community-based research. Another response is to use a medium that is more inclusive of people with diverse identities and experiences, such as arts-informed research. The initiative presented herein used both of these methodologies.

Arts-informed (arts-based) research has increasingly been used as method of qualitative research as well as participatory research within the social sciences (Bochner & Ellis, 2004). Arts may be used in various stages of the research process in a variety ways: for envisioning exercises during the planning phase; to generate knowledge through data collection or analysis; or to disseminate research results. This method allows those directly affected by the issue to document and express their concerns and their worldviews effectively (Finley, 2005). Participants become artists with the ability to create and the power to represent their worlds, deciding what to show and what to keep hidden (Foster, 2007). The process of making art can allow for the emergence of alternate and inclusive knowledge (Barone, 2001). While the exclusive use of words may limit research participants' expressions of multi-faceted realities, arts-based research offers more than one interpretive method for understanding their lives, challenges, and resiliencies. Consequently, the use of this methodology may increase research participation accessibility in allowing participants to engage with the research in multiple ways regardless of different abilities such as literacy level. Arguably, arts-based research is inherently political, and is thus often used to raise awareness about particular social issues (Eisner, 1997). The creative "results" from arts-informed research (e.g., film, photography) are more accessible and inclusive; they are more likely to have far greater potential to move people to action than would words in conventional position papers and journal articles (Wang & Burris, 1994). Community-based participatory research (CBR or CBPR) (Israel et al., 1998) is largely a response to the recognition that traditional academic research has often failed to appreciate the needs and interests of the communities in which research is conducted. The knowledge generated from these studies is often not returned to these communities, and members of stigmatized and/or marginalized groups frequently report feeling as though they are 'objects of study' within the research process. However, in recent years there has been a strong movement toward research that recognizes the strengths of the community as the core of research endeavors. Such an approach promotes the equitable involvement of all

{22}

partners in the research process in order to make research more action-oriented and relevant to the community in which CBR is conducted (Flicker & Savan, 2006). Consequently, CBR inherently aims for community or societal change, however small.

All of the projects in the collaborative were based on principles of CBPR (Minkler & Wallerstein, 2004) and aimed to make space for individuals with experiences of homelessness (or those at risk of becoming homeless). The participation of peer researchers[5] was crucial to the success of each of these projects.

Collaborative: "Homelessness – Solutions from Lived Experiences through Arts-Informed Research"

IN TORONTO, THERE HAVE BEEN SEVERAL cutting-edge, arts-informed, CBR projects on homelessness involving peer researchers conducted in the past few years. Despite their individual successes, these projects confronted similar limitations: often the results from arts-based research and CBR studies are only appreciated as "local" knowledge without much transferability to other settings; further, it is frequently the case that, upon completion of research, the scope of their dissemination efforts is limited due to funding constraints. Recognizing these issues led eight arts-informed CBR projects[6] to come together and draw upon our collective knowledge, resources and momentum and create social change to raise awareness and address the issues of homelessness in Toronto.

{23}

This unique collaboration called *Homelessness – Solutions from Lived Experiences through Arts-Informed Research*[7] aimed to synthesize and mobilize our collective knowledge while creating broader collaborative relationships moving toward more effective action and visibility of the issues. The eighteen collaborative team members included peer researchers, community agency staff, funders, artists, academics and two co-coordinators. Operating from empowerment and anti-oppressive perspectives (Gutierrez & Lewis, 1999; Sakamoto & Pitner, 2005), the Collaborative and its constitutive projects focused on the inclusion of peer researchers and recognizing them as "experts" of their own lived experiences with valuable knowledge to address issues of homelessness. Peer researchers, as well as other team members, worked together over a ten-month period, undertaking various roles related to the decision-making and implementation of multiple aspects of the collaboration. While salaried professionals were at the table as part of their work responsibilities, peer researchers were paid honoraria for their time and efforts.

Arts Methods

OUT OF THE EIGHT RESEARCH PROJECTS represented in the Collaborative, all used community-based, participatory action research approaches. One of them did not use arts in the research process, but the remaining seven are broadly construed as arts-informed research as they used arts for data collection, analysis and/or knowledge mobilization. Two projects were closely related. *The Street Health Report 2007* used a survey methodology to produce a report, which included still photos of some of the qualitative interview participants. The still photos and narratives of these individuals were then used to make the documentary, *Street Health Stories* to highlight the survey findings. (Editor's note: see http://www.youtube.com/watch?v=S_m7EK0_3Rs)

Various forms of arts were used as methods of data collection and analysis (e.g., Photovoice, staged photography) as well as for the dissemination of results (e.g., mural; staged photography; light box installation with sound; installation using bed mattresses to highlight Photovoice findings). Table 1 shows the details of the approaches used for each project.

Project	People/Agency[8]	Modality of arts used	How arts were used in the research process
A Day in the Life	York University (Nancy Viva Davis Halifax), Street Health (Erika Khandor), Peer researchers (Jim Meeks, et al.)	Photovoice; Photovoice findings (words and images) printed on fabric and hung for display	Data collection, analysis & dissemination
Asleep in Toronto	York University (Nancy Viva Davis Halifax), Street Health (Erika Khandor), University of Toronto Centre for Arts-Informed Research, Peer researchers (Jim Meeks, et al.)	Photovoice; installation of Photovoice finding vs (words and images) printed on fabric laid on single bed mattresses	Data collection, analysis & dissemination
Coming Together	University of Toronto (Izumi Sakamoto), Regent Park Community Health Centre (Josie Ricciardi), Sistering (Natalie Wood), Advisory board members (Brandi Nashkewa, Sheila Samuels, et al.)	Staged photography (storytelling, painting (murals), drama, photography); Posters and research report using the images and words collected; Photo-based storyboards created for display.	Data collection, analysis & dissemination

Project	People/Agency	Modality of arts used	How arts were used in the research process
Struggles, strengths and solutions: Exploring food security with young Aboriginal moms	Ryerson University (Cyndy Baskin), Peer researchers (Nadya Melanson et al.)	Mural that participants created to highlight the findings of the research	Dissemination of research results
I WAS HERE	National Film Board of Canada Filmmaker in Residence Program at St. Michael's Hospital, St. Michael's Hospital (Catherine Moravac), peer researchers	Photovoice, blog	Data collection, analysis & dissemination
Street Health Stories/ The Street Health Report 1997	NFB, Street Health, peer researchers (Jim Meeks, Brandi Nashkewa, et al.)	Video (still photos with voice over); light boxes of the still photos with sound installation	Dissemination of research results from *the Street Health Report 1997* and subsequent qualitative interviews

Table 1: The arts-informed projects represented in the Collaborative

Synthesizing arts?

WHILE THE COLLABORATIVE SHARED THE GOAL of coming together to raise awareness and promote social change around the issue of homelessness in Toronto, we faced the challenge of combining our projects in a way that would accurately represent the collaborative and contribute to our goals while also staying true to the specificity and uniqueness of each project. How we addressed this challenge is perhaps best described through a discussion of the joint policy report, "Homelessness – Diverse Experiences, Common Issues, Shared Solutions" that the group created.

In creating the joint policy document, the collaborative sought to distill the results gained from each of the projects in a way that would both raise awareness about the issues of homelessness and contribute to solutions. We thought that pulling together the text-based reports produced by each project was going to be fairly straightforward. However, the sub-committee of people who were working on this task (including the first author of this chapter) soon found out that it was a rather complex and labour intensive process. While most of the projects converged on large issues and solutions, many of the findings and recommendations were specific to particular populations that each project worked with (e.g., young mothers, transwomen, health issues). As a result, it became increasingly clear that the joint policy document would have to articulate the common aspects across the projects as well as the unique contributions offered by all the populations/issues represented in the Collaborative.

The next challenge in writing the joint policy document was to determine at which level we would synthesize the similar issues and solutions, and describe the unique issues experienced by each population while also doing justice to the individual projects (and the voices they represented). At this point, the lead researcher (Sakamoto) consulted housing research expert David Hulchanski and brainstormed different frameworks to pull together a myriad of findings and recommendations.

His suggestion was to start from the classic framework of solutions to homelessness: housing, income, and social supports. Applying this framework to the issues and recommendations from all the projects, the difference between the classic literature on homelessness and our Collaborative became clearer. In seeking to address these differences, the lead researcher came up with an image to conceptualize a bridge between them: a Venn diagram of three overlapping circles (housing, income, supports; *see page 29*), with multiple intersections to represent the way in which the different experiences of people with intersecting, diverse identities impact all three spheres at the same time. Based on these ideas, the sub-committee concluded that the main focus of the report should be on the need for inclusion and accountability and that the systems, services, policies and programs addressing homelessness should be inclusive of and accountable to people with lived experience of homelessness. The recommendations of each of the projects were organized according to the following four broad recommendation categories and further differentiated based on level of specificity and in correspondence to responsible implementing organization(s): 1) Ensuring policy-making planning and service delivery are inclusive of and accountable to diverse homeless people; 2) ensuring adequate incomes; 3) Improving and creating affordable and appropriate housing; and 4) Creating flexible and responsive health, social and community supports.

While the synthesis of the text-based components of the project proved to be challenging, pulling together the non-text based components proved to be no less so: how could we synthesize the arts while also preserving the diverse expressions and experiences that they represented? Although each of the projects addressed the issue of homelessness, the projects worked with different groups of people, on distinct issues and used various arts media in different ways within different stages of the project cycle. How to envision unity in this diversity? How could we pull together the arts created in each of the projects in ways that represented the collaborative while also staying true to the specific project?

{28}   The collaborative dealt with these issues in two ways. In the first case, the art from each of the projects was used to support the text within the policy document. The images, photos and quotes (including prose written by peer researchers) from the constitutive projects were inserted into the policy document text to further illustrate the points being made. Efforts were made to ensure equity of project representation and that the quotes, images and/or photos were placed appropriately in relation to issues being discussed. In this way, the pulling together of the art from the projects was done in an additive way to supplement a largely text based document.

In the second way, as opposed to a physical conjoining of the arts produced by each project, the collaborative sought to synthesize the projects by creating art as a consequence of collaborative meaning-making processes. This was done in two instances. In the first instance, the aforementioned framework to capture the solutions to homelessness forwarded by the Collaborative (that, in addition to the oft-mentioned securing of housing, income, and supports, accountability and the inclusion of diverse identities and experiences are required to ensure quality services that meet the needs of people they are meant to serve) was graphically captured with the help of a Toronto-based designer, Meera Sethi.

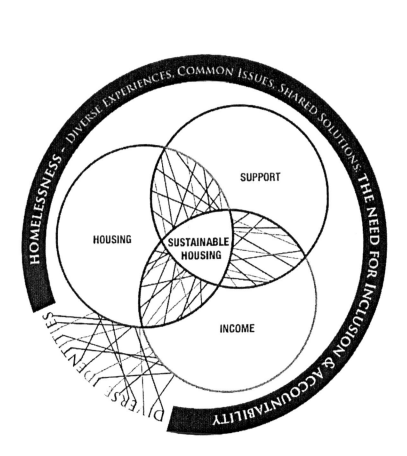

Image 2: Diagram by Meera Sethi. This image was used as the cover of the policy report and a more detailed description of the image can be found therein (Sakamoto et al., 2008, p. 8).

In the second case, the meaning making process that motivated the creation of art did not focus on the representation of the collaborative message but rather was occasioned by the challenge of how to conceptualize the eight individual projects as one. This process is discussed in the following section.

The Medicine Wheel

THE EIGHT PROJECTS THAT CAME TOGETHER had several things in common: they were all arts-based and/or CBPR projects; they all focused on homelessness and poverty in Toronto, and; they all sought to raise awareness and mobilize knowledge towards solving homelessness. Yet, despite these important similarities, the collaborative still struggled to come up with a way to conceive of the individual projects as a single group. The solution to this issue originated with one of the projects in our collaborative (led by the third author, Dr. Cyndy Baskin of the Mi'kmaq Nation) which focused exclusively on Aboriginal people in Toronto and was then supported by the many Aboriginal people who participated in the collaborative.

The suggestion made was to organize the exhibition of the arts created by research projects according to one of the versions of the teachings of the Medicine Wheel of the Anishinabe (Ojibwe) peoples.[9] The decision to implement this version of the Medicine Wheel was based on the commitment to acknowledge and honour the people on whose territory the collaborative members had the privilege to live. The collaborative also agreed that this framework was appropriate given that Aboriginal peoples are overrepresented among those with experiences of homelessness due to historical and contemporary processes of colonization. Furthermore, the use of the Medicine Wheel as a way to conceive of eight different project was especially fitting given that it symbolizes unity and the bringing of people together (in this case to find solutions to homelessness)

The projects were organized according to the principles of the Medicine Wheel. At the launch of the Collaborative at Metro Hall, Toronto, which involved the release of the Joint Policy Report and website as well as the unveiling of the Joint Art Exhibit, each of the projects was situated within the space in a specific direction in correspondence with the Medicine Wheel. Each direction of the Medicine Wheel (East, South, West, and North) has a specific meaning, and each of the projects in the Collaborative was matched to the most appropriate direction based on these meanings and the nature of the project. For example, the Southern direction speaks to the importance of developing relationships, so the *Coming Together* project, which focused on the social support that women and transwomen who are homeless lend to each other, was placed in the Southern direction of the round exhibit hall (Metro Hall Rotunda).

The collaborative sought to create posters for the launch to serve as a spatial orientation tool and to visually represent how the projects fit within the Medicine Wheel. In so doing, we consulted with John Hupfield, a Toronto-based, Anishinabe visual artist as to how best to achieve this goal. Hupfield then created nine posters: eight project specific posters visually representing how each project fit within the Medicine Wheel and a text explanation as to why the project was placed in that particular direction; and one larger general poster also with a visual of the Medicine Wheel and a text explanation as to why and how we chose to use it. A sample of these posters can be seen in Image 3.

Opposite page:
Image 3,
Medicine Wheel
poster created
by John Hupfield

{30}

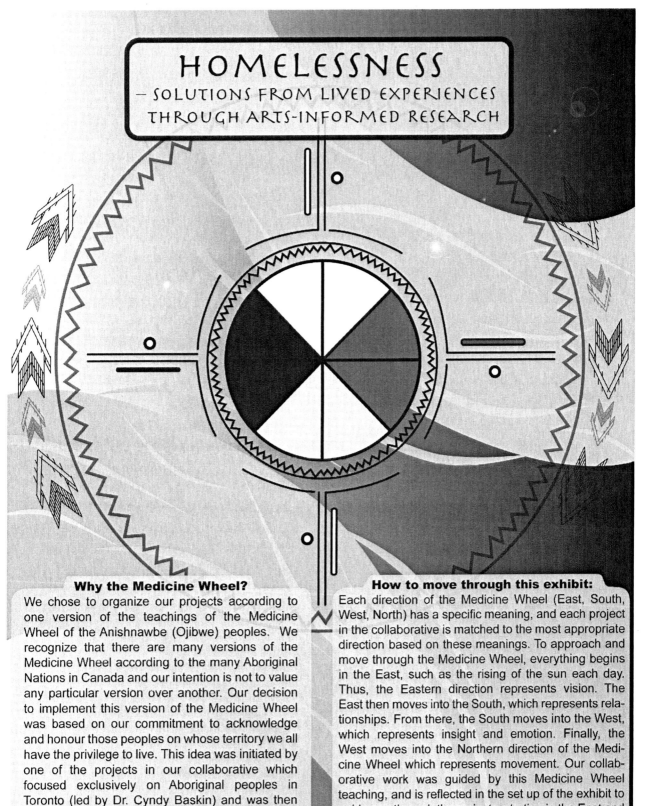

HOMELESSNESS
– SOLUTIONS FROM LIVED EXPERIENCES
THROUGH ARTS-INFORMED RESEARCH

Why the Medicine Wheel?

We chose to organize our projects according to one version of the teachings of the Medicine Wheel of the Anishnawbe (Ojibwe) peoples. We recognize that there are many versions of the Medicine Wheel according to the many Aboriginal Nations in Canada and our intention is not to value any particular version over another. Our decision to implement this version of the Medicine Wheel was based on our commitment to acknowledge and honour those peoples on whose territory we all have the privilege to live. This idea was initiated by one of the projects in our collaborative which focused exclusively on Aboriginal peoples in Toronto (led by Dr. Cyndy Baskin) and was then supported by the many Aboriginal peoples who also participated in our collaborative initiative.

How to move through this exhibit:

Each direction of the Medicine Wheel (East, South, West, North) has a specific meaning, and each project in the collaborative is matched to the most appropriate direction based on these meanings. To approach and move through the Medicine Wheel, everything begins in the East, such as the rising of the sun each day. Thus, the Eastern direction represents vision. The East then moves into the South, which represents relationships. From there, the South moves into the West, which represents insight and emotion. Finally, the West moves into the Northern direction of the Medicine Wheel which represents movement. Our collaborative work was guided by this Medicine Wheel teaching, and is reflected in the set up of the exhibit to guide you through the projects, starting in the East and moving clockwise as shown by the arrows.

Outcomes

ON OCTOBER 1, 2008, at Metro Hall[10], Toronto, several hundred people attended the Collaborative's launch of a joint art exhibit, policy report and website, which highlighted the pressing issues of homelessness through arts and stories. A highly publicized event, this launch attracted print media and radio coverage and a wide range of participants including politicians, bureaucrats, social service agency administrators, front-line workers, and people with experiences of homelessness. The Launch started with blessings offered by an Oneida Elder and an Anishinabe singer. Displaying the artwork from the various projects in one place allowed us to showcase the complexity and multiplicity of personal stories and representations of experiences of homelessness – for, while people who are homeless may share many experiences, those belonging to certain groups (e.g., young parents) may encounter situations that are different from those faced by other groups (e.g., transwomen). The Medicine Wheel provided the unity in our quest to seek solutions to homelessness, while acknowledging the diverse experiences within the eight research projects and among the people these projects sought to represent. At the Launch, representing the eight research projects on display, seven peer researchers spoke about their experiences of having been involved in arts-informed research/CBR projects and their own personal stories of homelessness and poverty.

The Role of Arts in Research and Knowledge Mobilization

THE USE OF ARTS WAS PARTICULARLY EFFECTIVE because it allowed for the meaningful inclusion of people who are homeless in the research process as peer researchers, and the artwork was created by those who have experienced homelessness firsthand. Further, various modalities and representations of arts made it possible to communicate the message of "the need for inclusion and accountability" for diverse voices, without bombarding people with words. At the Launch, the Executive Director of a grass-roots women's drop-in centre, Sistering – A Woman's Place, made this point eloquently:

> You're also seeing that art doesn't belong to an exclusive category, it doesn't belong to the privileged, that art belongs to people, it belongs to us. And in fact, art is what people who often don't have privilege have, to claim space, make voice, make their experience known and therefore it is why I want you to register your protest that art matters. That art is about social change, and that this group of men and women

has clearly articulated that in what you see around the room. (Angela Robertson, October 1, 2008)

Likewise, the majority of the audience members who filled out the evaluation forms provided mentioned that their most significant experience in attending our exhibit and/or event was listening to the personal stories of the peer researchers and witnessing the artwork created by people who experienced homelessness. In responding to the question "What will you remember most about the event?" some of the responses included: "The voice of homeless people was in the foreground. The variety of arts-based approaches will stay in the mind"; "the power of arts-informed research and the impact it has on people"; and "the power of the arts as a multi-modal form to enable these stories to be heard at different levels."

The participation of community members and peer researchers was critical to the success of each of the eight projects, as well as the Collaborative as a whole.

Conclusion

THE COLLABORATIVE 'Homelessness – Solutions from Lived Experiences through Arts-Informed Research' illustrates a particular case in which arts can be brought together in various ways to raise awareness and promote social change. In our Collaborative, arts were used in various ways to synthesize the eight CBR and/or arts-informed research projects. In addition to arts being used in the research process of each project (e.g., for data collection, analysis), the arts produced by each study were also used for the purpose of dissemination in the Joint Art Exhibit that took place in Metro Hall Rotunda, Toronto. Arts were also mobilized to enhance the words-based policy document as a means of providing alternate knowledge in support of the Collaborative's main message. Additionally, new arts were created to help synthesize the eight research projects represented in the Collaborative. In the first case, a single design was created to visually capture our main message (Image 2; emphasizing the importance of inclusion and accountability while also addressing more oft-talked-about solutions to homelessness: housing, income and supports). In the second case, the creation of arts to synthesize our projects was facilitated by the use of the Anishinabe Medicine Wheel as a "meta-art"/meta-framework to bring together eight projects based on their meanings (as opposed to their visual representations or art modalities). This, we believe, was a powerful and appropriate way of synthesizing our unique projects together under Aboriginal teachings.

{33}

IZUMI SAKAMOTO, Ph.D. is Associate Professor of Social Work, University of Toronto, and was the lead researcher for the Collaborative discussed in this article.

MATTHEW CHIN, B.A. (hon.) was the Project Co-Coordinator for the Collaborative, and is currently a Ph.D. student in the Joint Program of Social Work and Anthropology at the University of Michigan, Ann Arbor.

CYNDY BASKIN, Ph.D., Associate Professor of Social Work, Ryerson University, is of Mi'kmaq and Irish descent, and was the member of the Collaborative and its Creative Team.

{34}

References

CITY OF TORONTO. (2009). Frequently asked questions about: Moving to Toronto. Author. Retrieved on September 29, 2009 from HTTP://WWW.TORONTO.CA/FAQ/MOVINGTO.HTM

CITY OF TORONTO. (2003). *The Toronto report card on homelessness and housing 2003*. Toronto: Author.

EISNER, E.W. (1997). The new frontier in qualitative research methodology. *Qualitative Inquiry*, 3(3), 259-273.

FINLEY, S. (2005). Arts-based inquiry: Performing revolutionary pedagogy. In N. Denzin & Y. Lincoln (Eds.). *The Sage handbook of qualitative research* (3rd ed.; pp. 681-694). Thousand Oaks, CA: Sage.

FLICKER, S., & SAVAN, S. (2006). *A snapshot of CBR in Canada*. Toronto: Wellesley Institute.

FOSTER, V. (2007). 'Ways of knowing and showing': Imagination and representation in feminist participatory social research. *Journal of Social Work Practice, 21*(3), 361- 376

GUTIÉRREZ, L., & LEWIS, E. (1999). *Empowering women of color*. New York: Columbia University Press

ISRAEL, B. A., SCHULZ, A. J., PARKER, E. A., & BECKER, A. B. (1998). Review of community-based research: Assessing partnership approaches to improve public health. *Annual Review of Public Health, 19*, 173-202.

KHANDOR, E., & MASON, K. (2007). *The street health report 2007*. Toronto: Street Health

MINKLER, M., & WALLERSTEIN, N. (2004). *Community- based participatory research for health*. New York: Jossey-Bass.

RAFAEL, D. (2008). *Social determinants of health: Canadian perspectives* (2nd ed.). Toronto: Canadian Scholars Press.

SAKAMOTO, I., KHANDOR, E., CHAPRA, A., HENDRICKSON, T., MAHER, J., ROCHE, B., & CHIN, M. (2008). *Homelessness--Diverse experiences, common issues, shared solutions: The need for inclusion and accountability*. Toronto: Factor-Inwentash Faculty of Social Work, University of Toronto. ISBN: 978-0-9811128-0-0 (book). Also available at: HTTP://WWW.ARTSANDHOMELESS.COM/DOWNLOAD/HOMELESS_PROPOSAL_LR.PDF

SAKAMOTO, I., & PITNER, R. (2005). Use of critical consciousness in anti-oppressive social work practice: Disentangling power dynamics at personal and structural levels. *British Journal of Social Work, 35*(4), 420-437.

WANG, C., & BURRIS, M. (1994). Photovoice: Concept, methodology, and use for participatory needs assessment. *Health Education and Behavior, 24*(3), 369-387.

{36}

Notes

1   The City of Toronto defines homelessness as "a condition of people who live outside, stay in emergency shelters, spend most of their income on rent, or live in homelessness." (City of Toronto, 2003, p. 2).

It must be noted that "homelessness" encompasses a very broad range of experiences and identities and that the eight projects in the collaborative worked with people with diverse relationships to housing and homelessness. For instance, some projects worked with people who were at risk of becoming homeless, others worked with those who were marginally housed and some projects worked with individuals who (for varying periods of time) lived on the streets.

2   In 1998, the City of Toronto endorsed a declaration acknowledging homelessness as a national disaster.

3   In the 2006 Census, Toronto's population was 2.63 million (5.55 million in the Greater Toronto Area). (City of Toronto, 2009)

4   Those who are either at risk of homelessness or are not actively seeking social services are not accounted for in these numbers.

5   Peer researchers are people who have lived experiences of the social issues under study, in this case, homelessness.

6   All eight projects were community-based research, of which seven used arts-informed or arts-based research methods.

7   This project was funded by Social Sciences Humanities Research Council of Canada (SSSRC), Wellesley Institute, and Centre for Urban Health Initiatives at the University of Toronto. The project's organizational partners included Regent Park Community Health Centre, Street Health, Ontario Women's Health Network, Wellesley Institute, St. Michael's Hospital, Sistering – A Woman's Place, the University of Toronto, Ryerson University, and York University. For more information, visit: WWW.ARTSANDHOMELESS.COM.

8   While many more people were involved in conducting each of these community-based research projects, only the names of those who were involved in the Collaborative are given. For more information for each project, please visit: WWW.ARTSANDHOMELESS.COM.

Sakamoto · Chin · Baskin

9   We recognize that there are many versions of the Medicine Wheel according to the several Aboriginal Nations in Canada and our intention is not to value any particular version over another.

10 Metro Hall is one of the central municipal government buildings in the City of Toronto.

The Voice of the Artist as Researcher, Homelessness in Toronto

Writing Toward Homelessness, An Artist Researcher's Reflections

Nancy Viva Davis Halifax

To be an I means then not to be able to escape responsibility, as though the whole edifice of creation rested on my shoulders.

–Emmanuel Levinas

To disclose how things might be we must follow in the wake of the imagination.

–Kearney

I'm not falling through the cracks, it's where I live.

–Anonymous.

To be a poet is to practice sitting in front of memory, the ashes and embers.

–Davis Halifax

Is a room considered a home? Home is where the heart is, yes, that is true. But if I have a room and I don't have hot and cold running water or I am not allowed cooking, is that a home? I believe it is still a room. When I am in jail I am in a room. When I am in hospital I am in a room but it is not a home. So a room is still not a home. I always thought it was something like self-contained, hot and cold running water, where you could cook, that is a home. A room is not a home. It keeps you isolated.

–Ray

I ask you, who walk by poems
Like you walk by homeless girls
To attend.

Wipe the seeping walls of memory with rags.
Watch the rising,
Wring the waters into a cup,
Drink.

I LINGER NEAR AFFECTIVE INQUIRY and feminist reflexivity as I write toward home/lessness. I want to push the pieces of understanding, memory, body, knowing, into the world as each arises. Affect is a way of being in the midst of these fragments. Each arises, (sub)merges, traces a path that is mapped and embodied, erased-creating a palimpsest where tangled corridors displace their referents.

Like other feminist scholars, I am not convinced that inquiry dependant on binaries such as subject/object, knower/known, thought/feeling, political/personal separations is the only approach to contemporary knowledge creation (Stacey, 1988, Behar, 1996, Lather 2001). "Discussions of feminist methodology generally assault the hierarchical, exploitative relations of conventional research, urging feminist researchers to seek instead an egalitarian research process characterized by authenticity, reciprocity, and intersubjectivity between the researcher and her "subjects" (Klein, et. al as cited in ibid., p. 22). But I am also less than certain that experiential and relational knowledge creation through immersion in the field will not create its own conflicts (ibid.). I am left with the hope of a failed account (Carson, *Eros the bittersweet* – , Davis Halifax, 2009; Lather, 2001). "By working the limits of intelligibility and foregrounding the inadequacy of thought to its object, a stuttering knowledge is constructed that elicits an experience of the object through its very failures of representation" (Lather, p. 207).

Yesterday she lay on the
Shuddering ground as this broke-green earth circled.

Viva Davis Halifax

A fragmented writing parallels the reading. Performative writing is a practice that involves you deeply. Pelias reminds us that:

> Performative writing offers both an evocation of human experience and an enabling fiction. Its power is in its ability to tell the story of human experience, a story that can be trusted and a story that can be used. It opens the doors to a place where the raw and the genuine find their articulation through form, through poetic expression, through art. (p. 418)

Through writing, speech, and thought I forge sensuous relationships with the bodies of words. Affective inquiry brings "forth ghosted bodies and the traumatized remains of erased histories" (Ticiento Clough, p. 3). I fail. My tongue thickens and my thoughts dry as I consider what I have to provide and how best to serve it to the reader. Feminist reflexivity produces an exchange wherein we abandon the safety of "subjectivity based in a single perspective . . . [for] exposed vulnerable spaces" (Perreault, 1995, p. 111). Through reflexivity we abandon linear narratives where the subject is accessible for easy consumption (Lather, 2001). Instead I present a writing that repeats, erases, and loses focus.

RESEARCHERS ARE USED TO THINKING, researching, and representing the lives of others who live as homeless; our own lives are protected with authorial power. I do not want to create greater dispossession through writing and thinking. Here, I connect myself to others through theoretical, poetic and fragmented writing, knowing there is a history of homelessness that is shared. *And this is how it writes.* This announcement makes me uneasy, yet I grant that the unconscious of my writing is preoccupied with the moral consequences of abandoning the subjects of our perception, a question that absorbs my work. The notion that we abandon what we see and our capacity for visioning, prompts my phenomenological and moral search.

The shifting nature of research allows for greater researcher reflexivity and subjectivity. However, researchers' experiences haven't been fully explored within homelessness research. It is as if the two can't be brought together: homeless person, researcher, unless the word "peer" is in front of the word "researcher." *There are so many ways to make a person feel shame.*

Viva Davis Halifax

My own reluctance at times, at least, has to do with the incoherence I find at this site; my history is filled with sitting for hours and waiting at the door of memory as a supplicant. I sit in my red chair by a window, where today it reflects blue light.

The heat of estrogen startles them.
At 12 the daughter burns.
The mother, periomenopausal has had her fill.
Daily affirmations spoken into the mirror,
Come back as shrieked and sobbed accusations.
The fecundity is too much for the father,
He resorts to fists and drinking.
Their hopes to tame the girl with long tangled hair founder.
She lopes off to the hills to be with her pack.
Living in woods, at the edges of fields, sleeping
Under signs on highways,
In boxcars they bring each other up.

Old man, who works at the bottling plant,
Thinks the way she rounds the corner at 13 is beautiful.
He lets her and a friend sleep together
In a single bed in his walk-up flat.
He feeds them white bread, cheese whiz, and coke.

In stores, pale orange tomatoes sold in cellophane packages
Find their way into coats in the middle of winter.
The shopkeepers extend
Kindness toward hungry girls with no homes.

The guy who owns the pool hall lets her vacuum tables after hours.
And she picks up tricks to keep safe.
A few brothers accumulate around her.
Love and hate tattooed on knuckles, so cool.
Makes a family to live in the woods.

Viva Davis Halifax

The church choir is distant. The dream of a father and mother
Is quit. This is what it is.[1]

THE WORK I DO IS FRAMED by the idioms of homelessness, poverty, and difference and disability. Homelessness can be defined as:

> an extreme form of poverty characterized by inadequate housing, income and social supports. People who are defined as homeless include those who are absolutely homeless (i.e. temporary, intermittent or ongoing), as well as those who are at risk of homelessness (underhoused). The absolutely homeless may be living in shelters, out doors in public or semi-public spaces, with friends or relatives (couch surfing). Those who are 'at risk' of homelessness may be precariously housed, living in hotels, rooming houses or apartments, and transitional housing, but who may potentially lose their housing due to eviction, inadequate income or because they are fleeing violence.[2]

This broad definition reminds us of the multiple influences that can allow one to have or not have a safe, secure home, while remembering that the homeless also experience an additional level of precariousness that "is not simply physical dislocation or cultural rejection but political exclusion to varying levels" (Andrews, 2004, p. 18).

Homelessness cannot be considered separately from what critical scholars in disability are addressing. The United States Department of Housing and Urban Development defines the chronically homeless as those who are "disabled and either being continuously homeless for a year or more or having had at least four homeless episodes during the last three years." Their

---

1 *What it is.* This poem is from a series of autographical works (Perreault) that are part of a larger work in progress.

2 Taken from the draft York Ethics document Guidelines for Conducting Research with People who are Homeless, Nov 4, 2008.

definition attempts stability through creating categories for individuals and holds no nuances of related exclusions for homelessness or disability. Disability is fluid, intersectional, embodied, uncertain, ambiguous, messy; disability conjoins the social, the categorical confidences of policy, and the embodied. Disability as "undecidability is deeply unsettling to the cultural imaginary, particularly one that incorporates an image of the embodied self as whole, separate and invulnerable" (Shildrick, p. 763).

Establishing a context for arts research

THERE ARE SEVERAL SELVES that my artist researcher self calls upon as she writes and works, as well as one act. I will outline two of these selves, recognizing their provisional aspects, their creation and potential in the context of communities (Perreault). Imagining is the chosen act.

Before entering the academy I established my identity as an artist, although others might call me differently: mummy, worker, friend. At times the hours filled with art felt too small until I came to define art in a manner unlike the teachings I had come to embody. Teachings found in modernist EuroAmerican learnings had nestled in my bones, their language, their notions of who an artist could be were in my thought, the first arrived on my tongue, the ones that held my trembling brush against canvas. The dominant definition of art in the contemporary Western world occurring within a modernist paradigm suggested that art was: isolated, heroic, genderless, original, monumental, and timeless (Gablik, 1991, Pollock, 1994). In those years the visible exemplars of artistic achievement had been masculine, and women and minoritized groups were excluded and feminized, despite art's apparent lack of gender.

{44}

I learned the value of art as a potential object of consumption, display and/or investment but not "as a tool that can regenerate the lost, hidden, creative, spiritual, and intuitive aspects of human life" (Becker, 1994, p. 118). This value – and the notion that there is a transformative potential inherent in viewing, making, and researching art – had been discounted by the modernist paradigm.

Those years gave me no hope of becoming an artist until imagination and feminism came to my rescue. And yet, there is still no end to this modernist idea, for in communities where I work there is a denial of the self as creative, as artist, which is often related to these dominant definitions and their continued dominance. The people that I work with often do not hold their work, their handicraft, as valuable: they mirror the cultural values that split art and handicraft. Herein I do not separate art and handicraft but imagine the domestic arts as part of the finer arts.

Viva Davis Halifax

Being subject to the arts

My practice is deeply subject to the arts. My first home and comfort is found in form, and the lyricism of colour and line. It doesn't matter what media, as making art is as much about thinking as it is about the media through which the thought is formed. I define the arts broadly as both process and product, and like Becker above suggest that it has transformative and regenerative powers. Gablik (1991) in writing about art suggests,

> Community is the starting point for new modes of relatedness, in which the paradigm of social conscience replaces that of the individual genius. In the past, we have made much of the idea of art as a mirror (reflecting the times); we have had art as a hammer (social protest); we have had art as furniture (something to hang on the walls); and we have had art as a search for the self. There is another kind of art, which speaks to the power of connectedness and establishes bonds, art that calls us into relationship. (p. 114)

As an artist researcher working in communities I use the arts as form, method, analysis, and more, as the art/inquiry itself moves us toward social justice and equity: new forms of relatedness. My work does its best to be participatory and community based, but there are practical and economic considerations that need to enter the conversations. My work recognizes the long-term commitment, and hence understands the years it takes to work within and build relationships with and in communities. I also understand that the best conditions for this work are not always in place and so we must engage where we are invited, working with the limits of the contingencies of each project. Finally, I admit the importance of using art as process and product in communities, and how staying with arts practices, staying in the metaphors as they emerge, reveals significant personal and community shifts.

Figure 1

Figure 1 is a photograph of a house, taken in early evening, late winter. The depicted house is made of brick and has a white wooden porch, a simple fence, and sits on a corner lot. The sun is going down; it is barely above the horizon, as visible in the mid left. Snow crowds the sidewalks and streets, and there is a lone walker centred in the bottom left quarter of the photograph. They are walking along the unplowed road. The room illuminated through the window on the second floor of the house sends a warm glow to the street beneath. The three-story house occupies the right half of the photograph.

The house reads *home*. A warm, safe interior is imagined, and home becomes a place where we leave behind cold streets, pass a limin, and enter a sanctuary from the external world.

Look more closely and we see signs. One advertises the presence of "neighbourhood watch" and another tells us that no trucks are allowed on this residential street. Neighbourhood watch organizations ensure that people living in these houses know each other and will cooperate with police —a level of surveillance is tolerated to support the common interest of crime prevention.[1] Criminal or suspicious behaviour is noted and reported. People not from the neighbourhood are surveilled more closely. Their home is not here.

The concept of home is ordinary and complicated; it may not always conjure safety, warmth, or sanctuary. Avery Gordon writes that life's complications appear obvious yet we never seem to totally "grasp [this notion] in its widest significance" (2008, p. 3). There is power hidden within this idea and power and its fluid nature are not always recognized. In addition, Gordon suggests that there is a complexity of personhood for all of us who live in and outside of neighbourhoods: "it's about conferring the respect on others that comes from presuming that life and people's lives are simultaneously straightforward and full of enormously subtle meaning" (p. 5). The binary of *homeless* and *not-homeless* begins to unravel inside these contemporary practices, where complex personhood (Gordon, 2008) is bestowed on neighbours and strangers, and where complications are where crossings are made between homes and homeless, and ideas and theories about social relations and how power structures these. These thoughts and practices are central in the work I do exploring homeless and not-homeless alongside disability and poverty.

Arts Research in the area of homelessness, disability, and poverty

HOMELESSNESS IS INCOHERENCE that I gather. It staggers through my hands onto paper, and blisters my lips. It is an impossible structure; I do not have the tools that it wants. Homelessness wants me to split this paper and these words with something harder.

Lacking an ax or hammer, a level, wood, nails, insulation, I am left with what I collect. Words, memory, the words of others, images, imagination. This present moment that is filled with hauntings. For I lack other phrases. I have spent time without language, so much so that my discovery of it is a surprise. I find it shuddering in cold, damp parking lots behind storage units in industrial parks where food banks are on the edge (like their customers). Homelessness in all its vacant lot prettiness. I wear two or three tattered hoodies and stuff words like Mr. Noodles™ into my pockets.

---

3 http://www.cpatoronto.org/community_programs.htm#Neighbourhood%20Watch. Retrieved 1 September, 2009.

This – what you read – is a mirror, *broken* – the words exist as a gathering of a history that is still a-part. It is a walk through a history that is in pieces, in alleys, stuck in the sugary bottom of a teacup.

Homelessness is not even history for it is erased before it settles onto the streets, swept up. And this is troubling, this disappearance before shadows are cast. How can we respond to these "*stories and images that insist remembrance be accountable to the demand for non-indifference*" (Simon, p. 2, italics added). Simon writes something that helps. Although their working group's focus is on trauma, testimony, memory, and the Holocaust, I take their method and transpose it to the streets of Toronto.

They are looking to the past in order to understand what an "ethical practice and pedagogy of remembrance" and a "responsible historical consciousness" might be (Ibid.). "Opening anew to the actuality of enacting or deciding the range of possibilities within which we live as purposeful human beings" they engage in an exploration of Holocaust testimony, relationality, and public ethics (Ibid., p. 3). I ally my quest with theirs, albeit my quest is not far and distant but temporally and geographically close. Their work is hopeful as I move forward in the present with the ghosts/not/ghosts of the Citizen Homeless.

{48}   Simon writes of the necessity of being present with ghosts. I ask that we do something more difficult, and that is to be present with the living who have become ghosts through social neglect. Social exclusion.

For months and years I attempt this writing about working in the arts with homeless people and my hands stop. It is usually only when I am with the people I have worked with that words arrive. When we are together, listening. And so I conjure them through the lighting of candles, through silence, as the snow falls and lifts this spirit. This paper is hard. The ax can't split it.

I am haunted by absences. The lack of language, of politics, of people I once knew. If the people I speak to on the streets disappear who shall speak their words? If I have attended to their words, their gestures, then we can recuperate these. As Walter Benjamen teaches us: "every image of the past that is not recognized by the present as one of its own concerns threatens to disappear irretrievably" (1968, 255, cited in Simon, 2005, p. 148). But let's write it differently: "every image of the *present* that is not recognized by the present as one of its own concerns threatens to disappear irretrievably" (ibid., with "present" exchanged for "past").

We can theorize homelessness through notions of invisibility and occlusion, the exclusion of present citizens. We can critique the present discourse from within homelessness advocacy which has only one rallying cry: end homelessness. Homelessness as an occurrence in the lives of individuals and our larger society garners mortal and brutal attention. Yet, there is more, there are obligations, and rights that are only partially bestowed.

> Why is it that some people have so much and yet so many people do not have nearly enough to live or eat let along have life's luxuries or life's necessities? Wouldn't it be nice if all of us people could share and live and love and help one another without greed and strife? We all would have a much better place to live together. Through these eyes I can only see what is yet put before me . . .
>
> —Ray, 2007.

Homelessness, disability and poverty are concerns that can be understood as intersecting points in the lives of multiple citizens. Each one of these derives benefit from a complexity even without touching the axis of its others, and each in their vast numbers have become ordinary, invisible experiences. These can also be imagined as more than isolated problems; instead, perceive these as failed public attitudes, failed policy, and the success of a political system that blames individuals for their exclusion and will not perceive its structural faults and limitations.

{49}

IN THE STREETHEALTH REPORT (2006), *Failing the homeless*, the consequences of ignoring the realities of the barriers for disabled persons who are also homeless are highlighted using the context of Toronto, a large urban centre, in a country that has no national housing program. These consequences include early death, longer hospitalizations, poorer health, increased costs to the health care system, and longer stays on the streets.

To move from a state of homelessness, poverty and disability is a series of acts and imaginings that lack stability in terms of both internal and external locations. "Homelessness entails a loss of the network of relations that make up an individual's identity" (Arnold, 2004, p. 12). This loss is significant in that when looked at closely I read the context of family or work (in all of their guises) for instance and how this lack perpetuates precarious existence (Ibid.). And yet there is something in this statement of Arnold's that does not apprehend the relationships that exist in different spaces.

"The guilt we feel can be so overwhelming that it is either neutralized or turned back on to the homeless as contempt and rage (Arnold, 2004, p. 16).

> I hate this. All it does is makes us all feel guilty for something we as citizens have nothing to apologize for. We pay an exorbitant amount in taxes – I should never have to see any homeless on the streets of our city. You really want to help them? Circumvent their civil rights and force them into treatment – get them alcohol & drug free. How about workfare to instill some pride & money earned for work done? Oh yeah – that idea for a homeless/addiction house on the corner of Richmond & Peter? That's just about the stupidest idea I've ever heard.[4]

> - Das, T. April 2, 2007 @ 3:32 pm

Homelessness and disability unite as their frayed threads are caught under the wheels of our contemporary neoliberal values, the cultural imaginary. Their inability to contribute to market forces create them as abject (Kristeva, 1988), vulnerable to accumulated hatred.

{50}

First. Breathe.

As I commence I feel a familiar sensation to which I must turn. It is encompassed by an ordinary turning away, as if there was something that cannot be perceived in these words.

> As I walk over to him I catch his eye. His skin is dark with dirt, as well as the hours of being in the sun. I begin to hunker down beside him on the curb, asking if that is ok. He agrees, but minimally, with a small nod that seems to collapse his body. I ask another question, can I talk to him, and he responds with his embodied no; a slow turning from side-to-side. He is dressed in heavy clothing, camouflage gear pants, jacket, and a toque. It is a hot, humid day and the others I am with are dressed in light clothing. I thank the seated man and ask if I can get him a coffee or other drink, or food from the donut shop (we were in the parking lot) and he again shakes

---

4 This comment is directed toward a public art series by Mark Daye. Daye's work, a series of signs posted throughout Toronto, is exemplary public art in that it subverts the messages of officially posted signs while mimicking their form.

his body in what I came to understand as no. I thank him, stand up and walk away. I wonder if the encounter could have gone any other way.

In the work I do there may be numerous encounters like the one I have just described from a recent recruitment foray. An invitation is set out and either accepted or declined. And then I wonder.

I sit across from a woman. She is telling me her story as part of her testimony about homelessness. We record our interaction.

I'm twenty-one. I cannot keep on pulling myself up. I got a place yesterday but it's no bigger than a jail cell. I don't care, it's a roof over my head and a bed. I'd rather be in a jail cell then this place. It's a start, but . . . I'm scared to live on my own. Last year I was sleeping in the alley. If you go down the stairs, you'll see I put the seat of a van there, it blocks the wind, but it's just like, dark and dingy . . . just scary. At the beginning of grade ten I started drinking so I was just like, I was too drunk to go to school. Everything started really going downhill, it mostly happened when my father died. I just ended up giving up on life. It has not been easy. And I'm just, like, I'm all by myself. Since thirteen, living on the streets. I have been suicidal, I've been on mental wards but I'm still here. It's hard being a single woman on the street especially when you're so small. People take advantage of you at any time. I was raped and I just thought about it and I'm just saying it's not going to happen again. I've been wanting to go through Victim Services but I'm afraid to. Like, I mean, since I was thirteen, I been raped five times.

I bring you this, not in hope that these words will pin the subject to the paper, but in hope that it will release at least some small part of her. I do not claim that this is an authentic representation either, just words heard months ago that I am still trying to make sense from. This fragment comes from a project that explores poverty, health, and homelessness in a suburban area. Our purpose is clear. A small group of researchers are here, our presence requested by a poverty action group who want assistance in bringing stories forward in order to engender policy change. We want others to better understand the homelessness that is endured in this region. Our intent is to make a video, gather stills, shift the perception of homelessness from a charity model to rights-based one, and speak about homelessness and disability in the same breath. The initial findings suggest that the difference between poverty and homelessness in urban or suburban regions is both vast and minimal. Mortality, injury, trauma are exceedingly high for these citizens.

Second. Imagine.

Viva Davis Halifax

A table of women. There is a hum, a murmuring. Necks curled like ferns, faces down, toward a table. Awareness of each other is buried. Moments pass, breaths are drawn. We come together as a group and for a moment or more we exist in community. And then, an exhalation and there is a return to silence, murmurings; these are closed rehearsals. This constant round of inhalation and exhalation makes temporality perceptible and we become aware of the time that this community requires, and the necessity that we as artists need to learn to attune to their needs. We are teaching each other a new alphabet based on breath, silence, murmurings.

At the end of April 2009, I completed a Toronto Arts Council Access Grant as a member artist in a collective[5] located in a part of Toronto, Ontario that is being gentrified. These forces have not quite reached this area, this particular anonymous building, and these women. Women arrive at our tables[6] each week from areas as diverse as China, Somalia, Pakistan, Swaziland, the Maritimes, Ontario, and Toronto. Our skin colours range from brown, black, white, yellow; not all of us are English speaking. Our bodies are replete with differences. The work over the past months was ambitious, even too ambitious for the women, *whose pasts fracture their present*, housed in this shelter. The initial research and development project had to be slowed in order to attune to their needs. As we came to orient to the women our work began to emerge as a phenomenological arts project.[7]

{52}

---

5 The Red Wagon Collective is composed of artist/inquirers in Canada and includes myself and Liz Forsberg, and past members Loree Lawrence, Amy Kazymerchyk, and Noah Kenneally.
   http://gatheringspace.blogspot.com

6 These tables, these rooms, are given to our collaborative in exchange for the work we do with the people in the shelter. In Toronto many of the shelters are run by faith organizations, while the organizations themselves are run as charities. From a critical disability studies perspective a charity model is one that forgets the politics associated with disability and homelessness, and instead works on an individual model where persons are often blamed for their life circumstances. The power people encounter "is bureaucratic rather than democratic" (Arnold 2004, p. 14). The complexity of explicating the contexts for this work in shelters is the subject of another paper, yet to be written, while it exists in the form of the moneyProject.

7 We started in 2008 with an initial transformative goal, which was to create a garden and a mural. Over time we recognized that the goals articulated to the Arts Council and those languaged in the group were in tension, and that the women would be the ones we would be following.

Viva Davis Halifax

What is held in common across these two projects is homelessness, disabilities, and chronic health problems; violence, trauma, and oppression is a daily mark for the Citizen Homeless.

In this group we eat and drink, take photographs, draw, knit, crochet, braid our lives and selves together. We move in our roles from teacher to learner to teacher. To undertake this work is always to issue a warning or caution. As Audre Lorde stated, "I was going to die, if not sooner, than later whether or not I had ever spoken myself" (20). "[S]peaking/putting ourselves into words exposes us, makes us visible, and that opens us to various threats, some of them material" (Perreault, 1999, p. 25). Audre Lorde suggests that the risk is worth it. Though placing one's self into words may invoke some external risk there is a pressure that emanates from an interior: a summons is issued to sanction the writing and speaking of self.

Speaking the self through aesthetic texts provides a symbolic space where safety can be woven through metaphor and media. Speaking through the development of a collage, a knitted scarf, the creation of a series of friendship bracelets language unfolds.

When we sit down over our cups of tea, I listen to bodies and voices. I perceive frustration, the violence experienced because others do not listen. My work is to bring their stories to a broader community, and at the same time to maintain an ethical and safe space. So often there is only silence. It is the silence of trauma, the experiences that have as yet no language. That exist as gesture: these are the ones we collect and provide form for over the months.

"Born in the positivity of the experiential, the self is nonetheless formed in the material limits of its discursive context" (Probyn). But what if the discursive context is silence? What if the self, her body, trembling, drawn into history (Cixous) has stumbled into a room where there is no possibility for emergence?

Right: Imagined banner for exterior; digitally manipulated photograph.

What occurs "when those who have the power to name and to socially construct reality choose not to see or hear you" (p. 34 Rich cited in Perreault). What if there is no witness?

For those without housing there may only be silence. They are cast as Other, and as such their voices remain outside of the discourses that shape knowledge of them.

Walking to and from the shelter allows me time to think. I imagine a strategy that will allow us to work with the women in a productive and gentle manner, which will support the shelter's goals of transformation. We talk about it around the table, with hot cups of Somali tea. The making of banners that incorporate the women's art is one way of working between community, shelter and each woman's story. The women respond in a positive way to this notion. This way of working is in accord with Suzanne Lacy, who suggested that art be redefined less as a product and more as "a process of value finding, a set of philosophies, an ethical action, and an aspect of a larger sociocultural agenda" (p. 46). Working with these guiding principles we will be able to work toward social justice through the arts. We reach this solution as our funding comes to an end. We apply for additional funds, wait four months and find that we have been successful. Our work can begin again.

The work I do as an arts-informed researcher brings me to communities and peoples who have been displaced from their aesthetic and cultural powers and have either not been represented or been represented through cultural mechanisms over which they lack power. Members of these communities are chronically and profoundly homeless, lack secure access to food and employment as well as any sustained means of cultural production. They experience chronic health problems, disability, and more illness.

I am, and have been, drawn to work with people, and in communities where there have been significant displacements, where distress is an external appearance on the landscape and an internal circumstance of this citizenry. My responsibility is to work towards social justice, and equity, and to teach about the circumstances through writing and arts-informed research. The deaths of the most vulnerable on our streets haunt me. Every season provides new challenges. And always there is isolation, fear, shame, loneliness.

> Awkward child, arms and legs angled
> To catch every bruise thrown.
> Readied by lonely cigarettes at ten
> She finds a place behind a door
> Where her frame's slight strength
> Is shored up.

Viva Davis Halifax

Her copper hair
Less bright than the
Flame held under a spoon, where
She cooks and washes.
It is never right that she be there:
Other children held close behind doors
Their light framed by curtains and locks and homework.

Smoke rings drift from her lips,
Sometimes she falls asleep
burning. Awake her mouth opens to filch
The last touch of relentless dark
Later breathing it out,
Exhaling a lawn, two trees, a row of bushes.

Witch, criminal, mad girl, dreamer,
Lover, she is   {55}
Framed by dark relentless exhalations.

I work in artist collectives, and research teams, like the ones described above. However this writing
about the work is firmly situated and lead by my own preoccupations, shaped by my memories
and selves.

At eleven she began to take control, staying out later
Knowing the consequences on her slight frame like a bedtime story.
Locked in, she would open the window, crawl out
To the picnic table, jump down and scamper
Across the garden like one of the Flopsy Bunnies.
Good night moon, she sang to herself.

Staring out from the bushes feared he would drag her back she watched the car
Lights until they disappeared and then
To the next bush.

Viva Davis Halifax

The red roads illuminated by the sound of irate wheels
Wet interior of a beige car fumed with Rob Roys, poppied with mothers pills,
Driving through streets with names of Queens and Kings
The streets had names that wore crowns
And red gems while she wore flannel shirts and hoodies while
At her wrist a bracelet emerges.
My pulse races like a girl's as she travels red roads.
Questions, the shadows trailing the light.

To fully develop as citizen participants in a social democracy we must advance the imaginations of citizens so that they can begin to think critically and perceive solutions to problems – to do so we must ensure that they are involved in transformative and creative projects using the arts.

I write from a place I call home. Throughout, there are scattered points where silence accumulates. In these places I listen, with eyes closed, senses open to the possibility of translation/re/presentation, of bringing lives and others to language. This home is a site of my privilege. It is here that I take refuge, work with small sounds, minute gestures, pushing them into the world as language.

I write from a place I call refuge, with senses open to minute gestures and closed eyes. Throughout language the world is scattering.

Listen.

Viva Davis Halifax

NANCY VIVA DAVIS HALIFAX, PH.D, is an assistant professor of critical disability studies at York University and brings her interdisciplinary experience to her teaching and research, which is located at the intersections of health care, gender, embodiment, difference, and disability, arts-informed research, and pedagogy. She has worked broadly in health research using the arts and documentary, and participatory methods with economically displaced persons in Canada. Her research uses the arts for sustaining and creating conversations around social change, self-determination, social auto/biographies, and for engaging communities in cultural democracy.

{57}

Viva Davis Halifax

References

ARNOLD, K. (2004). *Homelessness, citizenship and identity: The uncanniness of late modernity*. Albany, NY: SUNY.

BECKER, C. (1994). *The subversive imagination: artists, society, and responsibility*. New York, NY & London, UK: Routledge.

BEHAR, S. (1996.) *The Vulnerable Observer: Anthropology That Breaks Your Heart*. Boston, MA: Beacon.

CARSON, A. (1993). *Eros the bittersweet*. Urbana-Champaign, IL: Dalkey Archive Press.

CIXOUS, H. (1993). *Three steps on the ladder of writing*. New York, NY & London, UK: Routledge.

{58} DAS, T. (2007). Comment. Spacing blog. Retrieved December 12, 2008. http://spacing.ca/wire/2007/04/02/homeless-signs/

DAVIS HALIFAX, N. V. (2009). *Disability and illness in arts-informed research: Moving towards postconventional representations*. Amherst, NY: Cambria.

GABLIK, S. (1991). *The reenchantment of art*. London: UK: Thames and Hudson.

GORDON, A. F. (1997). *Ghostly matters: Haunting and the sociological imagination*. Minneapolis, MN: University of Minnesota Press.

KRISTEVA, J. (1988). *Powers of horror: An essay on abjection*. New York, NY: Columbia University Press.

KRØJER, J., HØLGE-HAZELTON, B. (2008). Poethical: breaking ground for reconstruction. *International Journal of Qualitative Studies in Education, 21*, 1: 27 – 33.

LACY, S. (ED.). (1995). *Mapping the terrain: New genre public art*. Seattle, WA: Bay Press.

LATHER, P. (2001). Postbook: Working the Ruins of Feminist Ethnography. *Signs*, 27,1: 199-227.

LORDE, A. (1980). *The cancer journals.* San Francisco, CA: Aunt Lute Books.

PELIAS, R. (2005). Performative writing as scholarship: An apology, an argument, an Anecdote. *Cultural Studies, Critical Methodologies*, 5,4: 415-424.

PERREAULT, J. M. (1995). *Writing selves: Contemporary feminist autography.* Minneapolis, MN: University of Minnesota Press.

POLLACK, G. (1994). (1994). Inscriptions in the feminine. In M. Catherine de Zegher (Curator & Ed.), *Inside the visible: An elliptical traverse of 20th century art.* (pp. 67-87). Cambridge, MA: MIT Press.

PROBYN, ELSPETH (2004). Everyday shame. *Cultural Studies*, 18:2, 328 – 349.

RAY. (2007). Personal communications.

SHILDRICK, MARGRIT (2005). The disabled body, genealogy and undecidability. *Cultural Studies*, 19 (6): 755 – 770.

SIMON, R. (2002). Remembrance as praxis and the ethics of the inter-human. Culture Machine, 4: 1-27. Retrieved November 12, 2008. http://www.culturemachine.net/index.php/cm/article/view/272/257

SIMON, R. (2005). *The touch of the past: Remembrance, learning and ethics.* New York, NY: Palgrave, MacMillan.

STACEY, J. (1988). Can there be a feminist ethnography? *Women's Studies International Forum*, 2(1), 21-27.

STREETHEALTH. (2006). *Failing the homeless: Barriers in the Ontario Disability Support Program for homeless people with disabilities.* Toronto, ON: Streethealth. Available from: HTTP://WWW.STREETHEALTH.CA/ DOWNLOADS/FAILFULL.PDF.

TICIENTO CLOUGH, P. (2007). *The Affective Turn: Theorizing the Social.* Durham, NC: Duke University.

Viva Davis Halifax

WALTER R. MCDONALD & ASSOCIATES, INC. (2004). *Strategies for Reducing Chronic Street Homelessness.* Final
Report Prepared for: U.S. Department of Housing and Urban Development, Office of Policy Development
and Research. Sacramento, CA: The Urban Institute. Retrieved September 6, 2009 www.huduser.org/
Publications/PDF/ChronicStrtHomeless.pdf - 2007-10-30.

Viva Davis Halifax

Engaging Neighbors, Transforming Toxic Realities

Community Environmental Forum Theatre Using Augusto Boal's Theatre of the Oppressed to Promote Environmental Justice

John Sullivan

Theatre is a form of knowledge; it should and can also be a means of transforming society. Theatre can help us build a future, rather than just waiting for it.

Augusto Boal

"Games for Actors and Non-Actors"

In 2002, The Community Outreach and Education Core (COEC) of the Sealy Center for Environmental Health & Medicine (SCEHM)/National Institute of Environmental Health Sciences (NIEHS) at the University of Texas Medical Branch at Galveston launched a unique approach to community-based research practice, integrating the inclusive participatory principles, personal story focus, multiple view-points and embodied techniques of Augusto Boal's 'Theatre of the Oppressed' (TO), and the dialogic engagement of Paulo Freire's "democratizing pedagogy" into the design and implementation of environmental health research, community health care, and environmental public health education (Sullivan, *Local Environment*, p. 629). In collaboration with a variety of grassroots partner organizations, the NIEHS COEC's Public Forum & Toxics Assistance Division (PFTA) offers "Community Environmental Forum Theater" educational workshops and public performances, an inclusive, drama-based outreach modality, that clarifies and articulates local needs and integrates local knowledge into the agendas and design of community-based participatory research (CBPR). (*1. Animating Democracy hyperlink) The COEC has supported a series of Forum production workshops throughout the Gulf Coast region, and additional projects with NIEHS partners in Buffalo, New York and Chattanooga, Tennessee.[1] (*2. Behind the Fence, Community Arts Network hyperlink) COEC personnel offered CEFT training workshops at various EPA sponsored Community Involvement Conferences, National Estuary Program workshops, and numerous state and regional gatherings, such as the Louisiana Environmental Action Network annual meeting. (*3. EPA CIC hyperlink) In addition to serving the overt purposes of environmental health education and research capacity-building, these workshop / performance

---

* See hyperlink references, p. 85

projects model a more equitable relationship between science and communities informed by the working principles of Environmental Justice, and the expectations of sound CBPR practice.

Environmental Justice, CBPR & Paulo Freire: Complimentary Philosophies for the Forum:

THE U.S. ENVIRONMENTAL JUSTICE MOVEMENT grew from the struggle of residents in Afton, a predominantly Black community in Warren County, North Carolina, to close and clean up a toxic waste pit containing PCB-laden materials. (Bullard, pp. 30-32) As the movement spread, Environmental Justice activists incorporated the ideals and advocacy strategies of the civil rights movement and evolved a philosophical framework that resonates closely with Boal and Freire in the following concepts and principles:

☞ Disproportionate exposures to environmental hazards are direct outgrowths of systemic race and class oppressions.

☞ Inclusion is of paramount importance; efforts to expand inclusion may be difficult, but they are always positive.

☞ The "big picture" is inter-subjective and multiple points-of-view must be accepted: science or established law is not the final arbiter of reality as experienced by Environmental Justice communities.

☞ Narratives of struggle and mutual support are important sources of strength, as well as qualitative data in Environmental Justice communities.

☞ Place is unique and important; the site-specifics of toxic exposures, health effects and destructive social outcomes are not merely mechanistic puzzles for science to solve.

☞ Authentic engagement is an indispensible *sine qua non* when Environmental Justice communities, researchers and regulatory agencies agree to talk and work together. Authentic engagement usually implies agonistic respect and critical responsiveness. (Schlosberg, pp. 145-147)

Community-Based Participatory Research (CBPR) was conceived as a model for collaboration and dialogue among public health research stake-holders which emphasizes equity in issue focus and levels of participation, and provides necessary access to the resources and expertise of community, university and health care provider research partners (Sullivan, J. et al., *Local Environment*, p. 629). Defined as 'a collaborative approach to research that equitably involves all partners in the research process and recognizes the unique strengths that each brings', CBPR widens the angle of regard for public health research, acknowledging that community networks and leaders, adverse social and economic consequences of environmental degradation, and community beliefs and attitudes toward scientific collaboration are all vital factors that directly impact the efficacy of research and community outreach (Katz, D.L., 2004 [serial online]). The practice of authentic CBPR "challenges the positivist basis of science, the construction and uses of knowledge, the ethical role of researchers in engaging society, the role of agency and participation by the

El Teatro Lucha por la Salud del Barrio sets up a an image of exposure pathways in the near north Houston barrio at the top of a Community Environmental Forum Theatre production. (de Madres a Madres, T.e.j.a.s. and the Sealy Center for Environmental Health & Medicine at the Holy Name Auditorium; Houston TX 2005) Photo by Karla Held community, the importance of power relationships that permeate the research process, and our capacity to become a more just and equitable society" (Wallersten & Duran, p. 27). Community-based research represents a Freirean correction to the trend ceding policy-making to experts at the expense of meaningful citizen input; Frank Fischer calls this movement "popular epidemiology" and hails it as "not only an intervention in public health discourse, but also a method for critical praxis that can restructure the undemocratic expert / client relationship because hypotheses, analysis and interpretation directly affects the social power dynamic" (Fischer, *Citizens, Experts and the Environment*, p. 155-156).

Science enjoys a prominent advantage over a community's knowledge base in interpreting data, determining damage to health and ecosystems, and prescribing ameliorative measures, because highly technical processes – such as public health or regulatory risk assessments – depend almost entirely on scientific expertise for validity. In *Street Science*, Jason Corburn explains this "exceptionalism" in terms of expertise disparities and scientific claim to neutrality and objectivity.

"Technocrats argue that experience in a given area and training in specialized collection and systematic analysis of information allow them as professionals to tackle issues with neutrality and dispassionate objectivity" (Corburn, p. 39).

{64}   CBPR recognizes that the storied objectivity of science is never guaranteed for "science is infused with normative, subjective judgments" and attempts to dispel this "myth of exclusivity?" that undermines the credibility of community-initiated science by inviting community organizations to actively collude with researchers in framing scientific questions and designing research: including hypothesis development and co-design of research protocols, direct community involvement in data collection, collaborative interpretation of findings, setting timetables for public release of project information, and co-authorship of project reports and papers (Fischer, 192). Various public and non-profit sector public health initiatives, including projects sponsored by the Kellogg Foundation, the Centers for Disease Control (CDC), the Institute of Medicine (IOM) and various subsets of the National Institutes of Health (NIH), such as the National Institute for Environmental Health Sciences (NIEHS), now regularly promote collaborative methods and incorporate CBPR into their repertoire of funded outreach and evaluation modalities.

However, the most important convergence of TO practitioners, Freirean educators, environmental justice activists, and community-engaged environmental health researchers centers on a shared faith that a bidirectional (or transitive) relationship organically connects communities of co-learners – teachers to students, community member to researchers – in a collaborative enterprise of meaning-making. Using Boal's "arsenal of the Theater of the Oppressed," community workshop participants, environmental Forum audiences, and their research partners may collectively dismantle what Freire referred to as the "myth of an unassailable reality," a belief that oppressive (in this case, toxic) realities cannot be changed, and that powerlessness is a permanent fact of existence. For at the heart of Freire's pedagogy, Boal's dramaturgy, authentic CBPR practice and the struggle for environmental justice, is a shared commitment to progressive values and an overarching optimism. And the core of Freirean philosophy is rooted in an unshakeable first premise that "through serious, just, determined, untiring struggle, it is possible to remake the world." (Freire, p. 174)

Mirroring Nina Wallerstein's assertion that "…the paramount public health goal of eliminating disparities demands a research practice within the emancipatory (Freirean) perspective that fosters the democratic participation of community members to change their own lives," Community Environmental Forum Theatre was designed to be a community/science interface that enlarges the scope of research, increases the effectiveness of interventions and strives to integrate and infuse peer-reviewed science into the ongoing efforts of community environmental health advocates to educate, mobilize and defend their constituencies and influence environmental regulatory policy (Wallerstein & Duran, p. 29).

"Tox, Risk, and Stress": a TO Curriculum Incorporating Toxicology, Cumulative Risk, Vulnerability & Environmental Health

COMMUNITY ENVIRONMENTAL FORUM THEATRE OFFERS grassroots groups throughout the Texas / Louisiana Gulf Coast petrochemical belt an opportunity to use the tools of Image Theater, dramatic improvisation, and leading edge environmental science research to analyze and develop a wide range of useful toxicological concepts, to develop a working knowledge of the linkages among toxic exposures and human health effects, cumulative risk, and to understand how toxic exposures, risk burdens, and socio-economic factors contribute to environmental injustices impacting their families. This *"tox, risk, & stress"* curriculum incorporates basic (qualitatively framed) toxicology, community ethnography, social epidemiology and environmental justice covering concepts such as:

☜· **Tox**: Participatory image structures and sociometry exercises illustrate toxicology concepts germane to community needs for information. The "tox" component encompasses traditional exposure toxicology concepts such as: exposure pathways, dose response parameters – magnitude, duration, frequency, timing - susceptibility factors, vulnerable populations, bioaccumulation, bio-magnification, fate, transport and bioavailability, biomarkers of exposure and susceptibility, Persistent-Organic-Pollutants (POPs), chemical body burdens and a brief introduction to community-based, popular epidemiology. (Sexton, pp. 38-45)

☞ **Risk:** This component stems from an image-based community ethnography process in which participants build site-specific snapshots of exposure pathways, risk perceptions, risk & action priorities, personal experience with EJ and environmental health issues, community power dynamics, and create image maps of community assets, and stressors. Sociometry exercises allow participants to determine intra-group safety and toxic abatement priorities, as well as sampling the spectrum of group experience regarding the personal effects of toxic exposures (ATSDR, pp. 2(1) – 2(16)).

☞ **Stress:** Facilitator and participants use personal stories and community lore to create short scenes and improvisational exercises exploring the health effects of cumulative community stress burdens from chronic toxic exposures, environmentally-induced health effects, lack of access to needed health care and other well documented social-economic indicators of health, opportunity and justice disparities. Stressors originate from various sectors of our social-economic reality and Forum scenes illustrate how these burdens converge upon and oppress our most vulnerable communities. The concepts of multiple stressor effects, cumulative risk, and the influence of these factors on a community's ability to identify, mitigate and ultimately recover from chronic toxic assaults closely guides planning scenes for the public Forum (ATSDR, pp. 4(1) – 4 (33)); (NEJAC, pp.31-33). (Sullivan & Parras, *Theory in Action*, p. 22)

A kinetic image shows how bioaccumulation impacts neighborhood health and adds to the cumulative burden of environmental justice communities. (Citizens for Environmental Justice; Corpus Christi, TX; 2003) vPhoto by Dr. Jonathan Ward

A fence-line family "circles the wagons" for protection when one of the children is diagnosed with Acute Lymphocytic Leukemia. (Community In-Power & Development Association; Port Arthur TX 2004) Photo by Bryan Parras.

Making Images of Life in Community:
From Present Realities to Imagined Ideal Futures

IN ADDITION TO THIS THEATRE-BASED APPROACH to teaching environmental and social science concepts, Community Environmental Forum Theatre participant / actors also prepare images and short scenes to perform for an audience of their neighbors and community leaders. These scenes focus on themes and incidents that dramatize the significance of "tox, risk and stress" factors within each community's unique context. Throughout the course of an intensive workshop, actors create stop action photo images to represent site-specific social and toxicological characteristics of their own environmental justice community. Working in small groups, with one community actor alternately serving as "sculptor" and the others as "clay", participants build mockups of social life in their communities. The images they create fall into two major categories: 1) frozen actions showing people in relation to one another, involved in a process of doing or saying something (Action Images), or 2) pictures of the subtext or submerged significance of actions, events or relationships, such as sculptural tableaus depicting political marginalization, environmental racism, or feelings of community solidarity (Essence Images). These images become part of a larger ethnographic tool demonstrating community risk perceptions, attitudes toward activist engagement , existing social capital and local power dynamics, ultimately yielding embodied versions of what Clifford Geertz termed "thick descriptions" of community dreams and realities (Geertz, pp. 3-30). Eight primary image exercises form the core of a community portrait or ethnography that describes the look and feel of facts on the ground in environmental justice communities. Workshop participants are asked to collaboratively create group sculptures of the following concepts, situations, and scenarios:

> ☞ Images of our worst environmental fear." (risk perception, exposure priorities)

> ☞ Images of point-source or secondary source pollution in our neighborhood / community." (community hazard mapping)

> ☞ Images of how people come in contact with this pollution in our daily lives. (exposure pathways)

> ☞ Images of how my neighbors respond when I give them facts (bad news) about their environmental health. (community attitudes, beliefs, resistances)

☞ Images of how it feels to live in my polluted community. (affective witness: emphasis on site-specific situations)

☞ Images of the "power dynamic" that affects the toxic situation in our community: this includes power both within and without, culturally connected or Other,

☞ Images of community assets, cultural capital and where / how it accumulates. (community asset mapping)

☞ A wish-based image of what an environmentally healthy neighborhood would look like" (Real to Ideal transformation, sometimes called "my neighborhood of the future," that integrates aspirations and assets). (Sullivan & Parras, *Theory in Action*, p. 24-25)

'Views of a Secret: Something here is very wrong!' Workshop image shows the extent of a congenital heart disease cluster and various community reactions while an environmental health field worker tries to comprehend the scene and an

environmental health scientist quietly observes from outside the social dynamic. (Citizens for Environmental Justice / Corpus Christi, TX, 2003.) Photo by Juan Parras.

The information gleaned from image ethnography is normally inaccessible to population health researchers working from outside the local dynamics of place, culture and history. CBPR practice and the human rights framework of environmental justice – by questioning the "myth of exclusivity" – have leveraged a position of new prominence for situated, or local, knowledge in identifying focus issues. These ethnographies add value to the efforts of both researchers and communities by increasing the precision of estimates of disease incidence and explanations of culturally-determined exposure pathways, and by extending descriptions of cumulative risk beyond textbook categories and sociological jargon into the realm of real world pressures on families and individuals.

Ethnographic images clearly illustrate how "communities experiencing disproportionate environmental and disease burdens know more about what these problems mean in their daily lives than anyone else ever could." (Corburn, p. 58).

"Fire in the Hole": CIDA Forum actors create image of their worst case environmental scenario – an explosion and fire at a nearby petrochemical facility. (Community In-Power & Development Association / Port Arthur TX; 2004) Photo by Bryan Parras.

For example, the "image of my worst environmental fear" is an abstraction for most scientists, public health practitioners and middle-class environmentalists.UTMB-NIEHS has facilitated numerous workshops at university-sponsored Environmental Justice conferences, EPA Community Involvement conferences, NIEHS and PIRG meetings, etc. and the generality of this image is remarkably uniform. Environmental justice communities, however, go right to the core of their own site-specific problem and create detailed, recognizable images of hazardous waste sites, petrochemical facility fence-lines, or neighborhood cancer clusters that exist "right out the window." This physicalized ethnographic work is also useful in *laying bare* how the undercurrents of power can block or promote change in an Environmental Justice community.

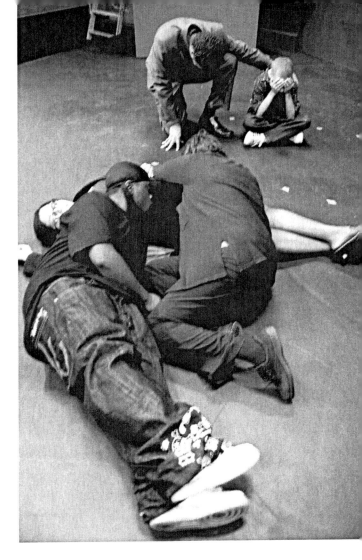

I can't watch my neighborhood die – a collective worst case environmental nightmare of lead poisoning and lupus near the 858 Ferry Street Superfund site." (Toxic Waste / Lupus Coalition – 858 Ferry Street Superfund Site / Buffalo NY). Photo by Bryan Parras.

The image of "how my neighbors respond" may focus on reactions from local businesses, politicians, regulatory agencies or the industrial sector when activists press for substantive pollution abatement, permit enforcement, access to health care or changes in an industry-biased tax framework. Used in this way, a reaction image segues smoothly into an overarching image of the local or regional power dynamic with respect to environmental justice. The image of an environmentally healthy neighborhood or community uses a special Boal image structure called the **Real to Ideal** image. Community actors morph images of their lived reality into ideal images of the community they would choose to inhabit. After creating a series of these images, individual actors alternate sculpting single images that synopsize a spectrum of everyone's ideal characteristics. This procedure, *Image of the Images*, provides a visual picture of possible goals for future actions. Another image structure, *Images of Transition*, may also be used to detail successive approximations of that ultimate goal, allowing the group to move more realistically through various stages of environmental and community reclamation. (Sullivan & Parras, *Theory in Action*, p.25)

Images may be used to illustrate a community's wealth of assets or need for additional mobilization in response to environmental challenges. Image and improvisational character development structures also provide the basis for performed scenarios that connect environmental toxicity to real life outcomes. Boal created techniques to "dynamize" freeze frame images, gradually awakening the characters inside the image by giving them personal gestures, then phrases, words and sentences – in an internal monologue – to accompany the gestures, finally asking them to move beyond the relatively static gestural movements while improvising dialogue. As they begin their unmoored movements, the characters relate to other actors in the original freeze frame and the image begins to resemble an actual scene in slow motion. (Boal, *Games for Actors & Non-Actors*, 176-203) Community Environmental Forum Theatre riffs on these techniques, using a sequence of three images called "Making a Dramatic Sandwich." (*3. wvm file hyperlink) This method begins with a *Core Conflict Image*, then immediately juxtaposes an image of the Past – *where did the actors in this conflict come from?* – followed by an image of the Future – *where did the characters go immediately after the unresolved conflict?* – to chronologically bracket the Core image. This "sandwich" comprises a complete scene; with some embellishments, this de-mystified process is often sufficient for making clear and coherent Forum scenes.

Boal's complete arsenal of interactive games, image techniques and improvisational structures is an immense body of empirical research in applied theatre. He considers each element of the TO process as equally crucial for arriving at the "final product": a Forum scene (or scenes) that effectively represents the effects of oppression on the actual lives of an oppressed group, and resonates with an audience, activating "spect-actors" to physically engage the issues on stage, and continue their involvement in dialogue and advocacy beyond the performance event. The tools and techniques commonly employed in Community Environmental Forum Theatre focus on moving quickly through toxicological concepts and image ethnography into the more traditionally dramatic realm of basic acting and devising scenes. In the process, we have borrowed moves from other forms of applied theatre – most notably Playback, and Sociodrama / Sociometry – and refined the TO menu to include a flexible *carte du jour* of methods appropriate to our environmental justice focus. Though far from exhaustive, the following list offers an overview of various methods and para-theatrical workshop formats incorporated into the practice of Community Environmental Forum Theatre:

☞ ***Basic TO Activation Games & Improvisational Exercises***: This segment of the workshop consists of physical activities: non-competitive games, movement routines, trust exercises, and improvisational character-based acting situations that promote awareness of physicality as an expressive tool, what Boal calls a "retuning of the senses" (Goodman & de Gay (Eds.), pp. 32-34). Boal places great emphasis on the importance of TO games, calling them mirrors of social life because of they "synthesize discipline (via rules) and liberty (via creativity, exuberance, improvisation), and serve as "apprenticeships for citizenship" (Boal, *Aesthetics of the Oppressed*, p. 37). Routines such as "I Got Your Back," "One You Fear / One Who Protects," "Carnival in Rio," "Homing Pigeons," "Glass Cobra," "Floating in the Circle," "The Amoeba," "The Empty Hand," "Image Machine," et al. are an essential foundation for developing embodied communication skills essential for the Theatre of the Oppressed.

☞· **Co-Piloting the Image**: This special image technique allows a story-teller and an interpreter to work in pairs, building their own image versions of the same story. The co-pilot often adds image details, or analytic twists to the original story that expand significance for the teller and the group. (Boal, *Rainbow of Desire*, 1995, pp. 87-89)

☞· ***Sociometry*** (*5. Sociometry hyperlink) A process of defining, mapping, measuring and evaluating choices and group dynamics. Viewing choices objectively allows groups to examine and characterize their organizations and networks. Sociometry exercises use movement through space to probe and query group attitudes, preferences and experiences with respect to choices, perceptions and priorities connected with the research. The results of sociometry exercises illustrate the difference between direct vs. vicarious experience of issues addressed in research, the relative value of affective vs. objective evaluations of experience, and the degree of connectedness to or marginalization from issues addressed in the workshop. Results may also be tabulated to provide quantitative feedback on the social characteristics of partnerships.

☞· **Systemic Image**: Small groups devise an animated and vocal image of systemic oppression that incorporates all the other workshop participants. These images are discussed as presented and a last group builds an image that incorporates characteristics from all the previous images using Boal's *Image of the Images* technique. This exercise, developed by Minneapolis educator, Victor Cole, provides a useful schematic for discussing the social power dynamic overarching environmental justice and other social equity issues.

☞· **Cops-in-the-Head:** An "introspective" image schema in Boal's *Rainbow of Desire* system, "Cops . . ." represents the multiple voices and shades of opinion that often cloud environmental issues and make it difficult to decide on competing courses of action. In addition to determining what these clashing voices say, the protagonist of the image sculpts actors into images of what the source of each voice looks like. If this image structure is used in a CEFT performance, spect-actors may step into the constellation of speakers and propose additional voices and sculptural shapes. The protagonist may accept, reject or modify these proposals to better represent the reality they actually experience. (Boal, *Rainbow of Desire*, pp. 136-141)

Community Forum at Bruce Elementary School in Houston TX uses an Image called "Cops-in-the-Head" to demonstrate how conflicting estimates of children's developmental risk from exposure to heavy metals at the nearby MDI Superfund site confuses neighborhood residents." (Mothers for Clean Air - 5th Ward Chapter / Houston TX, 2003) Photo by Bryan Parras.

☞ ***Rashomon:*** Based on the central premise of Akira Kurosawa's eponymous film, the same scene is played from multiple-character viewpoints. This is particularly useful in developing a sense of the complexity surrounding efforts to determine the environmental causes of disease, political strife over efforts to regulate polluting industry and the cumulative effects of multiple health and social stressors on life in environmental justice communities. This can also be used as a stand-alone image structure to take snap-shots of multiple points of view. (Boal, *Rainbow of Desire*, pp. 114-117)

☞ *Janaka's Double:* This image exercise, sometimes called the ***Inside / Outside Imag***e, represents the difference between reactions shown to the world and hidden, inner effects of living with the problems of environmental justice communities. Two actors are sculpted in close relationship to one another, showing how what is externally displayed may be different from what is really felt. This technique is especially revealing in analyzing the collateral toll of living with chronic health effects in toxic neighborhood. (Technique borrowed from Sri Lankan Theatre for Development)

☞ *Johari's Window:* Derived from the Theatre for Development – in common currency throughout Africa and South Asia – this image-based analytic procedure shows how community reality is organized in layers: that which is known to us and them, that which is seen only by them, that which is known only to us, and that which is effectively hidden from both them and us. This structure is especially useful – in tandem with close focus zoom and more distanced, wide angle images - in showing how a community's unique life-ways affect patterns of toxic exposure, belief systems and willingness to change environmental circumstances. Conversely, results of *Johari's Window* may also illustrate the futility of environmental efforts imposed on communities from outside the local power dynamic and culture. (McCarthy, J & Galvao, K, pp. 37-39)

{75}

No skin off my nose: Johari's Window image became the pretext for a scene representing how some citizens in Houston's 5th Ward deliberately ignore the toll of childhood lead poisoning and air pollution on the health of children in the community." (Mothers for Clean Air, 5th Ward Chapter/MDI Super Fund Site, Houston, TX, 2003.) Photo by Bryan Parras.

☞ *Hot Seats:* Antagonist, potential Allies and sometimes the protagonist sit in a chair surrounded by the other actors and answer questions about beliefs, motivations and intentions to deepen the effectiveness of Forum scenes. This technique is sometimes used prior to audience interventions in the Forum to open up these characters and give spect-actors character details they can use when they stop the action and enter the drama. (Technique borrowed from Gestalt)

☞ *Pairs & Fluid Sculptures:* Playback pairs and larger fluids are kinetic sculptures using actor duos or multi-character tableaus that embody both sides of an issue, or probe complex feelings relative to the issues. These sculptures are effective in representing blockages to effective action: excuses, misgivings, cynicism from previous failures to achieve positive results from environmental justice campaigns. (Salas, pp. 31-40)

☞ *Image Playback:* To conclude a show, Forum actors often form group images based on prompts from the audience. These suggestions range from feelings provoked by the performance to concepts such as sustainability, just regulations and accountability, community coexistence with industry, or solidarity in action. Sometimes forum actors will gradually assemble an additive concept sculpture and the facilitator will invite audience members to step into the image and "help it grow." Another alternative is a ***Real to Ideal Image***: audience members are asked to step up and revise a sculpture of toxicity and injustice into "somewhere they could choose to inhabit." (Boal, *Games for Actors & Non-Actors*, p. 185)

☞ *"Talking to Power*[3]*":* This sequential TO-based process combines a number of applied theatre techniques: the social atom, hot seating, analytic images, improvised dialogues, auxiliary allies, magic screen, enabling workshop participants to strategically choose which "power actors" in the real world dynamic they should engage in a dialogue (Sullivan et al., *Journal of Health Psychology*, p. 177). Actors experiment with various "readings" of the situation to effectively structure their rhetoric, choose useful allies for support, and magnify their presence (through image- making) to widen and empower their coalition of support. This complex technique allows community actors to make clear strategic decisions - weighing factors unique to the power dynamic they must work with and evaluating their power actor or ally options in terms of their ultimate environmental justice goals and objectives. "Talking to Power" is usually offered as a stand-alone workshop because it is both labor and time intensive; information gathered from such a session might be later integrated into a Forum scene. (Technique developed with *El Teatro Lucha por la Salud del Barrio*, 2005 as part of NIEHS funded EJ Project COAL: Communities Organized against Asthma & Lead.) (*6 El Teatro Lucha, Community Arts Network hyperlink) (Sullivan & Parras, *Theory in Action*, pp. 27-30)

From Private Murmur to Public Outcry:
How Personal Stories "Pluralize" as Forum Theatre:

JAN COHEN-CRUZ BEGINS A RECENT ESSAY on the act of witness, and the connections among personal stories and the emblematic, empowering tales of groups and movements, with a quote from Seyla Benhabib, Professor of Political Science and Philosophy at Yale University, that captures the nuanced tonalities of this intimate relationship.

> *All struggles against oppression in the modern world begin by defining what had previously been considered private, non-public and non-political, as matters of public concern, issues of justice, and sites of power. (Cohen-C, p. 103)*

Boal's dramaturgy follows the same arc of I becoming We. He calls his process, "pluralization," and Theatre of the Oppressed, "a theatre of the first person plural." The process of converting personal stories that resonate with a TO group's collective experience into more or less distanced, artfully constructed assemblages of images, dialogue and actions sculpted collectively by the group moves from first, targeting oppressions – a straight shot within the rubric of environmental justice – to eliciting personal stories using story circles, into image sculpting, and finally into a process of improvisation that molds character and plot in an "invitingly incomplete" scene for the Forum. (Cohen-C, p. 110)

These short scenes – characterized by Randy Martin as "a critique of what is imbedded in a proposal for possible futures" – are "forumed" (or processed) with the larger community, using Boal's conceptual device of audience members as ***spect-actors***. (Martin, p. 23) In Boal's dramatic system, these "self-narrated, inconclusive stories" are considered *anti-models* of what the community considers good (Cohen-C, p. 106).

A well-made Environmental Forum scene provides no personal closure for the protagonist or ally characters, and no satisfying resolutions to the environmental justice problems represented. Their very incompleteness and the resonance of issues and situations they represent activate

Charlton Park mothers rehearse a demonstration outside a City of Houston building for tighter control of diesel emissions in their neighborhood." (Madres para Aire Limpio / Houston TX). Photo by Rosalia Guerrero.

individual members of the Forum audience to stop the action as scenes are replayed, step onto the stage and insert themselves directly into the drama with new actions to effectively promote the health of the community and increase justice.

The Forum emphasizes replacing two major types of actors in these scenes: 1) the *protagonist* or central character whose efforts to change the situation in a positive direction are stymied; and 2) the *potentially effective ally* who would – under the right conditions – assist the protagonist in changing external circumstances for the better. *Effective ally* interventions are based on Theatre of the Oppressed scholar, Mady Schutzman's, concept of the *Invisible Witness*, a character that perceives an oppression but feels disconnected from the consequences, or paralyzed by personal fears or uncertainty over which course of action to follow. (Schutzman, p. 144)

The Forum process gives potential allies the chance to act beyond these normal restraints to develop an effective new rhetoric for presenting information and arguing their case. Rehearsing assertive action on behalf of their neighbors' health and the community's environment in the Forum, transforms participants who formerly accepted toxic assault and chronic social-political neglect as a fact of life in environmentally degraded neighborhoods. In a

West Port Arthur citizens confront refinery plant public relations officials after an explosion at their plant released hazardous air pollutants into the neighborhoods. (Community In-Power & development Association / Port Arthur TX). Photo by Bryan Parras.

sense, this transformative outcome mirrors the effects of social modeling - expanding range and comfort within new social roles - employed as a group drama therapy modality (Landy, pp. 52-55). Ally / spect-actors also have the opportunity to rehearse networking skills, to practice risk communication with their neighbors, and to question central assumptions of prevailing power dynamic: these activities are all sources of personal empowerment for the actors, for spect-actors,

A spect-actor enters the scene with a new plan for action to counter gentrification and consequent homelessness during a Forum run-through before the community performance." (Madres para Aire Limpio / Houston TX) Photo by Rosalia Guerrero.

and even merely witnessing these scenes unfold empowers other members of the audience to do likewise in the world beyond the Forum. As Augusto Boal claims, "The act of transforming, I always say, transforms she / he who acts. Theatre of the Oppressed uses the theater as a rehearsal for transformation of reality" (Boal, 2005, *Democracy Now*: radio interview).

An "ideal Forum" leaves actors, spect-actors and audience energized, motivated, actively vigilant and dissatisfied with the reality they've seen portrayed on stage. Freire calls this a state of "patient impatience," but Boal is less ambiguous. There is no place for passivity at a Forum; Theatre of the Oppressed primes spectators to apply their powers of critical awareness to deconstruct what they see and "prepare for action in and on the world." And with this activation comes a deep responsibility to channel and sustain the community's commitment to healing wounds and reconfiguring the power dynamic that maintains oppression. As Randy Martin puts it:

> When a theatre audience is politically committed, a demand is placed on the performance to treat the possibilities on stage as vehicles for advancing the audience's capacity to influence politics (Martin, p. 25).

During the intervention phase of a Forum, the *antagonist* is never replaced by *spect-actors*; Boal cautions against this because such a thing would never happen so automatically in the real world.

He calls this gratuitous shift in the antagonist's point-of-view **Magical Thinking**, reflecting Paulo Freire's caution: " I do not believe in the magnanimity of the dominant classes, as such…" (Freire, p.173). If the antagonist could change so drastically, of his/her own volition, the Forum would be unnecessary. The Forum facilitator assists this *spect-actor* intervention process, first activating the audience with warm-up games and exercises, leading the audience – after they've watched each scenario once - in voting for which scene they would like to run through the Forum process, and finally de-briefing the *spect-actor*, the other Forum actors, and the audience after each intervention. During this de-briefing, the facilitator asks five principal questions:

1. (*a two part question, for the audience*) What did you see? How was this different from the original scene? These questions invite the audience to quite literally describe the dramatic action as it just unfolded. From various points-of-view, the community assembles a multi-faceted record of the *spect-actor's* intervention.

2. (*for the spect-actor*) How did you feel during your intervention? This question opens the door for community members to express their frustration with the antagonist or apathetic potential allies who "just sat there and watched while they were beaten down." This moment also allows them to tell their neighbors how empowering they felt while engaged in the struggle for justice, regardless of the outcomes. The facilitator leads with this question because community members are seldom asked how both the negative and positive aspects of environmental justice actions feel, and in Boal's dramaturgy, feeling is the primary component.

3. (*a two part question, again, for the spect-actor*) Why did you choose this specific intervention and how would you evaluate the results?

4. (*for the other actors, especially the antagonist*) How did the spect-actor's intervention force you to change your own actions, or reconsider your beliefs (while remaining in character)?

5. (*for audience members*) What do you think of what happened?

This series of questions gives audience members the opportunity to offer their own evaluation of how effective they think each intervention would be in the real world. (Sullivan & Parras, *Theory in Action*, p.32-33)

These audience "talk-backs" after each intervention invariably introduce fresh perspectives and often uncover formerly submerged facts about the situation that weren't mentioned during the workshop, or included in the scenes. Audience members employed by polluting industries often mention facts associated with accidents, upsets or unsafe "standard practices" with toxic stock chemicals and waste products that aren't common knowledge in the community. Spectators with (usually former) connections to the public health, social services and political sectors often make similar revelations about economic redlining, or official "rationing" of local resources; these facts on the ground accumulate and add to the context and knowledge base for future environmental justice actions (Sullivan & Parras, *Theory in Action*, p. 33). Audience critiques of Forum interventions help the community to establish action priorities and develop a working agenda for a sustained campaign of collaborative advocacy. This dialogic process may be profitably extended when NIEHS scientists offer information on research pertinent to the Forum issues, or ask audience members to expand on previous comments about local disease incidence, exposure pathways, risk factors or social indicators of well-being at the end of the performance.

A Framework for Evaluating Outcomes from a Popular Arts Practitioners Perspective:

THE EFFICACY OF NIEHS PUBLIC FORUM & Toxics Assistance outreach efforts is measured in terms of outcomes supportive of scientific goals and objectives: (1) Did the forum provide useful community input for design of research and evidence-based interventions (integrating local knowledge)? (2) Does each forum promote an atmosphere of trust and dispel unwarranted community scepticism toward science (bridging)? (3) Did the workshop process effectively communicate toxicological concepts and assessments of reasonable site-specific risk, and how was this translational efficacy tracked and measured (translational education)? (4) Will this forum provide a platform for future collaborations (sustainability)?

But this narrowly focused lens offers little to assess the quality of the Forum experience for the community actors, and their audience of neighbors and "delegates" from the local / regional power structure. Viewed from the perspective of Community Arts practice, the qualitative goals of engagement, inclusion, dialogue, and empowerment assume critical importance. While this viewpoint is undeniably more subjective than science, the ultimate success of popular arts-based community science hinges directly on the scientific preparation, energy, facilitation skills and personal integrity of the community artist. The artist is the bridge among all the disparate groups that may participate in a CEFT project, and, in this context, should understand how all the pieces of this complex social jigsaw ultimately mesh, and facilitate an appropriate fit. (Goldbard & Adams, pp. 61 – 65).

This Community Arts framework employs the following series of questions to evaluate both efficacy and accountability: (1) Was the artist/facilitator sufficiently responsive to community needs and considerate of the inherent (race-class-gender-sexual orientation) power imbalances in doing this work? (2) Do participants show evidence of greater capacity to work as effective allies within the community? Can these allies also speak effectively to power structures? (3) Did the artist / facilitator truly activate the actors in workshop and the community during performance? (4) Did the artist / facilitator gather sufficient community input during networking phases of this project, in designing the performance, in facilitating the forum? (5) Is the NIEHS environmental science engagement ongoing, sustainable? Where does all the activated energy go next? (6) Did the efforts of the artist/facilitator promote and expand inclusion within the project? (7) Did CEFT validate the democratic creative and decision-making processes of TO, and increase the community's capacity to organize, and to deliver effective, clearly targeted messages that frame community issues in terms the community can accept and the public health-regulatory policy sphere will deem credible? (Sullivan, *Local Environment*, pp. 640-641)

Ultimately, Community Environmental Forum Theatre proves most valuable to science as a bridge process: each project increases scientific literacy within a given community and builds capacity for informed citizens and community-based organizations to collaborate on increasingly more complex public health research. For communities, a successful process unleashes a cascade of networking and energetic advocacy. In Gulf coastal Texas, a group of community-based organizations, who have hosted or organized CEFT projects, now serve as the nucleus for a new network of environmental justice advocacy groups convened annually for an *EJ Encuentro*. These groups support the human rights aspect of their EJ advocacy with references to public health disease incidence data, cutting-edge basic science, and the hinge concept of disproportionate, cumulative risk has gained currency throughout the network. And the cultures of community, research and frontline health care have developed new "rules of engagement" and a more authentic sense of mutual respect. Not that all the former barriers to knowing and appreciating the assets and limitations of the Other have magically diffused – neither Boal, nor Freire, nor any seasoned practitioner of CBPR could entertain that pleasant delusion. But we've met each other in this extraordinary aesthetic space to make images of our lives, to tell our stories, to listen and witness, to "pluralize" these stories from an I-view into a We-view, to devise and rehearse effective actions for change, to "gradually expand the space for pacts among groups, and consolidate a dialogue" (Freire, p. 175). And through this ongoing dialogue, to "penetrate the mirror of reality (in this case: toxic, lacking health, safety or justice) and transform the image we see in it, and to bring that transformed image back into [our lives]" (Boal, *Legislative Theatre*, p. 20).

JOHN SULLIVAN is currently an adjunct faculty member in the Department of Preventive Medicine and Community Health and an associate member of the Institute for Medical Humanities, and serves as Director: Public Forum & Toxics Assistance in University of Texas Medical Branch at Galveston NIEHS Center in Environmental Toxicology Community Outreach & Education Core. As an artist, John Sullivan has worked as a writer, playwright, director, poet, performance artist and arts educator. He is the recipient of numerous writing awards and honors including the "Jack Kerouac Literary Prize," "The Writers Voice: New Voices of the West Prize," two fellowships from the Arizona Commission on the Arts, a WESTAF Fellowship, and was the featured playwright at Denver's Summerplay Festival. He has performed at the Bisbee Poetry Festival, the Associated Writing Programs National Conference, and has presented at the National Psychodrama, Drama Therapy, Pedagogy & Theatre of the Oppressed (TO) conferences, and conducted training sessions in using TO in community engagement practice with regulatory personnel at EPA Community Involvement Conferences. In 2009, he was selected to participate in the Arts-Culture-Nature Mini-Think Tank in performance and arts-based methods (Art Matters Conference; U OR) He was Artistic/Producing Director of a bi-lingual company, Theater Degree Zero, in Arizona for five years, and Director of the Augusto Boal-based Community Outreach Wing at Seattle Public Theater. He uses Augusto Boal's Theatre of the Oppressed to teach basic toxicology, risk perception and communication concepts, and as a structure for stakeholder dialogue on environmental justice issues.

Hyper-Links

1. PUBLIC FORUM & TOXICS ASSISTANCE: Description of PFTA Division outreach activities posted on Animating Democracy Initiative web site (Program Profiles).
WWW.AMERICANSFORTHEARTS.ORG/ANIMATINGDEMOCRACY/LABS/LAB_080.ASP

2. "BEHIND THE FENCE" : Forum Theatre on Lupus, Lead Poisoning and Environmental Justice
WWW.COMMUNITYARTS.NET/READINGROOM/ARCHIVEFILES/2008/02/BEHIND_THE_FENC.PHP.

3. EPA CIC: Environmental Forum Theatre: Drama-Based Action Strategies for Community-Building, Issue Clarification, and Conflict Mediation.
WWW.EPACIC.ORG/2005/PROCEEDINGS.CFM

4. "MAKING A DRAMATIC SANDWICH": Main hyperlink for "Making a Dramatic Sandwich / applied theatre project in environmental justice / environmental health disparities": HTTP://WWW.UTMB.EDU/CEHD. This is the Home Page for the Center to Eliminate Health Disparities at the University of Texas Medical Branch @ Galveston TX. The specific link to the video file may be accessed by looking at the left menu column and selecting Social Determinants of Health, and this leads to a page that will include information on the "applied theatre project in environmental justice / environmental health disparities.

5. *SOCIOMETRY: EXPANDING ON the Meaning of the Term*, Hale, A.
WWW.SOCIOMETRY.NET/MODULES.PHP?NAME=CONTENT&PA=PRINT_PAGE&PID=20

6. EL TEATRO LUCHA por la Salud del Barrio:
WWW.COMMUNITYARTS.NET/READINGROOM/ARCHIVEFILES/2005/10/ACROBATS_OF_THE.PHP.

End Notes

1. COMMUNITY ENVIRONMENTAL FORUM THEATRE PROJECTS

☞ Barrio Segundo / Chavez HS Forum: SCEHM / NIEHS-UTMB, Unidos Contros Environmental Racismo, Nuestra Palabra, Talento Bilingue de Houston. Theme(s): School siting in high petrochemical emissions zone / plant safety / hazardous rail transport. June 2002.

☞ Bruce Elementary School / Mothers for Clean Air-5th Ward Chapter, SCEHM / NIEHS-UTMB. Theme(s): neurological effects of lead poisoning, MDI Superfund site / land use policies. April 2003.

☞ Citizens for Environmental Justice / Corpus Christi TX, SEED Coalition / Austin TX, SCEHM / NIEHS-UTMB. Theme(s): health of fence-line neighborhoods, local birth defect cluster, lax regulatory agencies. July 2003.

{86} ☞ Clean Air / Clear Lake, Clear Creek Unified School District, Armand Bayou Nature Center, Citizens League for Environmental Action Now, SCEHM / NIEHS-UTMB. Theme(s): fence-line air quality, organophosphate pesticide exposures, development encroachment on animal habitat. July 2004.

☞ Community In-Power & Development Association / Port Arthur TX, SCEHM / NIEHS-UTMB. Theme: fence-line air quality in West Port Arthur, lack of access to health care & social services, collusion of city-county government & industry in suppressing health effect facts. August 2004.

☞ Mothers for Clean Air / 5th Ward Chapter, Julia Hester House (Houston), Talento Bilingue de Houston, Ujima Theatre (Buffalo NY), Toxic Waste / Lupus Coalition (Buffalo NY), EPA, SCEHM / NIEHS-UTMB. Forum Theme(s): development / land-use policies at the MDI Superfund site in 5th Ward, gentrification and effects on low-income families; Forum title: *"Bamboozled!"* Forums in conjunction with production of Thomas Meloncon's "Restricted Area." April – July 2005.

☞ Project CEHRO: "Hurricane Readiness: a Way of Life of the Bayous." Community hazard assessment, peer-to-peer risk communication, environmental health / ecosystem advocacy. Inner Works, Inc., Bayou Grace, Bayou Interfaith Shared Community Organizing, Louisiana Spirit, S. Lafourche Levee District, S. Lafourche Unified School District, Gulf Restoration Network, EPA / Army Corps. Of Engineers, United Houma Nation.

Houma, Gray, Galliano & Chauvin LA, 10/2005 – 03/2007.

- Mothers for Clean Air / *Madres para aire limpio*, Charlton Park Community Center, SCEHM / NIEHS-UTMB. Themes(s): particulate & VOC air pollution / health effects, gentrification & dislocation of low-income families by metro transportation planning, effects of crime / violence on low-income barrios. Forum in conjunction with EPA / MfCA Collaborative Problem-Solving Project. March 2007.

- BISCO (Bayou Interfaith Shared Community Organizing) Regional Conference, Thibodaux LA: Racism & Environmental Justice; Co-facilitated with American Friends Service Committee; Forum in a Fishbowl / with wide-angle – zoom images used as to identify and engage effective allies. July 26th – 27th 2007.

- De Madres a Madres, Casa de Amigos (Harris County), El Teatro Lucha por la Salud del Barrio, City of Houston Lead Poisoning Prevention Program, Holy Name Parish, MECA, HISD, Latino Learning Center. Theme(s): healthy homes re: indoor air quality & lead poisoning prevention, neurological effects of lead poisoning and asthma triggers / respiratory disease pathogenesis. Multiple forum performances (>20) in conjunction with Project COAL – Communities Organized against Asthma & Lead (NIEHS funded). September 2003 – August 2007.

- Toxic Waste & Lupus Coalition of Buffalo NY, NY DEC, Environmental Justice Center of WNY, Ujima Theatre & Sealy Center for Environmental Health & Medicine present "Behind the Fence": a Forum workshop / performance focused on a Lupus cluster and high incidences of childhood lead poisoning in the neighborhoods proximate to 858 Ferry Street former industrial and hazardous waste storage site. October 26th – 30th, Buffalo NY, 2007.

- Alton Park / Piney Woods Environmental Justice Chattanooga TN) & University of Tennessee (Knoxville TN): a Community Environmental Forum Theatre / video documentary project focused on health disparities, cumulative risk and social issues stemming from the Chattanooga Creek Superfund site and collateral pollution from now-abandoned or scaled back industrial facilities. May 1st – May 5th, Chattanooga TN, 2008.

2. I FIRST RAN ACROSS THE "MYTH OF EXCLUSIVITY" in Dr. Marvin Legator's unique manual on popular epidemiology and grassroots data collection, "Chemical Alert: a community action handbook." In his own words: "I do not wish to minimize the importance of refined and specialized knowledge . . .I do suggest, however, that trained professionals do not have exclusive rights to their areas of investigation and that untrained

people can, in fact, perform early, simple epidemiological studies that will be as sound as those performed by professionals and that certainly will not compromise the scientific integrity of later investigations by professionals." He underscores his belief in the reasoning ability and integrity of non-scientist citizens with the story of Michael Bennett, a journeyman pipe-fitter at a Flint Michigan Fisher body plant who organized and conducted a credible and ground-breaking epidemiological study to determine a proportional mortality ratio from death records of his fellow workers, and equally remarkable tales of similar grassroots work by Occidental Chemical Company employees on the health effects of dibromochloropropane (primarily sterility), and Lois Gibbs of Love Canal fame. Dr. Legator helped found the scientific discipline of genetic toxicology, instituted the Division of Environmental Toxicology at University of Texas Medical Branch (Galveston), and was a tireless advocate for environmental justice until his death in 2005.

3. TO SEQUENCE USED IN "TALKING TO POWER / CHOOSING EFFECTIVE ALLIES":

1. Create Social Atom (Talking to Power): Regulatory, Governmental, Business-Industrial, Science-Medical Players important to your community-based organizations environmental issues & efforts. Protagonist arranges social actors around her or himself – protagonist is nucleus of atom. (Social Atom from work of Jacob Moreno)

2. Strategic Shift of electrons in the Atom to different shells based on approachability, leverage within the system, value in further networking, and values compatibility. Choose "Power Actor" to approach.

3. Chosen social actor sits in "hot seat" and answers questions from entire group. Answers to these questions provide values, intentions motivations & history for character. Group members fill in as "auxiliary voices" – based on what they know about this character - to help actor playing "Power." (Hot Seat from Gestalt)

4. Community Actor creates Real / Ideal Image of relationship to Power Actor. Group members help populate the images and offer proposals from their own perspectives on Real and Ideal. Discussion of ways to move closer to the ideal relationship influence strategies and content of dialogue in next step. (TO Real to Ideal Images, Images of Transition)

5. Dialogue with Power: When Power Actor has revealed enough character details, Community Actor engages the Power Actor in dialogue designed to persuade & enlist support.

Group participants assist the Community actor as auxiliaries to move the dialogue forward, offer new tactical perspectives, and try alternative arguments. (Auxiliary Sociodrama technique)

6.   Final Statement: Community Actor makes final uninterrupted statement to Power Actor to show how she/he feels about the issue & the unequal power dynamic that problematizes EJ progress. Process sequence of results with group. (Aside, Monologue or Magic Screen Sociodrama techniques)

(This sequence may also be used in much the same way to choose and activate potential allies within the social atom of the issue. The same procedure is followed though the criteria for shell shifting are somewhat different – experience with the issue on a grassroots level, community "authenticity" and levels of consistent activism (on this & other issues) would be added to the previous mix. Once again, the emphasis is on strategic choices and tactical models of discourse & argumentation.)

{90}

References:

AGENCY FOR TOXIC SUBSTANCES & DISEASE REGISTRY (revised 2005) *Public Health Assessment: Guidance Manual*; U.S. Department of Health & Human Services; Public Health Service (Atlanta, GA)

BOAL, A. (1995) *The Rainbow of Desire* (London, Routledge)

BOAL, A. (1998) *Legislative Theatre* (London, Routledge)

BOAL, A. (1992, revised 2002) *Games for Actors and Non-Actors* (London, Routledge)

BOAL, A. (2000) "The Structure of the Actor's Work;" in: L. Goodman & J. de Gay (Eds.) *The Routledge Reader in Politics and Performance* (London, Routledge)

BOAL, A. (2005) *Radio interview*; with Juan Gonzales (Los Angeles, CA, *Democracy Now; June 3rd 2005*)

BOAL, A. (2006) *The Aesthetics of the Oppressed* (New York, Routledge)

BULLARD, R. (1990, rev. 2000) *Dumping in Dixie: Race, Class & Environmental Quality* (Boulder CO, Westview Press)

COHEN-CRUZ, J. (2006) "Refining the private: from personal storytelling to political act;" in Cohen-Cruz, J. & Schutzman, M. (Eds.) *A Boal Companion: Dialogues on theatre and cultural politics*; pp. 103-113. (New York, Routledge)

CORBURN, JASON. (2005) *Street Science* (Cambridge MA, MIT Press)

FISCHER, FRANK (2000) *Citizens, Experts and the Environment; the Politics of Local Knowledge* (Durham, NC, Duke University Press)

FISCHER, FRANK (2009) *Democracy & Expertise: Reorienting Policy Inquiry* (Oxford University Press, New York)

FREIRE, P. (1992; reprinted 2002) *Pedagogy of Hope* (Boulder & London, Paradigm Publishers)

GEERTZ, C. (1973) "Thick Description: Toward an Interpretive Theory of Culture," *The Interpretation of Cultures* (New York, Basic Books)

GOLDBARD, A. & ADAMS, D. (2000) *Creative Community: The Art of Cultural Development* (New York, Rockefeller Foundation)

KATZ, D.L. (2004) "Representing your community in community-based participatory research: difference made & measured," *Prev Chron Dis* [serial online]

LANDY, R. (1993) *Persona & Performance: the meaning of role in drama, therapy and everyday life* (New York, Guilford Press)

LEGATOR, M. & STRAWN, S. (1993) *Chemical Alert: A Community Action Handbook* (AUSTIN, UNIVERSITY OF Texas Press)

MARTIN, R. (2006) "Staging the political: Boal and the horizons of theatrical commitment," in Cohen-Cruz, J. & Schutzman, M. (Eds.) *A Boal Companion: Dialogues on theatre and cultural politics*; pp. 23-32. (New York, Routledge)

McCARTHY, J. & GALVAO, K. (2002) *ARTPAD: a Resource for Theatre & Participatory Development* (Manchester, UK, University of Manchester Press)

NATIONAL ENVIRONMENTAL JUSTICE ADVISORY COUNCIL (2004) **Ensuring Risk Reduction in** Communities with Multiple Stressors: Environmental Justice & Cumulative Risks / *Impacts*; U.S. EPA; (Washington, D.C.)

SEXTON, K., NEEDHAM, L. & PIRKLE, J. (2003) "Human bio-monitoring of environmental chemicals," *American Scientist*; 92, pp. 38-45

SCHLOSBERG, D. (1999) *Environmental Justice and the New Pluralism* (Oxford University Press, New York)

{92}

SCHUTZMAN, M. (1994) "Brechtian Shamanism: the Political Therapy of Augusto Boal;" in: J. Cohen-Cruz & M. Schutzman (Eds) *Playing Boal: Theatre, Therapy Activism* (London, Routledge).

SULLIVAN, J. & LLOYD, R.S. (2006) "The Forum Theatre of Augusto Boal: a dramatic model for dialogue and community-based environmental science;" *Local Environment: The International Journal of Justice and Sustainability*; Vol. 11, No. 6, 627-646, December 2006

SULLIVAN, J. & PARRAS, J. (2008) "Environmental Justice and Augusto Boal's Theatre of the Oppressed: a Unique Community Tool for Outreach, Communication, Education and Advocacy;" *Theory in Action,* Vol. 1, No. 2, April 2008

SULLIVAN, PETRONELLA, BROOKS, MURILLO, PRIMEAU, & WARD (2008) "Theatre of the Oppressed and Environmental Justice Communities: a transformational therapy for the body politic;" *Journal of Health Psychology*, Vol. 13(2), pp. 166-179. 2008

WALLERSTEIN, N. & DURAN, B. (2003) "The Conceptual, Historical and Practice Roots of Community Based Participatory Research and Related Participatory Traditions;" in Minkler, M. & Wallerstein, N. (Eds.) *Community Based Participatory Research for Health*; (Jossey-Bass, San Francisco) 2003

Photography and Theatre in HIV Research

The Caregiving Network

Javier Mignone, Carla Pindera, Jennifer Davis, Paula Migliardi, Carol D. H. Harvey

THE CANADIAN PROVINCES OF SASKATCHEWAN and Manitoba have an increasing number of people living with or at risk for HIV. In Saskatchewan the number of confirmed cases jumped from forty cases in 2003 to 124 in 2007, while in Manitoba the numbers have ranged between eighty-one and 115 cases in the same period. Of particular relevance from a public health point of view are the characteristics of the people affected by the infection. The faces of people living with HIV/AIDS in these provinces include more Aboriginals, women, heterosexuals, younger ones in their reproductive years, and injection drug users. Many of the people living with HIV are isolated, disenfranchised, poor, and stigmatized, and thus they are socially invisible. Our study sought to better understand the social support and caregiving networks of people living with HIV in Winnipeg and Regina.

Our research used creative approaches in social science. When we collected data, rather than merely talking to people, we asked them to take photos of things important to them. When we talked to participants in the research about the photos they took, descriptions of their lives became more complete for us, with more detail. Explaining their photos helped participants remember what happened to them and assisted people who normally do not talk a lot to expand their ideas.

We discovered that among some of our participants there was an interesting network of care. No one seemed overtly to feel responsible for anyone else, yet they would work to support each other as a larger group. They would sleep at the house of whoever had accommodation that week; individuals would bring their friends lunch from the local soup kitchen; some would take it upon themselves to protect others from violence or abuse. Taking care of each other was simply taken as a matter of course within the group and few, if any, thought of it as caregiving. These networks were very loosely structured and often contained familial connections within them. They were not structured as families, but instead as large networks of individuals who bonded and watched over each other's physical needs.

Not all of our participants had such networks. Many were quite isolated from any supportive care outside of the formal systems. Some participants had moved to get away from dismissive or abusive family members and had not been able to develop trusting friendships; some had serious addictions and found themselves surrounded by others with similar addictions and were unable to find trusting relationships among them; some were so affected by the discrimination they faced as being HIV positive and/or gay and/or aboriginal and/or poor and/or struggling with addictions that they had difficulty developing supportive relationships with others. The analysis showed that these individuals relied quite heavily on professional people. Some participants photographed and named medical and social support professionals as their friends and even as family members, in some cases, without a single "informal" support person anywhere in their lives.

The least traditional but possibly most fulfilling form of dissemination of the findings of the study was the production of a reader's theatre. While academic papers and conferences certainly have their place, they are often inaccessible for the average person. A play can be brought directly to a community, and with reader's theatre, it can be brought alive by the community members themselves. Participants can hear their voices come to life and are able to be part of the sharing of their own words, photos and thoughts. They (the participants in the study) were the first people to see the play and were offered the opportunity to edit or comment on the work before it was shown elsewhere. In reaching a wider audience, this method of dissemination allowed for the study to become a catalyst for programmatic change, as well as one more step in enhancing the support networks of people living with HIV.

FAMILY SOCIAL SCIENCES, University of Manitoba Nine Circles Community
Health Centre, Winnipeg, Manitoba For more information on this project visit
WWW.NINECIRCLES.CA

Our Voice Through Pictures
Mother and Daughter

The Story of a Community-Based Latina Mother and Daughter Photovoice Intervention

Carolyn García, Sandi Lindgren

Las Fotos Son Nuestra Voz "Madre e Hija"

Los animales son una parte muy esencial en este mundo. Son un regalo de la vida y vale la pena cuidarlos.

En la más mínima planta puedes encontrar vida, ese es un regalo que nos ofrece la naturaleza. Para seguir preservándola tenemos que cuidarla y no destruirla.

Una religión es como una base, en ella están tus valores y algunas ideas. En una religión puedes obtener apoyo y amistad de otras personas.

A nosotros los Latinos nos gusta ser parte de la comunidad y enseñarles a los demás lo que tenemos y convivir con otras.

Una familia debe estar basada en el amor, la confianza, la amistad y todos los valores humanos que rigen al mundo. Es muy importante tener una base familiar porque así puedes mejorar el mundo. Si tienes una buena base familiar puedes transmitir eso al exterior.

Cuando utilizas un carro estás contaminando el medioambiente. Cuando utilizas una bicicleta conservas el medioambiente. Nuestro labor como humanos es cuidar del medioambiente. De ti depende en que planeta quieres vivir, así que tú tienes la elección.

Nuestra cultura es bien importante para nosotros los mexicanos. Es muy diferente - la religón, educación, valores, e idiomas. Como también la música y la comida, porque para toda persona es importante conocer sus costumbres.

Mediante la comida podemos dar a conocer nuestra cultura y a la vez hacer consciencia que debemos cuidar la tierra, ya que de ella extraemos nuestros alimentos.

Created by Estela y Liz, Ines y Maggie, Obdulia y Dulce July

I N THE UNITED STATES, health and social service providers are concerned with the mental health disparities apparent among adolescents. The growing Latino population in the US, has increased awareness and attention about the mental health of Latina adolescents. In this research, attention was given to using principles of community-based participatory research to promote success. Similarly, although grounded in theoretical understanding of behavioral interventions, the investigators explored non-traditional intervention strategies. Thus, a community-based photovoice intervention was developed for Latina mothers and their adolescent daughters.

The goal was to develop and pilot an arts-based intervention designed to improve levels of mother-daughter communication and connectedness. Secondary goals were to provide opportunity for the mothers and daughters to complete a photovoice project, document their combined perspectives in words and pictures, and present their findings to a community audience of friends, family, community leaders, and policymakers. The photovoice project topic, selected by a group of mother-daughter dyads, focused on preserving their culture. In this chapter we describe the nature of the problem we addressed, the development and implementation of the photovoice intervention, and our successes/lessons learned. Our experience using a photovoice-based intervention demonstrates how broadly the arts can be used to intervene and advocate for the health and well-being of individuals, families, and communities.

Why design an intervention with Latino mothers and adolescent daughters?

LATINO ADOLESCENTS IN THE UNITED STATES (US) are a fast growing proportion of the US population and in young adulthood/adulthood they will extensively affect the well-being of the overall US population (Guzman, 2001; U.S. Census, 2008). As with many health problems, disparities are evident in the rates of mental health problems, with Latino adolescents showing some of the highest rates, and disparities, compared to their peers (Ozer, Park, Brindis, & Irwin, 2003; Rew, Thomas, Horner, Resnick, & Beuhring, 2001). Latino adolescent females (Latinas) have high rates of suicide attempts compared to their adolescent peers, male or female (Eaton et al., 2008;. Zayas, Lester, Cabassa, & Fortuna, 2005). A high proportion of Latina adolescents report experiencing depressive symptoms, which are critical risk factors for mental health problems including suicide (Céspedes & Huey Jr., 2008; Garcia, Skay, Sieving, Naughton, & Bearinger, 2008; Mikolajczyk, Bredehorst, Khelaifat, Maier, & Maxwell, 2007).

Why Latino adolescents, females in particular, are reporting disproportionately high rates of mental health problems is not easily described. Complex factors are involved, which makes identifying solutions or possible points of intervention quite challenging. Bronfenbrenner's ecological model (Bronfenbrenner, 1979; Pantin, Schwartz, Sullivan, Coatsworth, & Szapoxznik, 2003) is a useful framework for realizing these complex factors. At the center of multiple

Garcia · Lindgren

concentric circles, the individual (Latina adolescent) has intra-personal factors (e.g. genetics, personality, beliefs) that may offer protection, or present risk, related to development of a mental health problem. The next circle, representing microsystem-level influences, includes family, school, peers, and for some, employment or religious institutions. Within the family a Latino adolescent might find protection in the cultural values that emphasize family priorities, togetherness, and community connection. On the other hand, the family may experience stressors related to acculturation differences, language preferences, substance use behaviors, or separation due to immigration (Garcia & Lindgren, 2009). At the macrosystem-level, potential stressors arise when societal values do not align with those of yourself, your family, or your culture.

Why is a relationship with mothers protective for adolescent females?

PARENT/CHILD CONFLICT IS HIGHEST IN ADOLESCENCE (Branje, 2008; Laursen & Collins, 1994). Parents are generally committed to the success and well-being of their adolescent children and parental bonding is known to be positively associated with adolescent well-being (Bucx & van Wel, 2008). For many adolescents, this developmental period is generally smooth; however, there are youth who struggle through the transitions, and can experience significant conflict with parents as part of the struggles. It has been consistently reported that most interpersonal conflict teens have is with their mothers, and that girls tend to have more interpersonal conflict than boys (Laursen & Collins, 1994; Laursen, 1995). High levels of conflict are problematic because they are associated with harmful adolescent behaviors such as depression, anger and substance use (Pasch et al., 2006).

Latina adolescents may be more vulnerable to conflict and tension with their mothers than other adolescent girls. Traditional Latino cultural values around family, women, and communication may conflict with the values Latina adolescents encounter among peers and in mainstream U.S. culture. For example, the emphasis in Latino culture on family (Romero, Robinson, Haydel, Mendoza, & Killen, 2004; Pabon, 1998) minimizes individuality although establishing self-identity is a normative adolescent developmental task (Steinburg, 1996). Generally the literature demonstrates familism to be protective for Latino adolescents, especially females, against high-risk behaviors including substance use and delinquency (Allen et al., 2008; Dakof, 2000; Martyn-Nemeth, Penckofer, Gulanick, Velsor-Friedrich, & Bryant, 2009; Parsai, Voisine, Marsiglia, Kulis, & Nieri, 2009; Romero et al., 2004; Unger, Ritt-Olson, Teran, Huang, Hoffman, & Palmer, 2002); however, in the context of mental health familism poses potential for risk as well as protection (Goldston et al., 2008). In addition, Latino culture may value particular traits in women, including being nurturing, quiet, and shy (Parsai et al., 2009; Quinones-Mayo & Dempsey, 2005) and may stand in contrast to the traits or behaviors valued or modeled by non-Latino peers, including open communication about difficult topics (McKee & Karasz, 2006).

In addition, there are less documented yet important factors contributing to risk for Latina adolescents with respect to mental health problems. For example, among immigrant Latina adolescents (over half the foreign-born in the U.S. are Latino; Bergman, 2003), susceptibility can occur when they experience separation from a parent for extended periods of time (Schapiro, 2002). For some adolescents who may be 'left' to live with grandparents or other family for years, being reunited with their parents can create conflicting emotions that are rarely adequately addressed or resolved (e.g. abandonment, anger, fear, or uncertainty). Parents may feel their adolescent children should be grateful for the opportunity of a better life and could unintentionally overlook the emotional effects and needs of their adolescents.

For many Latina adolescents, the processes of acculturation may vary from their parents, presenting risks that contribute to experiencing acculturative stress and conflict, and subsequent emotional distress (Eitle, Wahl, & Aranda, 2009; Schofield, Parke, Kim, & Coltrane, 2008; Smokowski, Buchanan, & Bacallao, 2009; Smokowski, David-Ferdon, & Stroupe, 2009).

Why does an intervention addressing the mother-daughter relationship make sense?

LEADING LATINO AND ADOLESCENT RESEARCHERS AGREE that successful behavioral interventions have common characteristics, including being school-based, family-centric, and promoting protective factors while reducing risk factors (Coatsworth, Pantin, & Szapocznik, 2002; Dishion & Kavanagh, 2003; Pantin et al., 2003; Resnick, Harris, & Blum, 1993; Rodriguez & Morrobel, 2004). One of these critical protective factors is a feeling of mutuality by an adolescent toward her mother. Mutuality is an indicator of the emotional bond between the adolescent-mother and in essence, the extent to which the adolescent can understand why her mother parents in certain ways (Turner, Kaplan, & Badger, 2006; Zayas, 2009). With higher levels of mutuality for adolescent girls toward their mothers comes greater connectedness and subsequently, for the adolescent, lower risk behaviors, including lower rates of attempting suicide (Zayas, 2009). We know that a close, trusting relationship with parents contributes to the healthy development of adolescents (Baer & Schmitz, 2007) and that a less tense relationship can facilitate reaching mutual goals, which can diminish interpersonal conflict between parents and adolescents (Marshall, Young,

& Tilton-Weaver, 2008). A healthy adolescent-parent relationship can protect against harmful adolescent behaviors including sexual risk-taking and substance use (Borawski, Ievers-Landis, Lovegreen, & Trapl, 2003; Dogan-Ates & Carrion-Basham, 2007; Mogro-Wilson, 2008; Trejos-Castillo & Vazsonyi, 2009).

We embarked on a collaborative process (Minkler & Wallerstein, 2003) to develop an intervention that would build on known successes, address the problems we have identified, and positively influence the mother-daughter relationship.

What was the study goal?

THE STUDY GOAL WAS TO DEVELOP and pilot test a photovoice intervention designed to improve communication and connectedness within Latino mother-daughter dyads. We aimed to provide a venue in which the mothers and daughters could spend time together with other mothers and daughters in a non-threatening and safe environment. We observed that the appeal of the project for the mothers and daughters was twofold: the opportunity to learn about and undertake a photovoice project, and the chance to improve their communication with each other without "therapy". {101}

Why was a community-based participatory research strategy used?

COMMUNITY-BASED PARTICIPATORY RESEARCH is a collaborative engaged research process that follows core principles assuring commitment, equity, mutual benefit, capacity building, relevance, and focus (Israel et al., 2003; Minkler & Wallerstein, 2003; Wallerstein & Duran, 2006). The university and community co-investigators comprised a trans-disciplinary team (nursing, social work) who have worked together since 2006. From the onset, this photovoice study was driven by the needs and desires of the community. The sincerity, trust, and commitment among the collaborators have grown over time and contribute to the likelihood of project success.

Why was photovoice the intervention strategy?

PHOTOVOICE, A TERM ORIGINATED BY CAROLINE WANG (Wang & Burris, 1997), is a process undertaken by a group of individuals who use photography to promote their voice on an issue they care about. Informed by the work of Freire and leading feminist theorists, Wang perceived photovoice to be more than photo-documentation with solely a descriptive or informative nature. Photovoice was originally developed with intention to serve those who traditionally may not have had or felt they had strong voices that could be heard by common stakeholders or decision-makers (e.g. legislators). Adolescents comprise a population that rarely has a voice regarding issues that influence their health and well-being.

Generally, photovoice projects are conducted with the purpose of advancing policy changes or health promotion efforts (Schwartz, Sable, Dannerbeck, & Campbell, 2007; Strack, Magill, & McDonagh, 2004; Wilson, Minkler, Dasho, Wallerstein, & Martin, 2008). A leading photovoice researcher has undertaken theoretical work to advance the ideas of photovoice beyond descriptive and policy implications to those of intervention (Strack, Lovelace, Jordan, & & Holmes, under review). Strack has coined the term "photovention" to describe the idea that photovoice is more than a process with an outcome (e.g., the product) and in fact, it is an intervention influencing those who participate in powerful ways (e.g., communication skills).

{102}

Our research team knew we needed to be creative to engage both mothers and adolescents. We talked with some adolescents about working together with their mothers, without actually talking about their problems (e.g., in therapy) and noted that the girls found this idea very appealing. Girls wanted to connect more with their mothers but not in traditional ways such as counseling or classes. Informal conversations with mothers consistently showed us that they too have a strong desire to spend more time with their daughters, to get to know them better, and to know more of what was going on in their lives. We decided to use photovoice as the core component of a group-based intervention to promote healthy mother-daughter communication and connectedness. In an intervention context, a photovoice project provides the group of mother-daughter dyads with a common goal that is not specific to their relationship. Instead, they indirectly 'work' on their relationship as they work side-by-side, practicing positive communication, observing the modeling of other mother-daughter dyads in the group, and mutually enjoying doing something together. Simultaneously, they complete a photovoice project with community-level health promotion implications.

How did the study unfold?

THE RESEARCH TEAM DETERMINED THAT the summer out-of-school months would be ideal for recruitment and engagement of mothers and daughters. Following appropriate processes to secure Institutional Review Board approval, our team began to recruit Latina students attending a public high school in an urban Minnesota city. We felt it was important to gain the interest of adolescents before inviting their mothers to participate. Three of the eight eligible and interested Latina girls (criteria included self-identifying as Latina, fourteen-eighteen years of age, and willing to commit to an eight-week program) were unavailable to participate because they were leaving Minnesota to visit Mexico during the summer. Four mother-daughter dyads attended an informational session held at the school. It became clear early in the recruitment process that the biggest logistical issue would be the various work schedules among the mothers. At the informational session we talked about possible days of the weeks and times that would work for everyone and established a schedule of meetings over a two-month period.

At this initial meeting, those who were interested in participating signed appropriate consent/ assent forms and completed baseline protocol data collection. The written survey (available in English or Spanish) inquired about demographics, emotions, coping behaviors, family connectedness and communication, and acculturation. In addition, a recorded communication task protocol was completed with each mother-daughter dyad (Sillars, Koerner, & Fitzpatrick, 2005). Each dyad was brought to a private room with a video camera. They were instructed to have a conversation about a topic they often disagree about for approximately ten minutes. It was after this task that one dyad made a decision to not participate in the project; the mother felt that their relationship and arguing were too intense to enable them to engage in the photovoice project with the other dyads.

{103}

What did the mothers and daughters do?

THREE LATINA MOTHERS AND THEIR ADOLESCENT DAUGHTERS enrolled in the project. Garcia and Lindgren outlined each session using a framework documented for prior photovoice projects (Strack et al., 2004). Initial sessions were designed to explain the purpose of photovoice, build comfort with the use of cameras, facilitate participants getting to know one another, and initiate a coaching conversation about the possible focus for their project. Subsequent sessions were focused on working with the photographs the participants had taken, facilitating a process of organizing photographs and creating meaningful messages. It should be noted that the process of facilitating conversation with the mothers and daughters was based on life coaching principles: the clients know best and are fully capable of using their own knowledge to come to decisions. The facilitator, rather than giving ideas or advice, guided the participants through listening and questioning. Generally each session lasted two and a half to three hours and followed this outline: 1) welcome and informal conversation, 2) download and organization of photographs on the computers, 3) presentation of photographs taken by each participants with explanation for what the photographs mean, 4) share a meal, 5) discussion of themes, categories, and messages, 6) strategize next steps and wrap up. In the final sessions, more time was focused on creating the lay-out of the photographs, firming up messages to accompany the photographs, and planning the final exhibit session.

All sessions were co-facilitated by Garcia and Lindgren, with the assistance of a Graduate Assistant. Following each session, field notes were written to capture the essence of each meeting, what was accomplished, and how it appeared the mothers and daughters were responding. Some of these notes are presented below.

{104} *Session One. The mothers and daughters sat expectantly around a table with the facilitators sharing sandwiches and getting to know each other. The girls knew each other, but not well. The mothers had not previously met. We explained what photovoice is, where it came from, and what the overarching goals or outcomes might look like. They were curious about the process, and about photovoice.*

Cameras were provided to participants and a photographer was present to explain the intricacies of use. Digital high quality yet easy to use cameras were purchased. Each individual was able to choose the color of their own camera, and each pair chose different colors so as not to mix them up. As each opened up their individual box containing camera and accessories, the feel in the air was festive. The daughters were quick to skip all instructions, and by knowledge or chance, put it all together (batteries, memory card, string handle, etc.). The mothers were careful, cautious; they quickly turned to their daughters for assistance. Each daughter explained to their mother (some with patience and some with exasperation) how to assemble the camera with the memory card and batteries. The facilitators circled the table filling in with explanations and assistance when needed. After all cameras were ready, one of the facilitators modeled the basics with an extra camera. Suddenly, the room was full of giggles and laughter, with more questions and answers as the group of individuals practiced taking photos, deleting photos, using the different photo categories. Individual and pairs were suddenly taking each other's picture, smiling for the camera. The daughters demanded to view the photo and then decided whether or not their mother could keep or delete that particular photo.

When they left the group that day, each was instructed to practice taking photos, getting to know their camera, and referring to the instruction manual when needed. The ethics of photography, including when and how to take photos of others, was carefully covered. They were instructed to take photos of what was important to them and to their community (without the facilitators or the group discussion or defining what 'their community' actually was). In this way, the group was guided toward what they would subsequently identify as the topic focus of their project.

SESSION TWO. This session was a show and tell. We had access to four Macintosh computers where we uploaded each person's photographs they wanted to share with the group (each selected 10-15 photos). Then, we had a narrative 'slide show' where each person was able to talk about the pictures she took, why she took them and what they reminded her of. One of the mothers had written down all her notes and photo descriptions in a notebook. This was the first mother to do so and seemed to set an example for the other mothers to take more time to explain their photos to each other. Each individual had sole rights to choose which photos were to be shown to the others.

We decided to split the group into two groups (mothers, daughters) for the initial conversation about possible themes to support the mothers' preference for talking in Spanish and the daughters' preference to use English. We also were curious as to the similarities or differences that each group would present in topic/theme ideas. Each group spent time talking about the topic, as well as related topics it informs and when the group re-joined the topics each proposed were similar and consistent.

The mothers discussed preserving the Latina culture and how hard it is living in Minnesota. One mother described how she still required the girls to have a 'chaperone' even when they went to the store for groceries, and the subsequent struggle to give in to her daughter's pressure to "please just let me go to the store by myself". To this mother, the preserving of culture, specifically a cultural expectation that girls have a chaperone, was a challenge in the U.S.. Another mother remarked that she gave up that struggle and regretted it because her daughter got involved with some people she didn't approve of and was subsequently exposed to drugs and alcohol. This mother stated that when she tried to 'pull back' into previous expectations, it was too late. And she felt she's all but lost her daughter but she was pleased that her daughter agreed to come to this group with her. The third mother stated that she's been in the U.S. a long time, and long ago gave up some of the traditions. However, she has not given up the importance of family, religion and culture. When the moms were joined by the girls the conversation continued to focus on the importance of preserving the Latino culture while living here in Minnesota. Although their perspectives were different, the girls also focused on the importance of preserving their culture, even when at times the culture seemed to constrain some of their desired behaviors or actions. This was a pivotal bonding moment for the mothers, and an equally important bonding moment among the daughters. The *open conversation paved the way for rich and honest conversations throughout the rest of the sessions. By the end of the session, the group had decided on the following overarching topic/theme: "Preserving Latino Culture and Tradition."*

SESSION THREE. *The goal of this session was to finalize and clarify the theme that the photos would depict, and the rationale for the importance of that theme to the group. Participants shared the photographs they had taken the previous week and began to expound their discussions of the categories within the theme. Some of the photographs portrayed religious symbols such as churches, religious figures, and traditional shrines dedicated to the virgin Guadalupe. Other photographs were taken of foods such as fruit, bread, vegetables, and sweet bread. The mothers and daughters consistently explained that these items are all significant in the Mexican culture.*

It was noted that most of the photos portrayed positive aspects of the theme. The facilitators led a discussion to explore additional photo ideas that would support their theme. Participants were asked to come up with examples of concerns or problems which may exist in their community that do not support the preservation of their culture. They shared the following examples: eating at a fast food restaurant instead of eating fresh vegetables or fruits, driving to the store instead of walking, and environmental pollution.

SESSIONS FOUR THROUGH SEVEN. *Session four was the only session that did not have perfect attendance; one dyad was not able to attend. It was observed in session four that photographs were increasing in quality and projected a clear understanding of the theme. The group genuinely appeared to be pleased to see each other.*

Throughout the discussions that ensued many categories surfaced, and the following are those they included in the final project: Latina Community; Religion; Family; Environment/Pollution; Nature; Food and Culture. Participants agreed to focus future photography efforts on examples that would fit within the selected categories.

IN EACH OF THESE SESSIONS, the mothers and daughters returned with new photographs to show and discuss with each other. Every week it was observed that the girls and mothers greeted each other more warmly and with ease. The group worked well together, downloading photos and then sharing a meal. The group talked about the type of layout they wanted to use to exhibit their photos and agreed to do a collage format that would include all themes on one layout. The mothers and daughters were quick to complement each other on photos they had taken.

As the photo sorting happened in preparation for the final exhibit, the group was hesitant to eliminate someone else's photos from the exhibit, even if there were duplicates. When this happened they (as a whole) were very respectful about which to choose or eliminate and generally left the choice to the photographer. They were also cognizant of making sure the exhibit reflected photos from each photographer.

In these last two sessions, there was increased group work and interactions. The mothers and daughters individually wrote messages for each theme. The messages were read aloud by each individual and then, as a group, parts of messages were used to create a final message. It was a difficult task for the group to narrow down their message on each theme to just one or two phrases.

Discussions during the shared meal time and informal picture-sorting time included a wide variety of informal topics: sharing family support community resources for Latino families, activities during the school and weekends, dating, chaperoning, drinking and drugs, boyfriends, and acculturation. Often mothers talked about these topics with daughters listening and occasionally offering their perspectives. These conversations were organic and appeared to be mutually beneficial to the mothers and daughters. These dialogues continued even after the sessions ended, with conversations continuing in the parking lot. There was no group facilitation required by the researchers, since the conversation was led and guided by the mothers and daughters. Periodically, one of the researchers would pose a question to clarify or deepen the discussion, and then the group would respond.

How was the photovoice project presented to the community?

THE GROUP OF MOTHERS AND DAUGHTERS decided that their title of the project would be: "Our Voice through Pictures: 'Mother and Daughter.'" They described the project in a flier that announced their final session and invited the public;

> "Preserving culture and tradition: A group of mothers and daughters created a presentation of photographs to show the importance of maintaining the Latino culture here in Minnesota. The project focused around the following themes: Religion, Culture, Latino Community, Nature, Animals, Food, and Environment."

The mothers and daughters were responsible for organizing the logistics of the final exhibit. During session seven, they determined the length of time for the exhibit and the strategies for inviting guests (e.g. flier, face-to-face invitation). They engaged in a discussion about what type of food would be offered to guests. Moms were quick to plan the menu, each one selecting what their family would contribute and make (e.g., rice and beans, juice, and salsa). Grant funding allowed for purchasing items the moms did not prefer to prepare (e.g. chicken, guacamole, chips, and chocolate-dipped strawberries). The mom of the research assistant was from Cuba and although she was not involved in the project she offered to make flan, a traditional custard-like dessert. The study participants felt honored that another mom would contribute her time and energy for their event. Despite the sudden death of a family member, and despite our efforts to release her from the obligation, this mother prepared beautiful flan, and arranged to have it delivered the night of the presentation.

In addition to planning the refreshments, the mothers and daughters talked about what they would wear and how they would present their project. By the end of the dialogue, each mother-daughter dyad agreed to wear a color of the Mexican flag (i.e. red, green, and white). The research team was impressed and amazed. We wondered what the likelihood was that at the onset of this project any one of these daughters would have agreed to don an outfit purposely matching their mother. One pair even went shopping together to buy matching tops. As we have informally shared this observation with colleagues and others who work with teens, they are universally surprised and concur that this 'evidence' speaks to the impact of the photovoice intervention on the mother-daughter relationship.

A few hours before the actual final presentation, the mother/daughter dyads arrived in matching outfits with homemade food. One dyad brought rice and beans (white rice with some 'green' mixed in as well as 'red' rice). The second dyad provided homemade salsa, made with red tomatoes, green jalapeños and white onions. The third dyad provided three kinds of traditional Mexican beverages (red, green, and white). They each brought family and friends with them, and everyone worked together in setting up for the meal and exhibit.

The exhibit began by sharing a meal with family, friends and community members. Then, Garcia provided a brief introduction about the project and introduced the mothers and daughters. Proud family members watched their mothers and daughters speak up about their photovoice project and the theme: "Preserving our Latino culture and tradition." They took turns explaining each of the categories while guests were able to observe many of the pictures they had taken, which were displayed as two large collage posters. An on-going slideshow of their selected photos was displayed on a wall near the posters.

The mothers and daughters took turns describing each category. The research team only assisted the process by providing note cards and making suggestions specific to the process, not the content. Examples of the phrases and photos representing the categories are presented below:

RELIGION. Religion is something very important for our community. It is a foundation of family values and principles of every family and has great impact on the beliefs and actions of every person.

CULTURE. The culture is a set of concepts that differentiate our community from others. For example: clothing, food, folklore, art, values, language, music, tradition and centers of support.

COMMUNITY. The community is the means in which we develop into being human. It

has great impact on our behavior, and the physical, emotional, and spiritual state.

NATURE. Nature is the environment in which we grow up; that which presents us with beautiful countryside, images of animals and plants and is the movement that teaches us that there is still life on our planet. Take care of it!

ANIMALS. Animals are an essential part of this world. They are a gift of life and it is worth it to take care of them.

FAMILY. The family is the nucleus or base of every society that forms love, respect and our values. We need to conserve this good family foundation and maintain our values, customs and traditions.

FOOD. Food is important to us, Hispanics, a part of the tradition. The Hispanic food

always has the colors of Mexico that we will always take with us no matter where we are.

Environment/Pollution. Pollution is what affects the environment like the cars, airplanes, etc. Human beings are inhabitants of this planet and we have to be conscientious and take actions to preserve it. For example, using bicycles or walking will not contaminate this planet which is ours and in which we live. Otherwise our future generations will not be able to live and enjoy this planet.

It was obvious to all observers that the mothers and daughters jointly owned what they had created and were proud to share it with their guests. Over fifty people attended the exhibit, representing family members, politicians, friends, and community leaders. A question was posed at the end of the presentation from a member of the audience: "Do you feel your relationship with your mother/daughter has improved as a result of being in this project?" The immediate nodding of every mother and daughter affirmed that they believed their relationships were stronger. One mother shared,

"I came to know my daughter better. She took beautiful pictures and I realized she has this sensitivity. I didn't know she was so sensitive, and I learned something new about her through the photos she took."

The group also had unintended positive support for the mothers involved. At the debriefing session the day after the presentation, one mother began crying when she shared with the others how important this group had been for her. It was an opportunity to spend time with her daughter and to receive support as a woman from other women in the community. She said that she often felt very isolated with no one to talk with or to share her concerns, and this group had been very supportive for her. She hoped (and the other mothers and daughters quickly agreed) that this group would gather again, so this would not be the last time they would see each other. They also exchanged names and phone numbers with each other, so they could continue to communicate with each other.

Successes and Lessons Learned

OUR PHOTOVOICE PROJECT YIELDED MANY PROMISING RESULTS and offered useful considerations for future projects. We observed numerous benefits to the participants including:

1. role modeling and support from other group members (mother-to-mother sharing experiences and resources.

2. daughter-to-daughter connecting and role modeling for each other.

3. mothers and daughters receiving information and support from other dyads by witnessing their interactions.

4.   those who traditionally may not have a voice that is heard are able to express themselves in photos, and words (a very shy mother became much more engaged and inclined to speak up over the course of the intervention).

5.   the power of a creative process that enables sharing your opinion, thoughts, ideas in a safe and supportive group environment.

6.   the power of presenting opinions formally to family members, friends, and community members who may have influence over the topic.

7.   mothers and daughters spending time together, working on a common goal in a non-threatening environment, which ultimately strengthened their relationship and communication with each other.

Additionally, there were key practical lessons learned that may be valuable to those interested in developing or implementing a similar photovoice intervention. These include:

1.   Establishing a firm date and time prior to recruitment rather than allowing group process to determine this. We were too flexible in that we tried to accommodate all schedules. Work and family responsibilities will always be a significant challenge to offering a group-based program such as this. However, the mothers in our project agreed that with advance notice and enough interest in participating, families would be able to commit and attend.

2.   Research-based data collection (e.g. survey, video-recording) should be completed prior to the first official session. When using objective data collection techniques (i.e. video-recorded communication task), time needs to be scheduled for preparing and debriefing participants.

3.   Facilitators/leaders need to be technologically savvy and should assist the group in selecting a final exhibit venue that is consistent with skill levels. In our experience, the creation of an electronic collage was time intensive and although the lay-out of photos was determined by the participants, the actual creation of this lay-out electronically was done by the research team.

4.   With a larger group of dyads more purposeful community building activities for the group and possibly mother/daughter dyads may be needed. The nature of a small group was conducive to natural, organic community-building but with larger numbers the process will likely benefit from more intentional activities. These activities should be well planned, led and debriefed by a skilled facilitator.

5.   The number and content of sessions needs to be carefully planned. Some groups will require more sessions. Also, some activities require more time (e.g. creating the invitation to the exhibit) and need to be scheduled appropriately in the curriculum.

6.   During the orientation to the project it should be emphasized that other family members should not attend the sessions if it can be helped because this can take away from the mother/daughter focus.

7.   As with any group-based intervention, an effective facilitator is necessary to provide guidance, appropriate levels of input, and reinforcement of successes and process. The ability of a facilitator to connect with participants so as to ensure a trusting environment is imperative for photovoice projects which may often address difficult topics or issues. Also, an effective facilitator will know when to step in and when to allow the group process to progress without assistance.

Application of Photovoice in Practice

THERE IS LITTLE DOUBT THAT the strengthening of a mother-daughter relationship or bond will have a positive influence on the social and emotional well-being of the daughters (and the mothers). Photovoice appears to be a useful intervention strategy for encouraging healthy mother-daughter communication and connectedness whilst maintaining the civic engagement emphases inherent in photovoice. Anecdotal information gathered from the mother/daughter dyad who had the most contentious relationship is consistent with the goals of the project: The dyad reports feeling closer to the other, reduced stress in their relationship, improved communication, and increased amount of time spent together. Photovoice is an arts-based intervention that may be useful to professionals in multiple disciplines who are addressing parent-adolescent relational issues, or more broadly, adolescent risk and protective factors. The use of coaching questions and techniques is not necessary in photovoice, yet proved valuable. Since the information and interpretation of the photos, as well as the creation of the themes was organically created by each individual and then the group together – the project outcome was 'owned' by the group and each individual.

There are numerous health and social issues that would be amenable to photovoice as an intervention technique. It is a technique that should be explored not only with mothers but also with fathers and their daughters or sons. Fathers attending our final exhibit expressed much interest in the possibility of a similar project that would provide them with the opportunity to do photovoice and foster improved connections with a son or daughter. Photovoice is a creative arts medium which has great potential as an intervention for health promotion and disease prevention. Our experience using a photovoice-based intervention with Latino mothers and daughters demonstrates how broadly the arts can be used to intervene on and advocate for the health and well-being of individuals, families, and communities.

{115}

CAROLYN GARCIA, PhD, MPH, RN is Assistant Professor in the University of Minnesota School of Nursing. She also holds an adjunct faculty appointment in the School of Public Health, and is a faculty advisor for the Center for Spirituality and Health. Carolyn's program of research addresses Latino adolescent mental health promotion and uses community-engaged processes to develop school-based interventions for youth and their families. Carolyn is currently conducting intervention pilot studies of a coping intervention for Latina adolescents and a photovoice intervention to improve communication and connectedness among Latina adolescents and their mothers. She received funding for a photovoice study in 2010 that will address the effects of migration on Latino adolescent well-being and family connectedness. Carolyn teaches public health nursing and qualitative research methods, and advises undergraduate and graduate students in Nursing and Public Health. Carolyn has expertise in mixed-method research, including the use of photovoice, a process of engaging community members to articulate health concerns they care about, with a particular goal toward policy changes.

SANDI LINDGREN, MSW, is a Licensed Independent Social Worker in Minnesota and a professional Life Coach certified through the International Coach Federation. She has worked with youth and their families for twenty-five years in various capacities including crisis work, juvenile probation, residential, case management, individual and family therapist, group work, school social work and life coach. Sandi has spent the last thirteen years working in the Minneapolis area mainly within the Latino community, providing bilingual services to youth and their families. She has been the high school social worker for the last six years at El Colegio Charter School in Minneapolis, MN. Sandi is an experienced national presenter and trainer for professionals working with youth and has expertise in the area of adolescents, adolescent females, and Latino families.

References

ALLEN, M. L., ELLIOTT, M. N., FULIGNI, A. J., MORALES, L. S., HAMBARSOOMIAN, K., & SCHUSTER, M. A. (2008). The relationship between Spanish language use and substance use behaviors among Latino youth: A social network approach. *Journal of Adolescent Health, 43*(4), 372-379.

BAER, J. C., & SCHMITZ, M. F. (2007). Ethnic differences in trajectories of family cohesion for Mexican American and non-Hispanic white adolescents. *Journal of Youth & Adolescence, 36*(4), 583-592.

BERGMAN, M. (2003). *Foreign-born population surpasses 32 million, Census Bureau estimates.* Washington: U.S. Census Bureau.

BORAWSKI, E. A., IEVERS-LANDIS, C. E., LOVEGREEN, L. D., & TRAPL, E. S. (2003). Parental monitoring, negotiated unsupervised time, and parental trust: the role of perceived parenting practices in adolescent health risk behaviors. *Journal of Adolescent Health, 33*(2), 60-70.

BRANJE, S. J. T. (2008). Conflict management in mother daughter interactions in early adolescence. *Behaviour, 145*, 1627-1651.

BRAY, J. H., ADAMS, G. J., GETZ, J. G., & BAER, P. E. (2001). Developmental, family, and ethnic in influences on adolescent alcohol usage: A growth curve approach. *Journal of Family Psychology, 15*(2), 301-314.

BRONFENBRENNER, U. (1979). *The ecology of human development: Experiments by nature and design.* Cambridge: Harvard University Press.

BUCX, F., & VAN WEL, F. (2008). Parental bond and life course transitions from adolescence to young adulthood.. *Adolescence, 43*(169), 71-88.

CÉSPEDES, Y. M., & HUEY JR., S. J. (2008). Depression in latino adolescents: A cultural discrepancy perspective. *Cultural Diversity and Ethnic Minority Psychology, 14*(2), 168-172.

COATSWORTH, J. D., PANTIN, H., & SZAPOCZNIK, J. (2002). Familias unidas: A family-centered ecodevelopmental intervention to reduce risk for problem behavior among Hispanic adolescents. *Clinical Child & Family Psychology Review, 5*(2), 113-132.

DAKOF, G. A. (2000). Understanding gender differences in adolescent drug abuse: issues of comorbidity and family functioning. *Journal of Psychoactive Drugs, 32*(1), 25-32.

DAVIS, R., & YONAS, M. (2008). Utilizing the creative arts as a tool for public health: Bridging cultural communities. Presented at the *American Public Health Association Annual Meeting.Oral Section 3151.0 Public Health Education Beyond Borders,* San Diego, California.

DELVA, J., WALLACE, J., J., O'MALLEY, P., BACHMAN, J. G., JOHNSTON, L. D., & SCHULENBERG, J. E. (2005). The epidemiology of alcohol, marijuana, and cocaine use among mexican american, puerto rican, cuban american, and other latin american eighth-grade students in the united states: 1991-2002. *American Journal of Public Health, 95*(4), 696-702.

DISHION, T. J., & KAVANAGH, K. (2003). *Intervening in adolescent problem behavior. A family-centered approach.* New York: The Guilford Press.

DOGAN-ATES, A., & CARRION-BASHAM, C. Y. (2007). Teenage pregnancy among Latinas: Examining risk and protective factors. *Hispanic Journal of Behavioral Sciences, 29*(4), 554-569.

EATON, D., KANN, L., KINCHEN, S., SHANKLIN, S., ROSS, J., HAWKINS, J., ET AL. (2008). Youth risk behavior surveillance --- United States, 2007. *MMWR, 57*((SS04)), 1-131.

EITLE, T. M., Wahl, A. G., & ARANDA, E. (2009). Immigrant generation, selective acculturation, and alcohol use among Latina/o adolescents. *Social Science Research, 38*(3), 732-742.

GARCIA, C., & LINDGREN, S. (2009). "Life grows between the rocks" latino adolescents' and parents' perspectives on mental health stressors. *Research in Nursing and Health, 32(2), 148-162.*

GARCIA, C., SKAY, C., SIEVING, R., NAUGHTON, S., & BEARINGER, L. (2008). Family and racial factors associated with suicide and emotional distress among Latino students. *Journal of School Health, 78*(9), 487-495.

GOLDSTON, D. B., MOLOCK, S. D., WHITBECK, L. B., ZAYAS, L. H., HALL, G. C. N., & MURAKAMI, J. L. (2008). Cultural considerations in adolescent suicide prevention and psychosocial treatment. *American Psychologist, 63*(1), 14-31.

{118}

Guzman, B. (2001). *The Hispanic population, census 2000 brief.* Retrieved 2/21, 2007, from http://www.census.gov/prod/2001pubs/c2kbr01-3.pdf

Israel, B., Schulz, A. J., Parker, E. A., Becker, A. B., Allen, A. J., & Guzman, J. R. (2003). Critical issues in developing and following community based participatory research principles. In M. Minkler, & N. Wallerstein (Eds.), (pp. 53-76). San Franciso, CA: Jossey-Bass.

Laursen, B., & Collins, W. (1994). Interpersonal conflict during adolescence.. *Psychological Bulletin, 115*(2), 197-209.

Laursen, B. (1995). Conflict and social interaction in adolescent relationships. *Journal of Research on Adolescence (Lawrence Erlbaum),* 5(1), 55-70.

Marshall, S. K., Young, R. A., & Tilton-Weaver, L. C. (2008). Balancing acts: Adolescents' and mothers' friendship projects. *Journal of Adolescent Research,* 23, 544-565.

Martyn-Nemeth, P., Penckofer, S., Gulanick, M., Velsor-Friedrich, B., & Bryant, F. B. (2009). The relationships among self-esteem, stress, coping, eating behavior, and depressive mood in adolescents. *Research in Nursing & Health,* 32(1), 96-109.

McKee, M. D., & Karasz, A. (2006). "You have to give her that confidence": Conversations about sex in Hispanic mother-daughter dyads. *Journal of Adolescent Research,* 21, 158-184.

Mikolajczyk, R. T., Bredehorst, M., Khelaifat, N., Maier, C., & Maxwell, A. E. (2007). Correlates of depressive symptoms among Latino and non-Latino white adolescents: Findings from the 2003 California Health Interview Survey. *BMC Public Health,* 7, 21.

Minkler, M., & Wallerstein, N. (Eds.). (2003). *Community-based participatory research for health.* San Francisco: Jossey-Bass.

Mogro-Wilson, C. (2008). The influence of parental warmth and control on Latino adolescent alcohol use. *Hispanic Journal of Behavioral Sciences,* 30(1), 89-105.

OZER, E. M., PARK, M. J., BRINDIS, C., & IRWIN, C. E.,JR. (2003). *America's adolescents: Are they healthy?* San Francisco: National Adolescent Health Information Center.

PABON, E. (1998). Hispanic adolescent delinquency and the family: A discussion of sociocultural influences. *Adolescence, 33*(132), 941-955.

PANTIN, H., SCHWARTZ, S., SULLIVAN, S., COATSWORTH, J., & SZAPOXZNIK, J. (2003). Preventing substance abuse in Hispanic immigrant adolescents: An ecodevelopmental, parent-centered approach. *Hispanic Journal of Behavioral Sciences, 25*(4), 496-500.

PARSAI, M., VOISINE, S., MARSIGLIA, F. F., KULIS, S., & NIERI, T. (2009). The protective and risk effects of parents and peers on substance use, attitudes, and behaviors of Mexican and Mexican American female and male adolescents. *Youth & Society, 40*(3), 353-376.

PASCH, L. A., DEARDORFF, J., TSCHANN, J. M., FLORES, E., PENILLA, C., & PANTOJA, P. (2006). Acculturation, parent-adolescent conflict, and adolescent adjustment in Mexican American families. *Family Process, 45*(1), 75-86.

POPULATION DIVISION, U.S. CENSUS BUREAU. (2008). *Projections of the population by race and Hispanic origin for the United States: 2008 to 2050.* Retrieved August 8, 2008, from WWW.CENSUS.GOV

QUINONES-MAYO, Y., & DEMPSEY, P. (2005). Finding the bicultural balance: Immigrant Latino mothers raising "American" adolescents. *Child Welfare, 84*(5), 649-667.

RESNICK, M. D., HARRIS, L. J., & BLUM, R. W. (1993). The impact of caring and connectedness on adolescent health and well-being. *J Paediatr Child Health, 29 Suppl* 1, S3-9.

REW, L., THOMAS, N., HORNER, S. D., RESNICK, M. D., & BEUHRING, T. (2001). Correlates of recent suicide attempts in a tri-ethnic group of adolescents. *J Nurs Scholarsh, 33*(4), 361-367.

RODRIGUEZ, M. C., & MORROBEL, D. (2004). A review of Latino youth development research and a call for an asset orientation. *Hispanic Journal of Behavioral Sciences, 26*(2), 107-127.

ROMERO, A. J., ROBINSON, T. N., HAYDEL, K. F., MENDOZA, F., & KILLEN, J. D. (2004). Associations among familism, language preference, and education in Mexican-American mothers and their children. *Journal of Developmental and Behavioral Pediatrics, 2*5(1), 34-40.

SCHAPIRO, N. A. (2002). Issues of separation and reunification in immigrant Latina youth. *Nurs Clin North Am, 3*7(3), 381-92, vii.

SCHOFIELD, T. J., PARKE, R. D., KIM, Y., & COLTRANE, S. (2008). Bridging the acculturation gap: Parent-child relationship quality as a moderator in Mexican American families. *Developmental Psychology, 4*4(4), 1190-1194.

SCHWARTZ, L. R., SABLE, M. R., DANNERBECK, A., & CAMPBELL, J. D. (2007). Using photovoice to improve family planning services for immigrant Hispanics. *Journal of Health Care for the Poor & Underserved, 1*8(4), 757-766.

SILLARS, S., KOERNER, A., & FITZPATRICK, M. (2005). Communication and understanding in parent-adolescent relationships. *Human Communication Research, 3*1(1), 102-128.

SMOKOWSKI, P. R., BUCHANAN, R. L., & BACALLAO, M. L. (2009). Acculturation and adjustment in Latino adolescents: How cultural risk factors and assets influence multiple domains of adolescent mental health. *J Primary Prevention, 30(3-4)*, 373-393.

SMOKOWSKI, P. R., DAVID-FERDON, M., & STROUPE, N. (2009). Acculturation and violence in minority adolescents: A review of the empirical literature. *J Primary Prevention, 30(3,4)*, 215-263.

STEINBURG, L. (1996). *Adolescenc*e. New York: McGraw-Hill, Inc.

STRACK, R., LOVELACE, K., JORDAN, T., & & HOLMES, A. (under review). Framing photovoice using a social-ecological logic model as a guide.

STRACK, R. W., MAGILL, C., & McDONAGH, K. (2004). Engaging youth through photovoice. *Health Promotion Practice*, 5(1), 49-58.

Trejos-Castillo, E., & Vazsonyi, A. T. (2009). Risky sexual behaviors in first and second generation Hispanic immigrant youth. *Journal of Youth Adolescence, 38*, 719-731.

Turner, S. G., Kaplan, C. P., & Badger, L. W. (2006). Adolescent Latinas' adaptive functioning and sense of well-being. *Journal of Women and Social Work, 21*(3), 272-281.

U.S. Census. (2008). *Census Population Estimates.* Retrieved 5/8, 2008, from http://www.census.gov/popest/national/asrh/NC-EST2007-asrh.html

Unger, J., Ritt-Olson, A., Teran, L., Huang, T., Hoffman, B., & Palmer, P. (2002). Cultural values and substance abuse in a multiethnic sample of california adolescents. *Addiction Research and Theory,* (10), 257-279.

Wallerstein, N. B., & Duran, B. (2006). Using community-based participatory research to address health disparities. *Health Promotion Practice, 7*(3), 312-323.

Wang, C., & Burris, M. (1997). Photovoice: Concept, methodology, and use for participatory needs assessment. *Health Education and Behavior, 24*(3), 369-387.

Wilson, N., Minkler, M., Dasho, S., Wallerstein, N., & Martin, A. C. (2008). Getting to social action: The youth empowerment strategies (YES!) project. *Health Promotion Practice, 9*(4), 395-403.

Zayas, L.(2009). Suicidal behavior in Latina teens: Prevention and research. *Adolescent Suicide: Addressing Disparities through Research, Programs, Policy and Partnerships. Expert Panel co-sponsored by CDC, IHS, and SAMSHA.* Rockville, MD.

Zayas, L. H., Lester, R. J., Cabassa, L. J., & Fortuna, L. R. (2005). Why do so many Latina teens attempt suicide? A conceptual model for research. *Am J Orthopsychiatry, 75*(2), 275-287.

{122}

Online Resources

☞ www.photovoice.org ☞ www.photovoice.com ☞ http://www.photovoicewyoming.com

Health Disparities in Our Community: Reflections in Art and Performance

A Community Based Participatory Approach with Arts as a Translational Bridge to Knowledge

Olga Idriss Davis

People who believe that they have no control over their health will have no motivation to engage in health promotion or disease prevention activities.

Witte, 1995

THE ROLE OF CULTURAL ART AND PERFORMANCE *in addressing the dilemma of health disparities offers a unique approach to community engagement and consciousness-raising efforts on issues of HIV/AIDS, substance abuse, and mental health. Health Disparities refers to the state in which marginalized communities lack access to healthcare and have fewer opportunities to obtain knowledge that can be integrated into personal wellness, health interventions, and treatment. Centering cultural art and performance in the context of health disparities, this chapter inquires, "How do arts-based communication channels serve as a "translational bridge" for providing communities the access to good science and researchers the access to important local knowledge?" A community-based participatory health communication*

Olga Idriss Davis
photo by Judy Butzine, Cultural Arts
Coalition, co-founder/co-director
WWW.ARTSCARE.ORG/CAC.INTRO.SHTML

approach to health literacy highlights the role that art and performance can play in intervention and offers a culturally-based model for replication in other marginalized communities.

HEALTH DISPARITIES IN THE UNITED States have affected the health and welfare of minority communities from the past century to the present. The 1985 landmark Secretary's Task Force Report on Black and Minority Health, published by the then U.S. Department of Health and Human Services (HHS) Secretary Margaret Heckler, spurred a concerted effort to address disparities impacting racial and ethnic minority populations at the federal level. That report identified specific racial and ethnic populations in the United States that were not experiencing the same level of health improvements as the nation. These were African Americans, Hispanics, Asian/Pacific Islanders, and American Indians/Alaska Natives. As Witte (1995) notes in the above quote, people of color have traditionally felt no agency in their own health care and thus have neither experienced interest nor worth of health promotion and prevention, continuing the cycle of determining factors which contribute to health disparities. The National Institutes of Health (n.d.) defines health disparities as "differences in the incidence, prevalence, mortality, and burden of diseases and other adverse health conditions that exist among specific population groups in the United States". Healthy People 2010 is a campaign which seeks to eliminate the disparities in six areas of health status experienced by racial and ethnic minority populations (infant mortality, cancer screening and management, cardiovascular disease, diabetes, HIV Infection/AIDS, and immunizations) however, little is being done to provide culturally-specific access to knowledge and awareness of health disparities among racially and ethnically diverse groups. Moreover, the lack of access to care uncovers the social, cultural, and environmental factors leading to higher levels of disease and disability thus revealing a broad range of issues that underscore the need for health disparities research. One potential source of these disparities is the lack of culturally and linguistically appropriate messages about the process of health and health literacy (Office of Minority Health [OMH], 2003).

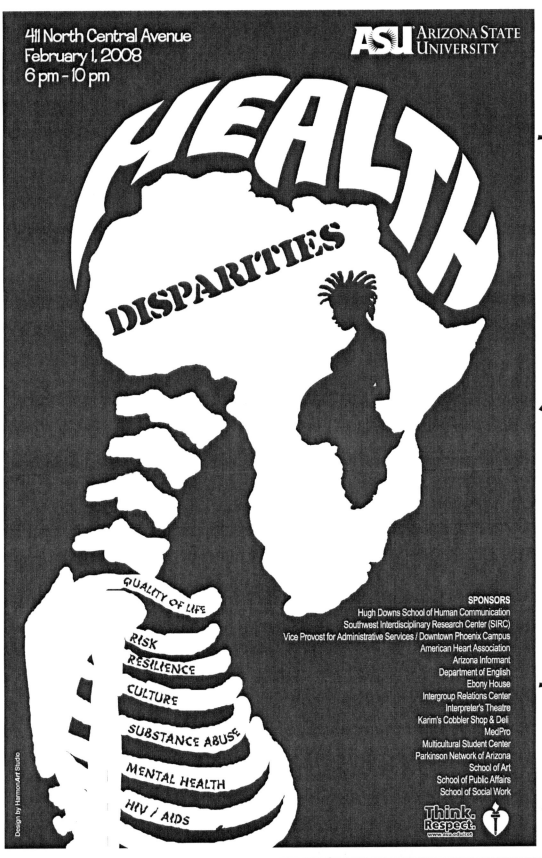

411 North Central Avenue
February 1, 2008
6 pm - 10 pm

ASU ARIZONA STATE UNIVERSITY

HEALTH

DISPARITIES

QUALITY OF LIFE
RISK
RESILIENCE
CULTURE
SUBSTANCE ABUSE
MENTAL HEALTH
HIV / AIDS

Design by HarmonArt Studio

SPONSORS
Hugh Downs School of Human Communication
Southwest Interdisciplinary Research Center (SIRC)
Vice Provost for Administrative Services / Downtown Phoenix Campus
American Heart Association
Arizona Informant
Department of English
Ebony House
Intergroup Relations Center
Interpreter's Theatre
Karim's Cobbler Shop & Deli
MedPro
Multicultural Student Center
Parkinson Network of Arizona
School of Art
School of Public Affairs
School of Social Work

Think.
Respect.
www.asu.edu/zet

Health Disparities in our community: Reflections in art and performance

{125}

These barriers to health care underscore the process of marginalization and disenfranchisement of numerous individuals, social groups, and communities whom are denied full privileges, rights, access, and power within the existing political system and social structure (Ray, 1996).

Health Disparities in African American Communities of Arizona

THE ARIZONA DEPARTMENT OF HEALTH SERVICES has produced a report every two years since 1997 called "Differences in the Health Status Among Ethnic Groups." Using seventy indicators, the reports rank Arizona's racial and ethnic population's health status using a scoring system – the higher the score, the worse the health status. Each year, the rankings remain the same. Asian/Pacific Islanders rank the most favorable, followed by White (Non Hispanic), Hispanics, American Indians/Alaska Natives, African Americans. Of all the racial and ethnic populations in the state, the disparity in health status is consistently worse for African Americans. This is indicated by the high rank, and the high sum of ranks. Unfortunately, African Americans have the worst ranking for: HIV Disease, Breast Cancer, Alzheimer's, Lung Cancer, Cardiovascular and Heart Disease. The causes of health disparities in health status are varied and complex. A simple framework below illustrates the personal and societal influences that impact health status, of which race and ethnicity act as only one variable, but is a proxy for other personal and societal conditions that can cause certain groups to have more disparity in health status than others. These determinants of health disparities serve as the impetus for community health workers and university health researchers in collaboration, to find health interventions that place dialogic communication at the center of socio-political and cultural influences that affect the African American community.

The unequal distribution of wealth, health, and life opportunities is heavily impacted by the interactions of social, political, cultural and economic factors that impact certain individuals and groups. Some are seen as not conforming to the "standards of normality" in society, and are thus marginalized and devalued, while their health concerns are treated differently than those in the dominant culture. These dynamics present challenges to effective communication efforts in making health-related messages available and relevant to all. This means understanding the dynamics of disenfranchisement and marginalization based on social class, or more frequently, in combination with other markers and social determinants such as race and ethnicity, gender, ability, and sexuality. The challenge to reaching those from diverse ethnic, racial, cultural and linguistic backgrounds, from different socio-economic strata, and those living in urban and rural locales is to recognize

Disparities in Health Status:
Personal and Societal Influences

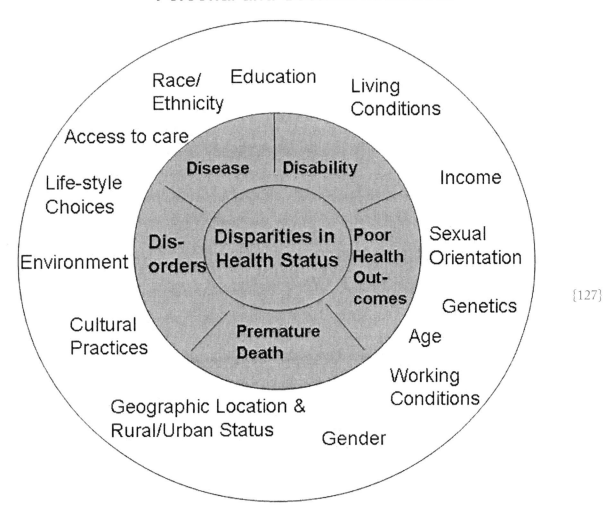

Figure 1. State of Black Arizona, (HHS, 2006).

the systems of inequality which prevent the maintenance of good health and preventive health practices and design new approaches to health communication interventions.

Arts and Performance as Health Intervention in the Black Community

Partnering with the community is necessary to create change and improve health.
– Center for Disease Control, 1997

ART AND PERFORMANCE HAVE ALWAYS BEEN a source of resistance, perseverance, and a coping mechanism in the Black community. The power of the spoken word in African and African American cultures has always been recognized as the hallmark of storytelling (Davis, 2008; Davis, 1999a, 1999b; Busia, 1988). Whether art is expressed in visual, dance, musical or literary contexts, the aesthetic dimension reveals human experience in the form of story. Human behavior is performative when the act is telling a story, creating reality, critiquing society, or remembering history through orality, the primacy of the spoken word (Fisher, 1987). Performance is a form of human communication and is considered an embodied, articulated, particularized and actualized dimension of the very core nature of human sense making. It has no singular definition nor is situated in any singular discipline of study. However, performance offers value and insight to theatre studies, to social sciences, and can be viewed through the lens of cultural and critical studies.

{128}

The arts as cultural performance illuminate how humans participate in political and cultural aspects of everyday life in creative and expressive ways. For example, oral history performance creates opportunities to understand the historical situatedness of culture and of navigating identity and discourse within a historical context of the times (Davis, 1998). Music and dance in the African American community have continued as important therapeutic means of helping Black people confront their struggles and to move toward healing (Wimberly, 1997). Through song and instrumental music, Black people have told and listened to stories of joy and struggle, and have accounted their successes to God's activity in their lives. For Africans living in America, various forms of ritual serve as a way to articulate the liminal space of cultural difference while illuminating the contested, the tensions, the complexities, and the commonalities of human existence and meaning-making within the context of social interaction. For example, the cultural heritage of African Americans in part, is grounded in food culture. However, competing narratives of traditional food and cultural engagement, and healthy eating continue to remain challenges to the health of African American communities. Of this dilemma Nettles (2007) articulates:

The threat of disease and death fails to quell the urge to prepare and consume foods that are valued as a positive part of a cultural tradition, that are valued as a positive part of our communal life . . . the plethora of light soul food cookbooks attempt to 'save' soul food by encouraging the retelling of narratives that honor family, love, and community while simultaneously advocating personal responsibility and restraint . . . We must begin to work collectively to bring about changes in the food system that will enable us to reclaim our food cultures in ways that honor our roots. Only in this way can we feed both body and soul without causing harm. (pp. 111-112)

What is considered a traditional soul food diet contains multiple high-fat and high-cholesterol foods that contribute to the risk factors for cardiovascular disease (American Heart Association, 2007; Center for Disease Control [CDC], 2007). Soul food is a metaphor of group identity and marks the emergence and rise of soul food restaurants in the 1960s in the U.S. During this time, soul food was adopted by millions of African Americans as a marker of ethnic identity (Brown & Mussell, 1984). Such food included foods high in fat, salt and sugar. Traditionally, meats and other foods are fried, and most vegetables are stewed with pork fat.

African Americans stand to benefit more from health promotion and disease prevention programs when those programs are conducted in ways that affirm and legitimate African Americans' cultural codes and meanings. Such affirmation of differences in health promotion activities in African American communities should be promoted (Airhihenbuwa & Pineiro, 1988). *The Health Disparities in Our Community: Reflections in Art and Performance* project is such a health promotion activity. Through the conceptual lens of culture and narrative theory, this project illuminates the ways in which health promotion centers African American culture of arts and performance to increase health literacy and to create a conversation about health in the African American community.

Culture and Story in Conceptual Frameworks

COMMUNICATING HEALTH FROM THE PERSPECTIVE of community-based participation encourages a culture-centered approach to health disparities research to conceptualize this project. Shared systems of belief, values, rituals, language, and various other aspects reflect the dynamics of the shifting cultural landscape and create the climate for multicultural health communication efforts (Brislin & Yoshida, 1994; Resnicow et al, 2002). Airhihenbuwa (1995) posits that health is a cultural construct and health theory and practice must be rooted in cultural codes and meanings, inherently tied to values. Situating culture and context at the core of public health communication practices underscores the intersections of culture, community, and health:

It has become common practice in the field of public health and in the social and behavioral sciences to pay lip service to the importance of culture in the study and understanding of health behaviors, but culture has yet to be inscribed at the root of health promotion and disease prevention programs, at least in the manner that legitimates its centrality in public health praxis. (Airhihenbuwa, x)

In the past decade, health communication theory and praxis has taken a turn towards incorporating culture in health communication (Dutta-Bergman, 2004, 2005, Dutta, 2007; Ford & Yep, 2003; Harris, 2001). A culture-centered approach attempts to place culture at the center of theorizing about health and health intervention practice rather than as an afterthought.

Similarly, narrative theory and cultural performance theory are alternative approaches to the understanding of communicative processes related to health and health disparities. The overarching social functions of narrative are especially attentive to the ways in which people tell stories to help them understand the world and make meaning of their everyday lived experiences (Fisher, 1987; Bruner, 1986; Davis, 1994, 1999, 2002, 2008). Storytelling is a particularly useful approach to the social construction of health for its functions of sense making, asserting control, transforming identity, and building community (Sharf & Vanderford, 2003).

Cultural performance theory is instrumental for galvanizing performance as a means for knowledge-formation and a force for intercultural exchange, understanding, and equality. Converging performance theory with traditional ways of knowing, offers performance as a framework for weaving together the social sciences and humanities in ways specific to understanding worldviews and ideologies. Performance implies an act of doing, practice, and theatricality, while simultaneously encompassing both subject and method of research. Created from perspectives on human behavior, culture, and ritual, cultural performance theory explores the relationship between the foundations of human experience: community, culture and performance. For African Americans, both narrative and cultural performance protocols embody the healing effects of community and self-identity, serve as means for understanding culture and cultural difference, and provide a context for the critique of issues related to health and access to care in their community.

Culture-Centered Approach and Dialogic Communication

THE CULTURE-CENTERED APPROACH EMPHASIZES the dialogical journey with cultural community members that foregrounds the voices of cultural members in articulation of health issues and relevant health solutions (Dutta & Zoller, 2008). The *Health Disparities in Our Community: Reflections in Art and Performance* (HDOC) project brought together health service organizations, artists, musicians, storytellers, community members, cuisine artists, and community members representing a cross section of metropolitan Phoenix. Dialogic communication offers community members to engage in participatory processes that solve the problems considered critical from within the community. A culture-centered approach centers dialogue that creates openings for the sharing of culturally-situated stories and narratives that provide possibilities for change (Dutta, 2008).

Intersectionality of Social Sciences and Culture: Southwest Interdisciplinary Research Center

THE SOUTHWEST INTERDISCIPLINARY RESEARCH CENTER (SIRC) at Arizona State University, an NIH/NCMHD Center for Excellence in the Study of Health Disparities, employs a Community Engagement/Outreach Core whose mission is to collaborate with a wide range of community partners in order to promote and improve health among minority populations of the U.S. such as Hispanic, Native American, African American, and Asian American/Pacific Islanders, and U.S.-Mexico border region and to reduce or eliminate their health disparities especially in the areas of mental health, HIV-AIDS, and substance abuse. Its goal is to promote an environment in which significant improvements in health among minority populations result in provision of health resources, care, and benefits equivalent to the majority of Americans. SIRC and its Community Engagement/Outreach Core support culturally-based, evidence-based research where translational research of knowledge into practice is valued in health intervention and promotion; taking into account risk behavior and resilience of marginalized populations of the Southwest. It centers resilience as a key tenet in the study of health disparities underscoring the inherent cultural aspects of how marginalized groups transcend the social determinants of health through indigenous cultural aspects inherent in their communities. Resilience refers to identifying the ways in which African American and other marginalized communities persevere, transform, and have the ability to recover from the misfortune of health disparities. The intersection of culture and social sciences encourages community-based health interventions that support an enactment of emancipatory projects (Zoeller, 2000) that ultimately creates a space for alternative voices to be heard.

Method

Community-Based Participatory Research (CBPR) is a methodology based ideally on flexible power relationships and the unobstructed flow of expert and local knowledge among project partners. Among social scientists the use of Community Based Participatory Research (CBPR) is widely spread. In health related fields there has been a recent increase in the incorporation of CBPR, although it still remains underutilized. Concerned with equity and the notion of participation, participatory research enables local people, or communities, to seek their own solutions according to their priorities while engaging social scientists in reflexive, flexible, and iterative characteristics of local knowledge and perceptions in the research process. The potential of success in CBPR depends on authentic dialogue among partners, free flow of information, and trust. Methods such as Theater of the Oppressed (TO), Photovoice, video, jazz, spoken word, hip-hop, visual arts, and performance art provide a strong, authentic voice for community values and needs, and ensures that methods and messages are rooted in local cultures and delivered clearly, directly, and respectfully.

{132}

CBPR allows scientists to gather the input from populations of interest, and use that knowledge to tailor interventions to targeted groups. Communities take an active role in the research process, giving them a voice. This type of research uses an iterative process that involves researchers, community members, professionals, and paraprofessionals that work with the target population. Usually, the research team drafts an intervention based on theory and their own knowledge of the population of interest; the drafts are presented to community groups; the community groups provide feedback and contribute their expertise concerning the subject, the look, readability, comprehension, and attractiveness of brochures and other materials that form part of the intervention (these could involve newspaper or TV ads, a school curriculum, a health intervention in a clinic or in a neighborhood), and they test all the materials (e.g. they complete worksheets, participate in activities). The information from community groups is integrated to the intervention model; the new draft is presented to the community for approval. This process goes on until the researchers in partnership with the community produce a final version of the intervention that reflects the culture, norms, and values of the target population. Feedback from the community is gathered through focus groups, one-on-one interviews, community surveys, and any other method that allows community members to voice their opinion and expertise concerning the intervention.

This method has been used successfully and proven to be effective. For example, the drug prevention program keepin' it REAL (Hecht et al, 2003) used CBPR to identify drug refusal strategies that felt natural and comfortable for the adolescents, and that were sensitive to their culture, values and norms, and created a culturally grounded intervention with the input of students, teachers, parents, and scientists from various fields. Students from a local high school wrote the scripts and produced the videos that are used in the intervention implementation. The intervention has been tested and proved to be efficacious (Freimuth, 1990) and was recognized as a National Model Program by the Substance Abuse and Mental Health Services Administration (SAMSHA). In large part, the success of the program lies in that the students' narratives were incorporated into the curriculum, and the prevention messages reflect the local, social, and cultural context of the community. The lived experience of students further helps to underscore the need to incorporate the experience and viewpoint of those whose ethnicity is being categorized and investigated. Similarly, in the HDOC project, CBPR provides an approach for incorporating the experience

Project Description

The *Health Disparities in Our Community: Reflections in Art and Performance* project was designed as a pilot project to be conducted in a large urban area during the annual recognition of Black History Month (Butzine, 2008; Traywick, 2008; White, 2008) in collaboration with the Community Organization of Black Artists (COBA), Artists of the Black Community (ABC), and health disparities researchers from the Southwest Interdisciplinary Research Center (SIRC) at Arizona State University (ASU). Beginning as a community-based, interpretative inquiry into implementing a model for cultural health promotion to find effective and innovative ways to reach vulnerable communities, the *Health Disparities in Our Community* project *(HDOC),* as it came to be called, would have, as its initial effort, increasing awareness of risk behavior and resilience in Black communities facing substance abuse, mental health, and HIV/AIDS. The goal was to experiment with using the oral tradition of storytelling, African interactive dance, jazz and Negro Spirituals, visual art, video montages, and cuisine, all culturally-appropriate strategies for African American culture, in an innovative way (Airhihenbuwa, 1995). The proposed project was to use a multi-layered approach of arts and performance in combination with a facilitation process that incorporated free blood pressure screenings from the Black Nurses Association, information booths

photo by Judy Butzine from a host of state, local, and university health service organizations, and a community-catered cuisine of healthy soul food for tasting.

The project examined two research questions. First, we explored ways to develop a creative, innovative, participatory health communication process that can be used effectively with African American communities and as a potential model for other health disparaged communities with diverse backgrounds and educational levels. Second, we incorporated the community-based participatory action research (CBPR) approach to ensure cultural appropriateness for the community, with community stakeholders; making the shift to a power-sharing/ empowerment way of relating and educating. The spirit of inclusion, mutual respect, and valuing of difference fueled the development of a plethora of creative work representing HIV/AIDS, mental health, from the community of visual artists, ceramicists, singers, jazz musicians, dollmakers, photo montage artists, dance and performance artists – from photo montages of slavery and its effects on mental health of African Americans, to an interpretive video autoethnography combining dance and narrative on the lived experience of HIV/AIDS Interpretive inquiry attempts to give voice to the needs, interests, and perspectives of the marginalized and disenfranchised communities, often

Davis

those who are most affected by health disparities, and supports the exploratory process and nature of learning through dialogue, mutual negotiation and balancing of ideas, needs, and constraints (Dutta-Bergman, 2004; Hubbard & Power, 1999). As a result, the HDOC project helped establish new partnerships and relations in the community and forged new associations between African American community members and majority institutional organizations of Phoenix, Arizona.

In addition to introducing the project to the African American community as an event for Black History Month during the first week in February of 2008, the collaborative consortium introduced the project to the First Fridays Committee of the City of Phoenix garnering public relations, marketing, public transportation, and a critical mass of interested, interactive audience members. By crafting an effective, innovative, and consciousness-raising effort in direct association with community members, the COBA, ABC, and university researchers believed the effort to reframe the role of arts and performance in a health setting would expand the effects of health awareness on the Greater Phoenix community at large. As participatory methodologies evolve, the arts have increasingly taken center stage as culturally fluent modalities for information, communication, advocacy and organizing.

On February 1, 2008, *Health Disparities in Our Community: Reflections in Art and Performance* brought together community partners and members, co-sponsors and university faculty, staff, and students to reflect on the dilemma of health disparities and the resilience of community to underscore the role of *voice* in community-based participatory health communication.

{135}

Drafting the Intervention "The Voice of the Drum"

In African cosmology, it is the beating of the drum that calls the community to unify, collect, and become attuned to the voice of the griot, or wisdom-bearer of the community. What lies at the heart of drafting a health intervention is the unifying call to address the concerns of the community. The impetus of the intervention was the high co-morbidity rate of African Americans in Phoenix, Arizona regarding health disparities.

In this phase, eight members formed the community group. These included visual artists of the COBA and ABC, representatives from ASU's Office of the Vice-Provost for Administrative Services, and health disparities researchers from SIRC. The intervention team met in September, 2007 to draft a plan of community participation, community mobilization, and community influence that addressed community health decision making and action in a creative, innovative way. The group dialogue format created a safe space for members to voice their opinions of health concerns in their community and to move toward action by way of an arts and performance health intervention. Group members participated actively in the session and built strong connections with each other. The group determined a health intervention that employed a cultural identity of arts and performance to address health challenges of the African American community in Phoenix, Arizona. Suggestions of the types of art involvement stemmed from the variety of expertise of the arts community membership as well as the potential organizations that would co-sponsor the event. Health challenges centered on HIV/AIDS, substance abuse, and mental health, critical to the plight of African Americans in Phoenix, Arizona.

Centralizing Community Dialogue: Participation of Co-Sponsors, Citizen Volunteers and Community Activists

CENTRAL TO THE SUCCESS OF A COMMUNITY HEALTH INTERVENTION is a partnership with co-sponsors, volunteers, and community activists. Co-sponsors, volunteers, and community activists created a coalition formation in the form of community member participation in community-based health promotion activities. This was characterized by an organization of individuals who represented diverse organizations or constituencies in an alliance to mobilize and achieve the enactment of the health intervention.

Co-sponsors

Many advocates of community-based health promotion efforts view grass roots CBPR organizing as the beginning of social change. As such, a collective of co-sponsors from health organizations to academic departments saw the efficacy of the *Health Disparities in Our Community* project and gave support to improve health literacy and other conditions in health disparaged communities (Bettencourt, 1996). Co-sponsors as members of the health community included the Black Nurses Association that conducted free blood pressure screenings to all attendees; the ASU health clinic and School of Nursing; Ebony House drug-intervention facility; Parkinson Network of Arizona; American Heart Association and its Cultural Health Initiative task force; and MedPro. Other co-sponsors included; Arizona State University's schools and departments and health conscious community caterer, Karim's Cobbler and Deli Shop.

Citizen Volunteers

The Campus Environment Team (CET) at Arizona State University recruited university student volunteers committed to the project's mission. Students ranged from undergraduate majors of public relations, nursing, communication, and social work. Their efforts ranged from welcome hosts to capacity organizers on the day of the event. They set up booths, tables, answered questions, and created an ambiance of invitation and courtesy. Other citizen volunteers from the First Fridays organization promoted community organizing efforts through bus shuttle service for event attendees, marketing applications to include brochures, flyers, and handouts, and security escort service.

Community activists

Community activists also found resonance in our project event. Several community activists performed as spoken word artists and visual artists in the evening's event. The support from activists of other disenfranchised groups (racial, ethnic, sexuality) also underscored the notion of coalition building efforts and how what happens to one group affects all. Activists attended when they felt a sense of community, saw their involvement as vital to the knowledge, skills, and resources of the project, believed issues as relevant and worth their time for mobilizing health decision-making and action, and viewed the process and climate of the event as supportive.

Organizing an Arts/ Performance Strategy: Creating a Safe Space For Health Intervention

AS RESEARCHERS AND PRACTITIONERS, creating a space for alternative voices to be heard is a challenge that may be met with minimal support. In the academic milieu, the research community is challenged to legitimate alternative research strategies such as ethnographic methodologies that can further health understandings from the perspective of culture, communication, and community. The social, cultural, and economic context of marginalized individuals and social groups creates unfriendly conditions for maintaining good health. The political context also offers an inhospitable environment for many vulnerable health disparaged populations. Shifting the context of health from an unfriendly environment to a safe space provides a framework for alternative discourses to reshape the role of health communication and health interventions in marginalized communities. Moreover, the arts and performance strategy reflects alternative ways of knowing and being in the world, pointing to the forms of expressions and understanding often embraced by culture-specific identities. For example, the African American oral tradition of jazz and blues and storytelling created a space for transformation. The First Friday event brought approximately four hundred attendees from a variety of cultural, ethnic, and racial populations providing knowledge of the health issues in the Black community.

The lobby of the ASU Downtown Phoenix University Center was a-blazing with hustle and bustle from neophytes to nurses, and activists to academics. Performers provided spoken word poetics on the topics of substance abuse, mental health, and HIV/AIDS, while personal narratives expressed the lived experience of health-related issues from a culturally specific domain. Singers of the Negro Spiritual genre told the story of resilience of the Black community through historical song. Jazz artists crafted instrumental music as a backdrop to the creative ambiance with blends of African beats and rhythms indicative of the cultural experience of this population. Cuisine artist prepared food in collaboration with the *Healthy Soul Food* cookbook from the American Heart Association, planning hoerdourves that considered the implications of cardiovascular disease and the ritual of New Year celebratory foods in the African American community. Displays of artists' conceptions of health disparities in the Black community underscored the transformative power of the aesthetic expression in community-based health communication intervention.

Voice as Empowerment and Participation: Centralizing a Translational Bridge to Community

Don't start with the notion that you have to "empower" us. Recognize that we are in power.
This is our community and when your program is gone, we'll still be here.
–Poole & Van Hook, 1997

THE NOTION OF VOICE POSITS the importance of effective engagement in the process of capacity building (Davis, 2008). Before individuals and community organizations can gain control and influence and become co-creators, players and partners in the development of a health intervention, they may need knowledge and skills of empowerment and participation in problem-solving efforts (Fawcett et al, 1995). Empowerment suggests that marginalized communities help to create a space for alternative voices to be heard. That is to say, through engagement in the social construction of the community's notion of what it means to be healthy, boundaries are crossed, difference is celebrated, and cultural empowerment becomes the source of citizen participation (Airhihenbuwa, 1995). Community participation became the translational bridge for co-creating meaning of the event into positive action of many attendees. For instance, in our project, there was a woman from the community who is HIV positive. She wrote and performed a personal narrative to reveal the richness of her lived experience and to underscore the importance of community support in her health challenges. With the event nestled in the First Fridays celebration, many people from across racial and ethnic communities initially came out to view the art – but they also heard the narratives – the stories of lived experience, dialogued with each other, and networked about ways to get involved in specific task forces, activist groups, and community organizations. Community is empowered when members can play an integral role in creating an intervention for promoting positive health behaviors. Translational research is the outcome that is engendered as a result of taking scientific knowledge and transforming it. That is, giving evidence-based, culturally-specific knowledge back to the community in ways that are affirming, validating, and resilient. For example, the *Health Disparities in Our Community* project involved community members in the development of spoken word performances, the selection of musical interludes, the activities of the interactive information booths, and the heart-healthy samplers of black-eyed peas, cornbread, {139} vegetable gumbo, baked chicken wings, and peace cobbler. Empowerment of the spirit, soul, and body was expressed in the nature of the gathering as well as in the intervention that centered the intersection of community, culture, health, and communication.

CONCLUSION

It is only through the way in which we represent and imagine ourselves
that we come to know how we are constituted and who we are
–Hall, 1997

THE REPRESENTATION OF THE COMMUNITY, by the community, and for the community was the underlying richness of the community-based arts and performance health communication promotion. The event served as a way for the Black community to represent itself and imagine the resilience that culture provides in overcoming life's obstacles. By bringing attention to health disparities, members of the African American community and other diverse communities in the metropolitan Phoenix vicinity took in the myriad of sensory perceptual activities related to health literacy and promotion. The planned organization by the community group to have free blood pressure screenings, free health giveaways (including free condoms), cuisine samplers, art, music, and performance served as a welcome call and a consciousness-raising effect for hundreds who attended the evening.

The nature of health disparities is defined as differences in the incidence, prevalence, mortality, and burden of diseases and other adverse health conditions that exist among specific

{140}

photo by
Judy Butzine

populations in the U.S. Healthy People 2010 (Office of Disease Prevention and Health Promotion, 2005) is a campaign which seeks to eliminate the disparities in six areas of health status experienced by racial and ethnic minority populations (infant mortality, cancer screening and management, cardiovascular disease, diabetes, HIV Infection/AIDS, and immunizations). To successfully address these disparities, researchers are realizing that they need to not only understand the nature of the community, but also involve community members in the research process (Minkler & Wallerstein, 2003). However, little is being done to provide access to health promotion and health literacy from a cultural perspective for racially and ethnically diverse groups suffering from disparities of health status. The *Health Disparities in Our Community: Reflections in Art and Performance* project offered a nuanced look at the possibilities of a culture-centered community-participatory approach to eradicate this dilemma.

Recommendations for Future Study

THE OUTCOMES AND IMPLICATIONS OF the success of this community-participatory health communication intervention focused on the African American community provides the opportunity to suggest several recommendations for the future of this project.

Expand the model to include other ethnically and racially-diverse communities. There is a paucity of knowledge among the African American community on the importance of taking better personal care earlier in their lives. The safe space of arts and performance along with interactive booths of health information construct ways to help marginalized community members successfully stay healthy and make healthy choices to address the problems facing their care. The initial project centered on the cultural experience of arts and performance as a health intervention in the African American community. However, extending this project might include alternative ethnic and racially-diverse communities, such as Latino and Native American communities, to explore the ways in historically disenfranchised communities create health interventions through cultural processes. Such inclusivity of the model also would allow more community members to become well-informed about HIV/AIDS, substance abuse, and mental health, adequate and appropriate care, and avenues of access.

Create opportunities for empowerment in marginalized communities to reduce and eliminate health disparities. An important aspect of this project was to demonstrate how the integration of information for one minority population might serve to empower its members, and as a result, provide the impetus to raise awareness and move toward action in accessing the health care system in the U.S. This project reveals the potential for health sustainability, community capacity building, transformation, and self-healing in African American communities. Strategies of cultural tradition, discourse, music, dance, visual arts, cuisine, and the gathering of community, empower individuals and create healing networks that may serve to disrupt the effects of the politics of health disparities. A recommendation to expand the project as a model to include emphasis on follow-up data to determine not only the degree to which community members responded to the empowering information, but also how they accessed adequate and appropriate health care in pursuit of improved health (e.g. regular blood pressure screenings).

Promote community-based participatory research (CBPR) in Health-Related Communication Studies (Minkler & Wallerstein, 2003). The role of Black visual arts and performance in the African American community points to the ways in which community-based discourse and community-informed research illuminate the study of African American health and the ways in which African American communities engage in a cultural discourse of health to eradicate health disparities. With the preponderance of racism and discrimination often experienced by members of the African American community, community-based health interventions such as the *Health Disparities in Our Community* allows members to heal from the constant experience of attacks to their identity by When community activists, performers, visual and cuisine artists were included in the creation of the health intervention model, they were able to: 1) identify co-sponsors, community volunteers, and a variety of artists for whom their voice underscored the success of the project; 2) raise consciousness of the health dilemma in the Black community; and 3) demonstrate the efficacy of community-based dialogue through creative arts and innovative practice.

Further, community health interventions have an emancipatory goal. Through these community-developed and community-enacted interventions, the marginalized community challenges the larger systems of domination, i.e. the social, political, cultural, and economic forces that function to preserve the power of the oppressors and continue the subjugation of the oppressed (Ford & Yep, 2003). In addition, community-based health promotion scholarship can begin to recognize a need to rethink alternative theories and praxis that take into account cultural forms of epistemology and ontology as ways to address health promotion in marginalized communities. As a result of community-based participation in this health promotion project, visual and performance artists are redefining their role by transforming art into health knowledge through a model of culturally-appropriate health communication intervention.

OLGA IDRISS DAVIS, Ph.D., is Associate Professor at The Hugh Downs School of Human Communication, Arizona State University (ASU) and Co-Principal Investigator of the Community Engagement and Outreach Core of the Southwest Interdisciplinary Research Center (SIRC) NIH-P20 Centre of Excellence grant for the Study of Health Disparities in the Southwest. Her research agenda is in the domain of critical cultural studies and performance studies in the disciplinary area of human communication. Her work explores the performative struggle of identity within the African Diaspora, the Black body as a site of racialized and sexualized oppression, the socio-cultural determinants of health disparities, and the function of memory as ritualized healing among survivors of the Tulsa Race Riot of 1921. Central to her work is the study of narrative-how narrative empowers, creates, and fosters cultural awareness to provide a space for social change.

{144}

References

Airhihenbuwa, C.O. & Pineiro, O. (1998). Cross-cultural health education: A pedagogical challenge. *Journal of School Health*, 58, 240-242.

Airhihenbuwa, C.O. (1995). *Health and Culture: Beyond the Western Paradigm*. Thousand Oaks: Sage.

American Heart Association. (2007). Disease and stroke statistics – 2007 update: A report from the American Heart Association. www.americanheart.org/presenter.jhtml?identifier=2007

Ball, L., Evans, G., & Bostrom, A. (1998). Risky business: Challenges in vaccine risk communication. *Pediatrics*, 101, 453-458.

Bettencourt, B.A. (1996). Grass roots organizations: Recurrent themes and research approaches. *Journal of Social Issues*, 52, 207-220.

Brislin, R.W. & Yoshida, T. (1994). *Intercultural communication training: An introduction.* New York: Sage.

Brown . L.K. & Mussell, K. (1984). *Ethnic and regional foodways in the United States: The performance of group identity.* Knoxville: U Tennessee P.

Bruner, J. (1986). *Actual Minds, Possible Worlds.* Cambridge: Harvard UP.

Busia, A. (1988). Words whipped over voids: A context for black women's rebellious voices in the novel of the African diaspora. In J. Weixlmann & H. Baker (eds.), Studies in Black American Literature, 1-41. Greenwood, CT.: Penkeville.

Butzine, J. (2008a). Photos of Health disparities Event – Health Disparities in Our Community. Cultural Arts Coalition.

Butzine, J. (2008b). Health disparities in our community: Reflections in art and performance. Online community website at: www.artscare.org/cac.event.30.shtml.

CENTER FOR DISEASE Control. [CDC] (1997a). Participatory research maximizes community and lay involvement. WWW.CDC.GOV/PHPPO/PCE/INDEX.HTML.

CENTER FOR DISEASE Control. [CDC] (2007b). Heart disease and stroke statistics—2007: A report from the American Heart Association. *Circulation,* 2007:115: e69--e171

CORBIE-SMITH, G., THOMAS, S.B., Williams, M.V., & Moody-Ayers, S. (1999). Attitudes and beliefs of African Americans toward participation in medical research. *Journal of General Internal Medicine,* 14, 537-546.

CORTIS,, J. (2003). Managing society's difference and diversity. *Nursing Standard,* 18, (14-16), 33-39.

DAVIS, O.I. (2008). Locating Tulsa in the souls of black women folk: Performing memory as survival. *Performance Research,* 12:3, (2008), 124-136.

DAVIS, O.I. (1999A). "In the Kitchen: Transforming the Academy Through Safe Spaces of Resistance." *Western Journal of Communication,* 63, (Spring 1999), 364-381.

DAVIS, O.I. (1999B). Life ain't been no crystal stair: The rhetoric of autobiography in black female slave narratives. In J.L. Conyers, Jr. (ed.), *Black lives: Essays in African American biography,* 151-159. Armonk, NY: M.E. Sharpe.

DAVIS, O.I. (1998). A black woman as rhetorical critic: Validating self and violating the space of otherness. *Women's Studies in Communication,* 21:1, 77-89.

DUTTA, M.J. (2008). *Communicating health: A culture-centered approach.* Cambridge: Polity.

DUTTA, M.J. (2007). Communicating about culture and health: Theorizing culture-centered and cultural sensitivity approaches. *Communication theory,* 17: 3, 304-328.

DUTTA-BERGMAN, M.J. (2005). Theory and practice in health communication campaigns: A critical interrogation. *Health Communication,* 18:2, 103-122.

DUTTA-BERGMAN, M.J. (2004). Primary sources of health information: Comparisons in the domain of health attitudes, health cognitions, and health behaviors. *Health Communication,* 16: 3, 273-288.

DUTTA, M.J. & Zoller, . (2008). *Emerging Perspectives in Health Communication*. New York: Routledge.

FAWCETT, S.B., PAINE-ANDREWS, A., Francisco, V.T., Schultz, J.A., & Ricter, K.P. (1995). Using empowerment theory in collaborative partnerships for community health development. *American Journal of Community Psychology*, 23, 677-697.

FISHER, W.R. (1987). *Human communication as narration: Toward a philosophy of reason, value, and action*. Columbia: U of South Carolina P.

FORD, L.A. & Yep, G.A. (2003). Working along the margins: Developing community-based strategies for communicating about health with marginalized groups. In Thompson, T.L., Dorsey, A.M., Miller, K.I., Parrott, R. (eds). Handbook of Health Communication. Mahwah: Lawrence Erlbaum Associates.

FREIMUTH, V.S. (1990). The chronically uninformed: Closing the knowledge gap in health. *Communication and Health: Systems and Applications.* Hillsdale, NJ: Lawrence Erlbaum Associates.

HALL, S. (1997). Representation: Cultural representations and signifying practices. London: Sage.

HARRIS, T.M. (2001). Student reactions to the visual texts *The Color of Fear* and *Rosewood* in the interracial classroom. *Howard Journal of Communication*, 12:2, 101-117.

HECHT, ML, MARSIGLIA, FF, Elek–Fisk, E, Wagstaff, DA, Kulis, S, Dustman, P.A. (2003). Culturally grounded substance use prevention: An evaluation of the keepin' it R.E.A.L., *Prevention Science* 4:4, 233–48.

HUBBARD, R.S. & Power, B.M. (1999). Living the question: A guide for teacher-researchers. Maine: Stenhouse.

MINKLER, M. & Wallerstein, N. (2003). Introduction to community-based participatory research. In M. Minkler & N. Wallerstein (eds), *Community-based Participatory Research for Health.* San Francisco: Jossey-Bass, 3-26.

NETTLES, K. (2007). Saving soul food. Gastronomica, 7:3, 106-113.

OFFICE OF DISEASE Prevention and Health Promotion. (2005). State of disparities in cardiovascular health in the United States. *Circulation,* 111: 1233-1241.

OFFICE OF MINORITY Health, US Department of Health and Human Services (2003). *National Study of Culturally and Linguistically Appropriate Services in Managed Care Organizations.* Retrieved September 30, 2009 from WWW.OMHRC.GOV/CULTURAL/MCOCLAS-1%20FINAL%20REPORT%20MAINI.PDF

POOLE, D.L., & Van Hook, M. (1997). Retooling for community health partnerships in primary care and prevention. *Health and Social Work,* 22:1, 2-3.

RAY, E.B. (ED.) (1996). Introduction. *Communication and disenfranchisement: Social health issues and implications.* Mahwah: Lawrence Erlbaum Associates.

RENISCOW, K., BRAITHWAITE, R.L., Dilorio, C., & Glanz, K. (2002). Applying theory to culturally diverse and unique populations. In Glanz, K. , Rimer, B. & Lewis, M. (Eds.). *Health Behavior & Health Education.* San Francisco: Jossey-Bass, 485-509.

SHARF, B.F., & Vanderford, M.L. (2003). Illness narratives and the social construction of health. *Handbook of Health Communication.* (T.L. Thompson, A.M. Dorsey, K.I. Miller, & R. Parrott). Mahway: Lawrence Erlbaum Associates.

STATE OF BLACK Arizona. (2006). Differences in the health status among ethnic groups. Tempe: Arizona State University. www.asu.edu/asuforaz.

TRAYWICK, C. (2008). Art and Engagement: ASU in the Community—Community Camera. Feature article. http://community.uui.asu.edu/features/art.asp

VAN RYN, M. & Burke, J. (2000). The effect of patient race and socio-economic status on physicians' perceptions of patients. *Social Science and Medicine,* 50, 813-828.

WHITE, D. (2008) Health Disparities in our Community: Reflections in art and poetry. Newspaper article, *Arizona Informant.* January 21, 2008.

WIMBERLY, A.S. (1997). Music and the promotion of healing in religious caregiving. *Journal of the Interdenominational Theological Center,* 25(2), 99-124.

WITTE, K. (1995). "Fishing for success: Using the persuasive health message framework to generate effective campaign messages." In E. Maibach and R. Parrott (eds). *Designing health messages: Approaches from Communication Theory and Public Health Practice* (pp. 145-66). Thousand Oaks, CA: Sage.

ZOELLER, H.M. (2000). A place you haven't visited before: Creating the conditions for community dialogue. *Southern Communication Journal,* 65: 2&3, 191-207.

ZOLLER, H.M. & Dutta, M.J. (2008). Introduction. In Zoller, H.M. & Dutta, M.J. (eds.), *Emerging perspectives in health communication: Meaning, culture, and power.* New York: Routledge, 358-64.

Creation of this manuscript was supported by Grant Number P20MD002316, Flavio F. Marsiglia, Principal Investigator, from the National Center On Minority Health and Health Disparities. The content is solely the responsibility of the author and does not necessarily represent the official views of the National Center On Minority Health And Health Disparities or the National Institutes of Health

{149}

PART 2

Performance in
Health, Embodied
Understandings

EDITOR'S NOTE: This personal story has been included in our text as an addition to our articles about the creative arts in action and practice for hope and change and is a profound illustration of the life giving and transformative potential of dance. It is also a testament to Lata Pada's indomitable spirit and resilience as one of Canada's most respected choreographers and leading arts advocates. We are deeply indebted to Lata Pada for sharing her story with us. CM

Revealed By Fire

A woman's personal story of grief, dance and transformation

Lata Pada

"Revealed By Fire" rejoices in the heroism of a woman's indomitable spirit and her transformation from subjugation to a place of individual power and freedom, it is above all else, a celebration for the world to share.

—Judith Rudakoff,
Playwright and Dramaturg, "Revealed by Fire"

"It was an ordinary day
I was rehearsing
The phone rang.."

—Rudakoff, J., 2000,
(excerpt from playscript "Revealed by Fire")

ON AN ORDINARY DAY, a singular event transformed my life forever. It marked the beginning of a journey of deep personal and spiritual transformation, a journey that would in time reveal dance as the metonym of my existence and a return to wholeness. My life in dance became a pilgrimage, a sacred pathway towards a new revelation of my inner being.

On June 10, 1985, I left Sudbury, a city located about a four hour drive from Toronto, for Bombay to prepare for an important solo dance performance scheduled in Bangalore in July of that summer. My husband Vishnu and daughters Brinda, 18 and Arti, 15 were to join me in Bombay in two weeks, after Brinda had completed her high school graduation in Sudbury.

On that ordinary day in June, as I rehearsed in my Guru's studio in Matunga, Bombay, I received the fateful call. Air India Kanishka flight 182, which was bringing my family from Toronto to India, had exploded over the Atlantic Ocean, killing all 329 aboard. A terrorist bomb placed in a suitcase had been suspected as being the reason for the downing of this flight enroute from Toronto and Montreal to Bombay.

An unknowing victim of a heinous act of terrorism, the safe world of my home and my nuclear family had been violently destroyed, my identity as wife and mother irrevocably altered. Life, as I knew it, had ended in the same fire that had consumed my loved ones. Plunged into the depths of despair and unspeakable pain, I was engulfed by the darkness and futility of my existence. Through the haze of sedation, pierced by searing memories of Vishnu, Brinda, and Arti's faces and voices, unanswered questions tormented me. Why me? Where and who can I turn to? How can I survive? Do I have a right to live? Life was a seemingly endless spiral of pain, anger, frustration, confusion, guilt and overwhelming emptiness.

I returned to dance, intuitively, instinctively. The dance of death was now my dance of life. As I danced, like a woman possessed, my conscious mind snuffed out the reality of my loss. While my world as wife and mother had been cruelly wrenched from me, I came to understand that my identity as a dancer had survived, an identity that no outside force could destroy. As I willed movement into my paralyzed arms and legs; step by step, gesture by gesture, my still body came to life. Dance became that singular lifeline that I clung to, my slow and painful return to normalcy was to plunge myself into dance, where the sheer physicality and fatigue left me spent, too exhausted to even contemplate my future without Vishnu, Brinda, and Arti. In this suspended state of a living death, I dealt with a debilitating sense of guilt for continuing to survive in their absence.

Encouraged by the calming presence and blessings of my guru and his wife, cradled by the love and compassion of my parents and siblings, I took my first steps on this journey of healing and renewal. Every movement and gesture became incredibly potent with meaning as the devotional lyrics and mythological themes that I learned interpreted and performed were experienced at a deeply metaphorical level. As I danced, inexplicably, the profound truths of these time honoured compositions resonated in my being, re-awakening the wisdom of the philosophy of my Hindu upbringing, ultimately giving me the tools to cope with the unfathomable pain.

I came to understand that "the path to wisdom begins with a broken heart". I was reminded of a nineteenth century minister, Henry Jackson Van Dyke, who wrote: "in some realms of nature, shadows and darknesses are the places of greatest growth. The beautiful Indian corn never grows more rapidly than in the darkness. The sun withers and curls the leaves, but once a cloud hides the sun, they quickly unfold, the shadows provide a service that the sunlight cannot".

After five years of intensive dancing and artistic re- awakening, I emerged from my abyss of pain, prepared to embrace "the gift of wounding". I have been inspired by this phrase coined by psychologist Andre Auw where he offers the rationale for internalizing spiritual and emotional wounding as a gift. Saints and mystics, Dr. Auw says, are not the only ones who integrate suffering into their lives; each one of us can grow beyond our pain to transform it into a hidden blessing. For many, the blessing is an opportunity to change direction and find new meaning in our lives and relationships, for others it is a window to re-connect with our inner selves, the gift of a spiritual journey.

I learned that the journey along the road to survival is marked by a number of intersections, where we must make a choice. There is not a single path that represents the perfect path. These paths lead us to many new destinations along our life's journey; for me the gift was the alchemic restoration of my inner spirit. Living through the darkness and stepping on to a new path liberated me from my past.

> I am the journey
> The only way out is through

In May 1990, I returned to Toronto to embark on a new journey – a path of new opportunities to define myself and establish a career in dance. Assuming the role of teacher and artistic director, I charted a new life for myself, establishing and investing my passion, energy and artistic vision in the Sampradaya Dance Academy and a professional dance company – Sampradaya Dance Creations. Dance became my tribute to Vishnu, Brinda, and Arti, filling the void in my life with the presence of so many young dancers, many of them the ages of my two daughters.

From that fateful day in June 1985, my agnipariksha (test of fire) had initiated a process of self- reflection and self renewal. I questioned my identity as a woman, my role as a wife and mother in society. At no point, earlier in my career had I felt so prepared to channel my regained confidence, my new sense of self, into a production that would result in an unimagined cathartic journey.

Nine years later, a new chapter unfolded in my life – the creation of my autobiographical work "Revealed By Fire". In the making of "Revealed By Fire", I stepped onto a difficult and uncertain path. This journey was like no other I had taken before. How would I negotiate the minefield of emotional, artistic and collaborative challenges, let alone protect my vulnerable, emotional centre? Undeniably, it would mean returning to a fragile past and possibly a state of emotional instability.

Artistically, it would mean entering an undefined territory that of staging a production based on a personal narrative.

So where was the genesis for this work? What was the process?

IN AN INFORMAL MEETING IN 1999, with photographer Cylla von Tiedemann, after a photo shoot for an upcoming production, we talked about some ideas of working together on a project based on the magnificent sculptures of South Indian temples. I was planning my annual visit to India, and Cylla wanted very much to return to India for a visit. It led to discussion about an idea that we should explore the nexus between dance and temple sculptures of South India. I was inspired by the potential for the dramatic visualization of temple sculptures (through Cylla's photography) and the re-interpretation of the origins of today's bharatanatyam in temple ritual (through my choreography). This was the genesis of the work; I must confess, a romantic notion that was quickly abandoned. The task of conceptualizing a work on the temple dance tradition and repertoire of the devadasis (ritual temple dancers) was treading delicate ground: a rather contentious and academically controversial subject.

{156}

Cylla and I then explored the framework for a work that would examine the goddess tradition in India and the issues surrounding the paradoxes in the veneration of the goddess and the denigration of women in society. Those were the tensions, we felt, that would be important to examine through western and eastern sensibilities, and to explore universal meaning for themes of goddess, divinity, and woman.

Through our extensive travel in the winter of 1999, Cylla and I shared our visions and dreams for this new work. She journeyed with me, photographing what my artistic eye knew needed to be captured as image, without questioning or need for clarification. Self-doubt and confusion plagued me at every step; why was this work so compelling, what new boundaries would I be crossing, even breaking? Did I have the courage to tell this story to strangers? Would I have the strength to dance it? Was it even important, relevant for anyone else beyond me? It was obvious that we approached the work, from often opposing cultural perspectives, often very close to abandoning it. It became apparent through prolonged discussions that Revealed By Fire was essentially centred in my personal journey through tragedy and the production would strive to communicate the transformation of my life experience into an archetype of universal relevance. What was brought into sharper focus, were the possible contradictions between stepping beyond the boundaries of prescribed norms for classical bharatanatyam in the creation of a work based on an autobiographical narrative. Finally, to my surprise, I surrendered to my strong instinct; I did not question the need for this work, I only needed to imagine how to create it.

> *Changing isn't easy. Ideas, beautiful things change; they know how to*
> *change, because to change is to go beyond pain, to change is to disappear*
> *one day and then fill the space within yourself!*
> –From Alphonse, by Wajdi Mouawad, translated by Shelley Tepperman

Upon our return from India, I invited Judith Rudakoff, playwright and dramaturg to help realize the creative vision of the work . We spent many afternoons over tea, with Judith encouraging me to tell my life story. Much as I willed it, I could not keep a journal. I struggled putting to paper each fragment of memory of my loved ones. Every time I was interviewed by Judith, each word I spoke recounting my beautiful life with Vishnu, Brinda, and Arti would come alive with sharp, unspeakable pain. So all I had were my memories, blunted with a subconscious urge to forget, to dull the pain.

> *Fire is a metaphor*
> *It is both a destructive and regenerative force*
> *We must all deal with terrible things*
> *Every culture talks about the test of fire.*
> –from Judith Rudakoff interview with Lata Pada

As Judith needed to understand the context of my journey; painstakingly, she and I worked through the themes for the narrative. The play text that Judith crafted (which came organically out of our discussions and her instinctive and intuitive understanding of my inner voice) was recorded in my voice and integrated in the sound design. I was allowed, through the play text, to become Lata the central character of the work, as well the storyteller who guided the narrative, infusing into it the nuanced metaphors of transformation.

The music for Revealed By Fire was a collaboration between R.A. Ramamani, a Carnatic classical music composer from Bangalore and Toronto's western classical composer Timothy Sullivan. I can never forget the afternoon, Timothy and I played a cassette recording of the last phone message, my older daughter Brinda left on a friend's phone system. It was a cheery message, and Brinda talked of the plane trip she was making to India that day. The friend had saved the message, recorded it to an audio tape and sent it to me months after the tragedy. I could not bring myself to listen to it and it lay unheard in the back of a drawer for years. Something told me that this message should be integrated into the sound design. Aided by an Excel program, I worked with Timothy and Cylla in the creation of a detailed storyboard that organized the multiple temporal, geographical, and psychological dimensions of the production. Partnering the storyboard that Judith had created, Timothy designed a multi-textured soundscape integrated into the polyphonic score that mirrored my traumatic journey.

Creating the choreography was one of the most difficult and emotionally draining challenges in designing movement for each of the sections. Even though my dancers had trained with me for several years, and had grown very close to me, they were understandably hesitant and anxious about participating in a work that was so different from any work they had danced ever before. They comprehended the need and demand for their complete surrender to the 'emotional world' of this new autobiographical narrative. My dancers wanted so much to honour me with being part of my story on stage and pledged their uncompromising commitment. Sitting down with my dancers, I explained the personal and artistic themes of Revealed By Fire in detail, as we broke down every so often dissolving into tears.

Revealed By Fire resulted in an incredible convergence of interdisciplinary artists who, through their multiplicity of perspectives and rich artistic backgrounds, created a work that speaks to the universal quest for identity and meaning, central to all our lives.

As a child raised in post-independence India, in a traditional South Indian family with modern aspirations, I questioned existing gender and social inequities that continued to exist in a society that had won its hard earned freedom from a colonial power, only to perpetuate oppressive patriarchal systems and codes of behavior.

These nagging inconsistencies continued to percolate through my life at a deeper level, as I made my home in Canada and stayed connected with India (through reading, communicating and my annual visits) with socio-cultural issues surrounding women in urban and rural areas.

In 1971, I received the shocking news of the loss of my twenty one year old sister's husband, and flew to Bombay on the next flight to share in my sister's very sudden and devastating loss and comfort her as she awaited the birth of her son, born posthumously. The rituals, both religious and social, surrounding the last rites of Mohan, were seemingly harsh and unjust, and I was scarred by that negative experience. Fourteen years later, my life was cruelly altered and I too experienced the hypocrisy and bias towards women who suddenly found themselves widowed and stripped of their place in society.

The production

"Revealed By Fire" premiered on March 8, 2001, International Women's Day at the Premiere Dance Theatre, Harbourfront Centre, Toronto. It is a multi-media dance theatre production that is a convergence of classical bharatanatyam, contemporary movement and physical theatre of personal and universal themes of the East and West and is performed by myself and five company dancers.

It is performed against the evocative and powerful visual design created by Cylla von Tiedemann; the projection on a large 20 x 16 foot screen of Japanese rice paper panels. The visual design is intended not as a backdrop but a partner in evoking the multi-layered worlds of emotion, memory and the spiritual realm of the goddess as it reveals the complex textures of my physical and subconscious realities of wife, mother, and woman. The recorded sound design integrates R..A. Ramaman's and Timothy Sullivan's music, ambient soundscapes of India, excerpts of radio reports on the Air India crash and the playtext is in my voice.

The production, organized in seven sections unfolds through a series of flashbacks as it traces the journey of self-transformation from tragedy to renewal. The choreography is derived from the movement syntax of Bharatanatyam, as well as movement generated from a process of improvisation by the dancers. Retaining the essential aesthetic of Bharatanatyam, the choreography extends the boundaries of the formalism and stylization of this dance form by incorporating elements of improvised movement, folk dance, physical theatre, and yoga.

Revealed by Fire for me became an important signifier of the reconciliation of innovation within a specific cultural and aesthetic tradition of bharatanatyam dance. It represented for me the inscription of my personal mythology over those celebrated mythic archetypes that I was trained to characterize in my dance.

Centered in the work is the recurring motif of fire, which becomes the metaphor for the twin energies of destruction and re-generation as it also references Sita's agnipariksha as the archetypal symbol for re-birth.

The production opens informally and unexpectedly; *the pre-set soundscape creates an ambience of Bombay's street sounds, with snatches of film songs, popular ghazals, and devotional Carnatic songs. I walk on to the stage for what appears to be a casual warm up routine. I light a lamp and walk with it around the stage in a square, defining my world and sanctifying the space. I start my rehearsal. As I dance the music is pierced by the shrill ring of the telephone. As the incessant phone assaults my mind, I rush to the back of the stage to pull down the panels of colored silk, as the color drains out of my life and the screen is consumed with images of fire and the frenzied burning images of my family. As if in a meltdown, I am hurtled through this vortex of inescapable doom. Through the haze of the smoke emerges the benign presence of the goddess revealed, whose intermittent appearance throughout the visual projection comforts and reminds us of her latent grace and benevolence.*

My journey of self discovery begins. In a series of flashbacks through my past of vivid memories of childhood and marriage and settling in Canada, the production moves into the heart of the fire, as my life changes irreversibly from the pivotal moment of the air crash, into a frightening and unpredictable future redeemed by the profound and cathartic impact of dance in my life.

Five dancers join me and as we drape ourselves with the fallen fabric, we enact the many manifestations of womanhood through stylized representations of woman as wife, mother, and goddess. As the visual design creates a landscape of my childhood, the drawing of a kolam, the verdant rice fields of Kerala, we enact and dance passages from my childhood.

Against the recollection of my grandmother's presence, I learn the rituals of everyday life.

{160}   **"Grandmother teaches me to make kolam. We draw carefully, her hand guiding mine. The bangles on my wrist catch the light as we watch the red dust colors stain the ground. I learn the jobs of being a woman. I learn the place of being a woman"**

In later scenes, the same dancers are the faceless, relentless forces of society that condemn and strip me of my identity as wife. Two dancers are also part of my most vulnerable past, my life as mother; they move through, ghostlike, in the scene where I reach out to fragmented memories of their tender presence in my past.

In the third scene, against the projected backdrop of the interweaving of the red and white wedding scarves, the dance elaborates the rituals of my marriage; as a young girl of seventeen, my dreams of becoming a doctor are put aside when I acquiesce to be married and move to a northern mining town in Canada. My heart voices its nervousness at this distant journey. Friends prepare me for the wedding ritual as thy anoint me with fragrant sandal paste, decorate my hair with a jasmine spray and guide me through the measured steps of the saptapadi around the sacred fire; the fire both witness to my new beginnings as wife and catalyst for my rebirth later in the production.

"All good Indian girls listen to their parents. There are seven steps between the past and the future. I try to step out of the circle. We circle the fire seven times. Saptapadi, our steps slow and measured. Let us take the first step.

There are seven steps in the circle. The first step for prosperity and fulfillment of all our aspirations and endeavours, individually and as a couple. In a distant dream I became a doctor before I became a wife. There are seven steps in the circle. Let us take the step for longevity. Let us take the step for life-long commitment. Who of us can guarantee forever?

I taste the snow on the tip of my tongue and remember who I am now. And I can't help wondering: How can I dance on the frozen earth? How can I dance when the ground is shifting?"

The idyllic world of my new life in Canada is shattered by the ominous rumbling of the devastating fireball that explodes on to the screen. Silence follows this rupture; I enter as harsh white lights up the stage. Disoriented, and numbed, I make my way downstage as the reality of my loss engulfs me. One by one, the dancers strip me of the symbols of auspiciousness, that marked my identity as wife. A dancer shrouds me with a white cloth, my life bleached of the vibrant red of sumangali. As the screen fills with the image of a raging fire, I hold up a cloth imprinted with red handprints, my final act of submission, or is it defiance?, against my newly imposed status of widow. Sita, the archetypal heroine of the Ramayana, subsumes my identity with her fervent appeal against the hypocrisy of the patriarchal world, her life, and those of generations of women who have borne silent witness to.

I walk, trancelike towards the rushing waves of the ocean, enveloped in its comforting arms to attempt to end a life of no purpose.

" She looked into the fire and the fire was terrifying. She did not pause for if she had, she would have never moved into the heart of the flames. And in the moment of greatest pain, she like Sita, saw that at the heart of the fire was its strength and its weakness, and so she embraced it and found that it embraced her"

"Let the fire reveal Sita. Her agnipariksha. At the heart of the flame is the voice of the soul."

The full import of my loss of identity overwhelms me, in the next scene. Hallucinated by fleeting and smiling images of Vishnu, Brinda and Arti, the obsessive images of fire taunt me. I snatch at elusive memories of Brinda's beautiful hair, Vishnu's party jokes;

"there are stories about Brinda's freshly washed hair, all I can think about is fire . . .

Two dancers, as Brinda and Arti enact a scene of tender playfulness, pulling me into their games only to lose them as they disappear from my grasp and I crumble to the floor. As if returning from a long journey, another dancer as Vishnu gently lifts me, we cradle each other in poses of intimacy and togetherness, locked in our love for each other, Vishnu leaves silently, never to return again.

Who am I? What am I?

"If you take my daughters, am I still a mother? If you take my husband, am I still a wife? Sumangali? No – inauspicious. Who will cross the road to avoid crossing my path? Widow, Black cat. Inauspicious. I stain the world around me"

In the black out that snuffs out my questioning of a fragmented identity, my feet are seen on the screen making my way through a craggy field of sharp rocks. Filling the screen with a larger than life presence, my feet search for balance, literally and figuratively.

In the foreground, silent ghostlike dancers take their place huddled on the floor as large round boulders. As I enter the stage with my tentative steps, one by one, the dancers spring into an attacking pose, blocking my passage. Ominous and menacing, they prevent any move on my part to navigate my difficult journey, often forming a collective wall of resistance. I fend their attacks, only to be beaten into submission. The rocks on the screen turn to a fiery red, glowing with the hostility of a society that is unforgiving to a widow. The dancers leave, I am alone, left to my destiny.

Weak and destroyed, I am enraged at the injustice and lack of compassion. My hands lash against an unseen force, my body spasms with rage. Centre stage, I am caught in a barred prison like light, the screen throbs with images of my agony, my physical and emotional worlds colliding. Through extensive use of improvised movement, I search for my destiny, dragging myself along sharp diagonal paths of light, running across the never ending paths, balancing myself at the razor's edge of insanity. As the harsh white lights flood the stage, I am drawn into a vortex of pain, outrage and confusion, I lose control and drop to the ground.

The stage is silent, is this the end? As I lie there, left for dead, a strange calm fills my body. My beaten body quivers, my arms search for a movement, my fingers carve out small gestures. As I rise, my legs fail me but are willed into balance. Hesitating and tentatively, I beat out footsteps and dance filling the pregnant space with my newfound strength.

Inexplicably, the drone of the tanpura, fills the stage with an indescribably epiphanic tranquility; the srichakra appears on the screen. Spiral wisps of sacred fire and smoke conceal the goddess; gradually she emerges revealing herself as the final witness to my journey of transformation.

The stage comes alive with a new energy, I am in my studio rehearsing and celebrating my re-birth through dance. My dancers join me and resume their rehearsal routine.

Their movements mirror mine, corrections are made and we together complete a passage from a tillana. The phone rings, this time it does not interrupt my dance. The answering machine plays a message.

"You have reached Sampradaya Dance Creations. For information on our production, Revealed By Fire, please leave a detailed message . . ."

Lighting the lamp again, I walk around the square of light, prepared to honour life and my new identity.

I have come full circle. I have traversed the path. I am the journey.

All my mothers. {163}
A line through me.
A sounding of voices.
Calling in colors.
Who am I?
I am the journey.
Arc across my sky.

All my mothers.
A line through me.
An ocean of faces.
Carried inside.
Who am I?
I am the journey.
The only way out is through.

All my mothers.
A line through me.
Beginning with ending.
End of all beginnings.
Who am I?
I am the journey.
I have always been here.

Postscript

REVEALED BY FIRE IS DEDICATED TO THE MEMORY of the 329 lives lost in the 1985 mid-air explosion of Air India Flight 182 over the Atlantic Ocean, one hundred miles from the south-west coast of Ireland. Flight 182 was enroute from Toronto to Bombay, India and disappeared from all radar screens on the morning of June 23, 1985. It has been determined that this was the largest aviation disaster in Canada's history.

Of the 329 passengers aboard the flight, 156 were Canadian. Three of those were Lata Pada's husband Vishnu Pada and daughters Brinda and Arti Pada.

"Revealed By Fire" took on new meaning after September 11, 2001; it has become a metaphor for the 'rising from the ashes' for the healing that can occur when audiences become co-participants and co-seekers in the journey towards enlightenment and meaning. Dancing this work was an empowering journey of self-renewal.

As Susan McNaughton has suggests in her research paper LATA PADA'S REVEALED BY FIRE: AN EMBODIED NARRATIVE OF TRANSFORMATION – " this explosion took the lives of her husband and both children resulting in a huge reconfiguration of both her personal and artistic identity. Though her intention was to avoid making a highly personal statement, she discovered that only by doing so, could she ultimately re-awaken a personal mythology –"

LATA PADA holds a Masters in Dance from York University and is currently an Adjunct Professor in York University's Master's Program in Dance. She is Artistic Director of Sampradaya Dance Creations, an award winning Canadian dance company recognized for its distinctive choreography spanning a dynamic range of classical bharatanatyam and contemporary dance works. Lata has trained with India's distinguished gurus, Kalaimamani K. Kalyanasundaram and Padma Bhushan Kalanidhi Narayanan. The Company and Sampradaya Dance Academy were founded in 1990. In January 2009, Lata Pada was conferred the Order of Canada. She has the distinction of being the first Indian artist to receive this national honour. She brings a contemporary worldview to her dance creations which have been recognized for their innovative, intercultural and multi-disciplinary choreography. Her choreographic works have been performed world wide in prestigious festivals and dance series. In her Academy, she has nurtured talented dancers, many of them who are performing professionally in Canada and internationally.

HTTP://WWW.SAMPRADAYA.CA/

{165}

For more information on Judith Rudakoff, visit: HTTP://WWW.YORKU.CA/FINEARTS/FACULTY/PROFS/ RUDAKOFF.HTM

A YouTube excerpt from "Revealed by Fire" can be viewed at HTTP://WWW.YOUTUBE.COM/ WATCH?V=_NKEWZVX7CW

Ethnodramas about Health and Illness:

Staging Human Vulnerability, Fragility, and Resiliency

Johnny Saldaña

WE ARE ALL VULNERABLE AND FRAGILE HUMAN BEINGS, regardless of situation, circumstance, or social context. Resiliency, however, varies from person to person depending on his or her personality. Vulnerability's root meaning is "to wound," with its most salient definitions as "defenseless against injury" and "open to attack or damage." Fragility's root is "to break," and is defined as something "easily broken or destroyed." In the context of this paper, fragility's other definitions include "delicate health" and "unusually susceptible to ill health or physical harm."

As for resiliency, there are multiple roots, including "to jump back," "rebound," and "leap." Though the first definition is "returning freely to a previous position, shape, condition," in the contexts of health and illness these ideas resonate: "capable of withstanding shock without permanent deformation"; and "to regain strength or high spirits after weakness or depression."

I am a theatre artist, and certainly not an expert in the quantitative and qualitative research literature about health and illness. But I speculate that themes of vulnerability, fragility, and resiliency weave throughout most of these studies, for they are most apparent in the related ethnodramatic literature.

Overview

IN THIS PAPER, I share a descriptive, selected literature review of thirty-eight ethnodramatic play scripts about health and illness.[1] A few of these titles are documented play productions but without available written play scripts for analysis. I include excerpts from exemplars of the genre, hoping that these may serve as a sampler of models for the reader's own ethnodramatic writing. I will focus on the four most frequently addressed topics in this genre: cancer, health care, HIV/AIDS, and substance abuse/addiction.

Before proceeding, definitions of two key terms are needed:

> Ethno*theatre* employs the traditional craft and artistic techniques of theatre production to mount for an audience a live performance event of research participants' experiences and/or the researcher's interpretations of data.... The goal is to investigate a particular facet of the human condition for purposes of adapting those observations and insights into a performance medium. Simply put, this is preparatory fieldwork for theatrical production work.
>
> An ethno*drama*, the written script, consists of dramatized, significant selections of narrative collected through interviews, participant observation field notes, journal entries, and/or print and media artifacts such as diaries, television broadcasts, newspaper articles, and court proceedings. Simply put, this is dramatizing the data. (Saldaña, 2005, pp. 1-2)

THE NON-THEATRE-GOING PUBLIC is perhaps more familiar with commercial films and television programs about health and illness. These titles include such works as *Philadelphia*, *Wit*, *ER*, *Grey's Anatomy*, and others. Illness may not play a central role in selected film plots but can become a major component of story lines in such fictional works as *Steel Magnolias*, *Angels in America*, and *Terms of Endearment*. Most ethnodramatic work about the subject originates from the academic and scientific communities, with a handful of works by theatre artists and performance studies scholars with social or personal investment in health and illness issues. The history of theatre and its contemporary forms include documentation of performance events and dramatic modalities with pedagogic albeit sometimes didactic goals. Medieval morality plays preached wholesome spiritual living to the European masses; puppet plays are performed in Mexico to teach children proper hygiene; drama therapy utilizes improvisational work for psychotherapeutic goals; and digital storytelling projects are conducted in children's hospitals with terminally ill patients.

Ethnodramatic representations and presentations of health and illness bring participants' vulnerability, fragility, and, in most cases, resiliency to heightened prominence. Perhaps more than the academic journal article, the ethnotheatrical performance – if well done for a receptive audience – holds potential to increase awareness, deepen understanding, and provide experiences that generate sympathetic and empathetic responses and memories for future applications and transfer into clinical practice and possibly health care policy. If the shared goal of theatre and qualitative inquiry is to explore and learn more about the human condition, then the outcomes are doubly if not exponentially increased when the two disciplines merge, bringing with them their best representational and presentational modes of expression to the dramatic text.

Categorizations of ethnodramas about health and illness can be approached from multiple angles, but in this paper I classify these selected works by the specific health or illness issue addressed in the plays.

Cancer

IN THE ETHNODRAMATIC BIBLIOGRAPHY, the majority of plays about illness address cancer, with women's breast cancer as the most frequent subtopic. This category includes works about:

- women's breast cancer (Gray & Sinding, 2002; Miller, 2006; Park-Fuller, 2003)
- prostate cancer's effects on men and their spouses (Gray & Sinding, 2002)
- an ovarian cancer survivor (Shapiro & Hunt, 2003)
- a gay man's comic struggle with cancer (Lobel, 2007)
- communications between a physician and a cancer patient (Paget, 1995)
- a father's cancer and his daughter's struggle with his illness (Mulcahy, Parry, & Glover, 2009)

{169}

Ethnodramas about cancer range from the monologic and realistic one-woman play, to dialogic and expressionistic ensemble work. Character representations include the cancer survivors themselves, their caregivers, and significant others coping with their loved ones' illness. A few plays include symbolic representations as characters, suggesting a need to abstract the magnitude of the illness in order to grasp and make sense of it.

Perhaps the most-performed play about women's breast cancer is Susan Miller's (2006) autoethnodramatic *My Left Breast*. The opening scene of her comedy-drama sets the tone of a woman both vulnerable and resilient with her immediate disclosure to the audience:

> *(Music begins in the dark. It continues as the lights come up. SUSAN comes out dancing. After a few bars, the music stops and she takes in the audience.)*

The night before I went to the hospital, that's what I did. I danced.

(Holding hands over her breasts:)

One of these is not real.

Can you tell which?

(Beat.)

I was fourteen the first time a boy touched my breast. My left breast, in fact. I felt so guilty with pleasure I could hardly face my parents that night. It was exquisite. Well, you remember . . .

(Beat.)

Anyhow, breast cancer.

(Beat.) . . .

Here's what I wear sometimes under my clothes.

(Take breast prosthesis from desk. Hold up to show audience:)

Oh, don't worry. It's a spare. When you go for a fitting, you can hear the women in the other booths. Some of them have lost their hair and shop for wigs. Some are very young and their mothers are thinking, why didn't this happen to me, instead? . . .

(Beat.)

{170}

I miss it, but it's not a hand. I miss it, but it's not my mind. I miss it, but it's not the roof over my head. I miss it, but it's not a word I need. It's not a sentence I can't live without. I miss it, but it's not a conversation with my son. It's not my courage or my lack of faith.

(Beat.)

I miss it, but it's not HER. (pp. 5-6)

As a dialogic example of ethnodrama (a form underutilized in the genre), Mulchay, Parry, and Glover (2009) researched people with cancer and created *Between Diagnosis and Death*. In this play, the Father is a composite character whose words are taken from multiple interviewees' transcripts, but Caitlin M. Mulcahy, one of the co-authors, served as the basis for the Daughter. Vulnerability and fragility are experienced not just by the ill but also by their family members. In the scene below, Father and Daughter are sitting on a park bench on a cold day. The Daughter is "haunted by a ghost she cannot escape" (p. 30), but the character appears onstage alongside her. Notice the italicized stage directions in the excerpt, evoking not just character action but subtext and irony for audiences:

(Her father coughs into his gloves)

FATHER: I was in bad shape when I was diagnosed.

DAUGHTER: Oh god. It's starting.

GHOST: What's starting?

FATHER: And I was not given a good diagnosis. I was told I may have two to three years to live. *(shakes his head)* There was no explanation. None. *(long pause)*

DAUGHTER: *(to Ghost)* Oh he's pausing, but he won't stop there. The story never ends. It's on loop. I don't know what he's looking for, but he never finds it.

FATHER: You're not prepared. When you get that diagnosis .. . . . the whole world goes out of whack! *(gestures wildly)* Everything goes crazy! Your mind goes through the worst scenario .. . . . It's just awful .. . . . we just deal with these horrible diagnoses and we don't have anything to help with something like that.

GHOST: (circling downstage right) It's hard to write about this stuff when you have a parent who has cancer. Your co-authors know that. They've both gone through cancer with their own parents. They'll understand.

DAUGHTER: *(snorts)* If you think the writing's hard, you should try listening to this stuff all the time. It's the listening that's driving me crazy. *(checking pockets)* Where's my iPod? Did I leave it at home? *(fumbles through pockets for iPod while Father continues)*

FATHER: *(sniffs)* When you're in treatment, cancer's in your face every day. It's impossible to be getting on with your life. Your life is on hold. And then, you finish treatment and then what, you know? *(wipes a glove across his nose)*

DAUGHTER: *(exasperated)* Where is it, for god's sakes?!

(He pulls out a fistful of Kleenex and blows his nose. She finds her iPod.)

DAUGHTER: Yes! *(puts headphones in ears)*

FATHER: I found it to be extremely isolating going through the treatments. And when you go to a clinic, nobody talks to anyone. They're in their own space. You know it's as if they were all on iPods, cancer iPods, or something. (She sighs and tucks her iPod back into her pocket.)

DAUGHTER: I guess that's the end of that.

FATHER: They're just in their own space .. . . . Or they're weak. Or they're nauseated or whatever. So people don't talk and people don't connect. It's very isolating. Very isolating. (pp. 32-33)

{171}

Saldaña

Health Care

THE SECOND MOST FREQUENT SUBCATEGORY OF ETHNODRAMAS address health care issues from the perspectives of both recipients and caregivers (though not necessarily within the same play):

- ☞ dilemmas of living without health insurance in the U.S. (Saunders, 2008)

- ☞ patient interactions with health care providers (Rosenbaum, Ferguson, & Herwaldt, 2005)

- ☞ nursing home care (McIntyre, 2009)

- ☞ ESL immigrant women's perceptions of health care (Nimmon, 2007)

- ☞ cross-cultural health work in Australia (Preisinger, Schroeder, & Scott-Hoy, 2000)

{172} ☞ stroke awareness in South Africa (Stuttaford, Bryanston, Hundt, Connor, Thorogood, & Tollman, 2006)

These ethnodramas, unlike those about cancer, tend to be more "documentary" in tone and construction, though the emotional urgency of participants is still quite vivid. Plays about cancer tend to be case study in nature, whereas ethnodramas about health care are polyphonic collages of mini-monologues – a revue, if you will, of people's perspectives frustrated with a vulnerable and fragile system.

As one example, Saunders (2008) reports on the dilemmas of United States citizens without accessible and affordable health care by first reviewing and contextualizing the statistics before the participants' stories are presented. A narrator tells the audience:

> The number of people without health insurance is HUGE – 46.6 million . . . That represents 15.9% of US residents – over one in seven. Let's try to imagine that number. It's greater than the populations of California, Missouri, and Alabama combined (U.S. Census, 2006). It would take over 900 major league baseball stadiums filled to the hilt to fit all of the people without health insurance. If every

mile while going cross-country represented an uninsured person, you could travel over 7 000 times from California to New York round trip. (p. 529)

But statistics in a report do not always have to be sweeping in scope. The smaller numbers we deal with on a daily basis can provide points of reference for understanding different situations. Below, a Canadian health care worker relates the costs associated with meals at a nursing home for the elderly as she reflects on her coffee house purchase:

> I laugh out loud when I realize that what I've paid – $4.65 with tax, for my grande tazo chai crème, my Saturday after shopping treat is 16 cents more than our per day resident food budget. Yeah, that's right – three meals a day, with a choice between two entrees at each meal in five different textures: regular, mince, puree, dental soft, and chopped. Plus, snacks with a beverage at 10:00, at 2:00, and before bed at 8:00. Plus, tea and cookies during the night for the wanderers. All that for $4.49 per resident per day. It's gone up 23 cents since 1993. Ten years and an increase in 23 cents per day per person. How much do you figure Starbucks has put up their prices in ten years? (McIntyre, 2009, n.p.)

Aside from the monologic narratives of people's dilemmas with health care, one play by Nimmon (2007) utilizes dialogue to highlight conflicting tensions. Monica is an immigrant still learning the English language and needs medical attention. Note her resiliency to get the help she needs:

> *(Monica is having an allergic reaction to something and she has red bumps all over her body. She tries calling a health center in Victoria and gets a recorded message on the answering machine.)*

MACHINE: (*speaking quite fast*): You have reached the Victoria Medical Clinic. I am sorry we are not available to take your call. We are open from Monday to Friday from 9 am to 3 pm. If this is an emergency, please contact this number at 351-5565 where somebody will respond to your call.

> *(Monica dials again because she can't understand the message. Monica is starting to panic. She dials twice more and on the fourth time she finally understands the message. Monica calls the number and speaks with a nurse.)*

MONICA: Hi, ummm . . .

NURSE: Please speak up dear, I can't hear you.

MONICA: Hi, um . . . ummm. Well, I am really scratchy.

NURSE: Scratchy? What do you mean? You mean itchy?

MONICA: Yes, ummm, itchy. I have little points all over my arm . . . I mean little dots. They are rad . . . no . . . red.

NURSE: (*It is sooo annoying when ESL speakers call here.*) Oh, you mean you have a rash. It's called a rash.

MONICA: (*This is incredibly embarrassing, I feel like a child.*) Yes, a rash. I am sorry. It's so uncomfortable. What should I do?

NURSE: You should go and see a doctor.

MONICA: You mean a specialist?

NURSE: Well, you have to go to a general practitioner first. And then you'll get a referral to see a specialist.

MONICA: You mean I can't just go to a specialist on my own? I know what is wrong with me . . . I need to see a dermatologist. (pp. 389-390)

HIV/AIDS

ETHNODRAMAS IN THIS SUBCATEGORY tend to assert more socially conscious agendas. The plays range from sympathetic portraits by performance studies scholars, to awareness training by researchers for health care providers:

- HIV/AIDS awareness and people with HIV/AIDS (Corey, 1993)

- HIV-positive women and related stigma (Sandelowski, et al., 2006)

- a chronicle, with music, of a man living with HIV/AIDS (Shapiro & Hunt, 2003)

- a gay man awaiting the death of his partner from AIDS (Dillard, 2000)

One of the most provocative and well-executed ethnodramas in the literature is Margarete Sandelowski, Frank Trimble, Elizabeth K. Woodard, and Julie Barroso's (2006) collaboration to create the DVD production, *Maybe Someday: Voices of HIV-Positive Women*. Intended as a training documentary for health care providers and social service workers, plus a resonating forum for HIV-positive women themselves, the rigorously researched literature on women with HIV/AIDS was used primarily by Trimble to write and weave informational narrative with reconstructed monologues based on interviews with HIV-positive women. The composite-based resilient characters in the DVD are two African American women, one White woman, and two Latinas. In one scene, a narrator's voice-over prompts the viewer:

> Some women struggle with issues beyond their HIV status. These include the extra stigma and discrimination connected with being a woman, being a minority woman, and being a mother. Sometimes women are looked down upon because people make assumptions that their illness is related to drug use, prostitution, promiscuity, poverty, or homelessness. (p. 1363)

Maybe Someday focuses primarily but not exclusively on the themes of stigma associated with HIV status, as this monologue relates:

> WOMAN #4 (African American): People talk about minority this and minority that. Well, let me tell you somethin'. You try bein' a Black woman with HIV and see how far you get. See the men, well, they HIV *victims*. You know, they may face some discrimination, but mostly there's concern and money and support. Then there's the people who caught HIV, you know, because they was doin' somethin' they shouldn't been doin' and got "caught," you know? Yeah, them's mostly minority women, or poor women, or women with too many children, whatever "too many" is. I am sick of that shit! I am physically sick and then I have to handle all that other shit on top of it. It's too much. It's just too much. So what if a HIV person ain't always been good, or maybe is still doin' some of that junk? Sure, a woman needs to change her life if it hurts her and maybe other people, but we have all been hurt by this disease and need to help make things better. But I keep doin' the best I can. Have to. Just have to. Because . . . my children, you know? You don't know me. No one knows me. But my children . . . they know me. And I want to keep it that way. (p. 1364)

Substance Abuse/Addiction

ETHNODRAMAS ABOUT ABUSE AND ADDICTION are explicit and raw in their tone and action, with most titles venturing into a surrealistic style with overt "theatrical" devices in their staging. The skewed, nightmarish reality that results from substance abuse and addiction seems to transfer into the script and staging of the issue.[2] Resilience in these plays' characters is minimal. Scripts include:

- ☞ alcohol and drug abuse, and detoxification (Mienczakowski, 1996, 1997)

- ☞ a woman's struggle with her boyfriend's meth addiction (Pust, 2008)

- ☞ a young man's battle with alcoholism (Caswell, 2008)

- ☞ a family's turmoil from the son's drug abuse (Yang, 2001)

In the monologue excerpt below, female playwright Tifani Pust (2008) unabashedly and graphically describes her relationship with her speed-/meth-addicted male lover in *The Demon*. Notice the vulnerability and fragility in both characters' psychological states and actions:

> we call it "the demon." he is fighting it and doing well now. but i must remain in secret private detective mode and not let my heart fall too quickly. i must check his pupils, and the way he kisses me, his vocabulary changes, and even his energy swings. when the demon is scratching his back, his energy shifts and he becomes a little more reckless, a little more twitchy. i am too naïve to know if these are withdrawal symptoms or craving symptoms. maybe it doesn't matter. maybe it's both. maybe that's the point.
>
> he told me about jail on our "second date," which really wasn't a date as much as it was – our second day together. suddenly i was aware that i was spending time with a convict. not an ex-convict mind you – a convict. i am currently aiding and abetting (literally) a fugitive.
>
> i am falling in love with a felon. a felon and a speed junkie. i am in graduate school and was raised southern baptist. middle class. white. educated. my parents are educated. my parents are educators. i wonder sometimes if we are the last remaining nuclear family. mom, dad, two kids, a dog, and a cat. no picket fence, but

the same house for thirty-eight years. thirty eight. i am thirty. he is thirty-three. i am a poet and a dreamer and a writer and i am falling in love with a felon speed junkie who craves it every weekend. ironically, he has no drug charges on his record. misdemeanors, petty theft, brandishing a firearm, which turned out to be a BB gun. he doesn't get arrested when he's high because he's always at home high, alone, or with a girl, naked – fucking. if he's lucky. usually, she wears out and he ends up on the couch, alone, with porn.[3] (n.p.)

Additional Ethnodramas about Health and Illness

LENGTH RESTRICTIONS OF THIS ARTICLE do not permit me to examine in depth other categories of ethnodramas about health and illness, but the listing below refers readers to the topics addressed in other plays:

Aging and Mental Health

- ☞ aging, autonomy, and mental health of older persons (McLean, 2004)

- ☞ Alzheimer's disease and dementia (Cole, McIntyre, & McAuliffe, 2001; Kontos & Naglie, 2006; Mitchell, Jonas-Simpson, & Ivonoffski, 2006)

Schizophrenia

- ☞ attitudes toward schizophrenia (Mienczakowski, Smith, & Morgan, 2002).

- ☞ mothers of schizophrenic children (Schneider, 2005)

Abortion

- ☞ an artist's abortion experience (Minge, 2006)

- ☞ a couple experiencing the abortion of their child (Ellis & Bochner, 1992)

Death and Loss[4]

› a woman's reflections on her daughter's birth and mother's death (Pineau, 2000)

› a woman's reflections on the death of her mother and its personal consequences (Spry, 2003)

› an oral historian's grief over the men she interviewed who later died (Case, 2005)

› university students and suicide (Taylor, 2006)

› a visual artist's cultural research and reflections on death (Montano, 2003)

Other

› women's eating disorders (Plourde, 2007)

› an anthropological fieldworker's hallucinogenic bout with malaria (Passes, 2006)

› patients with "unspeakable" illnesses (HIV, breast cancer, etc.) (Kaplan, 2003)

Recommendations

I OFFER THE FOLLOWING PERSONAL and subjective recommendations to those interested in writing and producing ethnodramas about health and illness:

First, writers with a theatre background, or health care workers/academic researchers who collaborate with theatre artists, tend to generate higher quality ethnodramas. Both practitioners bring their respective expertise to the project, creating a synergistic product that more effectively balances science and art. I encourage those in health care who wish to use the medium of theatre as a forum for their issues to actively seek and consult with playwrights, stage directors, or drama educators for creative guidance.

Second, I would encourage exploration of the scripted dramatization of some of the field's best qualitative studies in health and illness. In my ethnotheatre course at Arizona State University, students experimented with improvising, as studio exercises, scenes from such works as Michael Angrosino's (1994) "On the Bus with Vonnie Lee," a case study of a developmentally disabled adult. Is there ethnodramatic potential in dramatizing scenes from such books as Denzin's (1993) *The Alcoholic Society*, or some of the descriptively rich grounded theory studies in illness by sociologist Kathy Charmaz?

Third, I stated in an article of my own autoethnodramatic project (Saldaña, 2008) that you can't learn how to tell someone else's story until you first learn how to tell your own. The reflective practitioner, the autobiographical and autoethnographic examination of one's own career and practice, or even your own history and experiences about health and illness, is rich material for experimental writing of an original monologue or one-act play about your personal stories. In the future, I plan to dramatize the story of my recent and first ambulance ride to a hospital emergency room after a side-effects seizure from a high prescription dose of amitriptyline for my sleep disorder. Metaphorically, the experience was an epiphanic "wake up" call for me to critically examine the work overload in my life.

Closure

WHEN WE READ OR ATTEND ETHNODRAMAS about health and illness, what we gain from the event depends on our experiential backgrounds. If we are health care providers, we might learn more about an illness from the patient or client's perspective. If we share the same illness or health issue dramatized on stage, we might find resonance and comfort knowing we are not alone in our suffering because others face the same struggles we do. And if we are neither of these populations, we might come to a greater understanding of those affected by illness and health care matters by perhaps unconsciously acknowledging that the participant's plight could very well be our own some day.

Theatre artists and entertainers are taught several folkloric lessons in how to conclude an evening. Such words of advice include, "Always leave them wanting more," "End a show with 'heart'," "Make them smile as they leave the theatre," and so on. One of the most vital lessons I've learned as both a playwright and audience member is that, regardless of the play's story, subject matter, and themes, *end with hope*. This is not to suggest that there must always be an artificially applied happy ending, or that we sugarcoat or negate the seriousness of the problems and issues we address. I advocate that we need to write theatrical experiences with the sense that obstacles can be overcome. We need to know that we can endure, despite the odds against us. We need to know that vulnerable and fragile human beings can also be quite resilient, when necessary.

JOHNNY SALDAÑA is a Professor of Theatre in the School of Theatre and Film at Arizona State University where he has taught since 1981. He is a playwright, actor, and director of ethnodramatic work, and the author of *Longitudinal Qualitative Research: Analyzing Change Through Time* (AltaMira Press, 2003), a research methods book and recipient of the 2004 Outstanding Book Award from the National Communication Association's Ethnography Division; *Ethnodrama: An Anthology of Reality Theatre* (AltaMira Press, 2005), and *The Coding Manual for Qualitative Researchers* (Sage Publications, 2009), a handbook on qualitative data analysis. His forthcoming textbook, *Understanding Qualitative Research: The Fundamentals*, will be published by Oxford University Press in 2011. Johnny Saldaña is also an Advisory Board member for the International Journal of Creative Arts in Interdisciplinary Practice, IJCAIP.

Notes

1 The paper's References include titles that focus on physical and mental health and illness issues, and do not include works that are more social issues-oriented (e.g., domestic violence, natural disaster recovery), though I acknowledge that these too can induce negative physical and mental health consequences. The bibliography included in this paper is not proposed as a comprehensive but a representational one. Ethnodramatic productions tend to be locally produced and not often widely disseminated in print. Also, I have located over 60 related and synonymous terms for ethnodrama/ethnotheatre (e.g., "performance ethnography," "verbatim theatre," "non-fiction playwriting") in the literature across several academic disciplines. This makes online searches of related works and projects difficult to undertake. The author would appreciate any additional references to add to this list from readers who may be acquainted with relevant play scripts and/ or productions. Please e-mail any sources with as much bibliographic information as possible to: Johnny. Saldana@asu.edu.

2 For a YouTube clip collage of John Caswell's (2008) autoethnodramatic *Shots: A Love Story*, access: HTTP:// WWW.YOUTUBE.COM/WATCH?V=5KMIPKDIXZ0&FEATURE=CHANNEL. Caswell's alcoholic "character" is represented by a chorus of three women, with alcohol itself represented as a street-savvy male. The highly abstract and symbolic dance movement throughout the piece was sometimes juxtaposed with authentic text (e.g., verbatim passages from Alcoholics Anonymous manuals), and demonstrates that performance art can function as a legitimate style of ethnodramatic presentation.

3. The playwright is no longer in this relationship and is living and working in a different part of the country, though there is still communication between she and her former partner who is, at the time of this writing, on probation and in recovery.

4 The large number of ethnodramas about Death and Loss suggests extended discussion in this paper, but I have withheld from this since most of the plays deal with survivorship and personal memoir.

References

ANGROSINO, M. V. (1994). On the bus with Vonnie Lee: Explorations in life history and metaphor. In J. Creswell (2007) (Ed.), *Qualitative inquiry and research design: Choosing among five approaches* (pp. 251-263). Thousand Oaks, CA: Sage.

CASE, G. A. (2005). "Tic(k)": A performance of time and memory. In D. Pollock (Ed.), *Remembering: oral history performance* (pp. 129-42). New York: Palgrave Macmillan.

CASWELL, J. J., JR. (2008, February). *Shots: A love story.* Performance at Mesa Arts Center, Mesa, AZ.

COLE, A. L., McIntyre, M., & McAuliffe, K. (2001, April). *All about Alzheimer's: Who can tell what we know?* Performance at the 2001 American Educational Research Association Conference, Seattle.

COREY, F. C. (Ed.). (1993). *HIV education: Performing personal narratives.* Tempe, AZ: Arizona State University.

DENZIN, N. K. (1993). *The alcoholic society: Addiction and recovery of the self.* New Brunswick, NJ: Transaction Publishers.

DILLARD, S. (2000). *Breathing Darrell*: Solo performance as a contribution to a useful queer methodology. *Text and Performance Quarterly 20*(1), 74–83.

ELLIS, C., & BOCHNER, A. P. (1992). Telling and performing personal stories: The constraints of choice in abortion. In C. Ellis & M. G. Flaherty (Eds.), *Investigating subjectivity: Research on lived experience* (pp. 79–101). Newbury Park, CA: Sage.

GRAY, R. E., & SINDING, C. (2002). *Standing ovation: Performing social science research about cancer.* Walnut Creek, CA: AltaMira Press.

KAPLAN, C. (2003, March). *The unspeakables.* Performance at the Strand Theatre, Houston, TX.

KONTOS, P. C., & NAGLIE, G. (2006). Expressions of personhood in Alzheimer's: Moving from ethnographic text to performing ethnography. *Qualitative Research 6*(3), 301-17.

LOBEL, B. (2007, February). *Ball and other funny stories about cancer.* Performance at Arizona State University, Tempe.

MCINTYRE, M. (2009). Home is where the heart is: A reader's theatre. *The International Journal of The Creative Arts in Interdisciplinary Practice, IJCAIP* http://ijcaip.com/archives/CCAHTE-Journal-7-McIntyre.html

MCLEAN, C. (2004, August). *Awareness about aging and autonomy—"Remember me for birds."* Performance at the National Association for Drama Therapy Conference, Newport, RI.

MIENCZAKOWSKI, J. (1996). An ethnographic act: The construction of consensual theatre. In C. Ellis & A. P. Bochner (Eds.), *Composing ethnography: Alternative forms of qualitative writing* (pp. 244–64). Walnut Creek, CA: AltaMira Press.

MIENCZAKOWSKI, J. (1997). Theatre of change. *Research in Drama Education* 2(2), 159–72.

MIENCZAKOWSKI, J., SMITH, L., & Morgan, S. (2002). Seeing words—hearing feelings: Ethnodrama and the performance of data. In C. Bagley & M. B. Cancienne (Eds.), *Dancing the data* (pp. 34–52). New York: Peter Lang.

MILLER, S. (2006). *My left breast.* New York: Playscripts, Inc.

MINGE, J. M. (2006). Painting a landscape of abortion: The fusion of embodied art. *Qualitative Inquiry* 12(1), 118-45.

MITCHELL, G. J., JONAS-SIMPSON, C., & IVONOFFSKI, V. (2006). Research-based theatre: The making of *I'm still here! Nursing Science Quarterly* 19(3), 198-206.

MONTANO, L. M. (2003). Death in the art and life of Linda M. Montano. In L. C. Miller, J. Taylor, & M.H.Carver (Eds.), *Voices made flesh: Performing women's autobiography* (pp. 265–81). Madison, WI: University of Wisconsin Press.

MULCAHY, C. M., PARRY, D. C., & GLOVER, T. D. (2009). Between diagnosis and death: A performance text about cancer, shadows, and the ghosts we cannot escape. *International Review of Qualitative Research* 2(1), 29-42.

NIMMON, L. E. (2007). ESL-speaking immigrant women's disillusions: Voices of health care in Canada: An ethnodrama. *Health Care for Women International* 28(4), 381-96.

PAGET, M. A. (1995). Performing the text. In J. Van Maanen (Ed.), *Representation in ethnography* (pp. 222–44). Thousand Oaks, CA: Sage.

PARK-FULLER, L. (2003). A clean breast of it. In L. C. Miller, J. Taylor, and M. H. Carver (Eds.), *Voices made flesh: Performing women's autobiography* (pp. 215–36). Madison, WI: University of Wisconsin Press.

PASSES, A. (2006). Chaos theory—a footnote: an experiment for radio. *Anthropology and Humanism* 31(1), 75-82.

PINEAU, E. (2000). *Nursing mother* and articulating absence. *Text and Performance Quarterly* 20(1), 1–19.

PLOURDE, C. (2007). *The thin line.* Portland, ME: Add Verb Productions touring performance.

PREISINGER, M. A., SCHROEDER, C., & SCOTT-HOY, K. (2000, February). *What makes me? Stories of motivation, morality and me.* Interdisciplinary arts performance at the 2000 American Educational Research Association Arts-Based Research Conference, Albuquerque.

PUST, T. (2008). The demon. Unpublished manuscript.

ROSENBAUM, M. E., Ferguson, K. J., & Herwaldt, L. A. (2005). In their own words: Presenting the patient's perspective using research-based theatre. *Medical Education* 39(6), 622-31.

SALDAÑA, J. (Ed.). (2005). *Ethnodrama: An anthology of reality theatre.* Walnut Creek, CA: AltaMira Press.

SALDAÑA, J. (2008). *Second chair*: An autoethnodrama. *Research Studies in Music Education* 30(2): 177-191.

SANDELOWSKI, M., TRIMBLE, F., Woodard, E. K., & Barroso, J. (2006). From synthesis to script: Transforming qualitative research findings for use in practice. *Qualitative Health Research 16*(10), 1350-70.

SAUNDERS, C. M. (2008). Forty seven million strong, weak, wrong, or right: Living without health insurance. *Qualitative Inquiry 14*(4), 528-45.

SCHNEIDER, B. (2005). Mothers talk about their children with schizophrenia: A performance autoethnography. *Journal of Psychiatric and Mental Health Nursing 12*(3), 333-340.

SHAPIRO, J., & HUNT, L. (2003). All the world's a stage: The use of theatrical performance in medical education. *Medical Education 37*(10), 922-27.

SPRY, T. (2003). Illustrated woman: Autoperfomance in "Skins: A daughter's (re)construction of cancer" and "Tattoo stories: A postscript to 'Skins'". In L. C. Miller, J. Taylor, and M. H. Carver (Eds.), *Voices made flesh: Performing women's autobiography* (pp. 167–91).

MADISON, WI: UNIVERSITY of Wisconsin Press.

STUTTAFORD, M., BRYANSTON, C., Hundt, G. L., Connor, M., Thorogood, M., & Tollman, S. (2006). Use of applied theatre in health research dissemination and data validation: A pilot study from South Africa. *Health 10*(1), 31-45.

TAYLOR, P. (2006). *Beautiful menaced child.* Performance at the New York University Forum on Ethnotheatre and Social Justice, New York City.

{184}   YANG, Z. (DIRECTOR). (2001). *Quitting* [DVD]. United States: Sony Pictures Classics.

Performance Based Approaches and Moving Toward Kinaesthetic Understandings of Illness in Healthcare

April Nunes Tucker
Amanda Price

PERFORMANCE STUDIES AND HEALTHCARE both share a value for empathy and historically this value for empathy has been taught theoretically within the context of healthcare whilst the discipline of performance studies has approached it experientially. Over the past two years April Nunes Tucker and Dr Amanda Price (Division of Performing Arts, University of Bedfordshire, UK) have been working with Professor Christopher Johns (Institute of Health Research, University of Bedfordshire) on a research project which explores the use of performance techniques in conjunction with reflective practice narratives emerging out of healthcare contexts.[1] One of the aims of this work was to consider the potential impact of performance techniques upon the Nursing Curriculum. Throughout our work the concept of 'empathy' and the practical realization of 'empathic encounters' in performance has proved central to our development of reflective-based practice.

This paper aims to explore and demonstrate how performance-based methodologies or kinaesthetic approaches can help healthcare professionals to 'experience with' the symptoms and conditions of illness presented by those in their care. The paper begins by considering the ways in which empathy has, in many cases, been taught theoretically to the student healthcare professional, and then presents practical aspects of an empathetic response found in performance studies as a means of considering ways in which the disciplines might inform each other with a view to developing and enhancing practice. The goal of such an inquiry has a practical outcome; to develop methodologies whereby empathy may be taught experientially as part of the nursing curriculum.

---

1. Professor Chris Johns has a background in nursing and leads postgraduate courses in Clinical Leadership, Palliative Care and Reflective Practice. He is the author of numerous books on the use of Reflective Practice within a Healthcare context. He also works as a complementary therapist with people with cancer in both hospice and community settings.

Phenomenological Philosopher Edmund Husserl (1859-1938)[2], defined empathy as an ability "to read into another's actions, as an expression of inner states analogous to my own" (Moran, 2000:175). Similarly, in psychology, empathy constitutes a strong inter-relationship between emotion and action (Gallese, 2003:524). Theoretically, the idea of empathy is further supported by recent research in the area of neural science[3,] The abundance of theoretical ideas concerning empathy can be digested and discussed within the healthcare curriculum; yet, empathy taught only from a theoretical perspective is problematic. The precise nature of this problem emerged during a workshop that I (April) was asked to give to a group of healthcare professionals at a conference on reflective practice in healthcare.[4] The workshop was entitled 'Exploring Kinaesthetic Empathy' and had been initially developed as part of my dance practice in order to enhance dance students' awareness of the way they encounter and make relationships with the bodies of other dancers in performance. The need to negotiate and navigate in response to the bodies of others is an essential

2. See Moran (2000:175-176). Moran s text provides succinct information about Edith Stein who was a pupil of Edmund Husserl (philosopher of phenomenology 1859-1938). Stein s PhD, written in 1916 was entitled On the Problem of Empathy and proposes that, in the experience of empathy, one cannot truly know the other. Stein provides the following examples: I see someone blush and know she feels ashamed of herself; a friend tells me of the loss of his brother and I become aware of his pain (Moran, 2000:176). Stein claims: I can live in the other 's experience in an intuitive manner but I don t undergo that experience myself in an original fashion (ibid).

3. Neural scientist Daniel Glaser carried out research in 2003 involving members of the Royal Ballet which addresses the idea of 186 mirror neurons . His research showed that dancers who watch movement have the same neurons firing in their brain as when they perform movement. See Glaser, D. and Friston, K. (2003). Since this research in 2003 the dance community in the UK has collaborated with experts from the area of neural science and has begun the pursuit of a multidisciplinary project involving four UK universities and funded by the Arts and Humanities Research Council from 2008-2011. The project will explore how spectators respond to and empathize with dance movements and will directly draw upon the idea of kinaesthetic empathy. See www.WATCHINGDANCE.ORG

4. Nunes, A. (2008). 186 Exploring Kinesthetic Empathy: A Practical Movement-based Workshop . Unfurling Knowledge: The 14th International Reflective Practice Conference, Waiariki Institute of Technology, Rotorua, New Zealand.

skill for the dancer and I offered this workshop within the context of healthcare as a means of highlighting the 'bodily' relationship the healthcare professional engages in daily with those in his/her care.

The task began with the simple premise of one person physically moving the other. The person being moved lay supine and was instructed to "do nothing but breathe" whilst aiming to release tension in their muscles. The person moving the other person was instructed to "*listen* to the other's body and respond accordingly" while aiming to explore the range of motion of the main joints in the other person's body (i.e. the hip and shoulder joints).[5]

Graduates from the Performing Arts Degree Course at University of Bedfordshire UK practice the 'Exploring Kinaesthetic Empathy' exercise

5. A full description of how to carry out this exercise alongside further illustrative photographs can be found on WWW.NEWNESSDANCE.ORG.uk

In essence, the 'Exploring Kinaesthetic Empathy' exercise was developed to facilitate an experience of 'being-in-the-moment' a quality that accompanies empathetic experience. Chris Johns says,

> The idea of paying attention to self within the unfolding moment defines reflection-within-the-moment; the exquisite paying attention to the way the self is thinking, feeling and responding within the particular moment, and those factors that are influencing the way self is thinking, feeling and responding. Such self-awareness moves reflection away from techniques to apply to a way of being (2004:2).

The 'Exploring Kinaesthetic Empathy' exercise works on a feedback loop of reciprocal nonverbal communication between two bodies. If, for example, in the process of this exercise, the active participant (the person doing the moving) clings to the agenda of manipulating the other's limbs beyond the comfort levels of the passive participant (the person being moved) then the communication between the two becomes autocratic in nature. Empathy cannot survive under such circumstances and instead the exercise turns into merely a task of physical manipulation whereby the channels of communication are one-sided (i.e. the active individual acts as a director of the passive individual's movements). The problem with this is that the passive person's body becomes objectified and the intersubjectivity required for empathy is lost.

{188}

A number of healthcare participants at the conference workshop struggled greatly with this exercise in that they found both roles – passive participant or the active participant – challenging. Many of them found it uncomfortable and disconcerting to lie passively, relax, breathe and allow themselves to be moved, perhaps because this activity in itself goes against the grain of the healthcare professional's role which innately involves a sense of *doing*. Similarly, the ingrained characteristic 'to do' as opposed to 'to be' posed problems in the active role whereby the professional habit of 'managing' another's body overwhelmed the instruction to 'listen to' the other's body. Many of the participants expressed surprise at their inability to follow the simple instruction given at the beginning of the exercise, and were eager to discuss both the habitual response they had discovered through this encounter and the means by which they might begin to revise their relationship to the bodies they encountered daily.

An evaluation of this experience with research colleagues raised the questions; Could it be that there is more emphasis placed on *doing* over *being* in the healthcare curriculum? Does the value placed on theory over practice strengthen theory's role as a distancing tool from the intersubjective empathetic response when confronted with another? Like the body-mind complex in which we operate and exist, an experiential knowledge of empathy needs to be implemented alongside the theoretical learning within the healthcare curriculum.

Attending to Kinaesthetic Empathy

AN EXPERIENTIAL PEDAGOGY ADDRESSING EMPATHY would need to embrace the perhaps obvious but certainly vital view that the experience of empathy is embodied. Embodiment assumes that "consciousness is not 'pure', but exists within a membrane of flesh and blood" (Bullock & Trombley (Eds.) 1977:264). Gail Weiss, Professor of Philosophy and Human Sciences at George Washington University, adds, "The experience of being embodied is never a private affair, but is always already mediated by our continual interactions with other human bodies" (1999:5). The emphasis upon embodiment highlights, first, our corporeality and second, it exposes the fact that our corporeality is shared. This fact supports the proposal to teach empathy experientially as it illuminates the importance of our intercorporeality and our body-mind unity. Deane Juhan, a body-worker who promotes the functionally integrated body-mind, states:

> The body is the immediate precinct in which the early formative stages of perceptions unfold, so our current experiences of our bodies influence in decisive ways many of the qualities of the world that is finally deposited into conscious awareness. (2003: 390)

We all have a 'thinking body'[6] which takes into account the coupling of emotional and visceral responses found in *empathy*. In the area of dance, the term empathy is often used in tandem with the word *kinaesthetic* to place emphasis on the corporeal. One defining aspect of 'kinaesthetic empathy'[7], as articulated by dance practitioner Carol Moore, is "physical identification with the movement one observes being executed" (1988:53). Empathy has to do with defining other; it is therefore a register of otherness.

---

6. A term introduced in the early 1900s by bodyworker Mabel Todd (see Todd, 1937). The 'thinking body' is now widely used in the field of dance to describe the physiological and psychological unity of the human being.

A dance teacher describes her relationship to her students:

> I observe them, and I put myself inside their skin. I devote myself completely to
> listening to them, and it's as if I enter inside their bodies. The two bodies become
> one. I put myself into their way of doing things, and I feel their internal state when
> they move (Fortin in Shapiro (Ed.) 1998:59).

This is a description of kinaesthetic empathy where an embodied reaction occurs in response to
the softening of boundaries between self and other. Empathy has gained momentum as a concern
in performance practice today because of the need to understand one's own being in relationship
to the being of another.

Openness to Shared Experience

MOMENTS OF KINAESTHETIC EMPATHY TAKE PLACE within a shared experience, requiring that both 'you'
and 'I' share time and share space. Renaud Barbaras, Professor of Contemporary Philosophy at the
University of Paris-Sorbonne France suggests that, "There is no becoming-self except as becoming-
other, no conquest of identity except as openness to others, but in such a way that alterity always
maintains itself at the heart of this openness" (1991:255). Barbaras considers that behind this
intercorporeal experience found in kinaesthetic empathy there is intent, intent to engage in the
state of openness towards the 'other'. 'Openness' to shared experience constitutes a willingness to
engage with another as well as the aim to cultivate attention toward the other. Like any other skill
that is to be mastered, crafting of that skill must be facilitated.

For healthcare professionals this 'intent to openness' needs to be embedded within a
professional role alongside a range of other therapeutic skills and has been described as 'an
indicator of humanity' (Fairbairn 2002). In an article exploring nurses' empathic responses within

---

7.   A term used in Dance Movement Therapy to describe a skill that can be honed by the dance movement
     therapist as a means of developing a trusting relationship with the client/patient. See Hervey (2000:18)
     and Levy (Ed.) (1995:87). In earlier dance literature, the dance critic John Martin speaks about *kinaesthetic
     sympathy* (1935:13) in order to describe the relationship between the performer's intention and the audience's
     perception of that intention. See Martin (1935:13) and Maletic (1987:159).

a healthcare context (Morse, Bottorff, Anderson, O'Brien, Solberg 2006) the authors define the empathic impulse as the moment in which: "the nurse is engaged with the patient's experience of suffering, and the patient's suffering is embodied by the nurse, and suffering becomes a shared experience." (2006: 77). They distinguish this 'emotional empathy' from 'therapeutic empathy' which is a theoretical modelling of empathy borrowed from 'counselling psychology'. They argue that whilst therapeutic empathy has the advantage of being educationally accessible as: "a learned communication skill comprised primarily of cognitive and behavioural components which is used to convey understanding of the patient's reality" (2006: 75-76) the embedded professionalism of this approach advocates a distancing of the nurse from the patient's suffering, rather than encouraging 'openness' and acceptance towards the patient's distress. Having noted the limitations of an empathic model learned as theory (therapeutic empathy) the authors posit an argument for the more intuitive approach which emerges when the nurse engages at a human level with those in his/her care. The authors do acknowledge that the concept of 'emotional empathy' implies a level of risk for healthcare professionals, given the absence of any hard and fast guidelines for its application. They also acknowledge that the relationship between the patient and nurse, in empathic encounters, is one in which the nurse ceases to use his/her professional role as a defence against suffering and, in a moment of shared humanity, identifies with both the suffering and the patient in order to be able to respond appropriately to their experience. These responses (appearing as verbatim patients' observations) include verbal interaction, touch and silence but they are characterised by a recognition of the difficulty, uncertainty and awkwardness of the interaction. The nurse who forsakes the shield of professional responsiveness in the face of suffering takes the risk of 'not knowing' what his or her response will be and thus shares the moment 'authentically' with the sufferer.

{191}

Whilst ample verbatim evidence is brought to bear concerning patients' positive responses to the affects of 'emotional empathy' the authors, having argued the importance of an emotional response that is not learned 'by rote' in training, are unable to provide a model whereby nurses may develop their empathic skills prior to applying them in the context of the hospital environment. Here is the paradox: the skill of empathy appears to be embedded culturally and yet – like any performer attempting to transfer innately human skills into a public/professional arena – the nurse must relearn their empathic responses in order to apply them within a professional context.

Developing Empathic Skills

THE EMPATHIC IMPULSE, defined above as 'emotional empathy', is akin to the task undertaken by performers taking on a role. The impulse to empathise with an 'other' occurs in stages invoking varying degrees of risk for the performer as the commitment to empathic response deepens. In its first stage the performer accepts responsibility for a role which will involve him or her in a series of actions and decisions which may lie outside the immediate realm of his or her experience. This first stage may be defined as the 'condition' of the performer whose function is to "stand in for" (Ron Vawter cited in Savrin 1988: 114) characters – whether fictional or real – in order to communicate their reality within a dramatic context. This stage may be likened to the 'intent' of the nurse to acknowledge and identify with the suffering of those in his/her care in order to provide appropriate responses to, and thereby ease, their suffering.

The second stage of the empathic impulse is modelled within a 'safe space' and is defined as the 'rehearsal process' during which the performer will practise the actions of the role undertaken, and begin to make decisions about his/her responses to those actions. This 'rehearsal' period of preparation can be compared to the training undertaken by nurses and healthcare professionals in {192} preparation for the performance of their roles within a public context. At this stage the performer begins to take responsibility for the role and the success of the final performance is dependent upon the depth of commitment developed during this period. The aim of the rehearsal period is to achieve effective communication of the role to the spectators who, in turn, will be invited to empathise with the dramatic material. A shallow, or uncommitted, rehearsal process will leave a spectator 'cold'; it may be that technical virtuosity is offered in place of emotional commitment but this is rarely emotionally satisfying for an audience. One might liken this experience to that of the patient who has successfully undergone treatment within the healthcare context but at the cost of having been 'objectified' by the process. Put more simply, the body has been tended to but the emotional wellbeing of the patient has been neglected.

Performance theorist, Peggy Phelan, notes the 'need' of the spectator to participate empathically in performance and suggests the term 'witnessing' as a means of defining this engagement. The 'witness' to an event not only watches what unfolds before them but shares in the event by taking some degree of responsibility for the human drama they perceive. To 'bear witness' is to acknowledge the shared nature of our human experience and to refuse the option to be a passive recipient of action (Phelan in Etchells 1999:14). For a spectator to become thoroughly involved in the lives represented on stage they must feel that they are sharing in a spontaneous 'lived' moment *with* the performers.

Paradoxically, the benchmark of the committed performer is that they should not 'look' rehearsed. A good rehearsal period will, therefore, allow performers to explore a range of potential responses to the role they have undertaken, and offer them the technical framework to allow them to play each performance as if it were the first time they had encountered this particular set of circumstances. The technical framework is often referred to as 'blocking'; a process whereby the moves, actions and responses of the performer – emerging out of early explorations – are set and rehearsed until they can be repeated without conscious intervention. Once the blocking is complete, the performer commits to a personal 'score' or technical 'blueprint' for performance. The score provides a technical competency which allows for spontaneous responses to occur within its framework. This process is somewhat akin to driving a car; once the technical competency is in place the driver is equipped to respond spontaneously to the driving conditions he/she encounters. Without such technical competency responses would be hampered by a limited ability to respond to unforeseen events.

The rehearsal period provides the performer with the conditions for controlled spontaneity; these conditions include a theoretical understanding of the text, a structural understanding of the drama, a technical understanding of the staging of the drama, a professional understanding of the style and concept of the piece. The movement, delivery and *mise-en-scene* will, therefore, have been rehearsed as a technical discipline, drawing on a theoretical and practical understanding of their craft, in order to allow the performer to explore and make decisions moment by moment in performance. Without the ability of the performer to work spontaneously within the planned elements of the performance the work will appear 'cold', 'technical' or 'superficial' to an audience. It is the function of the actor, therefore, to embody a professional discipline in order to facilitate the moments of existential exploration and decision making which are central to the audience's appreciation of the piece[8].

In order for the nurse to be effective as a carer a similar process must occur during which the technical aspects of the role are embodied; a professional discipline and framework must be learned by rote in order that the moments of spontaneous caring and existential encounter may be facilitated. A committed performer will know that only when a secure technical framework is in place can the risk-taking activity of improvising 'in the moment' occur.

8.   John Harrop's introduction to the craft of acting (1992) offers a clear and accessible overview of the technical aspects of the actor's work in rehearsal.

Performance-based techniques for the development of empathic response vary. The development of naturalist drama throughout the twentieth century gave rise to debates concerning whether or not the performer needed to develop his/ her role by utilising an 'authentic' stock of memories and emotions carried as a result of the performer's life to date. The 'system' developed by Russian practitioner Konstantin Stanislavski detailed a range of exercises designed to allow the performer to enmesh his/her role with lived experience in order to optimise the potential for a spontaneous response to events enacted upon the stage. The practitioner working with this approach uses the central question 'what if?' in order to bring the experience of the 'other' closer to their own lives; in so doing they utilise lived experience – accessed through memory – as a means of gaining an understanding of the emotional conditions they are witnessing in the other.[9] Whilst this approach would appear to offer a potential model for empathic encounters within the healthcare context, it is problematic in its positing of an emotional relationship based on 'feeling for', rather than 'feeling with' the other. The German theatre practitioner, Bertolt Brecht, noted this problematic at the heart of Stanislavski's 'system' and asserted that empathic response based on 'feeling for' was nothing more than a 'confidence trick' played on the spectator. He considered that such a response allowed the spectator an emotional release but left the object of that suffering

essentially unchanged and untouched by the experience. In place of 'feeling for' (a condition closer to 'sympathy' than empathy) he asserted the need for theatre to provide scientific analysis of the social conditions which gave birth to such suffering. He rejected the positing of 'empathy' in place of scientific analysis as a theatrical trick which encouraged passivity in the audience by convincing them that suffering was an inevitable element of human life, rather than being a symptom of human politics.[10] He did however assert that 'feeling with' characters within a drama could occur, but only when the theoretical framework which contextualised their suffering was evident within the drama as a whole.

During the late twentieth century, a new approach emerged which attempted to reformulate the relationship of the performer to their role, and thus to the development of empathy as an element of rehearsal:

---

9. Shomit Mitter provides a detailed and accessible account of these techniques in action in (1992) *Systems of Rehearsal: Stanislavsky, Brecht, Grotowski, Boal* London, Routledge pp.6-41

10. Bertolt Brecht discusses this approach to theatre in 'A Short Organum For The Theatre' in Willett, J. (ed.) (1957) Brecht on Theatre London, Methuen pp. 179-205

My college Stanislavskian training had taught me to find and observe the other in the streets of Boston, the physical place I was living in at the time, but somewhere in this process I came to realize that I could only guess at knowing this other , I could only pretend. The other person was always a thing, an object. His subjectivity, with its inner freedom, escaped me. This observation of the other, as study for a role, froze and congealed any fluid essence. I realized that I could not, and did not want to, reduce others to that object, that study for the stage. I wanted to explore myself as other. I wanted to investigate my actions. I no longer wanted to pretend to be a character outside myself. The streets where I encountered this other were in my body and mind. The 'other' was the other in me, the constant witness, the constant consciousness of self. (Willem Dafoe cited in Gray, S. (1979): 35)

This approach made explicit the concern that whether as a performer, or healthcare professional, one could never really enter the subjectivity of an 'other' without limiting the other's subjectivity to the range of one's own experience, or objectifying that 'other.' Having posited the subjective identification with otherness as false 'knowledge,' Dafoe suggests that empathy can occur only when the performer acknowledges the 'other' which resides within the self. This alternative modelling of empathy sidesteps any possibility of empathy being confused with its sister concept 'sympathy' and returns responsibility back on the performer as voyager and risk-taker. The question remains, however, as to the means by which the performer prepares for, or practises this approach during rehearsals in preparation for performance. The search for the 'other' within oneself is an abstract concept – as least as abstract as the blending of subjectivities – and requires some solid 'earthing' in order to be of practical use.

{195}

As an example of this approach to empathic development I (Amanda) will draw on a performance process undertaken by Antje Diedrich, April Nunes Tucker and Amanda Price in collaboration with Professor Chris Johns in the Summer of 2008.[11] The narrative Chris wanted to work on with us took the form of a Reflective Journal documenting his own therapy with a woman who had been diagnosed with breast cancer. The narrative charts her diagnosis, and subsequent mastectomy followed by chemotherapy and radiotherapy. Chris worked with her throughout this period as a reflexologist.

---

11. *Climbing Walls* was developed in collaboration during the Summer, 2008 and was performed at 14th International Reflective Practice Conference, Rotorua, New Zealand.

As performance specialists we were confronted with a range of challenges in working with this text; the narrative was written in the first person of the therapist (Chris) and the figure of 'Ann' – his patient – was already mediated through his language and perceptions. Both the figure 'Ann' and her condition were unknown to us; we had a hazy knowledge of breast cancer but no subjective understanding of its impact upon the lives of its sufferers or their families. The text dealt with all the key components which are fundamental to drama – suffering, love, death – and yet it lacked a dramatic structure, or framework, which would communicate these issues to an audience using the theatrical conventions with which we were familiar. We were dealing with 'otherness' at all levels in this process and we had to go through quite a painful process of 'unlearning' first in order to achieve any degree of openness to the material.

One example of this 'unlearning' occurred early in the rehearsal period; we decided to try to impose our knowledge of theatrical convention upon the text in order to facilitate effective dramatic communication. We set up a naturalistic scene, therefore, in which I (Amanda) played 'Ann', talking to her reflexologist, 'Chris' (played by himself). Below is a reproduction of the text as it appears in the original journal by Chris in order to provide a context for subsequent discussion:

Sketch 1
Thursday July 5th

Lou says goodbye outside my study. Ann hovers in the corridor.
I say hovers because she seems reticent, uncertain.
I'm surprised to see her.
"You've come for your dissertation result?"
She holds a book in her right hand
And then I add, "the exam board is not till next week."
She says "I've come to return the book you lent me."
Sensing her disturbance I ask "What is it?"
Her eyes drop. "I have some news to tell you."
She enters the study
And sits on the chair I pull out for her
Her tears are close to the surface
She says softly, "I have breast cancer".
(Johns, 2008)

The result of a naturalistic playing of this scene in which I attempted to 'feel for ' Ann was an entirely shallow representation of the reality embedded in the text; I brought to bear my own emotional experience in order to attempt to create a picture of 'Ann' but, in the absence of dramatic structuring, and in the presence of a 'real' reflexologist, the effect was crude, inauthentic, and entirely ineffectual. The problem became clear to us: we wanted to create an empathic response to 'Ann' using performance techniques but we had no dramatic framework to aid us; rather we had a real person embedded within her reflexologist's text. How were we to connect with this vital figure in performance?

After our 'false ' start we began again with the acknowledgement that 'knowing' Ann, or identifying with her subjectively, was an impossibility. To not acknowledge this fact could only lead us down paths of inauthenticity in performance, forcing us to employ our professional virtuosity in place of spontaneous exploration of the text we were working with. We were, therefore, in the same position as the performer Willem Dafoe, who recognized the necessity to explore ourselves as 'other' in order to achieve an empathic response. In contradistinction to the twentieth century debates concerning empathic response, we decided to work from the basic tenet that we would commit to the actions of an 'other' without the safety net of either a dramatic structure/plot, or knowing why they behaved as they did, or how we would have responded in the given circumstances. Rather than 'feeling for ', or 'feeling as' we committed our bodies to the actions which constituted Ann 's journey through the text, as a means of exploring what would become of us in the process.

As a result of this decision, our rehearsals included very little discussion of 'Ann' her life, her character, her social context; rather they concerned themselves with the practicalities, noted in Chris' Journal, which circumscribed her life post-diagnosis. One particularly vivid example of this occurred in a section of the text in which both Chris and Ann comment on the headscarf Ann is wearing in order to cover her bald scalp.

Sketch 6
(Ann wears a headscarf which gives her a 'Parisian Bohemian' look)
"I love your scarf."
"My Parisian Bohemian look."
(she twirls and laughs)
She laughs but her life has not been a laughing matter
She reacted badly again to the chemotherapy . . . four days of hell . . . worse than before

. . . continuous vomiting . . . staring at walls . . . pins and needles, oral tablets thrown up. (Johns, 2008)

I (Amanda) asked Chris where I might find such a headscarf, and how it should be tied. He directed me to Google: "Type in Cancer Headscarf" he suggested. "It'll come up." It took several hours for me to find the courage to undertake this search, although the process presented itself to me as a busyness which precluded my sitting down at the computer to do it. Once the search terms were entered, the result was immediate, as was my terror at having to make the decision to click on the site itself. I procrastinated before accepting my commitment to the action. The site was in front of me (HTTP://WWW.HEADCOVERS.COM/SCARF-TYING.PHP); all the information was there, including the opportunity to buy a headscarf from it. I knew immediately that I would not buy from the site, because – I reasoned – I had a scarf which would do the job, but I did locate the style mentioned in the Journal text and memorized the instructions for tying. Next, I went into my bedroom and found, from the bottom of a drawer, the headscarf which I thought would do the job, and began to tie it according to the instructions. I didn't look in the mirror. As I worked, I suddenly remembered where the scarf had come from; a friend of mine who subsequently died of lung cancer gave it to me many years ago. There was a sense of sorts, a kind of symmetry to my choice of scarf and I felt relieved, vindicated in the sequence of decisions which had brought me to this moment. Then I looked in the mirror and felt sickened and terrified at what I saw. I tore off the headscarf, threw it back in the drawer and went downstairs to find a distraction via the television from the whirling and *incomprehensible* emotions which had begun to course through my body. This was not an experience I could rationalise away; I had to accept the severe discomfort afforded me by my actions. I had to live with it!

I recount this incident in detail because it seems to me to capture the essence of the work we did with Chris. The sequence of events arose from a practical necessity; the need for a scarf tied as described in the text. The commitment to the actions of the text enmeshed me in a process which was entirely new to me: finding out how to get hold of and wear the headscarf used by 'Ann .' I had no emotional engagement in this process at this stage. Having committed myself to the action, however, I found myself responding in ways which were completely unfamiliar to me. Suddenly I was unable to maintain a distance between myself and 'Ann'; this was not 'feeling for,' this was 'feeling with' Ann. I was acutely aware that this could be me; that I was part of this drama. My decision not to buy from the site was a defensive gesture. I had choices that were not available to 'Ann,' and my decision to use a scarf that had been given to me by someone who had died of lung cancer turned the apparel into a fetish, grounding or earthing my fears in

{198}

a ritual object. The sight of me in the mirror – in *my* mirror, not in a prop mirror – brought back the terror, however. My hair was gone; I was appearing as a breast cancer sufferer within the context of my own life; Ann was no longer a representation, she was there in my mirror, manifesting through me. The emotional response was incoherent and overwhelming.

In the performance the tying of the headscarf remained a moment of 'unknowing' for me. Antje, the director of the piece, noted that I seemed irritable and flustered as I put it on. We rehearsed the actions over and over but my initial emotional response to this action resolutely refused to be erased by professional discipline and remained, therefore, as a moment of empathic encounter in performance. We let it remain as it was in the piece: a moment of vulnerability, anger and uncertainty which was awkward and ungainly, charged with fear. As a performer I always approached this moment with trepidation, because it made me feel like I was out of control, at risk: which was, of course, precisely as it should be.

Experiencing and acknowledging the reality of 'Ann' within the context of my own life proved a disturbing and destabilising encounter which translated itself into the performance on stage. What I performed at that moment was not 'Ann,' nor was it 'Amanda'; rather it was an empathic encounter with the culturally specific fears encompassing the subject matter. Having had the encounter my relationship to the subject matter changed; I respected the powerful emotional reservoir which it had the capacity to stir up in me, and my attitude towards my own life changed as well: a fear had been acknowledged that could not be un-acknowledged. {199}

This modelling of empathic response clearly raises questions concerning the training of nurses and healthcare professionals. How can students prepare themselves for the commitment to care-giving which underpins this profession? What is the appropriate preparation for nurses who will work at the 'front-line' of suffering as an integral part of their daily lives? How do we create a balance in training which will allow nurses to 'rehearse' the potential for spontaneous interaction within the professional framework of their role? There are no easy answers to these questions, but the centrality of empathy and its application within the context of healthcare forms a cornerstone to ongoing discussions concerning the structuring of professional training.

APRIL NUNES TUCKER, University of Bedfordshire, Bedford, United Kingdom, is a Lecturer in Dance at the University of Bedfordshire in the United Kingdom. She holds an MA in Dance from the Laban Centre, London and a BA in Dance from the University of California Irvine. She is currently completing a practice-based PhD in Dance at Middlesex University, UK. Her research interests include: performance and reflective practice, site-specific choreography, Butoh and the influences of somatic practices such as yoga on contemporary dance techniques. APRIL@NEWNESSDANCE.ORG.UK

DR AMANDA PRICE, University of Bedfordshire, Bedford, United Kingdom is a Principal Lecturer in Theatre at the University of Bedfordshire in the United Kingdom. She holds an MA in Theatre from the University of Leeds and her PhD offered a comparative analysis of contemporary playwrights in Africa and the UK. Amanda is a founding member of Famous & Divine, a theatre company committed to exploring our contemporary relationship to the uncanny and has recently performed in festivals in Bristol, London, and Germany. Her research interests include: performance and reflective practice, energy and transformation in performance. AMANDA.PRICE@BEDS.AC.UK

{200}

References

ANDERSON, G., BOTTORFF, J., MORSE, J. M., O BRIEN, B., SOLBERG, S. (2006) Beyond Empathy: Expanding Expressions of Caring in *Journal of Advanced Nursing* 53 (1) 75-90

BARBARAS, R. (2004). (trans. Toadvine, T & Lowlor, L.) *The Being of the Phenomenon: Merleau-Ponty's Ontology.* Indiana: Indiana University Press. First published in 1991 as *De L'etre du Phenomene: L'ontologie de Merleau-Ponty.* France: Editions Jérôme Millon

BULLOCK, A. AND TROMBLEY, S. (Ed.) (1977) *The New Fontana Dictionary of Modern Thought.* London: Harper Collins Publishers

DIEDRICH, A., NUNES TUCKER, A., PRICE, A. (2009) "Reflecting on Performance" in Johns, C. (ed.) (2010) *Guided Reflective Practice.* London: Blackwell

FAIRBAIRN, G.J. (2002) *Ethics, Empathy and Storytelling in Professional Development. School of Care Sciences,* University of Glamorgan. Published on the web 25th September 2006. Retrieved August 21st 2009 from HTTP://WWW95.HOMEPAGE.VILLANOVA.EDU/TIMOTHY.KIRK/ETHICS,%20EMPATHY%20AND%20STORYTELLING.PDF

FORTIN, S. (1998). "Somatics: A Tool for Empowering Modern Dance Teachers." In Shapiro, S. (Ed.) *Dance, Power and Difference: Critical and Feminist Perspectives on Dance Education.* USA: Human Kinetics

GALLESE, V. (2003). "The Manifold Nature of Interpersonal Relations: The Quest for a Common Mechanism." In *Decoding, Imitating and Influencing the Actions of Others: The Mechanisms of Social Interaction.* Published on the web, 14 February. Retrieved July 17, 2006, from: WWW.JOURNALS.ROYALSOC.AC.UK

GRAY, S. (1979) "About Three Places in Rhode Island", *The Drama Review* 23 (1) pp. 31-42

HARROP, J. (1992) *Acting* (Theatre Concepts) London: Routledge

HERVEY, L. (2000). *Artistic Inquiry in Dance/Movement Therapy: Creative Alternatives for Research.* USA: Charles C. Thomas

JOHNS, C. (2004) *Becoming A Reflective Practitioner.* UK: Wiley-Blackwell Publishers

JOHNS, C. (2008) "Climbing Walls: A Reflective Narrative for Performance in Johns, C." (2010) *Guided Reflective Practice*, 2ed. London: Blackwell

KABAT-ZINN, J. (1994). *Wherever You Go, There You Are*. UK: Piatkus Books

LEVY, F. (ED.) (1995). *Dance and Other Expressive Art Therapies*. New York & London: Routledge

MALETIC, V. (1987). *Body, Space, Expression: The Development of Rudolf Laban 's Movement and Dance Concepts*. Berlin, New York: Walter de Gruyter

MERLEAU-PONTY, M.(1962). *Phenomenology of Perception*. London, New York: Routledge

MITTER, S. (1992) *Systems of Rehearsal: Stanislavsky, Brecht, Grotowski, and Brook* London: Routledge

MOORE, C. (1988). *Beyond Words: Movement Observations and Analysis*. London: Routledge

MORAN, D. (2000). *Introduction to Phenomenology*. London and New York: Routledge

PHELAN, P (1999) "Foreward" in Etchells, T. (1999) *Certain Fragments: Contemporary Performance and Forced Entertainment*. London: Routledge

RUDEBECK, C. IN Toombs, K. (2001) (Ed.) "Grasping the Existential Anatomy: The Role of Bodily Empathy in Clinical Communication" in *The Handbook of Phenomenology and Medicine*. The Netherlands: Kluwer Press

TODD, M. (1937). *The Thinking Body*. USA: Princeton Books

SAVRAN, D. (1986) *Breaking the Rules: The Wooster Group*. New York: Theater Communications Group

TOOMBS, K. (2001) (Ed.) *The Handbook of Phenomenology and Medicine*. The Netherlands: Kluwer Academic Press

VANMANEN,M.(2002).*PhenomenologicalInquiry*.Retrieved 7 November 2008, from WWW.PHENOMENOLOGYONLINE.COM/INQUIRY

WILLETT, J. (ED.) (1964) *Brecht on Theatre*. London: Methuen

Mining the Depths: Performing Stories of Home and Homelessness

How Theatre Can Create the Space for Deep Listening and Understanding

Ian Prinsloo, Jessie Negropontes,
Sarada Eastham, Christine A. Walsh & Gayle Rutherford

courtesy of George Hennig Photography

Setting the Stage:
How can we come together? What shared purpose can we develop?

Process Note: In theatre we always have the option of hiding. We put on costumes, do make up, become a character and we have the option of saying, "oh that's not me, I'm just playing someone". We also have another way we can hide; in that if it doesn't work out – the play, the role, whatever – we can say "no big deal, it's not my life, it's just a job."

The people in The Lower Depths Project have shown me a level of courage that is humbling. They were given no place to hide, and yet were always willing to stand forward and declare "this is who I am". They were always willing to give voice to their experience and share it with others. And I have also come to understand the risk that they each embrace. If the work we do goes badly, hits a rough spot in the process, there is no safe place in which to retreat. It is their very selves that are at stake in each moment. The work has a deep and personal cost. And yet everyone shows up each week, and takes that risk. I.P.

{204}

I N NOVEMBER OF 2008 ,a project was initiated by the steering committee of the Growing Home Conference: a national conference on housing and homelessness to be held in February of 2009 at the University of Calgary. It was the intention of this project to involve members of the homeless community and other advocates to develop a drama presentation that could explore the experience of home and homelessness for the delegates.

Using his knowledge of experiential learning theory training in theatre work, Ian Prinsloo guided a diverse group of individuals (several people with direct experiences of homelessness, employees of local social service agencies, and faculty from the University of Calgary Faculties of Social Work and Nursing) into a cohesive ensemble. By engaging in theatre practices, he sought to develop creative capacity among the participants and then focus that ability for 'deep listening' through a rehearsal process of Maxim Gorky's play *The Lower Depths* (1902). The concept of deep listening describes the intentional opening of the individual to their lived experience within the world as well as the sharing of these experiences with others.

The original play chronicles the lives and relationships of a group of people living in an underground lodging in Russia. Over a four-month period of exploration, the group created a staging that brought a play to life and simultaneously gave voice to the players' own experiences. The project made use of a multi-purpose room located within a large urban homeless shelter for its activities and preparation, which contributed a great deal of authenticity to the experience for the participants. By combining the lived experience of the ensemble and the capacity for deep listening developed through theatre practices, The Lower Depths Project, as it became known, aimed to create an opening to allow for a new understanding of the situation of homelessness to emerge both in the actors and the audience.

This chapter describes the unfolding of the Lower Depths Project with the goal of exploring how arts-based experiences contribute to teaching, learning and activism within the classroom setting. Research shows that at the community level, arts-based teaching and learning can be employed with special populations such as 'at risk' communities to increase collaboration, creativity and community among organizations (Rooney, 2004). It can also increase capacity through enhanced organizational cooperation and communication (Centre of the Study of Art and Community, 2000).

We frame our discussion using the metaphor of 'the play' to move through the experience of creating The Lower Depths Project. The six phases of the project: Setting the Stage, Casting, Rehearsing – Part 1, Rehearsing – Part 2, Performance, and Post-Show Blues structure the narrative of this chapter. Within each section we share underlying theory which informed our work, typical activities that were used to develop the work, and insights from the journal notes of the lead author and animateur of the play, in the form of process notes.

Deep Listening:
A Practice to Build Community

ACCORDING TO SOCIAL JUSTICE ADVOCACY experts, "stories provide a tremendous source of power – to both the narrator and those listening" (Cohen, de la Vega & Watson, 2001, p. 23). By enlisting the power of story, advocates and educators can help people connect to their own personal experiences and the experiences of others, create abilities to navigate life's struggles, and "inspire realistic hope that unyielding forces can be overcome" (p. 23). Using theatre practices, The Lower Depths Project sought to bring to the surface each participant's story of home and homelessness by creating the space for 'deep listening' and understanding.

The term 'deep listening' is used by various people and organizations; from Pauline Oliveros and her Deep Listening Institute, to many different spiritual and psychological practitioners. The meaning that we give the phrase is drawn from two separate, but related, sources. The first arises from the work of the Koori Cohort of Post Graduate Researchers from the Royal Melbourne

Institute of Technology in Australia. The cohort is a cluster of artists, Indigenous people and academics exploring new methods in research. Dr. Laura Brearley (2008), one of the coordinators for the cohort, explained that the term is derived from a concept among the Indigenous peoples of Australia with 'deep and respectful listening which builds community' as the closest English translation. Essentially, deep listening is the intentional space and attention we give to one another to allow our stories to be shared and heard.

The second source for understanding deep listening is the work of Otto Scharmer. In his 2007 book *Theory U: Leading from the Future as it Emerges*, Scharmer delves into this concept when he describes the four levels of listening with which people can engage: downloading, factual, empathetic and generative (p. 11-13). The first level, termed 'downloading', refers to the process of retrieving our already established position while the other person is talking and simply firing back our opinions when they are done. At the next stage, the 'factual' level, we listen in order to identify the new information within what is being conveyed, seeing how it differs from what we already know. As Scharmer observes, these two levels of listening account for the majority of our interactions with people. These ways of listening also place our being at the subjective centre of understanding. However, Scharmer notes, in all communication there is the potential for deeper, more significant ways of listening: the 'empathic' and 'generative' modes.

In empathic listening we move our attention away from ourselves; we stop observing facts that are interesting or new to us and open our hearts to the living person with whom we are in contact. Scharmer (2007) states if empathic listening occurs, "we feel a profound switch; we forget about our own agenda and begin to see how the world unfolds through someone else's eyes" (p. 12). Yet as profound as this shift in our listening can be, generative listening, the fourth level, takes us even deeper. On this level we are not only seeking to connect with another person but also to allow for that engagement to clear the way for possibility to emerge. As Scharmer (2007) describes it "our work focuses on getting our [old] self out of the way in order to open up a space, a clearing, that allows for a different presence to manifest" (p.13). It is this type of deep listening that allows us to understand another's story in a deeper way, which we propose creates the mental and emotional space for new learning to emerge.

Each of us can identify times in our own lives when we have engaged in this level of connection with people or situations and experienced the 'deep and respectful listening which builds community'. Often it occurs during the moments of extremity in our lives: after the death of someone close, facing a life threatening situation, or when we fall in love. We can remember the intensity of connection with the other person or situation, the depth of understanding that we reached at that moment, and the profound sense of community and possibility that opened up within us. But these moments of insight occurred through chance, not through our conscious effort. In order to address the complex challenges now facing our world, the ability for intentional deep listening becomes critical. Arts-based practice can contribute to intentional deep listening as it assists individuals in the development of creative capacity (New American Schools, 2003; Burton, Horowitz, & Abeles, 1999), enhancing their ability to comprehend symbols and relate their meaning to a 'bigger-picture' of their communities and the world (Psilos, 2002; Snyder, n.d.).

Our progression through the project mirrors Tuckman's (1965) stages of group development (Figure 1). These stages, while presented in a linear fashion actually form more of a spiral, often looping back through one another, and containing cycles-within-cycles. Similarly, in our project, over and over again, we were shown that the deeper we listen, the more that there is to learn.

Figure 1:
Tuckman's stages of Group Development as they relate to The Lower Depths Project.

Stage	Group Concerns the pattern of interpersonal relationships	Task Activity the purpose of this stage
Forming/Casting: Orientation, testing and dependence	Who is here? Do I belong? What are the rules?	Building a safe space; being present to individual differences; convening the ensemble.
Storming/Rehearsal 1: Resistance to group influence and task requirements	Who's in charge? What power do I have in this group? What are the boundaries?	Developing abilities; finding and testing boundaries.
		continued . . .

Stage	Group Concerns	Task Activity
Norming/Rehearsal 2: Openness to other group members	What is our collective identity? Shall I risk trying something new? Can I reveal myself? How are the situations, characters or relationships in the play representative of our experience?	Open exchange of relevant interpretations; intimate, personal, opinions are expressed; opening to the world of the play
Performing/Performance: Constructive action	How can we best support one another? What solutions are emerging? Channeling energy into the task at hand.	Testing the process that brought the play into being; honouring what is at stake.
Adjourning/Post-Show Blues: Disengagement	Who am I now that the project is over? What am I taking from this experience? How has this experience changed me? How can I reenter my life? What parts of this experience will end? What will continue on?	Reflecting and integrating learning; owning up and letting go; deciding on next steps.

Casting:
Who is here? Do I belong? What are the rules?

Process Note: We started off slowly. It was hard to warm people into the work. I think that was mainly because it was such a small group. There were three participants at the beginning. But after lunch when we were joined by the fourth person, and after we did the sharing of our metaphor objects, people opened up in a big way. They will always be reticent at the beginning but that is not a reason to hold back. One thing to consider is how I build the connection between people who have not met yet. What builds intimacy and care? What exercises foster that growth? I.P.

THE FIRST TASK IN OUR PROCESS was to gather the individuals who would become the ensemble for The Lower Depths Project. The term 'ensemble' refers not only to the cast of a play but also describes the group dynamic that the rehearsal process seeks to create. In theatre a group of individuals – each with different strengths, histories and expected responsibilities – are brought together to explore a situation, typically the play. The group is then led through a process, termed the rehearsal, which uncovers the possibilities inherent in the situations, the relationships and motivating concepts. As part of the process of inquiry, the individuals must come together collectively to create meaning out of the range of possibilities that emerge. The goal of moving through this collaborative exploration and creation process is the transformation of a disparate group of individuals into a cohesive ensemble. The ensemble is then charged with communicating the meaning discovered in the process to different groups of people (the audience).

During the process of creation the ensemble develops a fluid leadership structure, one in which the combined abilities of the individuals within the group supplant the need for a single leader. Engaging in the practices identified throughout this chapter can facilitate the creation of the ensemble. However, since group dynamics change over time, there is no end point or final state. Each project will develop its own level of ensemble which once achieved must also be maintained.

In creating the ensemble it is important that the members be brought from the whole system under investigation. The Lower Depths Project was about experiences of homelessness; therefore, the system we drew from included residents of a large homeless shelter, others who had previously experienced homelessness and individuals who work with and advocate for members of this community. In their book *Presence,* Senge, Scharmer, Jaworski and Flowers (2005) frame the relationship between parts and wholes, suggesting that conventionally, our culture adopts a worldview which:

> Leads us to think of wholes as made up of many parts, the way a car is made up of wheels, a chassis, and a drive train. In this way of thinking, the whole is assembled from the parts and depends upon them to work effectively. If a part is broken, it must be repaired or replaced. (p. 5)

This mechanistic conception of being treats living things in terms of their substantive properties, which cannot account for how "living systems, such as your body or a tree, create themselves. They are not mere assemblages of their parts but are continually growing and changing along with their elements" (Senge, Scharmer, Jaworski, & Flowers, 2005, p. 5). Senge et al. (2005) advocate for shifting of our mechanistic worldview to one that embraces the interconnected nature of our being in the world:

> The whole [is] something dynamic and living that continually comes into being 'in concrete manifestations.' A part, in turn, [is] a manifestation of the whole, rather than just a component of it. Neither exists without the other. The whole exists through continually manifesting in the parts, and the parts exist as embodiments of the whole. (p. 6)

When creating the ensemble, the players must each be different manifestations of the whole if a full picture of the situation is to emerge. Thus it was important that our ensemble was drawn from a wide range of individuals actively involved in meeting the challenge of homelessness. In The Change Lab Fieldbook, the act of representing the parts of a whole is called "assembling a microcosm of the system" (Hassan & Mille, 2005, p. 13). In theatre the microcosm is achieved by the characters designated in the play who represent divergent set of opinions and whose interactions result in a greater understanding of the situation. When this sort of diversity of voice is missing then the audience can feel that they are being told what to think about the situation, instead of being allowed the space to come to their own personal understanding.

Co-Learning: Navigating Beyond Diversity

IN ATTEMPTING TO 'ASSEMBLE A MICROCOSM of the system' through casting, the central concern is gaining entry and establishing trust. This was a challenge during the Lower Depths Project because often members of the homeless community have, out of necessity, developed a culture that protects itself from too much 'outside' interference. This assumption could be made about most marginalized or oppressed communities. In asking someone to engage in deeply meaningful and creative work, patterns of exploitation and broken trust must be challenged. Doing this from a place of deep listening creates platforms for trust-building which overtime offer many multiple points of entry.

Johnson (1984) define the stages of entry into any community as stopping, waiting, transition and entry. Stopping, they suggest, occurs at the onset of a relationship, whereby the 'researcher/ outsider' is impeded from entering a community through either formal or informal means. During this stage, the community closely observes the researcher and future stages of entry are defined according to how the researchers' choices, actions and intentions are interpreted by community members. In the subsequent waiting phase, the community assesses the researcher, and values such as trust and integrity may be questioned. In this phase the community makes a decision to involve the researcher or to sever connections. It is not until the transition stage is reached that the researcher is fully able to become an active part of community initiatives. At this point the researcher may transition toward becoming part of the community or be seen as an 'insider'. In the final stage of entry whereby full access is granted to the researcher, there is mutual trust and respect shared amongst research co-learners (both researcher and community members) (Kowalsky, Thurston, & Rutherford, 1996). Establishing a relationship of co-learning at this point in the process is crucial to the trust building that has been the focus of the all of the stages of entry. We must therefore be conscious how we are manifesting this relationship. Rutherford (2009) defines co-learning as:

- ☞ Sharing roles of expert, novice, teacher and learner
- ☞ Application, creation and re-creation of knowledge
- ☞ Mutually beneficial processes for addressing issues of importance to all participants
- ☞ Active involvement in deciding what and how to learn

Gaining entry into a community is not a linear process and may entail involved stages of entry at varying times with different members and groups within the community, at times shifting 'backwards' and 'forwards' or by making leaps that are dependent on circumstances and the depth of relationships that are cultivated (Kowalsky, Thurston, & Rutherford, 1996).

In The Lower Depths Project we negotiated the community entry through a partnership with a local social service agency and a large inner city homeless shelter that facilitated the entry of people experienced with homelessness. Participants needed to know that their autonomy and integrity was not going to be jeopardized and that the project was not intended to exploit or tokenize their experiences. Once several people accepted the project and joined the ensemble, they began issuing their own invitations, drawing other people into the project. It was through these people (our casting agents) that we were able to gain entry into the various communities, thus bringing together the microcosm of players to which we could listen deeply.

Rehearsal – Part One:
Who's in charge? What power do I have in this group? What are the boundaries?

Process Note: It was a very powerful and emotional session last week. I am not sure quite why but the sharing that occurred was deeply personal and, for two people in particular, very healing. Being able to bring new people into the process will become an ability of the group as we continue the exploration. So far how that is achieved has always proved fruitful for building the ensemble nature of the group. I. P.

IN THEATRE, THE REHEARSAL DEFINES the time spent in the process of creation. The etymological background of the word "rehearsal" is worth noting to understand the drive behind this process. Its root – hearse – is connected to the word harrow, an agricultural tool" . . . which is dragged over ploughed land to break clods, pulverize and stir the soil, root up weeds, or cover in the seed"(OED Online). Building from this meaning, the act of rehearsing is to continually return to a situation in order to break up your existing understanding so that new growth can be fostered. This meaning is at odds with the conventional use of the word which often connotes drilling or repetitive practice whose aim is to achieve perfection. Rehearsal, when it is engaged within the spirit of the original meaning of the word, is the rigorous work of cultivating understanding. It is this focused 'digging' that allows participants to intentionally enter into the space of deep listening.

During the first part of our rehearsal process, the intention was to develop participants' abilities in order to prepare them for the later work of exploring the text and giving voice to personal narrative. This phase of the work sought to open up in the ensemble new ways of listening to the world. The act of listening – of giving attention – draws out a new understanding of the world in which we live. As Scharmer (2007) cautions, when we remain at the level of facts or control, we receive only a limited view of the world. Deep listening both opens up and is opened by all the senses; touch, taste, sight, sound, and smell, emotion, spirit, intuition, etc. Therefore we need to shift our attention to other areas of our lived experience if we are to actively engage in deeper ways of listening.

In her article, "Holistic Learning / Teaching in Adult Education: Would you Play a One-String Guitar", Virginia Griffin (1991) creates a compelling description of multi-dimensional, deep learning:

Playing a guitar with just one string would soon become monotonous, and the music would be limited in scope. Playing a guitar with six strings allows beautiful and complex music, limited only by our skill to use the six strings and our imagination.

Learning is like playing a guitar. Most of us have been trained by our schooling to play one string – our rational mind. However, we have at least five other strings, and if we learn to play them well, and keep them properly tuned, we can make limitless music in our learning. (p.107)

She then identifies emotional, relational, physical, metaphoric or intuitive, and spiritual capabilities as the five other strings of learning. By developing our ability to attend to each of these strings Griffin asserts, we can increase the learning potential within any situation. These she suggests are the paths we need to follow in order to create the act of conscious deep listening.

In this project the ensemble explored a series of experiential exercises, based on the theatre practices, whose purpose was to focus on each of the areas identified by Griffin (1991), allowing 'new organs of perception' to open. Each of these exercises, depicted in Figure 2 and 3, asked each person to listen deeply to the situation, the group and, most importantly, their inner self. Engaging in these exercises also fostered the development of the ensemble as they invited everyone, regardless of their background, to move into new areas of experience. This also minimized difference in status and power and introduced a relationship of co-learning characterized by reciprocity, trust, respect and empathy. These qualities helped to create the space for deep listening, which, in turn, deepened these values.

Figure 2

Activity One: Five Levels of Awareness – Opening to Deep Listening as a Group

Objective: To increase participants' attention to physical sense details.
This exercise defies any attempt to stay within the cognitive realm. It asks participants to open up their sensual awareness of a situation and to trust what they learn by deep listening through their body. It also asks them to begin discerning between the various messages received through their physical bodies.

Instructions: Ask participants to walk intentionally around the room in which you are working. An intentional walk is at a speed slightly faster than a normal walking pace; how you walk when you are late for a meeting. By focusing participants on walking 'intentionally' we ask them to attend to the physical and thus to become present. Moving at the faster speed, ask the participants to begin paying attention to all of the information their senses bring. Begin with sight: what are the visual details of the room? How does light enter the space? What are the colours in the space? What are the dimensions of the space? And so forth. The goal is to attend to all of the visual information of the room – not to hold onto the list, but to utilize the list as a field of attention to which you are aware.

Next, instruct the participants to do the same thing with hearing, opening the field to take in all of the sounds in the space. After that, open the field of touch: Do I feel a breeze on my skin? Do I touch anything as I walk? How do my clothes feel on my body? Am I sweating? Then we open the field of smell, and finally the field of taste. As each sensory field is opened up participants are reminded not to lose connection with the previous field. During the entire exploration of the senses, the group must keep moving at the heightened 'intentional' pace.

After the exercise, debrief with the group. What was the challenge in keeping all of your senses open to the room? What was your experience of the room as your senses expanded? What physical differences do you feel after the exercise? How did your awareness of other people in the room shift in the course of the exercise?

String of Knowing – Physical: The exercise defies any attempt to stay in cognitive realm. It asks participants to open up their sensual awareness of a situation and to trust what they learn by deep listening with their body; to begin to discern the various messages received through their physical bodies.

Process Note: The first time the participants move through the exercise they may be overwhelmed by their senses and may not be able to keep one sense engaged without losing another. In the Lower Depths Project we engaged with this activity over many sessions. As time went on the group was able to slowly build their facility with keeping multiple senses engaged. I.P.

Figure 3

Activity Two: Counting to Twenty – Sharpening Intuition and Deep Listening to Group Members

Objective: To build on the ability to sense outside of the cognitive realm as well as to develop group cohesion.

Instructions: In this exercise the participants form a circle facing inwards and touching shoulders with each other.

Explain to the group that they will count from one to twenty, in random order, without giving each other signs. If two people say the same number at the same time, then the group must start again from the beginning. The initial reaction of the group is to try to cognitively understand how to proceed. Ask the group to try the exercise and see what happens without 'thinking too much'.

Ask the participants to begin counting. They will probably get a few numbers out and then begin to collide with each other. It is important to allow them to struggle through the counting.

After the participants have had the chance to wrestle with the exercise, ask the group to simply try to count as a group and sense each other as they count, instead of focusing on getting to twenty. Introduce the central concept for the inquiry: moving the participants from the habit of getting an exercise 'right' to focusing on process; that is to listen more closely with each other and increase their ability to meet the challenge of counting.

At various intervals layers of complexity can be added to what is being mastered. Once the participants have gained confidence and some mastery in the basic 'game', the participants can be asked to turn and face outward from the circle so that they cannot see each other.

The next level of complexity would be to take five steps forward so that there is no physical contact. With each new layer there is an initial drop in ability. Once the group reconnects to the process that underlies the exercise, their ability will once again begin to climb. The continual meeting of new challenges deepens the understanding of the process for the participants and allows for the building of confidence.

String of Knowing – metaphorical or intuitive: This is an exercise that focuses participants into opening up to the impulses they feel. The beginning point for every actor is allowing impulse to be valued and given voice. If they cannot learn to trust their non-conscious intuition in a situation, they can miss rich areas of insight with the process of rehearsal. This is the same for our participants. This exercise is about strengthening their ability to listen to impulse – intuition – and then trust it enough to act upon it. Being able to listen and value intuition is an empowering ability.

Process Note*: It is always wonderful to see the light in people's eyes as the exercise starts to happen and people feel the possibilities. Most people started the exercise with a look on their face that seemed to say, "yeah right, like this is going to work" but then slowly they begin to open up. I ask them to listen in a different way and they experience that it is possible. In a moment the world changes. Deep listening becomes a possibility – and even a probability. I.P.*

In this project as participants co-learned or rehearsed, roles of expert, novice, teacher and learner were shared and integrated. Power relationships shifted and became lateral, offering all of the participants access to choice, voice and authority and embodying an ensemble-based leadership model.

Rehearsal - Part Two:

What is our collective identity? Shall I risk trying something new? Can I reveal my true self? How are the situations, characters or relationships in the play representative of our experience?

Process Note: Two participants in particular found a connection between their experiences that helped to release them from a sense of isolation in which they had told themselves, "no one knows how I feel." It was a powerful moment of relational knowing made manifest. And for all of us who witnessed the connection, it was a moment to listen without trying to fix. I.P.

AFTER SPENDING THE FIRST SIX WEEKS of the process exploring the abilities that would allow for us to listen deeply and to learn from and with one another, we began to focus those abilities into our investigation of the play *The Lower Depths* by Maxim Gorky. We began by examining the physical actions of the characters in the first scene. This became a process of surfacing the line of physical actions in which the characters are engaged with over the course of a given scene (Stanislavski, 2008). By exploring the physical reality of the play in this conscious way we were able to draw a connection to developing attention at the various sense levels. The line of physical actions invites people to begin focusing on how they are physically listening to a situation. For ensemble members who had direct experience with homelessness, this process invited them to consider the physical reality that they encounter on a daily basis, and to actively reflect on those experiences. Building on the activities that we had worked through as a part of the rehearsal process, this exercise within the context of the play itself allowed the ensemble members to take their newfound awareness directly into the play. They began to understand the characters more deeply, and were able to bring their personal physical experiences directly to the role.

{217}

The participants without direct experience with homelessness were asked to imagine themselves into the experience of homelessness and asked to explore the gaps in their understanding. In order to help them move more fully into the experience one of the past shelter residents took individuals on a tour of shelter. This learning journey focused on the areas where the homeless community gathers during the day, and invited participants to become aware of the intricacies of shelter life. They noticed sights and sounds from an 'insider's' perspective and their understanding of the homeless experience grew. As a part of this process they consciously began to open up to an alternative way of knowing and started to allow that experience to inform their work in rehearsals.

In addition to enriching the physical experience of the cast members, this co-learning opportunity had the extra benefit of deepening the connection between ensemble members.

At this important stage of rehearsal we also experimented with reading the play to one another out loud. This act of communal storytelling created the space for people to ask questions and experience the interaction and relationship between characters in a way that was very alive. As theatre is based on an oral tradition much more than being literary art, it is through the spoken word that the situation of the play comes into being. For the participants in the project, speaking the story out loud to one another brought the play into being. It also highlighted the relational nature of knowing that becomes apparent through the process of theatre: we created our understanding as a group as a result of our interaction.

Through the process of speaking the play we focused on one question: how are the situations, characters or relationships in the play representative of the experience of this homeless shelter? For the participants who had or were living in the shelter, the question allowed them to share their knowledge and reflections with the other members of the ensemble; other members were able to ask questions and expand their understanding. This reading and relating of material began to open up relationships between the participants who could then "…forget about [their] own agenda and begin to see how the world unfolds through someone else's eyes" (Scharmer, 2007, 12).

Each cast member then identified a particular aspect of the script that had personal resonance for them and by doing so developed what Stanislavski (2008) would define as 'an analogous experience'. Building analogous situations is the conscious act of making connections between unknown 'given circumstances' (in our case, any aspect of the Gorky script) and our personal lived experience. The entry point to this act of creation is the word 'if'.

'If' is an invitation to participate, asking you to consider the situation presented for yourself: 'What if that happened to me?' The question 'if' links the given circumstances to our personal existence. Stanislavski (2008) also outlines the use of simple ifs, magic ifs, single story and multi-story ifs in showing how this phrase can be used within an entire system of creative inquiry. The systematic approach to creating connections between individuals and unfamiliar given circumstances develops the metaphoric knowing that Griffin (1991) identifies. By entering into metaphoric space, the participants are consciously moving themselves into empathic and deep listening. The analogous experiences developed by the participants were then recorded as personal reflections, and were gathered together to become the "real life" story that was woven into and between scenes from The Lower Depths play.

Process Note: Throughout this process we continue to play games, have conversations, and build the ensemble connection between the participants. It is this growing connection between the participants that I find the most wonderful to watch. The first half of our work sessions have gone very well and I look forward to the New Year when we dig deeper into the play. I.P.

Performance:

How can we best support one another?
What solutions are emerging?
Channeling energy into the task at hand.

Process Note: It has been interesting to see everyone begin to inhabit their characters. By embodying the situations that are described within the script, they begin to make deeper connections to their own experiences. It is not only the people who are embodying the situations, but also those who watch them; witness the experiences, who are going deeper in their understanding. I.P.

In theatre, the final performance plays an integral part in understanding the process through which the ensemble has journeyed. The performance tests the process which brought the play into being; becoming a fire which burns away the extraneous work of rehearsals, leaving only that which is essential. What remains at the final performance are those qualities, which contribute to the artists' ability to meet the challenge set by the play; whether it is a Shakespearean tragedy, a musical comedy, or a post-modern performance piece. For our process, the presentation of the completed play helped to test how the abilities developed through the two phases of rehearsal had prepared participants for sharing their understanding with an audience.

On the evening of the final performance, the participants engaged in their usual warm up work: physical stretching, sense awareness exercises, group listening and focus work. Coming into the warm up work they were all running high on adrenalin and nerves but by engaging in practices they had honed over four months of rehearsal, the group pulled the energy into focus and found themselves ready to perform. All of the abilities that had been developed over the previous months were brought to bear on the challenge they now faced within the actual performance. The ensemble was well aware what was going to be required from them throughout the performance, and what they would each have to personally offer and risk through their own performances. The ensemble was no longer a group of people who were merely hoping to make a connection with the audience through sharing moving material. Instead, they were a group confident in their ability to tell a story of personal importance and resonance.

Process Note: During the performance I found it most exciting to watch the ensemble's conscious ability to stay centered and speak from the depths of their personal knowing. They did not shrink back from their reflections or the situations that were presented through the play. When not directly involved in the scenes the ensemble members gave all of their attention and focus to the people who were engaged with the work on stage. I.P.

In the very first scene, the performers encountered problems onstage when one of the actors forgot to make an entrance, leaving the action onstage without the cue to move on to the next section of dialogue. In response, the actors onstage began to improvise, throwing out lines to cover the absence. Suddenly, one actor skipped ahead to another section of dialogue and everyone else moved with her, ignoring the mistake and instead choosing to work together as a team in a moment of difficulty. In that instant, they chose not to buckle in front of the audience, but instead stayed in within their characters and the context of the play and found their way through together.

{220}

The performance was of great importance to the ensemble because of what theatre is: a physical space that invites deep listening. In the theatre we are asked to listen deeply to the lives of the people we meet – we are asked to share in their experience and the possibility is opened for the opportunity of sympathetic experience, one in which a new sense of self and other can emerge. For this group of participants, being able to have a space in which to speak their experience and to have a group of people honour that sharing was a powerful act of inclusion and voice. Truly vocalizing oneself is not so much finding a voice itself, as it is having that voice honoured and given respect and space by listeners. As James Carse (1986) observes "unheard silence is not the loss of the player's voice, but the loss of listeners for that voice. It is an evil when the drama of a life does not continue in others for reason of . . . deafness or ignorance" (p. 32). The experience of being on stage is a moment of existential affirmation: you physically and emotionally feel yourself being heard, being seen.

The Post-Show Blues:

Who am I now that the project is over?
What am I taking from this experience?
How has this experience changed me?
How can I reenter my life?
What parts of this experience will end?

> *Process Note: I have realized how deeply inside this project I am; to not contribute would be to go against the ideals of the work. I have learned deeply what the cost of this exploration is for the people involved, and how aware I need to be of what it means to risk. It is at this point that the creative exploration in this situation departs from conventional theatre work. It is this departure from conventional theatre work and the courage of those involved in this work that I will be reflecting on now . . . I.P.*

AFTER AN INTENSE EXPERIENCE of engagement and group work, ordinary living can seem a bit pale. In anticipation of this change, the participants were told before the final performance that we would gather as a group again in a month to debrief and talk about next steps for the project. The purpose of this meeting was to make sure that everyone knew how the work could live on and to invite possibilities for the next phase of the project.

The ensemble was also warned about the possibility of 'post show blues' that well known sense of let down that can happen after such a large personal investment with the process and performance. By helping the participants become aware that the grieving process for what had been done was a normal part of the creative cycle, we offered importance to their process and offered them the experience of others to support their learning. By establishing a framework within which to move through the post-show aspect of the group process, we sought to continue the connections and friendships that had been established and to help foster new initiatives. The work that we had done had opened a space where other possibilities and projects were already emerging. It was now important to hold that space open long enough for those possibilities to take root and grow under their own steam.

This part of the process created a gateway that allowed the present work to draw to a close as it also pointed toward an opening for new initiatives. Within this stage we honored and let pass, while also holding a way forward. One practice, which clearly embodies this idea and offers the participants an opportunity to acknowledge and celebrate, is "The Well" (Figure 4).

Figure 4

Activity Three: The Well – Deepening and recognizing connection through closing

Objective: The purpose of the ritual of "The Well" is to ensure that we have not only honoured the work of the day but also to assure people that what was shared during the session together will be kept safe. It also serves to remind everyone that it is the responsibility of each member of the group to keep the learning safe. This activity also serves as a model for the final letting go process which must inevitably occur, the termination of the group whose primary purpose has been served, to celebrate victories and move forward.

Instructions: Bring everyone together into a circle.

Ask each participant to place their right hand into the centre for the circle.

With hands extended, ask each participant to grasp the pinkie finger of the person next to them with their thumb. This forms "The Well".

The facilitator speaks aloud: "here is the well. Into the well we place all that we have shared, and all that we have created today. We each stand at the edge of the well, connected, keeping it safe and sacred. Thank you." (The closing ritual can be different depending on the mood of the day and the learning's of the group)

Each participant shares one word, which is kept in the safety of the group until the next session.

Closing the Curtain:

What will continue on?

Process Note: Rehearsals let people explore very charged situations in a controlled manner; experiencing the emotions and situations in a visceral way but with the ability to come out and talk about the experience. This is not something we are often afforded in our daily lives.

THERE IS A CRUCIAL DIFFERENCE between the work that was created through the Lower Depths Project and that of a mainstream theatre company. In most mainstream theatre when people extend themselves into this sort of inquiry there is the safety net of knowing that it is "just a show". If it doesn't work out, the actors and creative staff may be upset by the lack of success but they move on easily to the next show. Within this project, the cast was being asked to engage in an exploration that confronted central questions about how they identify and how they operate in the world. Within this exploration, it is important to honour what is at stake. Knowing that the performers will stand in front of a crowd and share something personal is an act of courage. However through the fire of performance and the pressure of the situation of the play, all extremities are burned away and the performers come to a greater understanding of what they value.

{223}

Moving through the experience of the Lower Depths Project, the ensemble learned to utilize deep listening for personal and social transformation. Through this process, the participants experienced the capacity to awaken intentional space in allowing another to share their stories and be truly heard. Within this empathic deep listening, the participants experienced a profound transformation in which they were able to know the world through the eyes of another. By sharing this experience with a wider audience at the conference, a powerful dialogue was established between those who had personally experienced homelessness and those who had not. Deep listening held a space for both ensemble and audience to honour and embrace diversity.

According to research, arts-based learning increases self-esteem, self-efficacy and allows people to continually "invent and reinvent themselves" (Eisner, 2002; Ritter, 1999; Stonge, 2002). Art allows people to explore uncertainty, and the inherent creativity that is a potential within process and change. Indeed, arts-based co-learning practices have the potential to be utilized as a powerful strategy that "engages all [participants] in learning, regardless of language, culture and life experiences" and allows participants to simultaneously create, comprehend and express new and in-depth understandings of meaning (Rooney, 2004, p. 20).

IAN PRINSLOO, MFA, is a professional theatre director with over twenty years experience working across Canada with such companies as the Shaw Festival, Tarragon Theatre, Manitoba Theatre Centre, Citadel Theatre, Sage Theatre, and Ground Zero. As well as working as a freelance director, Ian was the Artistic Director at Theatre Calgary from 1997 to 2005. Recently Ian has been exploring theatre outside of theatre. His graduate research (MFA, University of Calgary) focused on how the alternative ways of knowing developed through actor training and the rehearsal process could be used by people outside of theatre to meet complex challenges. Presently Ian is working on an eighteen month project as the Experiential Learning Coordinator with Enviros; a social service organization working with youth and family. Ian has also worked with various non-profits organizations using creative inquiry practices to incite change.

JESSE NEGROPONTES is a student in the Masters of Social Work program at the University of Calgary. She is passionate about the arts as a tool for learning and social justice.

SARADA EASTHAM is a student in the Masters of Social Work program at the University of Calgary. She believes that art expands the human experience as it demands action and enriches possibility

CHRISTINE A. WALSH, Ph.D., RSW is an Associate Professor in the Faculty of Social Work, University of Calgary. Her research interests include studying the epidemiology of violence across the lifespan and contributing to understanding of experiences of marginalized populations using arts-based practices and community-based research. She is interested in promoting student learning through experiential, service learning and interprofessional practice.

GAYLE RUTHERFORD is an Assistant Professor in the Faculty of Nursing at the University of Calgary. Her background is in public health nursing and she focuses teaching, practice, and research on social justice issues and strengthening the voices of vulnerable populations.

References

ANNENBERG INSTITUTE FOR SCHOOL REFORM AT BROWN UNIVERSITY. (2003). *The Arts and School Reform: Lessons and Possibilities from the Annenberg Challenge Arts Projects.* Providence, RI.

BREARLEY, L. (2008, September). 1st Annual Organizational Theatre Exploratorium. Banff Centre for the Arts, Banff, Alberta.

BURTON, J., HOROWITZ, R., & ABELES, H. (1999). *Learning in and through the arts: Curriculum implications.* New York: Teachers College, Columbia University.

CARSE, J. P. (1986). *Finite and infinite games: A vision of life as play and possibility.* New York: The Free Press.

CENTRE FOR THE STUDY OF ART AND COMMUNITY. (2000). CSA&C Services. Retrieved March 19, 2004, from HTTP://WWW.ARTANDCOMMUNITY.COM/SERVICES.HTML.

COHEN, D., DE LA VEGA, R. &, WATSON, G. (2001). *Advocacy for social justice: A global action and reflection guide.* Bloomfield CT: Oxfam Publishing.

DONMOYER, R., & YENNIE-DONMOYER, J. (1995). Data as drama: Reflections on the use of readers theatre as a mode of qualitative data display. *Qualitative Inquiry,* 1(4), 402-428.

EISNER, E. W. (2002). What can education learn from the arts about the practice of education? *Journal of Curriculum and Supervision,* 18, 4-16.

FISKE, E. (1999). Champions of change: Impact of the arts on learning. Retrieved March 19, 2004, from HTTP://WWW.ARTSEDGE.KENNEDY-CENTRE.ORG/CHAMPIONS/PDFS/CHAMPSREPORT.PDF

FOGG, T., & SMITH, M. (2001). The artists-in-the-classroom project: A closer look. *Educational Forum,* 66, 60-70.

FRIERE, P. (2003) *Pedagogy of the oppressed* (30th Anniversary ed.) New York: Continuum. (Original work published in 1970).

{225}

GOETHE, J.W. (1983). *Scientific studies.* (Vol. 12) (D. Miller, Trans). New York: Suhrkamp Publishers.

GORKY, M. (1902). *The lower depths.* (L. Irvine Trans).Middlesex, TW: Wildhern Press

GRIFFIN, V.R. (1991). Holistic learning / Teaching in adult education: Would you play a one-string guitar? In Barer-Stein, T., & Draper, J.A. (Ed.), *The Craft of Teaching Adults* (pp. 105-131). Toronto: OISE Printing.

HASSAN, Z., & MILLE, B. (Eds.). (2005). The change lab fieldbook. Version 2.0. (Available from Generon Consulting, 1 Broadway, 14th Floor, Kendall Square, Cambridge, Massachusetts)

HEARSE. (2008). In OED Online. Retrieved October 6, 2009, from HTTP://DICTIONARY.OED.COM.ELIBRARY. CALGARYPUBLICLIBRARY.COM/CGI/ENTRY/50102829?QUERY_TYPE=WORD&QUERYWORD=HARROW&FIRST=1&MAX_ TO_SHOW=10&SORT_TYPE=ALPHA&RESULT_PLACE=1&SEARCH_ID=PEH6-NC1F57-10619&HILITE=50102829

HOOKS, B. (1994). *Teaching to transgress: Education as the practice of freedom.* New York: Routeledge.

JENKINS, D. & O'TOOLE, B. (1978). *Curriculum evaluation, literary criticism, and the paracurriculum.* In G. Willis (Ed.) Qualitative evaluation: Concepts and cases in curriculum criticism (pp. 524-545). Berkeley, CA: McCuthan.

JENSEN, E. (2001). *Arts with the brain in mind.* Alexandria: Association for Supervision and Curriculum Development. (1995/2000). Brain-based Learning. San Diego: The Brain Store Publishing.

JOHNSON, N. B. (1984). Sex, color, and rites of passage in ethnographic research. Human Organization, 43(2), 108-120.

KOWALSKY, L., VERHOEF, M., Thurston, W., & Rutherford, G. (1996). Guidelines for entry into an Aboriginal community. *The Canadian Journal of Native Studies*, 16(2), 267-282.

NEW AMERICAN SCHOOLS. (2003). The Leonard Bernstein centre for learning. Retrieved March 19, 2004 from HTTP://NASCHOOLS.ORG/CONTENTVIEWER.ASP?HIGHLIGHTID-57&CATID-189.

PSILOS, P. (2002). *The impact of arts education on workforce preparation.* Issue brief. Washington, DC. National Governors' Association, Centre for Best Practices.

RITTER, N. (1999). *Teaching interdisciplinary thematic units in language arts.* Bloomington, IN: ERIC Clearinghouse on Reading, English and Communication.

RUTHERFORD, G. (2009). *Creating a co-learning environment: Interprofessional education in the community.* (Doctoral dissertation). University of Calgary, Calgary, AB.

SEAMAN, M.A. (1999). *The arts in basic curriculum project: A ten year evaluation. Looking at the past and preparing for the future.* College of Education, University of South Carolina.

SCHARMER, C.O. (2007). *Theory U: Leading from the future as it emerges.* Cambridge: SoL (Society for Organizational Learning).

SENGE, P., SCHARMER, C.O., JAWORSKI, J., FLOWERS, B.S. (2005). *Presence: An exploration of profound change in people, organizations and society.* New York: Currency / Double Day.

SHORT, G. (2001). *Arts-based school reform: A whole school studies one painting.* Art Education, 54, 4-11.

STANISLAVSKI, K. (2008). *An actor's work* (J. Benedetti, Trans.). New York: Routledge.

STONGE, J. H. (2002). *Qualities of effective teachers.* Alexandria, VA: Association for Supervision and Curriculum Development.

SNYDER, S. (No date). Total literacy and the arts. Retrieved March 19, 2004 from WWW.AEIDEAS.COM/ARTICLES/TLANDARTS.

SPAULDING, S. B, BANNING, J. HARBOUR, C. P., & DAVIES, T. G. (2009). Drama: A comparative analysis of individual narratives. *The Qualitative Report,* 14 (3), 524-565.

TUCKMAN, B. (1965). *Developmental sequence in small groups.* Psychological Bulletin, 63(6), 384-399.

PART 3

Creative Arts in
Action and Practice,
Special Populations
Self Expression,
Identity, Community

Community media arts

Encouraging citizenship through creative self-expression

Lorna R. Boschman

MEDIA ARTISTS AND RESEARCHERS ACTING through community-led training workshops can support marginalized individuals to develop a sense of citizenship by engaging in a program of creative self-expression. Through participating in community-based media creation, novice directors and photographers strengthen their ability to advocate on their own behalf. Two community-based media arts projects are discussed as case studies within the larger social context of artists and researchers who use art as a tool to facilitate community expression and development. The case studies are introduced by examining diverse approaches to training community members in media skills with the intention of facilitating a dialogue, strengthening a community's identity, or mapping the opinions and observations of participants.

Introduction

FOR TWO YEARS, I was the director of a community-led media arts training workshop for self-advocates and their supporters called *this ability media club*. The term self-advocate is a designation that people with developmental disabilities use self-referentially in order to make explicit their ability to communicate on their own behalf. The project grew out of a collaboration between an organization representing self-advocates, the Burnaby Association for Community Inclusion (BACI), and the National Film Board of Canada (NFB). My initial role was to teach the group members, based on my previous experiences as a documentary director who worked with self-advocates. During the second year of the project, I obtained permission to study the media club as a researcher using a grounded theory methodology. I also began to examine how other artists and researchers had approached the question of working with communities to create media art works, and how the projects differed based on their intended benefits to the community.

All of the approaches to community media arts programs or research projects discussed here link citizenship with artistic creation. While some programs place more emphasis on the development of individual creative voices from inside the community, others train participants to articulate community concerns or achievements to policy makers or other agencies. In the two case studies discussed, a fusion of approaches led to the individual participants' enhanced ability to communicate using media tools, while still sharing the works with their community in order to enhance collective benefits. Additionally, the case studies are presented as a means of informing those who might undertake this type of program in the future.

Prior to discussing the two case studies of NFB Filmmaker-in-Residence (FiR) projects, four historical models are presented as precursors to the current programs. These four approaches are united by the underlying concepts that social hierarchies have stifled the articulation of social concerns, and that voices of marginalized people have not reached a wider audience. The historic influences on the contemporary FiR programs are the 1960's NFB *Challenge for Change* program, initiatives linking civic engagement and community identity characterized by Clemencia Rodriguez as citizens' media, and an action research method photovoice that combines images and stories to map community assets and problems, and programs that directly support community cultural development.

The Canadian legacy of **Challenge for Change**

IMAGINE SOMEONE WHO IS LEARNING to direct media productions: the novice director might attend classes at a university or college or apprentice to an experienced practitioner. Taking into account the many programs we've watched on television or in theatres or downloaded to our computers, we may imagine a director as someone who leads the production crew and guides the actors. The professional director creates works that are considered economically viable by the commercial marketplace because the works are of potential interest to a large audience. In contrast to the commercial world of broadcast television, technical novices from marginalized communities who decide to participate in media initiatives are actively encouraged to express viewpoints that might be absent from the mainstream media. While becoming a director, marginalized individuals learn to actively express themselves in the process of creating new media works, regardless of the commercial potential of the work. In the process of training a novice director, the artist, researcher, or artist-researcher makes the connection between self-expression and self-determination explicit, allowing the novice to apply artistic knowledge to their social relationships.

The historical connections of the NFB to community-engaged filmmaking illustrate how the contemporary FiR projects are part of a Canadian documentary legacy. The case studies below indicate that training novice directors to communicate about their lives using digital technology can impact positively on identity, while helping to reshape the public perceptions of the host community. In the *Challenge for Change* model, the filmmaker helps participants to develop technical and aesthetic skills. By working closely with community members and by helping them to articulate their own perspective, the filmmaker learns about local concerns and works to ensure that local viewpoints are represented.

The 1967 rationale for the NFB's *Challenge for Change* and *Société nouvelle* programs was "that participation in media projects could empower disenfranchised groups and that media representation might effectively bring about improved political representation" (Druick, 2007: 127). *Challenge for Change* began as part of the Canadian government's war on poverty. According to Zoe Druick, government documents at the time indicated the belief that social issues like poverty could be overcome by adopting new methods of communication such as film.

The unique contribution to documentary filmmaking of the *Challenge for Change* program was the idea of a feedback loop between the target community, its participants, an outside viewing public, and the federal government (Druick, 2007; NFB Filmmaker-in Residence, 2006; Smith, 2004). By discussing detailed moments of concern through telling their stories, participants created texts related to their communities. These films were recorded and edited by socially engaged filmmakers and were presented to diverse audiences, beginning with the communities where the participants resided. Ideally, through the process of engaging with the films in a feedback loop, governmental policy could benefit citizens more directly as a result of this form of consultation. However, as Druick notes "The highly vaulted 'process' was a public performance about liberal democracy and an expanded public sphere as much as (if not more than) it was for the benefit of the film subjects" (2007: 131).

One of the better-known examples of the *Challenge for Change* filmmaking experiments took place on Fogo Island, off Canada's east coast. Faced with a declining fishery, the islanders were threatened with eviction by the provincial authorities of Newfoundland because they did not have an economic basis for survival. In addition to a small film crew, two native islanders were part of a group who shot and edited footage, and then presented it back to the community (Druick, 2007). Druick cites the NFB's Colin Low who produced the Fogo Island project as saying the films were edited vertically (2007). Instead of inter-cutting between two viewpoints to create an artificial debate, the films were edited into portraits, building up characters rather than focusing on opposing perspectives. Public screenings were set up with islanders, along with "facilitated discussion on the issues of welfare and self-sufficiency presented in the film" (Druick, 2007: 145). When the Fogo Island films were presented to the government, instead of being relocated, the community was assisted in creating a co-operative fishery that still supports them.

Through programs like *Challenge for Change*, the role of the filmmaker shifted from being a concerned observer to being an interventionist who could "shape social relations in ways different from predominant mass media formats" (Rennie, 2006:47). Socially engaged filmmakers moved beyond simply recording the struggles of others to teaching members of marginalized communities to wield the power of communication directly. In her examination of international community media, Ellie Rennie states that "community broadcasting did develop in Canada, and it is now seen by many as the birthplace of the community broadcasting movement in the First World" (2006: 48).

The socially engaged filmmaker is an outside interventionist for social change, simultaneously working with community members as a collaborating participant. In her discussion of Bonnie Sherr Klein's 1969 film *VTR St. Jacques*, Druick observes the position of the filmmaker within Canada's first community-made project (2007). Although Klein is shown handing over the VTR cameras to community members, she continues to film the transaction. The interaction illustrates the conflicted role of the professional filmmaker in community-engaged productions. On the one hand, the filmmaker gives training and access to media tools to the community members so they can express their own concerns. On the other hand, the filmmaker is also obligated to ensure that the footage resulting from the exchange is framed as a story that the audience will understand in order to portray participants sympathetically.

Citizens' media:
Linking civic engagement and community identity

IF AGENCY MEANS TAKING ACTION with the expectation of meaningful results, then supporting individuals to exercise self-determination supports a wider tendency toward civic engagement. In her attempt to avoid the binary thinking implicit in framing community works as alternative or non-mainstream communications initiatives, Clemencia Rodriguez (2001) uses the term *citizens' media* to describe situations where participants exercise their agency as citizens to create works about their own experiences. Individuals from marginalized communities enact citizens' media when they express their own unique perspectives rather than being reliant on media portraits from an outsiders' viewpoint. Rather than repeating stereotypes, these media works "are contesting social codes, legitimized identities, and institutionalized social relations" (Rodriguez, 2001:20). In her study of citizens' media projects in Latin America, Catalonia, and the USA, Rodriguez further characterizes citizens as people who engage civically on a regular basis. By participating in community media experiences, participants re-interpret their culture and identity, reformulate social norms, and revise how outsiders view their community by giving an insiders' perspective.

While the *Challenge for Change* model encourages the filmmaker or trainer to actively engage community members in order to create a dialogue between the local community, the general public, and the federal government, citizens' media is more concerned with long-term local community development and reformulating collective identity. Both emphasize the development of civic engagement, as does the *photovoice* model.

While a benefit of the action research method is that participants are trained to become photographers and storytellers, *photovoice* primarily provides the instruction so that community assets can be mapped. Because community artistic development projects use a similar strategy of mapping community assets in order to more fully confront community liabilities, the two approaches will be compared. *Photovoice* and community cultural development both seek to train participants to find their voice on behalf of the community in order to encourage a wider discourse locally. Both of the FiR projects presented as cases used *photovoice* methods in order to engage with community members.

Photovoice:
Mapping community insights via engaged photography

IN THE EARLY 1990's, Wang and Burris developed a participatory action research method called *photovoice*, theoretically derived from Paulo Freire's critical consciousness philosophy, feminist research approaches, and the practice of activist documentary photographers. While the method has been successfully applied in participatory projects worldwide, it was originally developed as a health promotion strategy in an action research study among women in rural China's Yunnan province (Wang et al., 1998). Caroline Wang, co-developer of the method, has written: "photovoice integrates a citizen approach to documentary photography, the production of knowledge, and social action" (1999:187). Through assessing health needs from the perspective of community members, researchers are able to more accurately develop public health strategies.

The *photovoice* approach to indigenous knowledge creation allows participants to use artistic tools as a way of articulating community concerns. Following an orientation to the method and discussion of the ethics involved in creating images of others, *photovoice* practitioners ask community members to take photos that will open up a discussion that reflects how the images are interpreted locally. Wang and Pies worked with community members in Southern California in order to conduct a needs assessment of community values in relation to maternal care (2004). Although the neighbourhood Maternal and Child Health Agency had gathered statistical data, they had not previously had input based on the knowledge of those who lived in the area and used their services. Through asking low income community members to reflect on their lives in relation to maternal care by taking photographs, discussing them as a group, and exhibiting them to their own community and invited politicians, practitioners attempt to influence public policy. Wang and Pies report that participants experienced a sense of empowerment while the sponsoring agency was better informed in their strategic planning as a result of the project.

In order to affect public policy, author and artist Arlene Goldbard states that community cultural development is enhanced by encouraging participants to engage in dialogue both inside and outside the group: "Live active social experience strengthens individuals' ability to participate in democratic discourse and community life" (2006:143). Both *photovoice* and cultural development encourage participants to use creative expression in order to critically examine their lives in the context of community. When *photovoice* participants undertake a critical discussion of a photo they've taken, they also write an interpretation of the image to direct viewers' understanding of the image. Participants are also asked to suggest ways of addressing the problem or concern raised by the photo, in a process that resembles the feedback loop of the *Challenge for Change* films. Goldbard (2006) describes her participation in a series of community cultural development projects that were explicitly modeled on action research methods. The artist team gathered digital photographic self-portraits from people at a farmers' market and used a story circle to engage community members. Rather than leading the evaluation of community assets and problems, the artist team used a creative approach to determine a direction based on the active input of community members.

Although Goldbard recognizes conflict is inherent in cultural community development work, it is not always possible to reconcile differences through artistic engagement. Reciprocity and dialogue are integral to community development but they may not be enough to overcome a lack of individual or collective resources. Real social divisions must be acknowledged and worked with so that the community development process does not reinforce existing barriers. Community organizations and members, artists and researchers must ensure that community-based artistic development efforts help to articulate local political aspirations, rather than redirecting attention away from issues deemed significant by the community.

Wang and Pies discuss several limitations of the *photovoice* method, especially in relation to the public presentation of photographic materials. While all participants contribute to the exchange of photos and discussion of community assets and problems, specific images are selected for public dissemination so that policy-makers can become aware of the issues raised. The designated facilitators of the *photovoice* project must balance the community needs with the needs of the funding agencies and the research design when selecting images and stories to share with the public. As well, individuals who choose to participate in the *photovoice* workshops represent their own perspective, and may not be representative of the larger community, or of the community at another point in time. Because the participants were not studied beyond the photovoice workshops, it was not possible to determine if participants directly benefitted from the experience. Additionally, although images and stories were shared with policy-makers, it is not possible to determine if any programs or policies were affected by the photovoice project.

Goldbard also addresses the lack of funding for community arts projects, as well as a lack of support from more formal artistic disciplines in the United States. Funding for the National Endowment for the Arts has been dramatically reduced, and organizations representing professional artists have tended to consider community-based artistic initiatives as amateur productions, unworthy of the limited remaining funding. Goldbard cites these factors among others as reasons why the movement of arts for social change has been limited in her country: "the election of Ronald Reagan, the elimination of public service arts employment, drastic funding cuts in other agencies and the demonization of art with a social purpose" (2006:167). The situation in Canada for community-based media projects differs in that a small portion of funding from the National Film Board of Canada has been dedicated to producing works that are reflective of local discourse.

Case study 1: this ability media club

THE TWO CASE STUDIES DISCUSSED BELOW examine programs that were funded through NFB Filmmaker-in-Residence (FiR) programs, one based in Toronto, Ontario and the other in Burnaby, British Columbia (near Vancouver). Prior to the formation of the programs in 2005, the NFB Director General Tom Perlmutter instructed heads of his regional offices to contribute to the production of works that engaged with communities, in the spirit of *Challenge for Change* (Silversides, 2007: para.20). In February 2005, I was hired by the NFB to lead a media workshop for self-advocates, as people with developmental disabilities call themselves. The mandate of the Burnaby program was to encourage self-advocates to explore what citizenship meant to them and to use their films to demonstrate how they participated in the community. While the program

Michelle McDonald celebrates the launch
of her video "Be Kind to Spiders"

with BACI deliberately focused on the idea of "becoming a director," the perspective advanced by the Toronto project was one of *interventionist media*, a filmmaker working within the community to support ideas of social change presented by the participants.

Prior to the formation of a group that encouraged self-advocates to share their stories about citizenship, a shift in approach had occurred in the other sponsoring organization as well. The Burnaby Association for Community Inclusion (BACI), who would host the club, worked with consultants from *Philia – A Dialogue on Caring Citizenship* to change their orientation from that of a service provider to becoming a welcoming meeting place. Underlying the Philia perspective is "a notion of citizenship based on contribution, participation, relationship, and a commitment to the common good" (Philia, 2005a: para. 1). At the same time as the NFB, technical sponsor of the club, were trying to infuse the spirit of *Challenge for Change* into their current productions, BACI was trying to explore the ways that self-advocates contribute to the community. A collaboration between BACI and the NFB, *this ability media club* was a weekly training workshop for people with developmental disabilities.

Self-advocacy and self-determination

Since the late 20th century, activists have argued that social barriers prevent full participation of people with disabilities. Marginalized by lower than average incomes and fewer opportunities for advanced media education, people with cognitive and physical disabilities are confronted with systemic barriers to inclusion. However, Catherine Frazee, writer, educator, researcher and

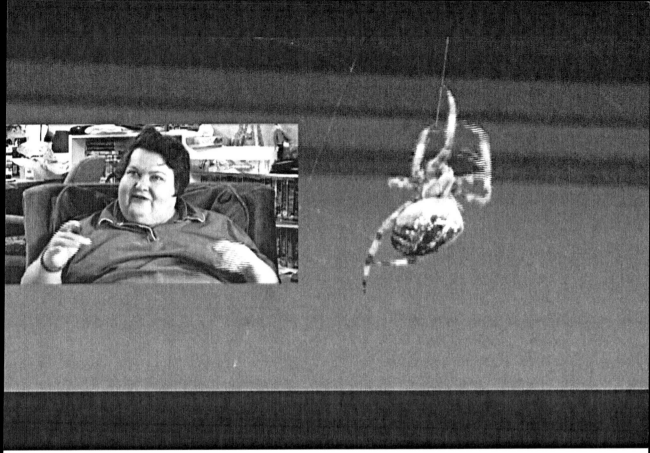

former Chief Commissioner of the Ontario Human Rights Commission, has stated that "For people with disabilities, the notion of citizenship is bound up with questions of access and entitlement, and with processes and structures that threaten to extinguish our identity and contribution. To be a citizen is to belong" (Philia,

"Be Kind to Spiders"
Director, Michelle Mcdonald,
Project director, Lorna Boschman
See http://citizenshift.org/be-kind-spiders?dossier_nid+1129

2005b: para 5). Involvement in community-led media programs have provided people with disabilities and others who are marginalized an opportunity to become civically engaged by creating portraits of their own lives. Hughes and Paterson suggest a transformation of the dominant social model of disability to include embodied experience, because of the "transformation of disability discourse from medical problem to emancipatory politics" 1997:326).

When self-advocates were trained to become media directors, they were also encouraged to learn self-determination, to become more civically engaged, to recreate an identity based on social inclusion, and to engage in a wider dialogue while considering community assets and difficulties. In a short documentary about the making of *this ability media club*, executive producer Rina Fraticelli states that in the past the NFB encouraged women, people of colour, and indigenous filmmakers to learn to express themselves through documentary film (Friesen & Boschman, 2006). She states that the time has come for filmmakers with disabilities to find their voice in order to create authentic media works reflective of their lives.

From the beginning, BACI and the NFB clearly stated that the *media club* was to serve the interests of the participants. It was designed to give the local community of self-advocates an opportunity to express themselves. However, unlike *photovoice* participants who were given free disposable cameras, free access to the professional digital video equipment was deemed impossible because of insurance concerns. The production package on loan from the NFB included a Sony PD170 digital video camera, Manfrotto tripod, and a microphone, but the equipment was required to be locked securely at BACI overnight in order to prevent theft or loss. The times set aside for the novice directors were limited to the weekly ninety minute *media club* or through appointment with the BACI liaison person and myself. When filming on location with club members, we travelled together with the equipment, but ideally the novice directors would have had access to equipment when they chose to shoot.

After discussions with a BACI staff member who worked as a liaison with the project, we began the group by advertising it as a 'Speaker's Corner.' At first, we envisioned that the function of the group was to give voice to the self-advocates' opinions. Initially, stories told by the participants were ones that seemed less spontaneous and more practiced: one told of his struggle to overcome alcoholism while another spoke of "the Richie Riches of the world" who drove cars and snubbed the disabled. Part of the filmmaking process was initiating a creative transformation that would allow participants to tell current stories about themselves. Initially, we offered refreshments and scrapbooking (visual art and still images pasted into a book) along with the digital production gear to those who attended but before several months had passed, the entire class was dedicated solely to learning how to use technology as a communications medium.

Initially, no clear outcome was imposed by the organizational sponsors – the eventual production could be a website or a video or could take any other form. As producer Tracey Friesen wrote in an internal NFB report, *this ability media club* was to be "an entirely process-oriented project, with no clear and pre-determined outcomes" (2005: 13). After several months in the program, our producers indicated that they would prefer to fund the sort of media works that could be distributed through a familiar method. As a result, six of the participants developed and directed their own short personal documentaries. The short films were launched in April 2006 and are available on the NFB's CitizenShift website at HTTP://CITIZENSHIFT.ORG/NODE/6321?DOSSIER_NID=1129.

The model of community-based filmmaking that was introduced at BACI grew out of the NFB's *Challenge for Change* era films. The process involves an experienced filmmaker teaching participants to prepare and ask questions during interviews and to provide leadership in directing and editing their own personal documentaries. The cognitive abilities of *this ability media club* group members varied, but most participants acknowledged memory problems as part of their disability. In order to address this and to support the formation of an identity as a director, personalized letterhead was created for each of the regular members of the group. The page was printed with their name and picture, identifying them as a director with *this ability media club*. The group also followed the idea of a feedback loop: after recording footage, members would show the unedited materials to the group and receive feedback. The letterhead was used to take notes during the weekly sessions. Each member had their own folder that was stored in BACI's offices during the week. Inside the folder, they collected notes, drawings, and photo stills along with extra copies of their letterhead.

In addition to engaging in self-determinant activities using digital media technology, club members also learned the discourse of directors by engaging in activities associated with professionals. When BACI held a launch for their community of supporters, the six directors were awarded simulated Oscars, and were invited by NFB producer Tracey Friesen to walk down a red carpet to accept their awards and make a short speech (Friesen & Boschman, 2007). Following the BACI launch, several public workshops were held to engage in a dialogue with a larger community. Before the public events, the directors practiced their verbal responses in class: what they'd like to say about themselves before the screening, what to say afterwards, and how to answer questions from the audience. During the workshops, two directors shared their short videos and then invited audience members to tell their own stories which club members recorded on video. As a result of directing the short films, members of the *media club* were recognized by others in their community because they were invited to speak on public panels, to help organize similar groups in other communities, and to help train new staff at BACI. In addition to demonstrating that self-advocates can direct their own short video projects, the group introduced members to the public presentation and organizational skills necessary to become a leader through civic engagement within their community.

Case Study 2:
Interventionist media at St. Michael's Hospital

INFLUENCED BY THE *CHALLENGE FOR CHANGE* ERA filmmaking practices, Katerina Cizek was the Filmmaker-in-Residence (FiR) at Toronto's St. Michael's Hospital for three years from 2005-08. In the Flash-based site she directed as part of her residency, she states: "I believe that filmmaking needs to start in the community too" (2006b: Section 2). Calling her work as a filmmaker *Interventionist media*, Cizek encourages people to take action as a result of their participation. Interventionist media emphasizes creating projects that will prompt social change as a result of the work. The completed media work represents a perspective that is relevant to the community: "media that can be used as tools to advance, enhance and achieve their distinct goals" (Cizek, 2006b: para.4).

From Cizek's perspective, interventionist media has a precedent. In the first section of her Flash site at WWW.NFB.CA/FILMMAKERINRESIDENCE, Cizek follows a mobile unit consisting of a police officer and a mental health nurse who respond to a crisis call on an early Toronto morning. Later she shows historic footage from one of the Fogo Island *Challenge for Change* films (Cizek, 2006b: Section 3). Black and white moving images of fishing boats and folk music play in the background as white text titles tell the story of filmmaker Colin Low. He and his crew shot interviews with the islanders, recording their opinions as well as their way of life. When the films were edited, islanders "were asked if the film reflected what they meant to say or if anything should be added or removed" (Cizek, 2006b: para.3). Cizek makes the connection between how filmmaking practices of the past are relevant to contemporary filmmakers and community-engaged programs.

In another section of the Flash site, Cizek travels to Malawi with doctors from Dignitas International whose project assists an African hospital with the distribution of anti-retroviral drugs for the treatment of HIV/AIDS. In addition to making a short film with one of the local organizers, Cizek engaged local youth in a *photovoice* project. The young people were encouraged to document and discuss their lives using photography and text. At first, the Malawian youth were asked to film happy moments; subsequently, they were asked to film what AIDS looks like to them. Each of the youth found one person who was willing to be photographed. When she returned to Canada, Cizek made a short film entitled *The Bicycle* about the Dignitas model of community health care. In addition to broadcasts in Canada and the US, the short film has been used by Dignitas as part of their community organizing and outreach activities (Cizek, 2006a).

On November 26, 2006 Cizek began entering information onto a blog attached to the Filmmaker-in-Residence site (Cizek, 2006a). She begins with a manifesto for community media production that clearly defines the collaborators' roles. While the community partner determines the goals and ideas for the project, the filmmaker's expertise in documentary form is used to experiment technically as well as to tell a good story. Through being a participant in the project, the filmmaker can assist the community in tackling political issues, keeping in mind that matters of ethics and consent should be discussed before filming takes place. According to Cizek, through working with community partners, the work will have a greater impact that will result in social change.

Subsequent to directing the previous works, Cizek continued to work with the St. Michael's hospital community by technically facilitating a young parents' photoblog I Was Here (HTTP://FILMMAKERINRESIDENCE.NFB.CA/BLOG/?PAGE_ID=9) and a photo installation with audio storytelling based on homeless people's health concerns. As Cizek observes "it's less about media training and more about what people do with their new skills" (Cizek, 2006b: section 6). Although photovoice has been used internationally, this may have been one of the first times that photos were accompanied by an online blog rather than written text. The text is important as it contextualizes the photos from the perspective of the participants.

Cizek concludes that the intentions of *Challenge for Change* and current programs are similar: to put media tools into the hands of people who otherwise wouldn't have access. What differentiates Cizek is her emphasis on the effort that follows the filming: working with the community to ensure that the work is shown and used to organize for social change.

Future work in community media arts

DRAWING ON THE LEGACY OF *Challenge for Change* and informed by well formulated research methods like *photovoice*, socially engaged media artists will continue to work with communities and train novices to become directors, photographers and storytellers. All of the approaches discussed here connect the idea that training individuals to express themselves will result in greater civic engagement and more inclusive social participation. While Cizek's interventionist media approach attempts to develop community by advocating for social change, *this ability media club* encouraged individual and organizational change by asking self-advocates to investigate the ways that they were a part of the wider community. Rather than trying to influence policy directly, the media club participants demonstrated that even if people are not able to communicate verbally, they are able to make a statement simply by being present. Researchers and artists working under the leadership of communities can identify social assets and problems. As Cizek and other socially engaged media artists have demonstrated, the real work of social change begins when the production is complete and the work is used to generate further discussion inside and beyond the community of origin.

LORNA BOSCHMAN has been a documentary and media artist for over twenty years. She directed *this ability*, a National Film Board (NFB) documentary (HTTP://CITIZENSHIFT.ORG/ABILITY) that grew out of a two year long community-based media program for adults with cognitive disabilities. In addition to being available online through the NFB's CitizenShift site and Canadian public libraries, *this ability* was featured at the 2008 American Psychological Association annual conference. Boschman's videos can be found in the collection at the National Gallery of Canada and have been shown at festivals internationally. She is part of a creative team awarded a public art commission through the City of Surrey, as a result of the city's designation as a Cultural Capital of Canada. Working with her team of artists she has created two Talking Poles, interactive sound sculptures that play back voices of the community members speaking on the themes of Love and Peace (WWW.SURREY.CA/LIVING+IN+SURREY/ARTS/PUBLIC+AND+COMMUNITY+ART/PROJECTS/TALKING+POLES+MAIN+PAGE.HTM). Currently, Lorna Boschman is completing a PhD at Simon Fraser University in the School of Interactive Arts and Technology.

References

CIZEK, K. (2006A). Blog. Toronto: National Film Board of Canada. Retrieved September 26, 2009 from http://filmmakerinresidence.nfb.ca/blog/?m=200611

CIZEK, K. (2006B). *NFB filmmaker-in-residence.* Toronto: National Film Board. Retrieved September 25, 2009 from http://www.nfb.ca/filmmakerinresidence/

DRUICK, Z. (2007) *Projecting Canada: Government policy and documentary film at the National Film Board.* Montreal: McGill - Queen's University Press.

FRIESEN, T. (2005). *National Film Board of Canada Pacific & Yukon Centre, Disability Projects, Initiatives and Community Outreach.* Vancouver: National Film Board of Canada Pacific & Yukon Centre.

FRIESEN, T (PRODUCER) & L. BOSCHMAN (DIRECTOR) (2006). *this ability* [Motion Picture]. Canada: National Film Board.

GOLDBARD, A. (2006). *New Creative Community: The Art of Cultural Development.* Oakland, CA: New Village Press.

HUGHES, B. & PATERSON, K. (1997). The social model of disability and the disappearing body: Towards a sociology of impairment. *Disability & Society* 12(3): 325-340.

NATIONAL FILM BOARD of Canada. (2006). CitizenShift - Reel Community - This Ability in *CitizenShift,* edited by R. Din. Retrieved September 23, 2009 from HTTP://CITIZENSHIFT.ORG/NODE/6321?DOSSIER_NID=1129

PHILIA (2005A). *Welcome to Philia -.* Philia. Retrieved September 26, 2009 from HTTP://WWW.PHILIA.CA/CMS_EN/INDEX.CFM?GROUP_ID=1000/

PHILIA (2005B). *A dialogue on citizenship -.* Philia. Retrieved May 15, 2007 from HTTP://WWW.PHILIA.CA/CMS_EN/PAGE1337.CFM/

RENNIE, E. (2006). Community Media: A Global Introduction. In *Critical Media Studies: Institutions, Politics, and Culture,* edited by A. Calabrese. Lanham: Rowman & Littlefield Publishers.

RODRIGUEZ, C. (2001). *Fissures in the mediascape: An international study of citizens' media.* Cresskill NJ. Hampton Press.

SILVERSIDES, A. (2007). Filming at the front lines of health. *Canadian Medical Association Journal CMAJ* 177(10): 1239. Retrieved September 23, 2009 from HTTP://WWW.CMAJ.CA/CGI/CONTENT/FULL/177/10/1239-A/

SMITH, B. (2004). This Ability: Revealing the contributions of people with disabilities. Canada: National Film Board of Canada. Retrieved October 17, 2008, from HTTP://CITIZEN.NFB.CA/ABILITY-REVEALING-CONTRIBUTIONS-PEOPLE-DISABILITIES/

STONEY, G. C. (Producer) & SHERR KLEIN, B. (Director) (1969). *VTR St-Jacques* [Motion Picture]. Canada: National Film Board.

UNITED STATES DEPARTMENT of Commerce. (2000). Falling through the net: Toward digital inclusion. Retrieved September 26, 2009 from http://www.ntia.doc.gov/ntiahome/fttn00/Falling.htm#61/

WANG, C. C. (1999). Photovoice: A Participatory Action Research Strategy Applied to Women's Health. Journal of Women's Health 8 (2): 185-192.

WANG, C. C. & C. A. Pies. (2004). Family, maternal, and child health through photovoice. Maternal and Child Health Journal 8(2): 95-102.

WANG, C. C., W. K. Yi, Z. W. Tao, & K. Carovano. (1998). Photovoice as a participatory health promotion strategy. Health Promotion International 13 (1): 75-86.

{247}

ACKNOWLEDGEMENTS

THANKS TO SSHRC Canada Graduate Scholarships (Masters) for their generous support during the research portion of this ability media club, to the NFB and BACI, and to the readers of versions of this paper, including Suzanne de Castell, Robin Oppenheimer, Suzan Kozel, Mary Bryson and Jim Bizzocchi.

"Rapping From the Inside Out"

Music Therapy and Rap Music with an Individual Diagnosed with Schizophrenia

Anthony DiGiacomo

THE PAST FIVE YEARS HAVE seen an increase in evidence-based research asserting the effectiveness of music therapy with individuals diagnosed with schizophrenia & like-illnesses. In *The Cochrane Database of Systemic Reviews,* a periodical that independently defines evidence-based practice standards, Gold *el al* (2005a) reports research that suggests "music therapy helps people with schizophrenia or schizophrenia-like illnesses improve their global state, mental state and social functioning". This research is supported in similar studies by Talwar *et al* (2006), Gold (2007) and Maratos *et al* (2008) with the added assertions that, with this population, music therapy has a particular affect on negative symptoms (depressive cognitions and depressed mood), and that music therapy, when added to standard psychiatric care, provides greater improvements in overall symptoms when compared to standard care alone.

In *Core Interventions in the Treatment and Management of Schizophrenia in Primary and Secondary Care (Update),* The National Institute for Health and Clinical Excellence [NICE], (Kuipers *et al,* 2009) lists music therapy under "Psychological Therapy and Psychosocial Interventions in the Treatment and Management of Schizophrenia". The evidence-based practice defining article in *The Cochrane Database of Systemic Reviews* (Gold *et al,* 2005a) also describes music therapy in the treatment of schizophrenia and like-illnesses as an intervention that assists in improving social functioning. In addition, most definitions of music therapy refer to an intervention that engages clients in psychosocial rehabilitation. The Canadian Association for Music Therapy [CAMT] (2005), in part, defines music therapy as a process that uses music "to facilitate contact, interaction, self-awareness, learning, self-expression, communication, and personal development". The American Music Therapy Association [AMTA] (2006), in part, defines music therapy as an intervention that uses music "within a therapeutic relationship to address . . . emotional, cognitive, and social needs." This chapter looks to report on music therapy as a psychosocial intervention and to support such evidence with a clinical case.

Treatment

In *Core Interventions in the Treatment and Management of Schizophrenia in Primary and Secondary Care (Update)*, The National Institute for Health and Clinical Excellence [NICE], (Kuipers *et al*, 2009) states that "emphasis has also been placed on the value of multi-disciplinary formulation and reflective practice, particularly where psychologists and allied mental health professionals operate within multidisciplinary teams". In exploring the further development of integrated treatment approaches to schizophrenia and psychosis, Alanen *et al* (2009) discuss "a more integrated understanding of the character and treatment of these disorders based on both neurobiological and psychodynamically oriented research". They go on to describe the most effective treatments of schizophrenia and psychosis as multidisciplinary and "utilizing a variety of approaches and perspectives". In discussing the treatment of schizophrenia and schizophrenia-like disorders, Mitchell (2006) describes the multidisciplinary treatment team as those in the role of providing clients with mental health strategies and developing a therapeutic relationship that will afford clients a sense of control in their own care. Perkins *et al* (2006) explore treatment for first episode psychosis and note that "pharmacological treatment continues to be the cornerstone".

However, they continue by recognizing that interventions such as various individual, group and family therapies my increase the likelihood of recovery. Deutsch *et al* (2005) comment on novel approaches to the treatment of schizophrenia and "acknowledge that in order to achieve optimal outcomes a multimodal approach involving and interdisciplinary team of providers will be required". Through the ongoing OPUS Trial, Petersen *et al* (2005), in looking at improving one-year outcomes in first episode psychosis, conclude "integrated treatment significantly reduced the proportion of patients with poor clinical and social outcome compared with standard treatment".

Schizophrenia, Interdisciplinary Treatment, and Psychosocial Intervention

There is an impressive and continuously developing evidence base for psychosocial treatments, added to standard psychiatric care, with this population. The National Institute for Health and Clinical Excellence [NICE] (Kuipers *et al*, 2009) acknowledges the research-based effectiveness of psychological and psychosocial interventions. They identify two main reasons for interdisciplinary psychiatric treatment, including psychological and psychosocial interventions. The first is that there is "growing recognition of the importance of psychological processes in psychosis" in onset and persistence of illness, and negative impact of individual well-being, psychosocial functioning and life opportunities. The second is recognition of the limitations of psychopharmacological interventions with limited response, in some individuals, to antipsychotic medication, a high incidence of disabling side-effects and poor adherence to treatment. In a National Institute of Mental Health (NIMH) workshop on definitions, assessment and research opportunities for social cognition in schizophrenia, Green *et al* (2008) recognize social cognition as a high priority in the study of schizophrenia. In their summary they focus on the importance of interdisciplinary research and treatment in this area and for this population. Miller *et al* (2006) state that "the advent of new-generation antipsychotics, led by clozapine, and of psychosocial interventions that demonstrably improve patient functioning and quality of life has made optimal treatment of schizophrenia very different now than it was a couple of decades ago". They continue by expanding on the integration of pharmacotherapy and psychosocial treatment for schizophrenia. Swartz *et al* (2006) take a less even stance by stating that most patients diagnosed with schizophrenia, due to the limited effects of antipsychotic medication, will need the empirically validated psychosocial interventions to cope with "disabling residual symptoms impaired social and vocational functioning". They go on to review the state of psychosocial interventions "designed to augment and complement treatment with medications".

{251}

Music Therapy in the Interdisciplinary Treatment of Schizophrenia

IN RECENT YEARS, there has been an increase in evidence-based research and literature promoting the effectiveness of music therapy in the treatment of schizophrenia and like-illnesses. This research is powerful in that it provides support and a rationale for the use of music therapy in the interdisciplinary psychiatric treatment of this population. The National Institute for Health and Clinical Excellence [NICE] (Kuipers *et al*, 2009) includes music therapy in its recommendations for the treatment and management of schizophrenia. In the clinical evidence summary, they conclude that consistent evidence exists to show music therapy is effective in reducing negative symptoms with medium to large effects lasting up to six-months in follow up. This effect was found in both inpatient and outpatient populations. They go on to acknowledge that at present, music therapy, among other arts therapies as well, "are the only interventions, both psychological and pharmacological, to demonstrate consistent efficacy in the reduction of negative symptoms". In the treatment of an acute episode and in promoting recovery, NICE recommends that music therapy be provided to all individuals diagnosed with schizophrenia, particularly for the alleviation of negative symptoms. Grocke *et al* (2008) investigate the role of music therapy in psychiatric care. They conclude that "music therapy is a viable options within the creative arts therapies for enhancing quality of life" in clients with severe mental illness. Through a detailed case study, Solli (2008) shows improved global and mental state through the use of music therapy in the psychiatric care on an inpatient diagnosed with schizophrenia. Cercone (2008) provides a meta-analysis of music therapy on symptoms of schizophrenia and other serious mental illnesses. She concludes that music therapy in the treatment of schizophrenia had some effect on positive symptoms, but that music therapy did indicate a moderate to large effect on general symptoms and a range of effects on negative symptoms. In an exploratory randomized control trial, Talwar *et al* (2006) investigate music therapy for psychiatric inpatients diagnosed with schizophrenia. They compare individual music therapy plus standard care to standard care alone. They conclude that there is a trend toward improved symptoms scores among the patients assigned to music therapy. The greatest trend was seen in general symptoms of schizophrenia. Gold *et al* (2005b) develop a protocol for a randomized control trial to explore music therapy for psychiatric patients with low motivation. In the protocol they propose that all participants will receive standard care and that the experimental group will have music therapy sessions biweekly over three months. As reported in the *Cochrane Database of Systemic Reviews*, Gold *et al* (2005a) achieve evidence-based practice status for music therapy in the treatment of schizophrenia and schizophrenia-like illnesses. They report that "music therapy added to standard care was superior to standard care alone for global state". They also report continuous data that suggests some positive effects on general mental state, negative symptoms and social functioning.

Music Therapy as a Psychosocial Intervention in the Interdisciplinary Treatment of Schizophrenia

In Core Interventions in the Treatment *and Management of Schizophrenia in Primary and Secondary Care (Update)*, The National Institute for Health and Clinical Excellence [NICE], (Kuipers *et al*, 2009) describe music therapy, and other arts therapies, "as a safe way to experiment with relating to others in a meaningful way when words can be difficult". They describe approaches and goals to highlight "expression, communication, social connection and self-awareness through supportive and interactive experiences". Ulrich *et al* (2007) report on additional therapeutic effects of group music therapy on inpatients diagnosed with schizophrenia needing acute care. In addition to the noteworthy effects on negative symptoms, their results show the significant effects of music therapy on individual evaluation of psychosocial orientation. They conclude that music therapy decreases negative symptoms and increases interpersonal contact. They close by stating that "these positive effects of music therapy could increase the patient's abilities to adapt to the social environment in the community after discharge from the hospital". Gold (2007) reports that adding music therapy to the standard care psychiatric treatment of those hospitalized for schizophrenia leads "to greater improvement in symptoms compared with standard care alone". He states that the strength of using a musical intervention, combined with a verbal reflection of the musical process, as a means of expression and communication may be helpful to individuals who do not easily benefit from verbal interventions alone. He concludes that music therapy enables individuals with schizophrenia to build social competencies by "improving some symptoms and areas of functioning with are not easily affected by traditional modes of therapy". Ceccato *et al* (2006) explore music therapy and cognitive rehabilitation in individuals diagnosed with schizophrenia. They begin by acknowledging the link between a diagnosis of schizophrenia and the impairment of cognitive and psychosocial function, and continue by developing a "specific music therapy protocol for specific components of attention and memory". Their results indicate that the subjects who were exposed to their specific music therapy protocol for attention and memory significantly improved their scores on the Wechsler Memory Scale and the Life Skills Profile. Valencia *et al* (2006) compare three groups of interventions: psychosocial therapy, music therapy and "multiple therapies" and measure both psychosocial functioning and global functioning. They conclude that psychosocial therapy and music therapy both show a larger effect size. They also conclude that these two groups display a higher degree of therapeutic adherence, and had lower rates of relapse and rehospitalization.

I am a music therapist and internship supervisor at the Centre for Addiction and Mental Health (CAMH) in Toronto, Ontario, Canada, working with adults with chronic mental illness and addiction concerns. What follows are excerpts from a case study with a client "John", (pseudonym) a man initially diagnosed with schizoaffective disorder.

Brief Overview of Psychiatric History

JOHN IS A TWENTY-SIX-YEAR-OLD MALE of Caribbean-Canadian descent, and has had a six year involvement with the psychiatric treatment system. As an outpatient receiving supportive and continuing care, John displays good insight into his illness and is able to express clear and logical thoughts; however, he is currently receiving inpatient psychiatric care and has been hospitalized for the past three months. John has five previous admissions for inpatient care, all of which have lasted approximately three months, with two inpatient admissions in the last six months. The majority of his admissions have been involuntary.

When acutely ill, John presents with psychosis and disorganization. At times, maintaining confusing and conflicting ideas can prove difficult and his speech and thoughts become disorganized and incomprehensible. Though aggressive at times, he has always denied homicidal or suicidal thoughts or ideation.

John is not currently employed and is on disability pension. Prior to his most recent hospitalization, he was working part time at a client-run café. However, before entering the hospital, John decided to quit this job. As an outpatient, John lives in his own apartment through supportive housing. He also moved into a new, larger apartment before his most recent hospitalization. These two stressful factors, employment and moving may have influenced John's most recent decompensation.

Treatment History

THROUGHOUT THE HISTORY of John's psychiatric care, his first line of treatment has been symptom management with psychopharmacological medication. Through six years of treatment, six inpatient hospitalizations and outpatient continuing care, John has received little else in terms of additional interventions. At times, as an inpatient, however, John attended recreation therapy programming and , in the past, has attended art therapy groups on the inpatient unit where he began to write self reflective poetry and draw pictures of famous rappers as well as create an album cover for a group of his own recordings.

Two years prior, John attended twenty-four sessions of individual music which I facilitated.

He was an outpatient for most of these sessions, but was briefly admitted as an inpatient. After a hiatus, John began attending the music therapy sessions once again, was discharged from the hospital and finished the sessions as an outpatient. During these sessions, John focused on turning some of his poetry into rap music lyrics. We worked together editing and reconstructing his poetry to fit into a song structure and collaboratively created, edited and recorded music and lyrics using samples, loops, a computer and digital recording software. As the sessions progressed, John began to write lyrics specifically for the music he envisioned, and he also took on the role of creative director in the music production. At first he merely gave hints as to how he wanted to shape the music and, as our sessions progressed, he would express how he wanted the music to sound and was able to successfully direct me in constructing the outcome.

Session Structure

Upon discharge from the previous music therapy program, John asked to be re-referred for another round of individual music therapy. After a wait of over one year, John was contacted to once again begin individual music therapy sessions. He and I arranged a weekly one hour session to take place in the studio. John and I agreed to twenty-four sessions. John continues to attend as an inpatient and his sessions are ongoing at the time of this writing. Goals identified for John through this program are:

1. To increase appropriate outlets for emotional expressions/containment of emotional release
2. To improve interpersonal skills
3. To improve impulse control
4. To expand range of affect

After approximately three sessions, a regular session structure emerged. John spends five to ten minutes discussing the previous week's events and then introduces an idea for a new song. We work on constructing and recording the music and/or lyrics for forty to forty-five minutes. Toward the end of the session, John and I review the work and burn a CD copy of the piece for him to take away. This provides John with the opportunity to work on the songs while not in session. All of his music is recorded to digital format.

Session Overview

John began the music therapy sessions by stating that he felt the previous sessions provided a solid base for the production and our therapeutic relationship and his development as a song writer. He said, in the upcoming sessions, he hoped to move into new and more creative directions. John and I were able to spend several sessions crafting newer, structured, more thematically and musically coherent songs. He was pleased with his progress and soon we began to produce songs more quickly and with greater precision.

Toward the beginning of the sessions, as an outpatient, John made a point of consistently bringing new lyrics to the sessions. Over the first three sessions, he created one song for his girlfriend titled "What My Eyes Can't See". On the heels of completing this piece, John moved immediately into an intense, dark and introspective piece he originally titled "Fake Friends". He came to the session with the chorus and the first verse intact. John and I spent the entire session producing music for the song. He said that, for the song, he wanted to create the music and did not want to use loops or samples. We worked together at the piano to develop a chord structure and bass line. The main structure of the song featured a repetition of the chords: D minor to A minor; D minor major 7 to A minor major 7. The bass part consists of the root notes of these chords. The chords and notes were programmed into the computer and John chose the synthesizer and bass sounds. We then programmed a down-tempo 4/4 beat at a tempo of eighty-six beats per minute to complete the song. John was very pleased with the music. Over the next three sessions, he wrote and recorded vocals for the intro, chorus and three verses. The song was mixed in the third session. At the song's completion, John decided to change his song title to "Who Do I Believe?" The lyrics to the song are as follows:

Who Do I Believe?

Busy as a bee making honey, had to put in time just to make this money
In every which way, an extra buck make it a brighter day
Lonely mind, body and soul, but at least I'm meeting some of my goals
Push harder, dig deeper, wide awake but I feel like a sleepwalker

If the heat is on, are you ready to burn
Knowledge expressed are you ready to learn
Five plus five equals ten, fake people on the block like to pretend
Run it back, run it back
Five plus five equals ten, fake people on the block like to pretend
Dead the smiles, dead the smiles, 'cos you know we ain't friends, and no we ain't twins
Born alone die alone, better off left alone, out of reach not even in your zone
No surprise that I had to call home, no surprise that I had to call home . . . no surprise

Chorus: 9-1-1 my mind's on fire

9-1-1 in a state of emergency

Oh, oh so crazy; Oh, oh so crazy

Oh, oh so crazy; Oh, oh so crazy

If God had a plan, yo, it wasn't for me

And if you don't understand it's 'cos you're not like me

I'm a problem with a problem, so how am I gonna solve them

Fake came close, but I don't need none of them

Walk in my way just to mess up my day

They played with my mind just to break me down

But no, Imma' hold my ground, stand tall, Imma' hold my ground

Won't let them back me down

I'm a man and I ain't no clown, wasn't lost so I'll never be found

I'm a man and I ain't no clown, wasn't lost so I'll never be found

(Chorus)   {257}

You don't like me, yo, I am what I am, pain circulate from the brain to the heart

Please don't let me use my hands, never been the type to lose my cool

At least not out of the blue, known to fall back and let it do what it do

Pain is my drive, the reason why I do what I do

Never had a father, always wanted one too, always wanted one too

Mamma held it down, but she won't let me grow, she do it all for the love

Her first-born and her only son, she won't let me die in the street

By a gun . . . now I'm done

(Chorus)

John discussed his feelings about this song stating that, at first, he wrote about not being able to trust people, but upon further refection he believed it became less about pointing the finger outside of himself to exploring these relationships and asking himself "Who *should* I trust . . . Who *do* I believe?". The lyrics are underscored with unsettling minor chords and a down-tempo beat.

John uses the song to express his emotions and voices his questions. He maintains a record of his thoughts in the form of printed lyrics and a CD copy to share with others if he so chooses.

John then returned to the sessions with a concept he had originally titled "It's All A Joke". He decided he wanted this song to have a more upbeat feel. Once again we sat down at the piano to develop the chord structure of the song. The main section of the song is written in two parts: The first with chords moving from C major to D minor to E minor to D minor and the second with chords from C major to D minor to E minor to F major. The client chose to use the horn section for the chords and acoustic bass playing the root notes. The chorus and the first verse were recorded in one session.

The following week John did not show up for his session. I was informed that he had voluntarily admitted himself as an inpatient. When John returned to our sessions he said he wanted to explore improvising the vocals or "freestyle rapping" to finish the song.

John and I finished mixing the song during the session.

Chorus:
Peep game when I speak game
Life is a joke, how dare you not laugh?
One by one my dreams are dying, living for the moment "cause time is flying
One way in and many ways out of my mind's at war please evil stay out
Can't count my blessings "cause I ain't got none
My mind is a weapon and I don't need a gun
Everything hurt like I don't know fun
Back to back cigarette like I don't need a lung
Déjà vu, Déjà vu like I've been here before
Déjà vu, Déjà vu like I've been here before
My life is hard, my memory is scarred
My life is hard, my memory is scarred
My brain's on fire can't take it no more

(Chorus)
Iddy, bitty me I pity the fool that hate me
I laugh so hard so you'll never see me cry
So happy I seem, but so many pain inside (sigh)
So happy I seem, but so many pain inside (sigh)

DiGiacomo

You all been fooled, I took you for a ride
Never be the same, all I know is pain
Vanity, vanity, I'm going insane
The party shut down when the truth came out
The belly of the best, that's my house
A fatherless past no joy to be found
Always bad news
Feed me, feed me, tell me something new
Feed me, feed me, tell me something new
It's like . . . like . . .
The future is mine . . . the future is mine and I'm walking in flames
To forever shine, the world is mine.

Through the progression of these songs and through music we enter John's world as he recounts life events and expresses the desire to rise above and claim "the future".

> *"It's a good way to express my feelings and get out what I really want to say, without saying it to someone else, but, like, make a song. That feels good, you know, creating something that you like to do and seeing other people do it, and then you come and do it. That felt good to have the chance to do that. That's what I like about it."*
>
> —*John*

John has used rap music conceptually as an appropriate container for his emotions. John was able to follow the music and fit his lyrics into the beat. Working cooperatively toward a goal and developing the ability to follow musical cues can also help John improve interpersonal skills and increase impulse control. The joy and enthusiasm John expresses at being able to create music, whatever his given capacity, assists in his ability to expand his range of affect. All of these goals make their way outside of the session with John when he leaves with a CD copy of his music. As of this writing, John has created nine pieces, all with very different musical styles and lyrical content. He is very pleased with each piece and feels that, musically, lyrically and as a song writer, he is covering new ground.

The research and scholarly literature are clear in documenting that interdisciplinary care is the preferred method of practice moving forward in treatment schizophrenia and like-illness such as schizoaffective disorder. Medicine can and will do its part in symptom reduction and maintenance. Psychological and psychosocial interventions including music therapy play their part by assisting clients in rebuilding social, emotional, educational, recreational and vocational skills and can lead to enhanced social functioning and quality of life. The Core Interventions in the Treatment and Management of Schizophrenia in Primary and Secondary Care (Update) by The National Institute for Health and Clinical Excellence [NICE], (Kuipers et al, 2009) make clear recommendations for the use of music therapy by promoting its benefits in the reduction of negative symptoms, facilitating new ways of relating to others and understanding feelings at a pace suited to the client. This paper supports the evidence and has demonstrated with examples how music therapy and methods such as songwriting and rap can bring individuals to a greater awareness of their situation while providing an outlet for concepts and emotions that they might otherwise have had some difficulty accessing. Music therapy, as demonstrated in this case example, can work as a media for both facilitation and communication.

ANTHONY DiGIACOMO is a music therapist and internship supervisor at the Centre for Addiction and Mental Health (CAMH) in Toronto, Ontario, Canada, working with adults with chronic mental illness and addiction concerns. Anthony holds a Bachelor of Arts degree in Psychology (research concentration), a Master of Arts degree in Creative Arts in Therapy (Music Therapy concentration), and a Diploma in Addiction Studies. Anthony is an Accredited Music Therapist (MTA) through the Canadian Association for Music Therapy (CAMT) and a Canadian Certified Counsellor (CCC) through the Canadian Counselling and Psychotherapy Association (CCPA). Anthony has served as Education Chair for the Executive Board of the CAMT, and Provincial Representative (Ontario) for the Creative Arts in Counselling Chapter of the CCPA. Anthony currently sits on the Editorial Review Board of the Canadian Journal of Music Therapy (CJMT) and the Article Review Board of the Canadian Journal of Counselling (CJC). Anthony has lecture, publication and research interests in: music therapy in mental health and addiction treatment, music therapy as an evidence-based intervention, music and mood, the creative process in therapy, client perceptions of therapeutic outcome, media/technology and spirituality/cultural implications for therapeutic interventions.

References

ALANEN, Y. O., GONZALEZ DE CHAVEZ, M., SILVER, A. S. & MARTINDALE, B. (2009). Further development of treatment approaches to schizophrenic psychosis: An integrated view. In Y. O. Alanen, M. Gonzalez de Chavez, A. S. Silver & B. Martindale (Eds.) *Psychotherapeutic Approaches to Schizophrenia Psychosis: Past, Present and Future* (pp. 357-376). New York: Routledge/Taylor & Francis Group.

AMERICAN MUSIC THERAPY ASSOCIATION. (2006). *AMTA member sourcebook.* Silver Spring, MD: Author.

CANADIAN ASSOCIATION FOR MUSIC THERAPY. (2005). *CAMT member sourcebook.* Waterloo, ON: Author.

CECCATO, E., CANEVA, P., & LAMONACA, D. (2006). Music therapy and cognitive rehabilitation in schizophrenia patients: A controlled study. *Nordic Journal of Music Therapy, 15*(2), 111-120.

CERCONE, K. A. (2008). *The effects of music therapy on symptoms of schizophrenia and other serious mental illnesses: A meta-analysis* (Doctoral dissertation, SUNY Buffalo, 2008). *Dissertation Abstracts International, 68*(09B), 6293.

DEUTSCH, S. I., WEIZMAN, A., & HERESCO-LEVY, U. (2005). A "work in-progress": Novel approaches to the treatment of schizophrenia. *Israel Journal of Psychiatry and related Sciences, 42*(1), 2-4.

GOLD C., HELDAL T. O., DAHLE T., & WIGRAM T. (2005a). Music therapy for schizophrenia or schizophrenia-like illnesses. *The Cochrane Database of Systematic Reviews 2005* (Issue 2, pp. 1-21). London: John Wiley & Sons, Ltd.

GOLD, C., ROLVSJORD, R., AARO, L. E., AARRE, T., TJEMSLAND, L., & STIGE, B. (2005b). Resource-oriented music therapy for psychiatric patients with low therapy motivation: Protocol for randomized controlled trial. *BMC Psychiatry, 5*, 39.

GOLD, C. (2007). Music therapy improves symptoms in adults hospitalized with schizophrenia. *Evidence Based Mental Health, 10*, 77.

{262}

DiGiacomo

GREEN, M. F., PENN, D. L., BENTALL, R., CARPENTER, W. T. GAEBEL, W., GUR, R. C., KRING, A. M., PARK, S., SILVERSTEIN, S. M., & HEINSSEN, R. (2008). Social cognition in schizophrenia: An NIMH workshop on definitions, assessment, and research opportunities. *Schizophrenia Bulletin, 34*(6), 1211-1220.

GROCKE, D., BLOCH, S., & CASTLE, D. (2008). Is there a role for music therapy in the severely mentally ill? *Australian Psychiatry, 16*(6), 442-445.

KUIPERS, E., KENDALL, T., ANTONIOU, J., BARNES, T., BHUI, K., BIRD, V., BRABBAN, A., FLANAGAN, E., GARETY, P., HOPKINS, S., LI, R., MARATOS, A., MAVRANEZOULI, I., MITCHELL, J., NAZARETH, I., PRATT, J. P., ROWLANDS, R. P., SEALEY, C., SIN, J., STOCKTON, S., STRATHDEE, G., TAYLOR, C., TRAVIS, C., TURKINGTON, D., WHITTINGTON, C., WOODHAMS, P. (2009). Schizophrenia: Core interventions in the treatment and management of schizophrenia in primary and secondary care (update). *National Clinical Practice Guideline 82.* London: National Institute for Health and Clinical Excellence.

MARATOS, A., GOLD, C., WANG, X., & CRAWFORD, M. (2008). Music therapy for depression. *The Cochrane Database of Systemic Reviews 2008* (Issue 1, pp. 1-19). London: John Wiley & Sons, Ltd.

MILLER, A. L., McEVOY, J. P., JESTE, D. V., & MARDER, S. R. (2006). Treatment of chronic schizophrenia. In J. A. Lieberman, T. S. Stroup, & D. O. Perkins (Eds.) *The American Psychiatric Publishing Textbook of Schizophrenia* (pp. 365-381). Arlington, VA: American Psychiatric Publishing, Inc.

MITCHELL, Y. (2006). Schizophrenia and schizophrenia-type disorders. In I. Peate & S. Chelvanayagam (Eds.) *Caring for Adults with Mental Health Problems* (pp. 145-159). New York: John Wiley & Sons Ltd.

PERKINS, D. O., LIEBERMAN, J. A., & LEWIS, S. (2006). First episode. In J. A. Lieberman, T. S. Stroup, & D. O. Perkins (Eds.) *The American Psychiatric Publishing Textbook of Schizophrenia* (pp. 353-364). Arlington, VA: American Psychiatric Publishing, Inc.

PETERSEN, L., NORDENTOFT, M., JEPPESEN, P., OHLENSCHLAEGER, J., THORUP, A., CHRISTIENSEN, T. O., KRARUP, G., DAHLSTROM, J., HAASTRUP, B., & JORGENSEN, P. (2005). Improving 1-year outcome in first-episode psychosis: OPUS trial. *British Journal of Psychiatry, 187*(Supp 148), s98-s103.

SOLLI, H. F. (2008). "Shut up and play": Improvisational use of popular music for a man with schizophrenia. *Nordic Journal of Music Therapy, 17*(1), 67-77.

SWARTZ, M. S., LAURIELLO, J., & DRAKE, R. E. (2006). Psychosocial therapies. In J. A. Lieberman, T. S. Stroup, & D. O. Perkins (Eds.) *The American Psychiatric Publishing Textbook of Schizophrenia* (pp. 327-340). Arlington, VA: American Psychiatric Publishing, Inc.

TALWAR, N., CRAWFORD, M. J., MARATOS, A., NUR, U., McDERMOTT, O., & PROCTER, S. (2006). Music therapy for in-patients with schizophrenia. *The British Journal of Psychiatry, 189*, 405-409.

ULRICH, G., HOUTMANS, T., & GOLD, C. (2007). The additional therapeutic effect of group music therapy for schizophrenic patients: A randomized study. *Acta Psychiatrica Scandinavica, 116*(5), 362-370.

VALENCIA, M., MUROW, E, & RASCON, M. L. (2006). Comparison of three types of treatment for schizophrenia: Psychosocial Therapy, music therapy, and multiple therapies. *Revista Latinoamericana de Psicologia, 38*(3), 535-549.

{264}

Music and Songwriting
for Closure at End-of-Life

Amy Clements-Cortes

"SHARON" WAS A FORTY-YEAR-OLD FEMALE diagnosed with breast cancer that had metastasized. She had two small children. When Sharon became progressively more ill, she and her family moved back to Canada from the United States so she could be closer to her extended family. When I met her she was a paraplegic and suffered from facial palsy, poor hearing, and diminished vision as a result of the metastasis. Sharon was initially very optimistic about her illness and wavered between thinking she was going to recover and realizing that she might not. She expressed her feelings through a song written for her children, and this also served her goal of wanting to leave something special behind . . .

Through song choice, lyric discussion and improvisation, Sharon identified feelings about her illness and expressed the anger that she felt. Additionally, the music helped her reminisce about important events and times in her life.

The use of songs written by clients provide rich data and the songs are meaningful to those who compose them and the song recipients. I am blessed to have been part of these processes. I do feel that through my engagement in this research project I have learned more about the importance of relationship completion at the end-of-life, and I am becoming increasingly aware of the need for members of the palliative care team to help clients with this issue. In bringing information about relationship completion to the forefront for music therapists and the palliative care team, we as health care workers, may begin to better understand how we can truly help our clients at this very important stage of life. It is my belief that we must devote attention to end-of-life, much in the same way that we devote attention to life's beginnings.

AMY CLEMENTS CORTES, Ph.D., Mus.M., BMT, MTA
is a Senior Music Therapist at Baycrest, Toronto.
WWW.NOTESBYAMY.COM

An After School Theatre Programme

Community, Hope, and Transformation
for a Hard of Hearing Student

Theresa Webber, George Belliveau, and Graham W. Lea

With My Hands I Can

With my hands I can
Fly a plane,
Pluck a guitar,
Shout,
Tell a story,
            Cry…

With my hands I can
Frown,
Dance,
Smile,
Take a chance…
Tell me what you can do with
your Voice?

By Maria Grace Okwara (as quoted in Adams and Rohring, 2004, p.75)

T HIS CHAPTER EXPLORES in a case study the experiences of 'Lisa[1]' a student with severe to profound hearing loss, in a high school drama program and musical, exposing her pitfalls and triumphs while investigating the role of language on her participation and

---

1. All names, including that of the school, are pseudonyms.

non-participation within these communities. The study draws from an extensive open-ended interview with Lisa and the reflections of the first author. At the time of the interview, Lisa was a nineteen-year-old college student who graduated from Carson High School two years earlier. She attended Carson for grades 11 and 12 after having been home schooled for her grade 10 year. The interview was conducted in person (at Lisa's request) in a park near her home.

Bourdieu (1991) places great credence on not only words spoken but on the person who speaks them. He brings to light the social dynamics at play during communication – the power of one's words is accredited to the value given to the person speaking them. Therefore, if a person is unrecognised, her words are not heard, regardless of their value. This creates a great dilemma for the hard of hearing person who must find membership within a hearing world before she may contribute to it. One must negotiate this power through the use of language (Norton, 2000) but before power can be negotiated, it has to be imagined. Anderson (1991) coined the term "imagined communities" in the political context defining nationalism as a product of our imaginations, largely due to the fact that a sense of community is created amongst a group of people who will never meet. Their connection is a creation of the mind. Pavlenko and Norton (2007) adapt imagined communities to the study of second language learners. They discuss the inequitable access to cultural communities – the legitimate membership of second language learners into the target community is sometimes never achieved due to the invisible nature of minorities within the dominant group (the *unimagined* membership). Education researchers Dagenais (2003) and Kanno (2003) explore the role of schools and parents in the creation of imagined communities. It is integral for a society to imagine the future collectively in order for dreams to shift from the mind to reality; the hearing world must dream for the inclusion of a deaf and hard of hearing community. For community to be created, the dominant group must dream *with* the non-dominant group, creating a third space (Gutiérrez, Baquedano-Lopez, & Tejeda, 1999).

Lisa's experience in Carson High School's drama program offered the opportunity for the emergence of this third space. As such, drama functioned not necessarily as a methodology but as a space offering possibility, hope, and transformation for Lisa.

Within the deaf and hard of hearing community, a movement has emerged, in which many positioned themselves as a cultural linguistic minority as opposed to a group of people deficient due to a sensory loss. In the 1980s, Carol Padden, a deaf activist, fought for the definition of "culture" to include the deaf community, but membership was not determined simply by one's inability to hear; rather, it was determined by one's *ability* to use sign language (Adams and Rohring, 2004). Socially, young hard of hearing individuals often suffer from severe loneliness and isolation due to a lack of communication with their hearing peers. One study noted that "deaf students in the mainstream frequently reported not being invited to parties and other social events attended by their hearing peers" (Mertens, 1989 as quoted in Holcomb, 1996, p. 184). Upon reflection of his mainstream experience, one student in the study said, "I was feeling lonely because no one seems to ask me to participate" (Holcomb, 1996, p.191).

The arts have long been used as a process through which to develop community. In Lowe's article, *Creating Community: Art for Community Development* (2000), a drama project is studied to understand its impact on participants. The community comes together to create a play, and through the process a collective identity is forged. The group of neighbours that were divided by culture, language, and age in Lowe's study were brought together with a shared interest in the arts, which gave them the opportunity to interact socially and develop relationships. Lowe posits that it is the arts that combat the isolation that is too often found in society.

Similarly, community may be developed as students create new roles for themselves both onstage and off in the production of high school theatre. This community development is not restricted to those working on-stage. As an integral member of the production team, a student working backstage can experience a great sense of satisfaction and value. Identities, as shown by Norton (1995, 2006), are continuously shifting; thercfore, society's prescribed identities are often limiting to a young person's complex and often contradictory perception of self. Through the creation of a drama production, young people learn that role negotiation both on and off the stage may transfer to role negotiation in real life.

Booth (2003) contends that theatre is essential in the education of young people because it teaches them that they are valuable contributors to society. A great deal of literature examines the influence of performance on the lives of the actors (Boal, 1995; Boehm et al, 2003; Conrad, 2005; Elam Jr., 1997; Gallagher, 2000; Gonzalez, 2006; Hatton, 2003; Heathcote, 1984; Lev-Aladgem & First, 2004; Lowe, 2000; Wolff, 1999), but more studies are needed on the people who work behind the scenes. Drawing on Booth's theory that participation in theatre and the tension that accompanies it teaches those involved that "everyone matters," (2003, p. 19) this chapter explores the experiences of Lisa as she searches for self-value and integration into the high school community while working backstage in a high school musical.

Before Carson

LISA BELIEVES THAT SHE WAS BORN HEARING and when "I got to be one and a half, my parents started to notice [my hearing loss] . . . And then by the time I was two and a half, three, I got my first

Webber · Belliveau ; Lea

hearing aids. I had a little bit of speech, but it wasn't much at all. I had speech therapy. I had walking therapy. Everything" (Participant interview).

Her parents decided to place her in a mainstream school rather than a school for the deaf and hard of hearing. To cope within a hearing classroom, Lisa developed strategies to keep pace with the other students. "I was always relying on lip reading skills. I would also rely on my ability to follow the leader, and go with what everybody else was doing. It was a lot of guessing" (Participant Interview). While the hearing students focussed on their learning and socialising, Lisa spent an enormous amount of energy simply trying to understand the many voices around her.

Her connection to the hearing world was threatened further when she experienced a sudden increase of her hearing impairment which led to a decrease in tolerance for sound. Her frustration levels increased, while her hearing aid gave her access to the hearing world and allowed her to participate within it, Lisa became incapable of using it at the level to which she had become accustomed.

Verbal communication became extremely difficult for Lisa. Sign language was finally introduced to her in grade nine and she was given an interpreter for two of her eight classes.

{270}

> It just opened up a whole new world for me, and I somehow . . . I understood the language . . . It was interesting because the minute that I met my interpreter and the minute she started signing, it was almost like a light went on in my head. It was like I understood. (Participant Interview)

Lisa was no longer expected to guess and follow the lead of others. She was given the opportunity to participate – to hear with her eyes and speak with her hands.

Sign language simultaneously connected her to the hearing world and kept her from it; sign language connected her to the deaf and hard of hearing world, yet she had no one other than her interpreter with whom to communicate in sign. Hovering between two incomplete communities, Lisa, with the support of her parents, elected to undergo surgery in order to be fitted with a cochlear implant in an attempt to hear. The implant essentially converts natural sound to electronic sound (Wilson et al. 1991). As a result, Lisa would have to relearn how to interpret sound at the age of fifteen. In an attempt to become a participating member of the hearing world, Lisa would first have to experience a complete disconnect from everything and everyone she once knew.

A cochlear implant isn't like regular hearing at all . . . the sounds are so different. I heard some with it. It's more that you have to train your brain how to hear with it. It would take me a while to decipher exactly what that sound was. So, like, for example, water running, I would have to be cognitive. I think the frustrating part for me was that I knew what water running sounded like. You know. It sounded so funny with a cochlear implant. It didn't sound like water running at all. It was noise . . . Everything was just noise. (Participant interview).

Lisa and her parents recognised that the process of re-learning to hear would be difficult. In an attempt to alleviate some of the ongoing challenges, Lisa was home schooled for her grade 10 year. During this time, Lisa was being trained to hear, and so did not have an interpreter. Her access to sign language was gone. She had high hopes that the cochlear implant would give her the gift of sound, but she was unprepared for the ironic silence that accompanied it and the painful emotional journey she would experience. Lisa needed to find an escape. Without her hearing aid, she had lost sound. With her cochlear implant, she heard only unrecognisable noise. Her escape from the silence was music.

I was lucky enough that I could hear music without my hearing aid . . . Yeah, that's what got me through, because that was the only thing I heard. Like, for ten months I could barely hear my parents' voices. [Music] was my way of getting through it. (Participant Interview)

Music gave her strength to persevere, foreshadowing what would help her to survive two years at Carson – the school musical.

After experiencing high levels of stress following her cochlear implant surgery and a year of home schooling, Lisa re-entered high school. The adjustments would be vast as Lisa would have to attend school without the use of her hearing aid for the first time and adjust to having an interpreter. However, Lisa's interpreter would not come without a cost. Because the school board had a limited number of available interpreters, she would have to change schools. Beyond being identified as the "deaf girl," Lisa would also have to develop strategies to cope with being the "new girl." Her imagined community (Pavlenko & Norton, 2007) was not going to offer automatic membership upon arrival.

With a great deal of stress, Lisa started grade eleven at Carson Secondary, located in an affluent multi-cultural neighbourhood in the lower mainland of British Columbia, Canada. The school has an approximate enrolment of 1200 students. A large part of the population is categorised as E.S.L. (English as a Second Language) learners. Among her other courses, Lisa was enrolled in Grade 11 English and drama classes taught by the first author.

Lisa's integration into the school was not smooth. The extent of her isolation was only revealed when her mother related her great concern over her daughter's severe loneliness and sense of isolation. She described Lisa spending her lunch hour hiding in the bathroom, crying, waiting for the miserable sixty minutes to end. In an attempt to avoid these painful lunch hours, Lisa's mother drove at least thirty minutes to school each day to pick up her daughter at lunch. As considerate as this gesture was, it would only exacerbate the problem. Lisa was painfully aware that she was not connecting to her peers in a meaningful way, but says that "it helped me knowing that I had somebody [the interpreter]. That I wasn't responsible for trying to figure everything out. Somebody was being my ears for me for once" (Participant Interview). She was connecting more than she had ever connected before.

Drama Class

DESPITE THESE COMMUNICATION BARRIERS, LISA attempted to succeed academically and make friends in a new school. This was particularly difficult in her drama class. For the majority of the class, Lisa was left to fend for herself without an interpreter in an environment that produced even greater obstacles than an academic class.

Lisa was not as comfortable with her drama interpreter, "Ellen" as she was with her English interpreter, Joan. Lisa explains why she felt distant with Ellen suggesting that "[Joan] was the person who introduced me to [sign language]. She was the person whose signing I had gotten so connected with. And to have someone else come in was hard" (Participant Interview). When Ellen left, Lisa appeared to become more socially involved, although great improvement was still needed. It was hoped that the lack of adult involvement would encourage her hearing peers to include her more fully.

As drama/theatre is a collaborative art, group work was a daily routine in the class. After discussing the theme or topic of the day, students would work in small groups to create scenes. Their scene work was inspired by group dialogue, and then the scene would take shape as movement and gestures were added. Music was occasionally used to add another sensory layer onto the performance. To facilitate her ability to participate in a verbally dominated curriculum, Lisa was asked to share with the class how to communicate with her most effectively. She was nervous, but agreed, telling her classmates that

> She needs to see you to "hear" you.
> She lip reads.
> If everyone speaks at once, it's difficult for her to follow along.
> If her back is turned and you need her attention, just tap her on the shoulder.
> She is capable of hearing some of what is said. She is not deaf.

By standing in front of the class to explain what could facilitate her participation, Lisa positioned herself as a leader. She turned the tables so that she was the person in power, self-representing, as opposed to accepting the imposed representation of "disabled deaf girl."

Lisa's approachability improved, but mainly on a superficial level. Students would talk to her when they shared an assignment together, but

> it was hard. It was really hard . . . I was just so awkward. I was angry, I think, a lot. I was very hurt and confused. It was such a hard year for me alone in grade 10, and I didn't really trust people. And I was still getting used to the fact that I could hear again. It was overwhelming for me to start a new school, that late too . . . Like, I knew people. I think people knew who I was. I was never bullied or anything like that. I was just kind of there. I was just there. (Participant Interview)

{273}

Lisa imagined herself as a person who contributed to life at Carson, not simply a person who sat on the outskirts, yet the other students did not recognise her as a person who had anything to offer. Lisa was viewed as a person who required assistance, but she was unable to construct an identity as a person who could offer assistance. How could Lisa independently integrate herself into the social world of Carson? The catalyst came in the form of the annual high school musical.

The School Musical

SOME OF THE STUDENTS WHOM Lisa identified as her imagined community belonged to the theatre department, so it seemed a logical choice to involve Lisa in some way in the school musical. She was asked if she would like to work backstage as a dresser, helping to organise costumes and assisting actors with quick dress changes. The position required a commitment that would involve rehearsals after school, including one Saturday, and six evening performances. When the drama teacher approached her with the invitation, she happily agreed to participate.

By coincidence, the parent in charge of costumes was also hearing impaired. While she had a very minor hearing loss in comparison to Lisa's, simply seeing another person wearing a hearing aid allowed Lisa to recognise that she was not alone. Furthering this, one of the directors of the musical also wore a hearing aid. Two adults with hearing impairments became, without realizing, role models for Lisa demonstrating that hard of hearing people could make valuable contributions to the world, even in a musical. As both role models held positions of high authority, all of the actors showed great respect to them and Lisa was able to witness them function in a hearing society, and follow their lead.

Theatre is a collaborative art in which all participants must work together to reach a common goal. If one person stepped away from the challenge, all would feel the effect. Actors needed to remember lines and dance choreography, stage crew needed to change set pieces, technical crew needed to control sound and light, musicians needed to work collaboratively with the singers, and dressers needed to ensure that each actor stepped on stage with exactly the right costume at exactly the right time. Lisa found the demands of working as a dresser were

{274}

> a good way to break through in the school . . . At the time I was so isolated from everything. And I just needed something that I could be involved with that was something that I could not focus on my problems and my feelings, and could just focus on something else for a change, and just get my mind off of everything. And, you know, it was just so nice to be able to help somebody else for a change. (Participant Interview)

Lisa became an essential part of the theatrical team. The actors, many of whom she identified as her imagined community, depended on her contributions. Lisa gained power by defining herself as helpful in the eyes of her peers. Her identity began to shift from someone who needed assistance to someone who offered assistance.

The assistance Lisa was able to offer extended beyond her duties as dresser to providing emotional support to the actors. As actors were usually anxious and nervous on performance nights, they became very dependent on their dressers to help them during high stress scenes. On opening night, the lead actress, who Lisa had been assigned to dress, suffered from a serious case of stage fright, hyperventilating backstage. The play could not start without her. The audience waited in anticipation, but the curtains did not open. The lead was in the dressing room desperately trying to regain her composure. "I was there for her. She almost fainted, right? . . . I was her dresser, and I was trying to calm her down, not to freak out. It was nice to be there" (Participant Interview).

Lisa witnessed a student in an extremely stressful situation, and she saw her emotionally breakdown. This showed Lisa that breaking under pressure can happen to anyone. Fear is a part of everyone's life. Fortunately, with the help of Lisa's consoling manner, the lead gathered her inner strength and performed magnificently. Throughout the production, Lisa witnessed mishaps: one girl broke her tap shoes, and microphones went missing. No longer on the sidelines, Lisa was part of the chaos: she witnessed, she consoled, she problem-solved, she laughed – she took part.

Lisa's work on the musical was rewarded by recognition from members of her imagined community. One of the actors was particularly appreciative of Lisa's efforts. When the production was over, she approached Lisa, presenting her with a gift to thank Lisa for her kindness. Lisa describes another instance in which

> one of the guys comes up to me and goes, 'You know, we're all going for bubble tea. You should come.' And, you know, this is a grade 12 guy asking me to come to something. I was flabbergasted. I wanted to scream inside. I was so happy. My mom was picking me up and I didn't want her to go all the way back, so I said, 'No, unfortunately, my mom is on her way. I can't make it.' And he goes, "Ah, that sucks. Another time.' And it was so funny, because I just felt connected with something there. And everybody treated me so nicely. The next night I asked [him], 'Oh how was bubble tea?' And he goes, 'Oh, it was great, but you should've been there.' It made me feel so good. I wish I did get the chance to thank him for that because it meant so much. (Participant Interview)

The simple gesture of a grade 12 boy helped Lisa feel connected. The continuous acknowledgement of her existence and the gratitude she received for her contributions by actors and crew members helped re-shape Lisa's identity. She was a significant member of the backstage crew. She was part of a team, part of a community.

No longer did Lisa need to hide in the bathroom; she became visible. Her strengths were seen, valued, acknowledged, and respected. Lisa made connections with her peer group; however, a few days of working on the school musical would not necessarily grant Lisa legitimate membership within her imagined community. But it did provide seeds of potential friendships.

Grade 12

In grade 12, with the encouragement of one of the actors, Lisa became a peer counsellor. Lisa proudly stated that "I think I was the first hard of hearing person at [Carson] to ever be a peer counsellor" (Participant Interview). As a peer counsellor, she was considered a mentor to grade 8s who were new to the school. This position provided Lisa the opportunity to expand on the leadership skills she gained from the school musical.

Lisa expanded her involvement in the musical during her grade 12 year by becoming a production assistant. She was delighted to be part of the team, acting as a leader to the backstage crew and supervising the costume crew. Lisa held meetings at lunch hour with volunteers, created a schedule of their shifts, and answered any necessary questions. She also worked collaboratively with a graduate from the previous year to supervise dressers on performance nights.

Working backstage in a musical is particularly difficult for a person with a hearing impairment. The limited light made it difficult for Lisa to lip read and many of her cues were sound cues (e.g.: a spoken line or the end of a song). Because Lisa was unable to hear the cues, she was forced to ask for help. She understood that performing well as a head dresser would situate her as capable in the eyes of her peers. Therefore, she asked questions and found answers; she reviewed the script; she memorised songs; she watched the backstage monitor; she read the scene orders posted backstage. She took initiative in her interactions with other people, no longer waiting for someone else to begin dialogue. She did everything she could to ensure her success.

{276}

Backstage, many of the crew members would get up and dance to their favourite songs in the musical. Lisa always joined in dancing to music that she could only partially hear. The repetition of rehearsals and performances allowed Lisa to not only participate in the backstage dancing, she was able to lead. Lisa could watch each night, follow the pattern, and begin to predict the events. The performance was the same every night, so she began to learn during which scenes everyone would get up and dance. After a couple of nights, she was the first to participate.

Despite her efforts, Lisa would occasionally get lost or confused. This is when two actors, "John" and "Alan," in particular reached out. "[They] knew some sign so sometimes when I didn't understand something, they would finger spell, or they would sign what they knew to me . . . . They knew some and it was amazing" (Participant Interview). Lisa knew that for the musical to be successful she would have to take initiative in her interactions. Similarly, John and Alan understood the necessity of Lisa having the correct information; without it, she may not perform her job properly, which would in turn affect them. As a result, they were willing to take the risk of signing poorly if it meant that Lisa would receive the information. The power dynamics shifted.

The hearing students had to learn how to communicate with a hard of hearing person, as opposed to the other way around. Lisa was thrilled to learn that she could share her language with two of the actors. Their acknowledgement of sign language was an acknowledgement of her identity.

After School

After high-school, Lisa continued her peer counselling role, becoming involved in a buddy program in which she works with deaf and hard of hearing children. She visits a child for two to four hours once a week, spending quality time with one another while signing. The mentoring Lisa provides benefits the parents as well as the deaf or hard of hearing child. The parents are given exposure to a young adult who has already encountered and survived much of what the child will likely experience, providing parents exposure to the deaf and hard of hearing community which they may not have otherwise.

Lisa also worked as a camp counsellor for deaf and hard of hearing children during the summer. Her experience working at the camp reinforced her decision to pursue social work at university. Lisa praised the opportunity to work with the deaf and hard of hearing children at the camp suggesting that "it was the best experience of my life so far. I really enjoyed it" (Participant Interview). The other staff members were all deaf, so for the first time, Lisa was able to immerse herself in a community of people who communicated with sign language.

Lisa has had social work as a career goal for many years, but her latest experiences have altered her plans. She had previously wanted to work with youth at risk, but now she would like to work within the deaf and hard of hearing community. She applied and has been accepted into a social work program at a university which caters to deaf and hard of hearing students.

Lisa credits the after school drama program for the shift in her sense of self

> Having drama there, it made me feel like, okay, I'm not alone. There are other people
> out there. Maybe we won't ever be the best of friends, but it's just nice to know that
> there's someone else there . . . I think that's what started me on so much more . . . If
> I didn't have that, I'm not sure everything else would have followed . . . It changes
> your life. (Participant Interview)

When Lisa learned that she had meaningful contributions to make within the hearing world, it gave her the confidence to seek the deaf and hard of hearing world; it was no longer a community she was forced to take part in, it became a community that she chose. Lisa voiced her gratitude to the drama program which taught her that she can successfully and meaningfully participate among fully hearing people. She does not romanticize her experience by suggesting that she made lifelong friendships, but recognises that being a part of the school musical changed her life by acting as a stepping stone.

> I think [the drama program] taught me for the first time in a really long time that I could do things. I could belong and I was important. I felt that when I dressed all those people, and I did a good job at it, and people were telling me that, I felt like I was part of it. I felt like I'm not invisible. I do exist here. It gave me that much more confidence to be a peer counsellor. It gave me that much more confidence to be in the school, to want to go to school. I fully admit, grade 11, I skipped. I hated it. I did not want to be in school. There wasn't anything that anybody could have done at that point, until the drama came along . . . to make me stay. I just did not want to be there, but then knowing that I had responsibilities, knowing that people were counting on me. Me! Knowing that it was me that was important, and not everyone could do what I was doing. It made me feel special. (Participant Interview)

After graduating, Lisa continued to take part in the school musicals, returning to the production team as Carson alumni. Because the program was so beneficial to her development, Lisa committed to helping other young people find a place to belong through theatre at Carson. By continuing to volunteer, she reinforces her self-value, and is able to help other students who may be experiencing school in the same way to feel part of a community, passing on to others what she has gained.

> I think that's why I wanted to come back and help so much. It helped me so much. Good memories. It really taught me that, I don't know, we're not all alone in high school. It looks like we are, but there's a lot of people there who just feel the same way. (Participant Interview)

Because theatre is a collaborative art requiring the participation of many, a community is formed. Making theatre has the potential to shift identities, create relationships, and build communities. Through theatre, Lisa was no longer alone and is helping to show others that they too are not alone.

This program, drama . . . I think more kids deserve something like that . . . Everybody just wants to feel like they belong somewhere . . . high school can be, it can be the hardest place in the world . . . It's hard to feel confident in who you are when everyone's telling you who you should be. (Participant Interview)

Throughout Lisa's time at Carson and her years since, she has envisioned multiple communities for herself: the school musical, the theatre company, peer counselling, college, a deaf and hard of hearing university, and social work. Having found access to these communities, Lisa envisions another imagined community in which her parents communicate with her through sign language; however, she doesn't "think that they realise that it's that important to me" (Participant Interview). She emphasized that she does not blame them for their choices but believes that if her parents were able to communicate with her in sign language, it would symbolise their acceptance of her identity as a hard of hearing person. Just as Lisa's parents shared Portuguese and Italian with her in order to give her a piece of their identities, she too would like to share her language in order to share a piece of her identity.

Conclusion

LISA'S HEARING LOSS HAS EXCLUDED HER from groups for a multitude of reasons. Hearing students did not know how to communicate with her. To overcome this, Lisa needed to learn the importance of initiating. She needed to educate those around her, and she will likely have to do this for the rest of her life. It is a reality of her hearing loss; therefore, it is essential for teachers to help equip students with the necessary skills to do this. Opportunities for education and leadership must be opened to deaf and hard of hearing students. Teachers have the power to create opportunities, but it is ultimately up to the student to use them.

Bourdieu (1991) and Miller (2002) argued that a person must be recognised as a legitimate member by the target community before being granted full license to operate within that community. Prior to her experience in the musical Lisa was invisible to her hearing peers because they were unable to recognise her communication practices. It would require a great risk on the part of hearing students such as John and Alan, who are situated comfortably as members of a dominant culture, to enter into a dialogue in which they are unaware of the rules. Hard of hearing students need to be educated on the insecurities that exist around them, not only within them.

Because Lisa displayed communication practices that situated her as "other," she was not viewed as a legitimate owner of English. Norton (1997) quotes Leung, Harris and Rampton as saying, "there is an abstracted notion of an idealised speaker of English from which ethnic and linguistic minorities are automatically excluded" (p. 123). If Lisa could not claim ownership of English, and her fluency in sign language was somewhat limited, in what culture or linguistic community could she be accepted?

Assuming Bourdieu's argument to be true, one's words are only valued if the speaker is valued, the teacher then has to investigate ways in which to provide value to the hard of hearing student in the eyes of the target community. The student needs to be given a position of public leadership. It is necessary that this position is recognised, because recognition raises the awareness of cultural difference. In addition, it promotes the value of the individual's voice on a large scale. Presenting a hard of hearing student with a position of power and leadership is not enough. When considering the potential discomfort involved for a hearing individual to approach one with a hearing loss, the meeting of the two is unlikely to take place unless the exchange is necessary, when the person in power has needed symbolic or material resources.

Lisa's job as a dresser provided a clear position of leadership. The actors communicated with her out of necessity in order to enter the stage prepared, her symbolic resources included the comfort and reassuring words she offered to highly anxious and nervous actors during performance, and finally she participated with a larger group to achieve the collective dream of a successful theatrical production.

Lisa moved from seeking symbolic power to giving symbolic power (friendship) because she imagined the possibility. She saw herself as being capable and helpful, yet she needed her hearing peers to recognise this in her before she was able to contribute to this community.

Making theatre is not only a construction of a story, it is the construction of a new reality. When Lisa became a necessary figure in the production of multiple musicals, she became part of a culture which values the contributions of a hard of hearing person. Her contributions were not fictional. She was no longer invisible – she was an integral part of the play-making process. She found a legitimate way to participate in her school.

When she could not hear the music, Lisa danced. When she could not hear the words, she signed. Theatre, at its best, is social dreaming, on the stage, behind the scenes, in the audience, and outside the theatre walls. Reality is limited only by the dreams we dream together.

THERESA WEBBER has an MA from the Department of Language and Literacy Education at the University of British Columbia. She heads the theatre program at Magee Secondary in Vancouver, Canada, where she also taught English for many years. She, in collaboration with a committee of teachers, originated the Leaders cohort program at Magee.

GEORGE BELLIVEAU, Ph.D. is Associate Professor in the Faculty of Education at the University of British Columbia where he teaches undergraduate and graduate courses in Theatre/Drama Education. His research interests include research-based theatre, drama and social justice, drama across the curriculum, and Canadian theatre. His co-authored book with Lynn Fels, *Exploring curriculum: performative inquiry, role drama and learning* (2008) is published by Pacific Educational Press. He is also an Advisory Board Memeber for The International Journal of Creative Arts in Interdisciplinary Practice, IJCAIP.

GRAHAM W. LEA has an MA in Theatre Education from the University of British Columbia. He has presented and published on research-based theatre, theatre and additional language learning, Prince Edward Island theatre history, and Shakespeare in elementary classrooms. He has extensive experience as a theatre practitioner both on and off the stage.

References

ADAMS, J. W. & Rohring, P. S. (2004). *Handbook to Service the Deaf and Hard of Hearing: A Bridge to Accessibility.* San Diego, California: Elsevier Academic Press.

ANDERSON, B. (1991). *Imagined Communities: Reflections on the Origin and Spread of Nationalism.* New York, N.Y.: Verso.

BOAL, AUGUSTO. 1995. *The rainbow of desire: The Boal method of theatre and therapy.* Trans. Adrian Jackson. London: Routledge.

BOEHM, A., & Boehm, E. (2003). Community Theatre as a Means of Empowerment in Social Work: A Case Study of Women's Community Theatre. *Journal of   Social Work*, 3(3): 283-300.

BOOTH, D. (2003). Towards an Understanding of Theatre for Education. In K. Gallagher & D. Booth (Eds.), *How Theatre Educates: Convergences and Counterpoints with Artists, Scholars, and Advocates.* Toronto, Ontario: University of Toronto Press.

BOURDIEU, P. (1991). *Language and Symbolic Power* (G. Raymond & M. Adamson, Trans.). Cambridge, Massachusetts: Harvard University Press.

CONRAD, D. (2005). Rethinking 'at-risk' in drama education: beyond prescribed roles. *Research in Drama Education*, 10(1), 27-41.

DAGENAIS, D. (2003). Accessing imagined communities through multilingualism and immersion education. In Y. Kanno & B. Norton (Eds.), Imagined communities and educational possibilities [Special issue]. *Journal of Language, Identity, and Education*, 2(4), 269-283.

ELAM, JR., J.J., (1997). *Taking It to the Streets: The Social Protest Theatre of Luis Valdez   and Amiri Baraka.* Ann Arbor: The University of Michigan.

GALLAGHER, K. (2000). *Drama Education in the Lives of Girls: Imagining Possibilities.* Toronto: University of Toronto Press.

GONZALEZ, J. B. (2006). *Temporary Stages: Departing from Tradition in High School Theatre Education*. Portsmouth, NH: Heinemann.

GUTIÉRREZ, K. D., Baquedano-Lopez, P. & Tejeda, C. (1999). Rethinking Diversity: Hybridity and Hybrid Language Practices in the Third Space. *Mind Culture, and Activity*, 6(4), 286-303.

HATTON, C. (2003). Backyards and Borderlands: some reflections on researching the travels of adolescent girls doing drama. *Research in Drama Education, 8*(2), 139-156.

HEATHCOTE, D. (1984). Teachers and Teaching. In L. Johnson and C. O'Neill (Eds.), *Dorothy Heathcote: collected writings on education and drama*. London: Hutchinson.

HOLCOMB, T. K. (1996). Social Assimilation of Deaf High School Students: The Role of School Environment. In I. Parasnis (Ed.), *Cultural and Language Diversity and the Deaf Experience* (pp. 181-198). New York: Cambridge University Press.

KANNO, Y. (2003). Imagined communities, school visions, and the education of bilingual students in Japan. In Y. Kanno & B. Norton (Eds.), Imagined communities and educational possibilities [Special issue]. *Journal of Language, Identity, and Education, 2*(4), 285-300.

LEV-ALADGEM, S. & First, A. (2004). Community Theatre as a Site for Performing Gender and Identity. *Feminist Media Studies, 4*(1), 38-50.

LOWE, S.S., (2000). Creating Community: Art for Community Development. *Journal of Contemporary Ethnography*, 29(3), 357-386.

MILLER, J. (2000). Language Use, Identity, and Social Interaction: Migrant Students in Australia. *Research on Language and Social Interaction*, 33(1), 69-100.

NORTON, B. (1997). Language, Identity, and the Ownership of English. *TESOL Quarterly*, 31(3), 409-422.

NORTON, B. (2000). *Identity and language learning: Gender, ethnicity and educational change*. Harlow, England: Longman/Pearson Education.

NORTON, B. (2006). Identity: Second language. In K. Brown (Ed.), *Encyclopedia of language and linguistics,* Volume 4 (2nd ed.) (pp. 502-508). Oxford, England Elsevier.

NORTON PEIRCE, B. (1995). Social Identity, Investment, and Language Learning. *TESOL Quarterly*, 29(1), 9-31.

PAVLENKO, A., & Norton, B. (2007). Imagined communities, identity, and English language teaching. In C. Davison & J. Cummins (Eds.), *International Handbook of English Language Teaching.* Netherlands: Kluwer Academic Publishers.

WILSON, B., FINLEY, C., Lawson, D., Wolford, R., Eddington, D., and Rabinowitz, W. (1991). Better speech recognition with cochlear implants. *Nature*, 352(18), 236-238.

WOLFF, D. (1999). Drama Behind Barbed Wire. In Rovit & Goldfarb (Eds.), *Theatrical Performance during the Holocaust.* (pp. 145-150). Baltimore: The Johns Hopkins University Press.

PART 4

Narrative and Story

To be Human with Other Humans

A Caregiver's Narrative

Susan K. MacRae

FOR THE PAST EIGHTEEN YEARS, in my role as a nurse, a clinical ethicist, the Deputy Director of the largest ethics centre in Canada and now as a transpersonal psychotherapist, I have increasingly come to understand the power of narrative as a form of healing.

For many years, I have personally experienced a powerful relief in the expression of my own stories. Perhaps these stories are powerful because they challenge the oppressive flatland and scientific efficiency that still defines healthcare despite many knowing that caregiving is an endeavor of human capacity. Perhaps the power of these stories is in acknowledging that I am not a robot and that the human, emotional, psychological, and spiritual dimensions of what I do are key if I want to be fully present as a caregiver.

Narrative as an art in health has far more potential for hope and change than simply a personal healing or confession. This became obvious when I started speaking these narratives in small groups and at large conferences over six years ago. I received standing ovations, and fearful confrontations from clinicians (who I imagined had been triggered into their own guilt, shame or fear of caregiving) and I realized that the narratives were giving people space to release tension and address unresolved experiences in their own practice. Forgotten and forbidden content was allowed to breathe.

When I started the narrative ethics group at the University of Toronto's Joint Centre for Bioethics, I began to understand that such narrative practice allowed a more robust and deeper human inquiry to emerge beneath the layers of intellectual dialogue about ethical issues in healthcare. The layers of reality that a narrative exploration uncovered added significantly, in my opinion, to the intellectual discussions we were having as clinical ethicists on notions of right and wrong.

Narrative is a form of peeling back beneath the ideas of what is happening in the external world of healthcare to reveal more of the internal world of caregiving. We know, for example, very little about the internal action of caregivers and what motivates them, what inspires them, what shuts them down and what causes them to leave the healthcare setting all together. We still understand very little of people who endure sickness and even less about those who care for them.

What is missing is the inquiry into the "I" and the "We" beyond the massive "It" that runs the mechanics of healthcare.

So this paper is a qualitative research endeavor of personal experience and "meaning making" in my own case. I reflect on and share a story made up of a series of shorter stories (taken from my own journals) that describe some of my experiences as a caregiver. My goal with this effort is to share these narratives and my own journey of "meaning making" (up to this point) in the hopes that perhaps they may spark one or two or ten other clinicians to tell their own stories and begin to bridge the intense isolation that I think is a tragic as well as inevitable part of the caregiver's experience. Maybe by telling these stories we may find something in our own individual and collective experiences that will lead us to deeper resources and directions that at this moment may not be obviously available to us. This has certainly been true in my own case. And since many of the narratives I use in this article are from my experience as a student nurse, I particularly hope that these stories may support students beginning clinical practice and provide a model for them to express and validate their inner experiences in their early training. I share these stories most importantly because I hope this dialogue enriches the discussion around a comprehensive understanding of what it truly means to be a caregiver.

So let me begin my story.

As a clinician, while my colleagues concerned themselves with diagnosing and treating disease, I instead found myself fascinated with relationship. In my thirteen years in clinical practice, I became increasingly interested in what actually takes place in the known and felt experience of those who are sick and facing life-threatening illness and those who care for them and how they relate to one another.

Like most clinicians, I have deep within me an impulse to serve, to help people, to make people feel better, to feel better in myself, to give, and most fundamentally to get to the bottom of something about what living has to do with Wellness or Peacefulness or Happiness. I want to be a "good" nurse.

So early on in my clinical training as a nurse, I reveled in relationship with others – my patients and my colleagues. Intuitively it seemed like the foundational basis for all healing and caring. But nothing could have prepared me for the actual experience of relationship that I encountered once I entered the clinical years. Relationships in that instance came with a bizarre, almost alien and disappointing feel to them. I spent a lot of time trying to get to the bottom of what a healing clinician-patient relationship looked like in healthcare so I could be good at the thing that mattered to me most. But it was challenging.

As my training progressed I noticed more about relationships. My relational contact seemed to circle around medications, equipment, laundry, schedules, staff availability and incidents of one form or another. I soon realized that there was nearly no time built into the clinical routine for connectable human time with patients and even less for families. In that context, miraculously some clinicians still found a way to engage, while other didn't bother. And in response to this hectic pattern, some patients became fearful and demanding while others shut down, asking for nothing. I knew in my gut that contact, trust and relationship between people had to be a key to healing somewhere but soon learned I had no clue how to be a good caregiver or how to navigate these relationships in this context. So I watched and listened to those around me for guidance.

"Don't let them get to you," a resident once said to me on a night shift, when a patient of mine, riddled with head and neck cancer, exsanguinated – bright red blood pulsating across the room through her trach. The resident pushed me up to her face saying "Talk *to* her". I mumbled, "It will soon be over my dear, soon be over." I think it may have been that same resident who, shortly after the patient died, brought me into the coffee room for a few moments before his "code" beeper went off again. "Don't let them get to you," he said. And then touched me briefly on the right shoulder, almost connecting but not quite, and then spun around and left me under the fluorescent lights in a room smelling of burnt coffee.

Don't let them get to you? It seemed like bizarre advice under the circumstances.

When I arrived home my father asked, "How was your work last night honey?" I stood at the bottom of the stairs before heading for the dark basement where I would block out the light of the sun so I could fool my body into thinking it was night time. That morning, I was aware for the first time of the gap that existed between those of us who do this kind of work, and those of us who don't. It was also the moment that I began to realize the amount of distress, pain and intense suffering that I was being asked to bear and endure in my role as caregiver.

Ann was eighteen, and she had been driving in a car after a party with her boyfriend. She had been drinking a little. She swerved on the road to miss a raccoon and crashed into a telephone pole, killing her partner Brad, who had been riding in the front seat beside her. She had spent several days unconscious in the ICU and when she came to my unit she was covered in bruises from head to toe, bones all over her body had been smashed leaving her body swollen and sore to touch. She faded in and out of consciousness because of the amount of drugs that she took for pain. I cared for Ann for two weeks as her primary nurse and each time she would awaken she would inquire about her boyfriend. I lied to her forty times. I lied to her because her doctor and lawyer had strictly instructed me not to inform her that Brad had been killed, to allegedly protect her from the tragic news while she was still so terribly unwell.

On Friday April 14th, 1991, I met a policemen and her doctor coming out of Ann's room as I returned from my coffee break. Both of their faces were fierce and hard and when I asked them what was going on, the policeman informed me that he had just told Ann that she was facing manslaughter charges for Brad's death. "Did you know that she didn't even know that Brad had died?", I said to the doctor. He paused and said, "Oh well, she should have thought of that before she drank those beers." I fell backwards to lean against the wall and hit instead a metal cart, my weight knocking some stacked blue absorbent towels onto the floor. "Better clean up that mess", the doctor said to me. I stood outside the door a deep trembling starting somewhere in the lower half of my body and then felt a suffocating tightening all the way to my throat. I was falling and no one was going to catch me.

"Don't let them get to you"

EMILY'S FECES WERE THE FIRST THING I remembered about her. That morning I surprised myself with the insight that it had taken very little time in my role as a student nurse to get used to seeing other people's feces. Shit was an inevitable part of nursing, I realized, and some part of me just accepted that. Seeing someone else's feces was as commonplace now as seeing the naked human body. When I first saw Emily, she was lying in her own crap and she had smeared it, in the fifteen minutes or so before I arrived into her room, on everything within her limited paralyzed reach, including into her mouth and all over her face. When I found her, my initial reaction was disgust. But as I turned to look into her face, I was drawn into her joy with the whole experience of it. "Look what I've done!" she seemed to say proudly, (in a world where I can do so little). My disgust eased into a strange sense of compassion and I began to laugh.

From behind me, a large voice boomed over this intimacy, as Emily's primary nurse arrived. "Emily, you are a disgusting pig," she said. As the nurse grabbed Emily's wrists, and tied them tightly in cotton gauze to the bedrail, her smile faded into shock, sadness, and humiliation. Emily was sobbing. "Shut up Emily," the nurse said "you did this to yourself." The nurse then turned to me coldly and said, "Come on, get a basin, and clean up this shit."

"Don't let them get to you"

AS A STUDENT NURSE, my first impression of some other nurses was that the valve inside them that controlled expression or human emotion was nearly shut off.

MacRae

We had been told in the morning during our orientation to this new unit, that the far hallway of the unit was where they did abortions. "Some of them are 2nd trimester abortions requiring an actual labour so don't be surprised if you hear screaming," my clinical supervisor said calmly. We were then given our clinical assignments and released to the unit to find our patients. Later that morning, looking for a washbasin to help my patients wash up, I walked into the clean utility room. There directly in front of me, on the steel waist high table lie about a twenty-six-week-old fetus gasping for air in a round silver washbasin. His small round belly was shiny and taught as he pounded for air – filling and collapsing as his fists weakly pounded on either side of the cold basin. I met his struggle in utter disbelief , my mind racing back and forth. I don't now remember my other reactions. I only remember turning around and walking out.

Moments later I met my instructor in the hall. "There is a dying baby in there you know," I said to her as she came closer to me. She looked behind me into the sterile room full of supplies and cold empty basins. "Oh," she said. "Yeah, like I told you, that's what happens here." And then she just turned and walked away.

"Don't let them get to you"

{291}

THE EXPERIENCES FROM MY EARLY DAYS as a nurse were not always tragic. They could be equally intense however.

I remember Ben more clearly than any other patient I cared for. Ben had asked me to help him die. Squirming in pain from post polio syndrome, we cared together for his paraplegic body day in and day out for months. For the first few weeks, he would ask me for extra medication to put him out of his misery. "For all I care," he said, "You can smash me over the head with a hammer." I don't remember doing anything special for Ben but something in our relating was noticeably different than it was with other patients. At first it was just a connection that was based on regular contact, care, and communication. This was a far cry from the usual dissociated busyness that occupied most of my days in the split second encounters my shift schedule allowed for me. Without any additional effort, Ben and I found something in our relating – a way to be together in our different roles. I eased his suffering in the only ways I knew how. It was a job we shared. Without realizing it or preparing for it, I found what I had always been looking for – a real healing relationship.

When I told Ben that I was leaving for a year to travel, which meant I would no longer be his primary nurse, the last words he said to me were "I will wait for you before I die."

In the end Ben waited one year to die. He passed away quietly in his sleep one week after I returned from my trip.

"Don't let them get to you!"

SOME MOMENTS OF CAREGIVING DELIVER me to a place bigger than myself – perhaps to a place where we all share something transcendent and beyond everyday reality.

I remember doing a dressing change for a large abdominal wound on this jolly janitor patient who always lifted my spirits with his inquiring curiosity. He was the kind of man who could make every moment last longer than it really did. I remember he said, "Stop! Look! Sue . . . No, I mean really look!" This man I cared for, his abdomen now healing from a wound six inches deep and eight inches wide that took three hours to dress each morning, said "Can you believe this body? It's fucking amazing. It's healing all by itself. I'm not doing anything." My face covered up to my nose with a mask, he looks into my eyes and calls me to his world. I look . . . and then I say, "Wow.""It is amazing! "Hmmm, **we** are amazing!"

Let them get to you!

IF THERE WAS LITTLE TIME BUILT IN for contact with patients and families, there was no time whatsoever dedicated to peer discussions about the emotional, psychological and spiritual challenges that were a regular part of this work. Instead I was told by my colleagues not to take things personally. I was told not to be weak. I was told not to be so sensitive and emotional. I was told, *Don't let them get to you.*

But what if they did? And they did. Then what?

I could cope with the busy schedule, and the regular stress of the busy job, but I couldn't find an outlet for my inner feelings that were trying to make sense of this intense, unusual world. I soon found out that I couldn't talk about my vulnerability and I had no outlet to express myself. Eventually, I gave up looking for that experienced mentor because he or she did not exist. Instead, I learned to keep such things to myself. In fact, I did more than that. I started to believe that I was too sensitive, too emotional, too "something" and maybe wasn't cut out for this work. I eventually started to doubt my own inner moral compass and stopped believing in myself.

I felt morally abandoned. I called it moral abandonment because the abandonment of my inner experience felt like a dismissal at some core level of human goodness – It seemed like defamation of what I felt was an obvious requirement in the caregiving guild – a necessary capacity

MacRae

to feel ourselves and others and be *with* suffering. But more often than not, the inner world of self and other was dismissed. And this dismissal had an impact. All the caregivers around me were experiencing significant amounts of stress, many of them coping with unacceptable levels of suffering in a field that is supposed to be about healing and well-being. There were no offerings of support. I couldn't help but think if all caregivers continued to abandon each other in this way and no other forms of support were offered, in the end this could lead to a dismissal of the importance of moral and relational inner life all together.

And it had only taken a few years out of my university training to find that my job had become about survival as I tried to deal with feeling victimized, helpless, powerless, heartbroken, angry, and shut down. Finally that same cool clinical objectivity I resented in those clinicians took over and left me with a vicarious coldness that seemed unnatural to my own heart. The "Don't let them get to you," had succeeded in my own case, but I was still aware enough to know that the cost it carried was enormous.

I decided to "get away" and take a break and go traveling. I didn't know where my career in nursing would take me; I just knew I wanted to leave it for a while.

That was when I began writing. For a year, I wrote in my journal about my experiences and relationships as a caregiver and stared to examine my own responsibility in what was happening to me. At first the memories were like a blur. Emotions and fragments of stories spilled out on the blank pages in my journal. But I remembered what a poetry teacher has once said to me "you have to write thousands of pages before your own story starts to tell itself." So I kept writing.

As I wrote the stories and told the stories to others over and over, at some point the art of storytelling and writing allowed me to reclaim aspects of myself that I had deeply buried. I started to write myself back into the meaning of my work. I started to reflect on the difference I had made and to remember moments in my work when I was engaged in healing at my best. I started to discover what being a nurse really meant to me.

Near the end of my travels I found myself walking off a street into a small rural hospital in Nepal and asking if there was anything I could do to help them. Once they discovered I was a nurse from Canada they asked me to "set up" and run a recovery room in their OR. No experience since has given such a clear caregiving perspective. The teaching I experienced there was that "real relationship" flows out of real life and that this flow can't hide away from anything. True caregivers walk through the middle of suffering in the best way we know how and sometimes the only support a person has is a nurse or a doctor. That clinician is a lifeline. The treatments, the pain relief, the techniques we offer are important. But the true power of this human to human relationship in caregiving comes from the simple truth that we all will get sick and die one day.

And somehow if caregivers can connect to the privilege of meeting a person who is sick or dying as part of this larger journey we are all taking together, then it is a journey that is most profound indeed.

Recovering in Nepal

I have found myself
working as a nurse
in the recovery room
in a hospital
in Nepal.

I just received a call
from one of the anesthetists
who told me they just
brought in a man
attacked
by a leopard.

Last week
it was
the missionary worker
whose hands were cut off
by the Maoists
and the tiny malnourished child
with a litre of pus
in her abdomen
with abscesses
of unknown cause.

Over an oxygen mask
I try to decipher
perhaps
the last few words

of a man
dying from cancer
of his voice box
and then
try to look at the floppy
stillborn baby
long enough
to send a few brief wishes.

The absurdity of it all
for me
can be summed up
by the amputated leg
left in a bucket
in the recovery room
for all the pre and post op
patients to see.

Meanwhile the doctors stand
ankle deep in blood in thongs
in the operating theatre
while patients share bloody gowns
 between them.

But for the first time
I honestly feel
deep in my heart
like a nurse!
Despite the excuse for technology,
the language barrier
the unlikelihood that
oxygen, electricity and water
would all be working at the same time,
I finally feel like I am making a difference.

MacRae

It is the being here that matters
nothing more!
Nothing more
than standing
eyes fixed on yours
appreciating and feeling grateful
for the relationship
we all share
in belonging here
in our shared humanity.

And when I leave the hospital
past the pile of garbage
where cows avoid the dirty needles
to eat cardboard,
I walk along the ridge
lined by the great Himalayas
and the deep gorges of the Seti river
where bodies burn on the banks,
And realize that there is space here
and room in between the birds
and the butterflies
that seem to stick to the air
that is invisible to the rest of us.

And as I think
of the tragic stories from the day
and see suffering all around me,
the children
playing on the road
run to my side
and hand me flowers
and say "hello" or "Namaste"

MacRae

or "What is your name?"

Motorcycles and
buses loaded with people
on the roof
honk as they go by each other
which wakes me up to a feeling that
mostly I don't know much more
than those cows eating cardboard
behind me
and my life could easily
dissolve into this moment
or any other.

But I do know
that there is an amazing beauty
in watching these moments
float by
into infinity
and to feel the longing
that tries to hold them here.
 And realizing that
the hardest thing in life
is that a broken heart
is the only way I seem to grow.

Just then
I run into a monk friend on the road and
ask him,
"What can we hang onto
when we're dying?

He says,
only one thing

No object
No person
No belief
Only,
"Your Goodness"

By the time I returned to Canada, my inquiry into "real relationship" had evolved beyond anything I had learned about the clinician- patient relationship in my training as a nurse or in my regular work-life. Deep inner reflection and narrative show me that "real relationship" happened in moments where I felt humble and grateful. It appeared in moments where there was a widening, a deepening, perhaps an opportunity, no matter where I was, to put more space around all the "doing". I realized that "real relationship" flowed out of a sense of awe when I stayed open to the possibility for transcendent moments that flow from simple activities, such as dressing changes and ordinary contact with patients – when I stayed open to my own heart's capacity for depth of relationship, love and compassion. But it is also required that I approach suffering differently. I've had to continue to learn how to stand in the middle of it with others and with myself and deepen in my capacity to bear it. And by realizing that suffering can't be ultimately overcome, I have had to find a bigger context to understand the human drama unfolding on the stage in new ways that doesn't ignore my vulnerable mortality.

When I eventually did leave nursing some years later it was for different reasons than I set out in my original decision of disengagement. I left nursing to go into clinical bioethics – a place where my interest in moral life and human relationship could become the focus of my work. This eventually led to my work in psychotherapy where I now deal almost exclusively with the inner inquiry of living.

My narrative work leads me to seek answers to the question, How can we stop driving empathetic, humane, compassionate, loving responses out of clinicians in the first place?

I believe it is time to create safe spaces for people to share their honest experiences with other colleagues who can support them and normalize these experiences – students, new grads and seasoned practitioners alike. We also need to share and gather collective wisdom about how to manage the challenges in healthcare from a place of practical wisdom that honours the self-evident experience of practitioners. And we need leaders who will support this.

We need to find better advice for our colleagues than "Don't let them get to you." We must allow each other the room and respect to face and process our experiences. We must heal ourselves long before we can hope to heal those we work with and care for.

Susan (Sue) MacRae, RN,. is a Registered Nurse and has been working in the field of patient centred care and clinical ethics consulting and program development for sixteen years. Her fellowship training at University of Chicago MacLean Center for Clinical Medical Ethics and at the Picker Institute in Boston positions Sue with a unique perspective that marries the needs and perspectives of patients with the views, responsibilities and duties of healthcare professionals and administrators. Until recently Sue was the Deputy Director at the University of Toronto Joint Centre for Bioethics (JCB) and during her seven year tenure there (2000-2007), was instrumental in forging its vision and ensuring the transformation of this centre into an internationally regarded organization. Sue is a champion of patient-centred ethics, narrative ethics and an innovator in building ethics and relationship centred competencies and capacity, a leader in scholarship in her work in clinical ethics program development and systems thinking and an innovator in education by virtue of her contributions to the growth of the highly acclaimed professional Masters of Health Sciences in Bioethics in Toronto. Sue was the lead on the narrative working group at the JCB: a group focused on encouraging clinicians and bioethicists to write about their experiences. These and other accomplishments have been formally acknowledged by the Joint Centre for Bioethics in 2007 with an endowed yearly lecture created in Sue's name on ethics and patient centred care. Sue currently works as a clinical ethicist at the Centre for Clinical Ethics, (a joint venture of Providence Healthcare, St. Joseph's Health Centre and St. Michael's Hospital) in Toronto promoting values integration in hospitals and runs her own psychotherapy consulting practice.

Creative New Directions in Dietetics Research and Education

A Voice for Change

Catherine Morley

M Y WORK COMBINES ORIGINAL and historical research in nutrition and dietetics, filmmaking, and textile arts. After twenty-five years of working as a registered dietitian in clinical care, public health, and as a consultant, I was moved to study textile arts at Capilano University (Cap U) in North Vancouver, British Columbia by the untimely death of a colleague, and because I was frustrated by what I experienced as a lack of opportunities for dietitians trained and with experience beyond entry level. While in the textile arts program, I learned about the newly-shortened Cap U documentary film program and decided to do both diplomas.

I was drawn to study textile arts and filmmaking to expand the reach of research findings. I wanted to find ways to share ideas and to invite collaborative connections with diverse audiences including individuals and families experiencing illness, dietitians and other health and human service workers, students, and decision makers to overcome the one-way flow of communication inherent in writing and making presentations.

My explorations are primarily in three areas: family dynamics related to eating and illness; dietetics education (particularly approaches to and evaluation of client-centred nutrition education, and training dietitians to participate in practice-based research); and historical studies of the food supply, the invalid's dietary, and training of dietitians. In the future I will use film and visual arts for online and installation multimedia presentations that invite others to contribute their experiences as a means of social comparison and mutual support. I am excited about the prospect of combining creative approaches in my work such as emerging film distribution approaches (e.g., online; house parties; People's Cinemas), virtual and installation textile works, collaborative art partnerships, and new forms of inquiry. My goal is to contribute to new understandings of approaches to training so that dietitians can better support the people with whom they work while ultimately stemming the loss of human capital in dietetics.

> CATHERINE MORLEY, PhD, RD, FDC has advocated for, and piloted innovations in dietetic education throughout her career, especially in the areas of nurturing critical reflectivity in practice, enhancing nutrition education and counselling skills, and building capacity for practice-based dietetic research.

Mapping Resiliency:
Building Bridges Toward the Future

An Experiential Arts-based
Narrative Inquiry with Dietetics Professionals

Jacqui Gingras, Jennifer Atkins

RESILIENCY HAS IMPLICATIONS for the way dietitians do their work and the relationships they cultivate. This research explored dietitians' experiences of resiliency in the context of their professional practice. The project enlisted dietitians in an experiential, narrative inquiry through use of a *Resiliency Map*. Three themes emerged: disconnection, workplace conflict, and relational resiliency, which were further informed by gender, emotionality, and burnout. These findings demonstrate the ways in which workplace stress remains mediated by relational contexts as informed by the organizational culture of the profession. Moreover, it demonstrates that loss of connection, conflict, and suppression of emotions limits capacity to build relational resilience. {303} There is a demonstrated need to constructively engage with these issues in the workplace. Fostering relational resiliency in professional practice could improve workplace outcomes for dietitians.

In this chapter, we discuss resiliency in dietetic practice as constituted by relational contexts and mediated by gender, emotionality, and the organizational culture of the profession; contexts that inform workplace stress, burnout, and work engagement. The current work builds on previous studies in the area by examining through experiential and arts-based methods the intersection between expectations for a career in dietetics as established by professional education and the experience of practice, namely those experiences of work stress, burnout, and resiliency.

This inquiry is informed by subjective and relational dimensions of dietetic identity as constituted through dietetic undergraduate education and further complicated by the exigencies of practice. Previous work indicates that dietetic student identity is influenced by discourses and perceptions of health and the body and that these perceptions shift and change as students progress through dietetic programs (Atkins & Gingras, 2009).

In an effort to privilege relational resilience and experiential ways of knowing we incorporated relational activity as a central method. Accordingly, a large floor map was used as an experiential means to elicit narratives of practice. The map was divided into concentric circles referring to self (the centre circle) in relation to emotions, family, community, and organizations (circles moving out from the middle). As participants walked over the map, an experienced map facilitator posed guiding questions that elicited personal and professional narratives. While this process was occurring, the other participants sat around the map as witnesses to the map narratives and were encouraged to contribute to the narratives when and/or if it felt meaningful.

As one of the participants remarked at the beginning of the first meeting, "That's my dream is to really give . . . a sense of, of what this work can be like, the emotionality, the relationality, [and] the political nature of it. The richness of it, it's incredibly rich. And so . . . what this circle for me represents is a coming together to share stories."

Along with using the map over the course of three separate meetings, participants engaged in artmaking activities in order to build rapport, establish trust, and explore symbolically/visually the impact of their work. The mapping method was an essential frame through which personal and professional narratives became woven together with experiential (embodied) truths and collective resilience regarding dietetic practice.

Dietetic theorists have claimed that dietitians' practice is organized around several key features; it is traditionally structured to privilege science-based epistemologies, it is constituted by professional nutrition discourse, and it neglects to acknowledge the emotionality of dietetic practice. Specifically, DeVault (1999) describes the professional training that dietetic students receive as a structure that produces isolation from families and communities so that students learn to suppress emotions. Liquori (2001) elaborates on this theory to describe the science-based and experiential types of knowledge that dietitians possess as being in competition with one another, which has implications for "how members of the profession learn their place in it and their value as women and men, practitioners and scientists" (p. 234). These pedagogical and professional contexts have implications for the way dietitians do their work, the challenges they face, and the resilience they cultivate in the process. This research was initiated to make visible these realities in a way that honoured the emotional aspects of dietetic beingness – a subject that has not received any significant attention in the past.

{304}

Background

A DIETITIAN'S BEING IS CONSTITUTED through educational and institutional regulation. That the dietitian's gendered body is performative, however, suggests that the dietitian has no being apart from the various acts that constitute her dietitian reality. These acts create a deliberate illusion that is maintained for the purposes of its own regulation (Butler, 1999). Dietitians are implicated by their practices; they are trained as expert purveyors of abstract nutrition knowledge and yet all are also subjects of that knowledge through the visible, everyday experience of eating. In other words, dietitians possess a clinical gaze as a direct result of their education and at the same time they exert self-scrutiny (self-surveillance) as a result of their affiliation and participation in a culture that values slimness, femininity, and compliance. Foucault (as quoted by Menzies Lyth, 2000) would claim that "the [dietetic] body is constructed by, shaped and reshaped by, the intersection of a series of disciplinary discursive practices" (p. 24). Consequently, there is much at stake for dietitians in making visible their bodily experiences of being.

Butler (1997) theorizes the subjection dietitians might experience if they come to make explicit their bodily experiences in relation to their work. Previous inquiry has determined the passion and commitment dietitians bring to their work, whereby their practice becomes the object of their love (Gingras, 2009). When the dietitian discovers that her passion for the object of dietetic practice is based on false promises, inevitably the dietitian experiences feelings of grief and loss (Gingras, 2009). Unresolved grieving of losing the object of their passion – loss of love for their practice – is related to profound feelings of sadness and melancholia. Dietitians describe these lived experiences as "spiritual injury" and "living death" (Gingras, 2009). If a dietitian believes that her identity is fixed, then she embraces her performativity as given and unchangeable; there is no effort expended to transform and *status quo* is preserved (Levinson, 2001).

This melancholic identity, however, does not necessarily preclude agency, but is in itself a potential site of subversion (Salih & Butler, 2004) since the melancholia inspires reflexivity when the subject "turns back upon itself" (Butler, 1997, p. 168). Melancholia contains the possibility of regenerated or renegotiated subjectivity, a dietitian being in-process.

The concept of resilience and agency is well documented in nursing and other social sciences (Wicks, 2006; Hodges, et al., 2005; Waddell & Bauer, 2005; McGillis Hall, et al., 2004; Kulig, 2000), but less so in dietetics. Since the origin of the concept in the nineteenth century (McAllister, & McKinnon, 2008) resiliency has taken on many varied definitions. Most commonly, resiliency is the ability to recover from traumatic experiences or to achieve good outcomes in one's life after experiencing significant hardships (Hartling, 2003).

Relatively recently, resiliency has transcended its former boundaries of child and youth-based inquiry to research with adults in various stages of health (Denez-Penhey, & Murdoch, 2008) and, as it relates to experiences of adults in their place of work (Jackson, Firtko, & Edenborough, 2007). This transition has been paralleled by a conceptual transition. The earlier focus on primarily individual-based characteristics and attributes of resilience whose perspective holds that resiliency is some "thing" that the individual possesses or not, has given way to an alternative view through

{305}

which, resiliency can be understood as a relational endeavour. Jordan (1992) thus reconceptualizes resilience as a fundamental human capacity that is developed through growth-fostering relationships; a position complemented by consideration of ecological factors that present both risks and protective measures in the pursuit of resilience (Masten & Powell, 2003).

Recent research (Denz-Penhey & Murdoch, 2008) suggests that there are five main factors which support adults in cultivating resilience: social connectedness, connectedness to family, connectedness to the physical environment, connectedness to experiential inner wisdom and, connectedness to a strong psychological self (p. 394). It has been argued that these dimensions remain true for health care professionals wishing to strengthen and sustain resilient responses to stress in their profession (McAllister, & McKinnon, 2008).

Methods

THIS ETHNOGRAPHIC PROJECT ENLISTED DIETITIANS in a reflexive, artistic, experiential exploration of self and other through use of *The Resiliency Map*. The map – originating from exploring resiliency with front-line AIDS workers, "is a 16'x16' floor blanket or quilt with concentric circles depicting self (centre), emotional reactions/relation to others (next circle), community /social networks (third circle) and the socio-political environments (outside circle)" (Perrault, n.d. p. 2). In the creation of the map, the red lines represented "life lines" that move participants between the realms of self, relationship, community, and then broader social realities.

During three separate, four-hour sessions, six female dietitians who had previously consented to participate were invited by an experienced facilitator to literally walk along the map's different circles as they explored and wove together various aspects of their personal (and by extension – professional) narratives of workplace adversity and subsequent manifestations of resilience. All sessions were audio-recorded, transcribed verbatim and subjected to thematic, feminist discourse analysis using NVivo 7.0 software (QSR International, 2006) to organize the data. A feminist analytical perspective offered a lens that permitted researchers to "attend to the emotional dimensions of social organization and to the dynamics of participation and exclusion" (Devault, 1999, p. 167). Given the nature of the research question and the anecdotal challenges associated with the dietetic profession (competition, poor representation of diversity, horizontal violence), feminist discourse analysis was a means to make visible the contributing factors to these issues, expand the critical dietetics literature, and offer questions for further inquiry.

The Resiliency Map was created by the AIDS Bereavement Project of Ontario. Reproduced with permission. More details available at: HTTP://WWW.ABPO.ORG/INDEX.PHP/RESILIENCY_INITIATIVE/

RESILIENCY MAP

To begin, the map was prepared by four participants who individually took one corner and unfolded the map, layer by layer. The map was specifically aligned to have the word "motivation" pointing to the east. "Motivation" was the word that most participants stood on first as they were invited to share their response to the question, "What motivated me to enter this field?"

The purpose of the distinct circles was for people to notice what they were attached to, what relationships had meaning, and which social principles had meaning. The meanings shared in relation to those circles informed the construction of each participant's life story. As the map facilitator indicated, "Certainly there's no prescription about how to use it, we just try and you know treat it with respect to the best degree that we can. It is done like a talking circle to the extent that when one person is on and they are speaking a story then the time is [hers] until the point that [she] either asks a facilitator for help or [she] puts a question out to the group."

For some, their time on the map took the form of quiet, deliberate contemplation as they shared their stories. At times participants laughed together, prompted by the nostalgia and humour emerging from their past. For others, their time on the map took a meandering, more inquisitive feel with rhetorical questions posed to the storytellers' witnesses. Others were overcome by the experience stood strongly, clench-fisted, crying, and overwhelmed by the narrative the map evoked. And a few physically knelt to the ground, resting on each space that held meaning, finding themselves unexpectedly amidst the vulnerability of public healing.

An experiential, arts-based approach is decidedly uncommon in dietetic practice-based research; nevertheless, it has been piloted with other human service workers (Perrault, n.d.). Proceeding with experiential, arts-based dietetics inquiry speaks to the call from former president of the American Dietetic Association to be creative in our pursuits of knowledge:

> Creativity, innovation and new ways of looking at what we do, both individually and as an association, are necessities ... As dietetics professionals we have the right stuff for creativity ... (Coulston, 1999, p. 108).

Moreover, the experiential and collective nature of this inquiry draws upon and reminds us of the relationally embedded nature of dietitians' work (DeVault, 1999).

Participants transitioned between artmaking, mapping, and lunch with a guided breathing and visualization process that was offered by the map facilitator. In this way, participants were invited by the map facilitator to become more aware of "the sense of increasing spaciousness for holding all of the stories, and appreciating what [was] still resonating from the stories ... just heard." As well, participants were called to "register the sensations and the memories" activated by being a witness to others' narratives and to "take inventory of the things that [were] most prominent." The facilitator encouraged a reflexive, empathetic tone with these words, "Your witness is there to say 'Yes, I noticed and I'm going to keep noticing. Yes, I was touched by, and I'm going to continue to let myself interact with [these women and their stories]'." Within this meditative and narrative context, a creative space was enacted and articulated by the facilitators and co-participants. In this space, several themes emerged from the mapping narratives, the artmaking, and the transitional visualizations.

Findings

PARTICIPANTS OF THE *MAPPING RESILIENCY PROJECT* were compelled to participate in the research for the opportunity to connect with one another as dietitians, who for one reason or another struggled to reconcile their experiences within the profession of dietetics. Participants represented varied aspects of the field with their experience ranging from clinical dietetics, to community, public health, industry, research, and education. The length of time in the profession also ranged from a few years to more than two decades. Despite this diversity, participants arrived for similar reasons. They came to share their observations of personal, professional, and/or organizational issues through experiential narrative. In this way they explored strategies of resiliency in response to the struggles they encountered. They collectively rediscovered ways in which to apply this experiential learning in an effort to sustain the passion and meaning that they valued, yet found lacking in their work.

The narratives unfolded in non-linear patterns, overlapping, intersecting and, at once remaining distinctly unique. Each person was invited to enter the map along the axis of motivation, speaking to what brought her to the profession, and from there she moved to other areas of the map that spoke to relevant pieces of her story. The time was unmonitored, leaving participants to explore their experiences at their own pace, and exiting the map when and from which section they desired.

Three themes emerged through our participants' dialogical journey: disconnection, workplace conflict, and relational resiliency. These themes were infused with subtexts of gender, emotionality, and burnout.

Disconnection

THROUGHOUT CONVERSATION, disconnection emerged AS an immensely meaningful and pervasive theme. In each session together, the theme of disconnection offered dimension to narratives of the self, relational, organizational and social/political context of the women's personal and professional lives. A notable grieving and curious, questioning-spirit accompanied the stories of disconnection as the women moved together through their dialogical journey.

According to Kobel (1997), the choice to enter dietetics is highly influenced by a "personal interest in nutrition", the "opportunity to help others", the potential health promoting benefits of nutrition and, diverse work environments (p. 256). Participants expressed similar sentiments, yet struggled to reconcile the fact that there was a profound disconnection between their ideals and values of professional practice and the limitations imposed by their prescribed role in practice.

DISEMBODIMENT

A participant's interest in nutrition was related to the potential for empowerment and a sense of control over food. Entrenched in experiences of oppression, women who found their bodies and eating habits under the scrutiny of family, friends, and romantic partners; they sought to master that which brought to them violent condemnation and judgment of their self-worth. Thus, they found themselves wanting to learn more about food and health as an escape from abusive patterns and as a means to take control over their bodies and relationships. Carol shared:

> There was a lot of control and surveillance over my body and so I was really looking for a way to alleviate some of that scrutiny by shrinking my body smaller, smaller, always smaller (short pause, on "emotion"). And the emotions that went on with that (short pause) quest (Pamela nods at this term). It wasn't, it didn't feel like heart felt passion, for the field, it felt like a quest, like some kind of quest for knowledge. It was very disconnecting, disembodying.

This experience is echoed as the foundation of interest in the field of dietetics for Pamela as well, who remarked:

> I was also in a relationship . . . there were control issues and I was um, feeling a lot of, ya a lot of need to control my weight and um, um, (long pause) ya just not eating enough and really feeling a lot um (short pause) a lot of issues with that and I thought that going into nutrition would help me.

And for Emily who painfully reflected on where she initially gained interest in nutrition and its capacity to shape bodies and lives:

> My dad put me on a diet when I was eight (standing on "family"). And, and started off that sort of focus, I really didn't get it because I was eight, but he would weigh me almost every day (exhaling and beginning to cry).

In contrast to their hopes for emancipation, the women were confronted with the conformity demanded of professional discourse, and continuously struggled to "fit into the picture of the dietitian" (Emily). That experience was accompanied by a sense of disembodiment, leaving participants unable to reside fully in themselves without risk of critical judgment. Moving perspectives were recounted about the efforts that were made to "fit in" to the world of dietetics and the impact of this experience on sense of self.

Specifically, dietitians spoke about how they felt implicated by "what dietitians should look like" (Pamela), and the ways in which their bodies, historically speaking, had come to serve as a barometer of professional competence and knowledge amidst the critical gaze of both colleagues and the general public alike:

> You know my weight was up and down and all over . . . as a dietitian . . . struggling with that, patients would comment and colleagues would comment and (deep inhale) and, you know it was tough. This is all very sad (breaks into tears) (Emily)

Emily elaborated and summed the sentiment nicely, saying:

> [You're] always trying to, trying to, to, to bend and be, you know the way you're supposed to be, and I don't know where that came from in the beginning who said you have to be that way, but probably it goes all the way back to internship and, and, and just that socialization.

Kathy speculated that much of the surveillance that she and others had been subjected to through their careers was related to the gendered nature of the profession:

> I think it's a very female dominated profession, so there's a lot [of] . . . expectations . . . about body size. [It's] just feeling kind of exposed all the time and having lots of comments about my size . . .

Kerfoot (as quoted by Driver, 2008) argues that, "the body becomes a project to be fashioned and refashioned amid different [organizational] discourses" (p. 914). Internalization of such discourse is inescapable. This was evident in the way that the conversation remained saturated with comments of seemingly resigned acceptance of the professional discourse, "I felt the same thing – self criticism – it's just part of the profession to be critical." (Pamela)

Carol offered just how "disruptive" and "decentering" this body surveillance was to one's sense of self, stating "I couldn't connect because it [dietetic work] was taking me away from myself . . . there's a lot of covering up of self."

Martin (2006) contends that unconscious conformity and performance of gendered roles are common in workplace contexts. Surveillance and regulation of women's bodies prevail, masked in and protected by the safety of professional norms, but nonetheless oppressive, exuding elements of social control (Martin, 2006).

Gendered oppression and accommodations made on behalf of women in health disciplines have historical underpinnings. Like dietetics, nursing, a female-dominated profession underwent significant transition from a profession marked by 'feminine' attributes of philanthropic, empathetic, intuitive and moral endeavours to one of 'masculine' superiority swathed in objective, professional, bureaucratized expertise which privileged scientific truth over subjective knowing (Bashford, 2000). In its wake, emerged the culturally-constructed and scientifically defined body, newly vulnerable to rationalist discourse (Bashford, 2000) and moralistic judgment. This scrutiny of the body continues today and places no greater judgment than on the bodies of dietitians who, above all others should 'know best' how to control their weight and appearance.

ISOLATION FROM FAMILIES

Severance from an embodied sense of self was but one facet of disconnection. Another site of alienation was in the context of family. Here, descriptions of the emotional demands of dietetic work were further amplified by the stress and energy required by the still largely female-dominated
realm of child-rearing and family management. Collectively, these challenges, coupled by the perceived negligence of the profession to offer support, rendered the women unable to fully participate in the experiences of their families. For some, it came with a sense of hypocrisy and often left the women with a subsequent and enduring sense of guilt:

> I'm teaching people what to do with their babies and how to be with their kids and everything and my kids are being totally ignored . . . I'm feeling really guilty I'm feeling pulled in a lot of different directions . . . like it's just, it's the whole profession, I've found was unsupportive of me as a [mother] (Heather)

Similarly, Pamela spoke of her strain to balance motherhood with the weight of full time work:

> It [was] busy going back to work full time and you know going home to pump (giggles) . . . it's just a few different layers of things, right? You've got [to] raise children and work full time and then deal with . . . these issues and . . . [the] emotions that go . . . with . . . the kind of work I'm doing."

Moral Strain

The moral nature and integrity of 'people work' adds further compounding effects to the gendered and disembodying aspects of dietetic practice. Participants drawn to dietetics by the opportunity to help others voiced disappointment regarding the discontinuity between their expectations of their profession and the realities of their practice:

> It seems like we don't all agree on what contributes to health . . . you know what's actually important (Dawn nods). And, the old-guard nutrition says that if we tell people . . . the right things to do, how to eat, they will be healthy. (short pause) And yet, there's all this research that says . . . that people's social conditions and economic conditions are primary contributors to their health . . . but . . . you can't find a place (Dawn nods) to talk about that, it's very difficult to find a place to talk about that" (Pamela)

Dawn commented with similar frustration:

> I don't even have the language to describe how ludicrous it is to me that [place of work] with all these resources, and all our money and all our skills are not doing the most fundamental things in the community (raising her tone with more frustration).

Kathy concurred highlighting the fact that "We're just not reaching out . . . it's like something's missing," questioning: "doesn't anybody else see it?!"

"Stress of conscience" (Glasberg, Eriksson, & Norberg, 2006, p.392) has been documented in recent research as the moral strain that results for health personnel when they are unable to perform their work in a meaningful way, Participants time and again referred to the moral strain of their work, making reference to the "warring" tensions (Carol), and citing that "on the one hand you know what the party line is that you're supposed to be towing (short pause) and on the other hand there's [your] personal integrity that's at stake on a daily basis."(Emily)

The consequences of this strain are significant and are evidenced by Glasberg, Eriksson, & Norberg (2006) to contribute to over 40% of the variance for emotional exhaustion, the first phase of three in Maslach's Burnout Inventory (MBI) and highly predictive of turnover intention (Cropanzano, Rupp, & Byrnc, 2003; Houkes, Janssen, de Jonge, & Nijhuis, 2001).

This disconnection thus takes on particular salience in dietetics and begs inquiry into emotionality and conflict in the dietetic workplace, areas which bear evidence of gendered relationships and which serve to perpetuate self-regulation and professional compliance.

Workplace Conflict

CONFLICT IN THE WORKPLACE is inevitable. Professional relationships in healthcare work are impacted by several factors, which among the most prominent are professional status (Adams, 2004) and interpersonal challenges that often result in an individual feeling devalued (Jackson, Mannix, & Daly, 2001). Professional conflict arises in many facets of dietetic work. Interprofessional conflict in dietetic practice dates back to some of the earliest moments in the profession as evidenced by the words of a clinical dietitian, who, over eighty years ago, recognized the need to navigate workplace conflict:

> The dietitian must speak the language and practice the suspended judgment of the scientists whose findings she is using practically before she can hope to be counted among those who rank with officers in the medical army (Morgan, 1925, p.175).

The interprofessional conflicts that arise in clinical hierarchies persist today (Kelly, 2006) and represent one realm of dietetic practice that bears witness to professional divisions of power and authority. Bureaucratic organizational cultures common in government offices and services are also entrenched in dietetic workplace conflict and unrest (Kelly, 2006). Here, management and leadership positions typically remain reserved for dietitians whose position, by virtue of their training (Master's degree) and professional credentials, have come to be endowed with work that receives higher value and esteem, while internship-trained dietitians in the same field, are relegated to relatively subordinate positions which receive relatively less autonomy and authority in their work. The impact of hierarchical structures and the perception that "some people think they're better than others" (Heather) has potentially devastating consequences on the relationships between colleagues:

> When you're working on a project or you're in a meeting, or you're in a relationship and one person is paid more and what they say is respected and they're given more opportunities and they have a better workspace . . . the imbalance is very um (short

pause) it erodes your sense of worth and who you are, and . . . leaches into your personal life and it's very demeaning. (Dawn)

Adams (2004) contends that vying for authority and power through interprofessional conflict is an integral part of professionalization. His research investigates the evolutionary distinction between the male-dominated discipline of dentistry with the relatively recent profession of female-dominated, dental hygiene. In the process, he describes the tensions that unfold as, "occupational leaders seek claim to professional status – defined as the power to elicit respect . . . [and, which] possess[es] characteristics that are socially esteemed and which entitle group members to special treatment" (Adams, 2004, p. 2245). One might find comparable professional distinctions and the subsequent conflict they inspire, with the current tensions emerging between Master's educated and internship educated dietitians' work.

Conversations that emerged as participants walked the map frequently returned to the frustration with their attempts to work collaboratively across intraprofessional distinctions. Heather remarked, "[but] it became very clear to me (short pause) that I was a dietitian and she was a nutritionist. I hadn't even heard of that, I thought we were all together, you know, and we weren't."

How dietetic work comes to be de/valued is not merely a matter of interprofessional divides within medical hierarchies, nor of intraprofessional divisions of credentials, but is also informed by place of work. Kathy, a former clinical dietitian who transitioned to work in the community setting and whose credentials remained the same throughout her transition articulated the dismissive comments she encountered by colleagues as she prepared for her new role:

> I . . . moved from the hospital into the community . . . which is not as respected, absolutely not as respected . . . You know being told, well you know 'it won't be as challenging but that's nice" like that's "*nice* work (giggles) – it's *nice* work out there in community'.

The invalidation experienced in such comments bear negative implications for one's sense of self worth manifesting as feeling devalued and/or underutilized in one's work. Emily describes her longing to make meaningful contributions to her work, to have them embraced by her colleagues and, the "sadness" at the dismissal of her ideas:

I can contribute and how come [they] don't want that? I think that's a shame . . .
I feel sadness because I think that there are many of us who are just here to give, you
know. And it's not, it's not going to being capitalized upon and it's a waste.

Dawn shared a similar sense of grief and loss in observing how enthusiasm and ideas are lost
to hierarchical politics and old-guard approaches to nutrition work. She reflected on the efforts of
fellow energetic colleagues who" would quickly find "their passion being dismissed because it was
not in the book, [or the original] plan". The responses shared are similar upon reflection to recent
research by Munn-Giddings, Hart, & Ramo (2005) who found an association between feeling
undervalued at work and higher degrees of burnout as measured by Maslach's Burnout Inventory
(MBI). For some, efforts to resist or confront workplace conflict were met with punitive responses.
Pamela rhetorically warned participants, " . . . and, you know, don't have a big mouth, because
. . . you'll be in trouble, you'll feel, you'll be squashed, you'll be marginalized, you'll be nothing".
She added further caution:

{316}
> So, you challenge those people a couple of times and . . . you put yourself in the line
> of fire a couple of times, then you realize that oh, okay – emotionally, I can't take
> that . . . spiritually . . . you know . . . you just have to protect yourself, and I'm - so I'm
> learning more about protecting myself.

EMOTIONALITY

Fineman & Sturdy (1999) remind us that "the social negotiation of position, authority and status
is very much an emotional and sometimes passionate process" (p. 659). In every action of an
employee's complicity or resistance, or management's expectations for emotional suppression,
emotionality inevitably plays a dominant role in the fabrication of one's identity (Coupland, Brown,
Daniels, & Humphreys, 2008). Game (2008) echoes this notion arguing that management and
leadership are fundamentally emotional and relational processes. Fineman & Sturdy (1999) go
on to argue that the emotionality of workplace relationships can be particularly "charged" (p.660)
within the intersection of employment and gender. In their ethnographic study of environmental
regulatory inspectors, they juxtaposed the well-established requirement of emotional regulation
in the workplace with the concept of emotions (and its regulation) as a profound strategy of
organizational control. Moreover, they posited that being controlled can have deeply impactful
emotional consequences (Fineman & Sturdy, 1999)

Thus, it is not surprising that despite the inevitably of workplace conflict, it is most often met with avoidance strategies, and accommodations which require emotional suppression (Kelly, 2006). This is arguably even truer for the female-dominated profession of dietetics, where women are already well-versed in the art of interpersonal diplomacy, demanded of their respective gender. Indeed, Marquid & Huston, as cited in Kelly (2006) argue that "Women, more than men, are reluctant to engaged in conflict as they feel they may be dismissed as 'emotional women'"(p.24).

The dietitians who participated in the study spoke repeatedly of just such a fear. Dawn spoke of feeling "totally exposed" while engaging in conflict management in the workplace and her fear that "They'll just think I'm an idiot". She went on to share how after many years of tight emotional regulation, she might be ready to speak with her adversaries:

> I think I'm getting to the point where I might be able to [speak to] them without
> . . . just screaming at them and swearing or by just breaking down and crying . . .
> I don't really want to do that with them, because I'm not interested in showing that
> [crying] to them.

This example demonstrates the interplay between emotions and the contexts in which they are, or are not expressed. It is argued that emotions serve to fundamentally influence social interactions and power distribution, a process which dictates what is and is not acceptable in any given context (Coupland, Brown, Daniels, & Humphreys, 2008). The point of reference for acceptable emotionality in dietetic work seemed to be that of those in positions of power. Pamela remarked, "People who make it into positions of power don't show their emotions, they don't get emotional".

Some exasperatedly shared the frustration of trying to brave the ever-delicate and always daunting task of speaking with those in power. Heather remarked with frustration, "I don't have a voice…I'm not valued (moves to "values" on map). I'm not valued at work." Later reflecting on a time when she had found her voice, "I'm actually talking, like I'm talking and I'm *still* not even heard. So it's that whole thing, how do I do this so that I'm not seen as a babbling idiot".

Others had long given up the effort to speak and navigate the emotional rules of engagement. Pamela spoke about leaving meetings with headaches, "I can't say what I would like to say, I can't speak up". In a similar fashion, Kathy, who described her visceral response to the project as "volcanic activity" reflected, "You know and, and why can't I say anything? Because maybe I've seen people be reprimanded, or I have been reprimanded before that . . . so you plan and plan and plan how you're going to say it and how you can say it in a way that's not perceived as you know (short pause) wrong". These remarks illustrate that which Fineman & Sturdy (1999) term the "historically situated" elements of emotional control (p. 659) as well as the necessity for strategic planning in approaching management in the workplace.

This emotional discourse also seemed to be a hallmark of professionalization. Heather commented with dismay about an intern's confession to her after a long conversation they had shared:

> I had an intern and she just finished up and she said "This is the first place I've come to where I actually, could talk and give my opinion and people listened" She was shocked! She was totally shocked.

While the dynamics of social control through emotional regulation are often subtle and dynamic (Fineman & Sturdy, 1999), some participants voiced insights into the "power" that resided in the unknowing, unknowable, unspeakable. Emily implicitly spoke to the impact that so many years of emotional regulation held over her and questioned "I was like, okay, do I open the door [and engage in discussion], because it's unknown, but I, I do know enough to know that it's going to be tough". Carol meditated on some words spoken at a recent conference, pondering its application to the women's time together in building relational resilience:

> She said over time, being in, in academics, that [she'd] learned how to speak power to power. She's learned how to use power in the face of power. And now it's more important for her to speak truth to power.

At the same time, however, Carol spoke with realization that, "speaking truth seems to be a very emotional thing to do . . . there's a sense . . . of being vulnerable in that. Like trying to connect with this [truth] without having to protect myself . . . just trying to speak the truth. It's incredibly hard."

Nevertheless, truth, it seemed was what the group session had come to host for many of the participants. And, the participants dared to enter vulnerable spaces in which to begin the first stages of meeting power with truth, in finding resilience in their experience. Kathy shared this poignantly in saying, "Some of those things that we've talked about I haven't spoken as openly about before, and then once you have, you start, then, it becomes like a truth".

Relational Resiliency: Building Bridges

Bill Wilkerson, CEO of a Global Roundtable on Addiction and Mental Health and special advisor at the Institute of Mental Health at McGill University states, "Frustration and rumination – seething – are the two major social effects of chronic job stress. They are a prelude to depression" (Jacobs, 2008, p.1) which "flows from a protracted sense of . . . perceived illogic and unfairness – even injustice – in the affairs and leadership of the organization by [one] is employed" (Wilkerson, 2004, p.10). In this context, the loss of resiliency renders no other "fallback", but depression, a loss of control and sense of place (Wilkerson, 2008, p. 1). Wilkerson likens the progression to this end as a "migratory sequence between stress, burnout and depression" (Jacobs, 2008, p.1). Burnout itself has been theorized as a spectrum which mirrors this progression as stages of emotional exhaustion, depersonalization and diminished personal accomplishment (Cropanzano, Rupp, & Byrnc, 2003, p. 160). Common to the origin of each spectrum, is stress.

Reflecting on the journey of our participants, there is evidence of extreme stress in the context of dietetic work including: disembodying work (isolation from self), isolation from family and colleagues and relentless moral tension where ideals fall subject to constrained prescriptions of practice. Furthermore, participants spoke of the utter physical, spiritual, mental, and emotional fatigue, the latter a particular hallmark of the first phase of burnout and subsequent depression (Glasberg, Eriksson, & Norberg, 2006; Cropanzano, Rupp, & Byrnc, 2003) that came as a consequence of their work and left them longing for something different.

Hope for something different remained central to the gatherings. "It's the hope too," Emily remarked. At many stages throughout the conversations, a sense of eager hopefulness and optimism arose within the group intent. Emily commented with intrigue, "I have left the profession twice now and I have come back. There's something really strange there . . . it's rich and how do we navigate to where we do find some joy [in it]?" Similarly, another dietitian who had left the profession only to return and "reclaim" the professional status of dietitian, commented on the potential to change the experience for dietitians of the future . . . Dawn spoke of the way in which the dialogue born of the project would contribute to this process:

> I think that the gains that they made from my generation and those before me sort of clear[ed] the path a little bit, so um, I find it um, wonderful to work with younger people and I'm um, and um, I'm just so interested in this [project] because I want to join this conversation…I want to…figure out.. how can I protect those people [future generations of new dietitians].

{319}

Similarly, Kathy reflected, "I like nutrition . . . I like the things that I'm doing but it's finding a place to do them where I'm going to feel like it's effective . . . and valued." She likened her journey to "trailblazing" wherein she strove to carve out a niche in which her unique collection of skills might somehow be recognized.

Revisiting the challenges endured in the profession seemed to serve as an integral component of building relational resiliency. Through the course of reflection, the women came to describe a myriad of resilient activities they had undertaken in order to cope with the challenges they faced. Kathy shared, "I keep my feet [and] . . . my hands in different pots to, you know, try and find something that really resonates".

Heather who at the outset had "jokingly call[ed] this [coming together] . . . [her] dietitians' bereavement group" described the creative resilience she brought to her counselling sessions with clients, "flying under the radar" behind closed doors, seeking professional development events, writing, teaching and taking in interns to whom she felt she could extend the relational style mentorship she had found so lacking in her professionalization. "I still think it's a good field, it's very interesting . . . there's lots of things going on" she added. Dawn resonated with Heather adding, "I'm always trying different things."

{320} For some, "trying different things" meant a change in how they practiced in dietetics. Many ventured into education of various kinds (Carol, Heather, Dawn, Emily), others sought creativity, and the opportunity to "inspire young minds" (Emily & Heather).

Still others, like Pamela who had "spent most of [her] career as a dietitian with one food out the door" remained hopeful of employment opportunities outside of nutrition, "maybe I'll be more valued, I'll be able to make a difference . . . and influence nutrition . . . from the outside, 'cause it's too hard to do it from within." Yet, at the same time, she felt hopeful that nutrition might still hold a promising potential to do work that possessed, "a sense of ethics and . . . social justice . . . [a space for] doing things because they actually make a difference in people's lives."

The five points of resiliency (Denz-Penhey, & Murdoch, 2008) - connection to social support, family, the physical environment, experiential inner wisdom and, a strong psychological self, are critical to preventing the migration along Wilkerson's proposed spectrum from stress toward burnout and depression. Yet, a significant portion of the conversation shared amongst the women spoke to the disconnections they had endured in their profession. It was evident from the speakers and listeners, that there was a critical need to reconnect, to counter the isolating costs of disembodiment, loss of family and collegial connections and, melancholia over lost ideals for the profession.

Social support is essential to mitigating the effects of workplace stress (Jackson, Firtko, &

Edenborough, 2007). Indeed, a lack of social support and negative relationships with professional colleagues has been found to be consistently associated with interpersonal conflict and increased turnover intention (Houkes, Janssen, de Jonge, & Nijhuis, 2001). Moreover, it is a primary predictor of emotional exhaustion (Houkes, Janssen, de Jonge, & Nijhuis, 2001).

The very act of coming together, in shared vulnerability to speak of their experiences seemed to mark a critical, hopeful moment of reconnection with self, and others for the dietitians of this study. In essence, assembling together was an act of resilience. Much like the way conversation shed light on "truth" (Kathy) of experience for participants intertwining narratives unveiled the collective nature of shared experiences and, previously unnamed acts of resilience. Pamela shared, "I always think "it's just me", and really, being, talking to this group I think "maybe it's not just me".

Further evidence of relational resiliency emerged between the dietitians as they spoke. Kathy commented on "connecting some of the dots . . . based on some of the conversations that we've had here". Pamela, in a moment of self reflection commented, "[I'm] thinking about . . . sharing information and experiences and, and what does that mean for me and . . . I don't know I guess it's um, ya, just a bit, I feel like there was some growth going on for me, just, you know, this is helping me grow let's say." {321}

Others remarked on the strength and validation they received in finding other dietitians who demonstrated "shared values . . . around justice and fairness and . . . significance of relationship in our work" (Carol). Likewise, Pamela spoke of the power in finding people with shared values, while Emily credited it with giving her the energy she needed to remain in the profession, remarking that "it comes back to this (moves to "shared values" on the map) shared values as well for me . . . the connections with other people are what keeps me here".

Conclusion

LOSS OF CONNECTION LIMITS CAPACITY to build resiliency. The women in this study highlighted the ways in which they had, through dietetics, come to experience a profound disembodied sense of self, a loss of connection with family, a severed connection with colleagues, and grief at the loss of professional ideals.

Coming together, in a narrative space of both shared vulnerability and values, the women were able to cultivate relational resilience in response to each of the previously mentioned aspects of disconnection how together, they had moved toward strength, healing and the ability to endure.

This research thus positions workplace relationships as central to reconciling the experience of disconnection, workplace conflict and a lack of resiliency within dietetic work. Moreover, this creative, arts-informed research demonstrates the ways in which relational resiliency may buffer the consequences of the emotionally-demanding, gendered nature of dietetic work and the risk of subsequent burnout. Equally creative and embodied approaches to primary prevention of burnout in undergraduate educational contexts are also required (Atkins & Gingras, 2009).

Previous research has affirmed that fostering resiliency is critical to health professionals and that it must be a collective, relational effort (McAllister, & McKinnon, 2008). It argues that resiliency must be built into the professionalization process, in a participatory way that prompts self-reflection on emerging professional identity, inspires artistic, narrative, and creative thinking and coping strategies and encourages constructive ways to engage in work relationships that will serve to model future generations of workplaces (McAllister, & McKinnon, 2008).

In similar fashion, a recent literature review highlights "emotional intelligence, nurturing positive professional relationships, positivity and becoming more reflective" (Jackson, Fitko, & Edenborough, 2007, p. 1) as strategies to cultivate resiliency. These characteristics speak to some of the elements featured in the growing trend to "refashion" management skills (Hatcher, 2003) where it is argued that in order for workplaces to remain successful, they must embrace a feminized approach which welcomes and recognizes passion, emotionality, an emphasis on "connection with other human beings" (Hatcher, 2003, p. 399) and "a shift to relational rather than competitive values"(Barrett, as cited in Hatcher, 2003, p. 402) as imperative skills that will favourably impact workplace settings.

Dietetics remains a female-dominated profession, yet, given the privilege of emotionally-suppressive, rationalist, deductive, scientific and disembodied demands of our work, how might this refashioning be made relevant to dietetic contexts?

Implications for Practice

RESILIENCE CAN BE LEARNED. One randomized control trial (RCT) (N= 150) demonstrated that training in personal resilience and resilient relationships (PRRR) had significant and positive outcomes for participants (Waite, & Richardson, 2004). These results are promising.

Given the resounding expression of isolation within dietetic work among these participants, how might efforts towards relational resiliency enable change? How might the context of dietetic work be relationally re-imagined? Continued research in response to these questions is essential to the future of dietetic work and the health of its practitioners. Specifically, qualitative, feminist, institutional ethnography, which "explores the social world as it is known experientially . . . as people's activities or doings in the actual local situations and conditions." (Smith, 2007, p.411) might be considered.

Carol deplores, "[I'm] lacking the sense that [our] stories speak for themselves, I keep wanting to have more stories told. And say "see", "see", "see, these are real experiences, I'm not just making this up."

The effort toward change in dietetic practice is not a naïve aim to smooth over the complicated contexts of workplace relations. Instead, it is to recognize the intricate, dynamic, and human elements in which dietitians work, acknowledge the unique challenges and discourses that constitute dietetic work, and cultivate relational resiliency as both generative and fulfilling as we learn to respond to these emerging workplace challenges. As we move toward new creative and experiential approaches to relational resiliency in dietetic work, we may enrich dietitians' personal and professional experiences beyond responses to workplace adversity and inspire untold possibilities for the future.

JACQUI GINGRAS, PhD, RD is an Assistant Professor at the School of Nutrition, Ryerson University, Toronto, Canada. Her research involves theoretical and experiential explorations of critical dietetics epistemology. She has a particular interest in how dietetic students' and professional's subjectivities are constituted by power and discourse to inform advocacy, policy, and pedagogy. Her research engages autoethnographic, narrative, and arts-informed methods as a means for situated and particular understandings of dietetic theory, education, and practice. Her work appears in *Food, Culture & Society, Radical Psychology, Feminist Media Studies,* and *Journal of Agricultural and Environmental Ethics.*

JENNIFER ATKINS, MHSc, RD is a dietitian at Access Alliance Multicultural Health and Community Services, Toronto, Canada. Her professional interests include exploration of the ways in which food and relationships intersect, the profession's role in social justice, the discourse around professionalism in dietetics and its role in situating identity of those represented by the profession. As a research assistant, she has worked directly with students and dietitians to explore their experience with dietetic education & practice and its pedagogical role in influencing subjectivity and ability for research and action. She has been published in the Canadian Journal of Dietetic Practice and Research.

References

ADAMS, L. T. (2004). Inter-professional conflict and professionalization: dentistry and dental hygiene in Ontario. *Social Science & Medicine, 58*, 2243-2252.

ATKINS, J., & GINGRAS, J. R. (2009). Coming and going: Dietetic students' experience of their education. *Canadian Journal of Dietetic Practice and Research, 70*(4), 181-186.

BASHFORD, A. (2000). Modernity, gender, and the negotiation of science in Australian nursing, 1880-1910. *Journal of Women's History, 12*(2), 127-145.

BUTLER, J. (1999). *Gender trouble: feminism and the subversion of identity.* New York: Routledge.

BUTLER, J. (1997). *The psychic life of power: theories in subjection.* Stanford, CA: Stanford University Press.

COULSTON, M. A. (1999). President's page: Creativity – blocks, crayons and erasers. *Journal of the American Dietetic Association, 99*(1), 108.

COUPLAND, C, BROWN, D. A., DANIELS, K. & HUMPHREYS, M. (2008). Saying it with feeling: Analysing speakable emotions. *Human Relations, 6*(3), 327-353.

CROPANZANO, R., RUPP, E. D., & BYRNC, S. Z. (2003). The relationship of emotional exhaustion to work attitudes, job performance and organizational citizenship behaviors. *Journal of Applied Psychology, 85*(1), 160-169.

DENEZ-PENHEY, H., & MURDOCH, C. (2008). Personal resiliency: serious diagnosis and prognosis with unexpected quality outcomes. *Qualitative Health Research, 18*(3), 391-404.

DEVAULT, M. (1999). Whose science of food and health: narratives of profession and activism from public-health nutrition. In A. E. Clarke & V. L. Olesen (Eds.), *Revisioning women, health, and healing: feminist, cultural, and technoscience perspectives.* (pp. 166-183). New York; London: Routledge.

DRIVER, M. (2008). Every bite you take . . . food and the struggles of embodied subjectivity in organizations. *Human Relations, 61*(7), 913-934.

FINEMAN, S., & STURDY, A. (1999). The emotions of control: A qualitative exploration of environmental regulation. *Human Relations, 52*(5), 631-663.

GAME, M. A. (2008). Negative emotions in supervisory relationships: The role of relational models. *Human Relations, 61*(3), 355-393.

GINGRAS, J. (2009). *Longing for recognition: the joys, complexities, and contradictions of practicing dietetics.* York, England: Raw Nerve Books.

GIORDANO, B. (1997). Resilience: A survival tool for the nineties. *Association of Perioperative Registered Nurses Journal, 65*, 1032-1036.

GLASBERG, L. A., Eriksson, S., & Norberg, A. (2006). Burnout and 'stress of conscience' among healthcare personnel. *Journal of Advanced Nursing, 57*(4), 392-403.

HARTLING, L. M. (2003). *Strengthening resilience in a risky world: it's all about relationships.* Stone Center Works in Progress #101. Wellesley College, Wellesley, MA.

HATCHER, C. (2003). Refashioning a passionate manager: Gender at work. *Gender, Work & Organization, 10*(4), 391-412.

HODGES, H. F., KEELEY, A. C., & GRIER, E. C. (2005). Professional resilience, practice longevity, and Parse's theory for baccalaureate education. *Journal of Nursing Education, 44*(12), 548-554.

HOUKES, I., JANSSEN, M. P., DEJONGE, J., & NIJHUIS, J. N. F. (2001). Specific relationships between work characteristics and intrinsic work motivation, burnout and turnover intention: A multi-sample analysis. *European Journal of Work and Organizational Psychology, 10*(1), 1-23.

JACKSON, D., FIRTKO, A., & EDENBOROUGH, M. (2007). Personal resilience as a strategy for surviving and thriving in the face of workplace adversity: a literature review. *Journal of Advanced Nursing, 60*(1), 1-9.

JACKSON, D., MANNIX, J., & DALY, J. (2001). Retaining a viable workforce: a critical challenge for nursing. *Contemporary Nurse, 11*, 163-172

Jacobs, D. (2008). Mental Illness a crisis with no end in sight: expert. Ottawa, Canada: *Ottawa Citizen*.

Kobel, A. K. (1997). Influences on the selection of dietetics as a career. *Journal of the American Dietetic Association, 97*(3),254-257.

Kulig, J. C. (2001). Community resiliency: the potential for community health nursing theory development. *Public Health Nursing, 17*(5), 374-385.

Levinson, N. (2001). The paradox of natality: teaching in the midst of belatedness. In M. Gordon (Ed.), *Hannah Arendt and education: renewing our common world.* (pp. 11-36). Boulder, Colorado: Westview Press.

Martin, Y., M. (2006). Practising gender at work: Further thoughts on reflexivity. *Gender, Work and Organization, 13*(3), 254-276.

Masten, A., & Powell, J. (2003). A resiliency framework for research, policy and practice. In: Luthar, S. (Ed.), *Resiliency and Vulnerability: Adaptation in the Context of Childhood Adversity.* (pp. 1-29). Cambridge: Cambridge University Press.

Maslach, C., Jackson, S.-E., & Leiter, M.-P. (1996). *Maslach burnout inventory*, 3rd edition. Palo, Alto, CA: Consulting Psychologists Press.

McAllister, M., & McKinnon, J. (2008). The importance of teaching and learning resilience in the health disciplines: A critical review of the literature. *Nurse Education Today*, doi: 10.1016/j.nedt.2008.10.011.

McGillis Hall, L., Waddell, J., Donner, G., & Wheeler, M. (2004). Outcomes of a career planning and development program for registered nurses. *Nursing Economics, 22*(5), 231-238.

Morgan, A.F. (1925). College Education and the Food Specialist. *Journal of the American Dietetic Association, 1*, 174 – 178.

Munn-Giddings, C., Hart, C., & Ramon, S. (2005). A participatory approach to the promotion of well-being in the workplace: *Lessons from empirical research. International Review of Psychiatry, 17*(5), 409-417.

{327}

NEWMAN R. (2003). Providing direction on the road to resilience. *Behavioral Health Management, 23*(4), 42-43.

PERRAULT Y. (N.D.). *AIDS bereavement project of Ontario.* Retrieved January 2, 2009 from WWW.ABPO.ORG/IMAGES/UPLOADS/RESILIENCY_FRAMEWORK.PDF.

SALIH, S. & BUTLER, J. (2004). *The Judith Butler reader.* Malden, MA: Blackwell Publishing.

SMITH, D. E. (2007). Institutional ethnography: From a sociology for women to a sociology for people. In N. S. Hesse-Biber (Ed.), *Handbook of feminist research: Theory and praxis* (pp. 409-416). Thousand Oaks, CA: Sage Publications.

WADDELL, J., & BAUER, M. (2005). Career planning and development for students: building a career in a professional practice discipline. *Canadian Journal of Career Development, 4*(2), 4-13.

WAGNILD G., & YOUNGE H. (1993). Development and psychometric evaluation of the Resilience Scale. *Journal of Nursing Measurement, 1,* 165-178.

WAITE, J. P., & RICHARDSON, E. G. (2004). Determining the efficacy of resiliency training in the work site. *Journal of Allied Health, 33*(3), 178-183.

WICKS, R. J. (2006). *Overcoming secondary stress in medical and nursing practice: a guide to professional resilience and personal well-being.* New York: Oxford University Press.

WILKERSON, B. (2004). Text of keynote speech by roundtable co-founder and CEO Bill Wilkerson to the Ontario Medical Association Annual Meeting. Toronto, Ontario, Canada: Global business and Economic Roundtable on Addiction and Mental Health.

The Convergence of Expressive Art Forms and Community Based Cancer Education

Bringing What's On the Inside Out

Melany Cueva

CANCER IS THE LEADING CAUSE OF DEATH among Alaska Native peoples. As we talked about cancer, we coloured luminarias out of paper bags. Each bag became a living sculpture, as together we discussed our experiences with cancer, sharing tears and laughter through drawing. A participant shared, "If you can't say it out in sentences you could put it in drawing, put your feelings out, to help bring out what you have in your mind...it makes it easier to talk about." Each paper bag luminaria had an important cancer related message. One elder drew a home clouded with tobacco smoke with children inhaling all the illness associated with breathing second-hand smoke. A youth coloured the importance of eating traditional foods to prevent disease. Another participant drew her hopes that people would take care of their physical health. Each participant was given a candle as a symbolic way to add light to share their message. Additionally, the candle symbolized a variety of ideas among participants including: "peace", "hope", "knowledge", "a dedication to our ancestors", and "self care". One participant shared, "you are in control when you light your candle and when you blow it out to prevent burn out".

Learning is more than an extension of cognitive ways of being. The expressive arts bring a heart and soul connection to learning. In collaboration with diverse adult learners, I continue to explore and discover the ways that engagement with the expressive arts enriches cancer education and wellness course offerings."

MELANY CUEVA, RN, Ed.D., is a nurse, researcher, and public health educator working with and for American Indian and Alaska Native peoples. Dr. Cueva has focused her research efforts in the past ten years on developing and providing culturally respectful cancer prevention and education with American Indian and Alaska Native peoples. Dr. Cueva works with the Alaska Native Tribal Health Consortium, based in Anchorage, Alaska, and is pursuing the convergence of expressive art forms and community-based cancer education as part of a mentored research scholar award from the American Cancer Society.

Creating A Place for the Arts in Healthcare Management Education

Sherry Fontaine

Introduction

MANAGEMENT PROGRAMS IN HIGHER EDUCATION are looking towards the arts to cultivate the leadership skills and attributes necessary to succeed in the current marketplace. The application of the arts in management education encompasses cross-sector leadership skills that include collaboration, team building, communications, innovation and creativity; with the intent of strengthening these skills through arts-based learning. The trends affecting health care leaders are similar to the trends that fostered the adoption of arts-based learning in management education. Health care leaders face a rapidly changing environment, technological advances that significantly influence health care operations, and the heightened importance of managing teams of health care professionals whose collaboration is essential in providing quality health care. This chapter will explore of the application of arts-based learning in healthcare management education and how this pedagogy can be utilized to strengthen the leadership skills of health care managers.

Leadership and the Arts

A GLOBAL ECONOMY, an increasingly competitive marketplace, rapid advances in technology and societal changes require leaders that are able to be adaptive and responsive to the rapid changes occurring around them. Responding to change necessitates greater creativity and the ability to develop new and innovative ideas that respond these new challenges. Creativity is at the core of the artistic process. Through the study of art and/or being involved in creating art, leaders can further develop their own abilities in innovative and creative thinking, and problem solving. Arts-based learning is a particular pedagogy that is used to integrate the arts into a wider range of disciplines. By integrating the arts and humanities into multi-disciplinary curriculum and coursework, arts-based learning deepens the knowledge base and awareness of learners in differing disciplines (Fontaine, 2008).

Management educators have increasingly turned toward the arts, in the form of arts-based learning, as a means to build and strengthen leadership skills among business students. Leadership theories identify a set of leadership skills across sectors that are integral for effective leadership. These cross sector leadership skills involve collaboration, team building, communications, innovation and creativity (Kouzes and Posner, 2002 ;Yukl, 2006; Puccio, Mordock, and Mance, 2007; Northouse, 2007). The application of the arts in management education encompasses the aforementioned cross-sector leadership skills and provides a means of deepening these skills through arts-based learning .

Collaboration and Team Building:

ACTORS, DANCERS, AND MUSICIANS – performing as ensembles – have developed team-based collaborative skills to a much greater extent than have most managers (Adler, 2006: 491)

The performing arts offer valuable insight in acquiring and sharpening collaborative and team-building skills. Gold and Hirshfeld (2005) describe how improvisational jazz provides a metaphor for collaboration and improvisation in management. As the authors note, improvisational jazz starts with the ability to listen and requires that musicians assume dual roles of leading and supporting to create great jazz. The same acts of listening, leading as well as supporting are also essential for great leadership. Similarly, studying how a symphony conductor leads a diverse group of musicians provides a deeper understanding of how leaders can communicate a shared vision and inspire both individual and collective performance (Mockler, 2002). Music is by no means the only artistic medium that is used to teach methods of collaboration and team building. The skills employed in improvisational theatre are utilized to allow students to experience ways of achieving spontaneous collaboration and teamwork (Greene and Burke, 2007). Another example is Wharton's MBA workshop which uses dance to explore improvisation and collaboration (Adler, 2006).

COMMUNICATIONS: Corrigan in his book, *Shakespeare on Management*, examined the leadership skills learned from Shakespeare's plays. In Shakespeare's plays, one successful leader is depicted, Prince Hal in *Henry V*. A key attribute of the character Prince Hal was his ability to communicate with the people he hoped to one day lead. His ability to communicate and motivate his subjects was based upon his desire to understand the peoples' language and culture; foundations upon which meaningful communications are built. Corrigan tells us that the leadership lesson learned in *Henry V* is that to become a good leader one must learn how to communicate effectively and to recognize what constitutes the basis of effective communication (Corrigan,1999).

CREATIVITY AND INNOVATION: The connection between arts-based learning and creativity and innovation is an area often explored in management education. Daniel Pink's (2004:21) assertion that the "MFA is the New MBA" took account of the new economic realities of a competitive marketplace that requires artistic aptitudes. While an artist's aptitudes, such as the ability to differentiate products by making them aesthetically desirable, is important from a management standpoint, how the arts can be utilized to expand creative thinking and innovation are considered critical skills in successfully competing in a global marketplace. Nancy Adler in her article *The Arts & Leadership: Now That We Can Do Anything, What Will We Do?* contends that in light of current global and market trends and the concomitant need for new ideas and innovative business practices, now is the right time for a cross-fertilization of the arts and leadership (Adler, 2006:487). One of the trends Alder mentioned is the decreasing cost of experimentation. To remain competitive, businesses need to transform ideas quickly into new products and services. With a decreased time span necessary to test ideas the important resource at present are individuals that are able to create and bring forth innovative ideas for products and services.

Creativity and innovation are frequently mentioned in the management education literature as one of the most valued outcomes of arts-based learning for leadership development (Bartelme, 2005; Boyle and Ottensmayer, 2005; Adler, 2006; Barynek and Carboni, 2006). The application of arts-based learning in developing creative and innovative thinking is accomplished by instilling the creativity found in artistic expression within the management curriculum. These attributes include experimentation, questioning and challenging assumptions, risk-taking, exploring alternate possibilities and options, and empowering and enlisting others to pursue a shared, ideal vision for the future. (Puccio, Murdock, and Mance, 2007). The artistic mediums of music, drama, and literary arts all offer transferable creative skills that strengthen creative thinking and the innovative ability of leaders in managerial settings.

{333}

Arts-Based Learning and Healthcare Leadership

THE APPLICATION OF ARTS-BASED LEARNING in health care is mainly occurring in medical and allied health education. Medical humanities, which was in the past generally offered as a stand-alone elective in the medical school curriculum, is increasingly becoming integrated into the curriculum (Wear, 2006). Utilizing arts and humanities courses and faculty at their own institutions, medical schools are adopting arts-based learning as a complimentary pedagogy in medical education. In medical and allied health education, arts-based learning instills the professional attributes of empathy and compassion for patients strengthens the communication skills essential for good physician-patient relations, and sharpens health care providers observational, interpretive, and diagnostic skills (Boisaubin and Winkler, 2000; Macnaughton, 2000; Wiencke, 2007). As in management education, arts-based learning in medical education builds upon a strong interdisciplinary foundation; using disciplines such as the visual arts, literature, philosophy, and music to compliment the medical sciences.

A comparative review of the literature of arts-based learning applied to health care management education indicates that this is not an area in which arts-based learning has been actively pursued. The relative lack of arts-based learning practiced in healthcare management education is surprising in that health care management includes courses that draw from the disciplines of management and health studies. As previously discussed, the attributes of creativity and innovation, communications and collaboration and team-building are representative of the leadership and management skills that are strengthened through arts -based learning. The aforementioned skills are equally important for healthcare leaders. Given that providing optimal patient care is the primary objective for healthcare administrators, deepening the attributes of empathy and compassion for the patients they serve is another valuable contribution arts-based learning offers in the education of future healthcare leaders.

Daniel Pink (2006) in his book, *A Whole New Mind*, stressed the importance of several right brain aptitudes in our current Conceptual Age; one of which is empathy:

What will distinguish those who thrive will be their ability to understand what makes their fellow woman or man tick, to forge relationships, and to care for others (p.66).

In a discussion of values for health care executives, the President and CEO of the American College of Healthcare Executives, Thomas Dolan, expressed that health care leaders need to understand that the patients want to know that the health care organization that they are entrusting themselves and their love ones to is a compassionate and caring one (Buell, 2008:22).

Greene and Burke (2007) explored the potential application of arts-based learning specifically within health care leadership education. The authors found that the trends affecting health care leaders are similar to the trends that fostered the adoption of arts-based learning in management education. Health care leaders face a rapidly changing environment, technological advances that significantly influence health care operations, and the heightened importance of managing teams of health care professionals whose collaboration is essential in providing quality health care. Moreover, health care organizations are mission-driven and have an obligation to a customer base which the authors describe as the "range of humanity". Thus, the authors believe that the unique characteristics of the health care sector intensify the relevance of an "artistically informed healthcare leaders" (p. 383).

Green and Burke offer two methods for introducing arts-based learning into the health care leadership curriculum. The first method is an embedded method in which arts-based learning is offered within existing courses. An example the authors provide as an application for health care administration programs would be to use literature and/or poetry that reflects leadership attributes within a health care course to teach about leading change in a health care organization. The second approach is to offer arts-based learning as a separate focus. For example, an artist offers students specific training in drama or painting to enhance their artistic aptitudes. An artistic project or course would stand-alone and not be integrated within a health care specific course. An arts project or course allows for what Taylor and Ladkin (2009) refer to as a transfer of skills that focuses on the process of creating art rather than a final product.

Both approaches have strengths and weaknesses. An embedded approach provides a stronger linkage between theory and application, as well as a more direct application of problem-solving skills. However, an embedded approach can simplify the arts form as well as the artistic experience. In addition, an embedded approach most often limits arts-based learning to a specific class within a course. Alternately, utilizing the arts as a separate focus allows the learner to experience the creative process. The limitation of the stand-alone approach is that the emphasis is not on the practical application in health care management but rather on the artistic experience.

{335}

Application of Arts-Based Learning

As evidenced in the review of the application of arts-based learning in management and medical education, the skills and aptitudes that result from the application of arts-based learning as a complementary pedagogy are equally valuable for educating current and future leaders in healthcare management. As an educator in a graduate healthcare leadership program, I had the opportunity to explore how arts-based learning could be used to strengthen the healthcare leadership skills among my students. My overall goal was to utilize arts-based learning to instill in students an awareness of multiple perspectives in administrative decision-making in order to create an impetus for more informed and inclusive administrative decisions.

I was specifically interested in providing students with the broader perspectives of physicians and patients. Maintaining positive physician relations is one of the foremost concerns of healthcare executives. In the U.S. health care system, physicians drive hospital admissions and therefore are integral to the financial health of a hospital (Press Ganey Associates, 2006). The mission of any healthcare organization is the care of the patient and the optimal means of providing that care. Yet, those that hold administrative and managerial positions in healthcare organizations are often removed from the patients they serve. To understand the patient perspective, hospital administrators usually rely on patient satisfaction surveys which cannot fully convey the patient experience. As examples from the literature have demonstrated, visual and narrative arts have been successfully used to provide a voice for patients and a means of expression for physicians; providing an illustrative medium for understanding both perspectives.

Administrative decision-making in itself has multiple dimensions. Since our program focuses on healthcare leadership, decision-making is considered through the lens of leadership and specifically those skills and attributes that contribute to success in a healthcare leadership role. The leadership skills and attributes referred to are those that were described earlier as benefitting from arts-based learning in management and medical education, namely, collaboration and team-building, communications, innovation and creativity , and empathy. The aforementioned leadership skills and attributes are integral to a well-rounded and comprehensive curriculum in healthcare management and, in particular, healthcare leadership education. Thus, the task as an educator was to find a means of integrating arts-based learning into healthcare leadership courses.

Integration of Arts-Based Learning in a Healthcare Leadership Program

THE MASTERS OF HEALTHCARE LEADERSHIP PROGRAM (MHL) offered at Park University serves as an example of how one approach to arts-based learning was integrated into a healthcare leadership course. The MHL program offers a curriculum that is common to most healthcare management programs with a specific emphasis on healthcare leadership. The program is designed for students who are currently in managerial and/or leadership positions and for those who or aspire to be future leaders of healthcare organizations.

An embedded approach was initially chosen as the optimal means of integrating arts-based learning into the curriculum. The embedded approach allowed for integration into the established curriculum without the addition of credit hours. The embedded approach also complimented the existing course content in the core courses on health care strategy and the organization of health care delivery systems. All students enrolled in the core courses have a common understanding of the foundations of healthcare management and the leadership responsibilities of healthcare administrators. The primary programmatic goals of the MHL Program are not only to develop the managerial skills and competencies necessary for health care administrators but also to develop leadership skills that can guide health care systems in new directions. Given the programmatic goals of the MHL Program, the aforementioned health care courses within the MHL curriculum easily accommodated integration of arts-based learning and provided an instructional basis for applications to a health care setting.

Objectives for Integrating Arts-Based Learning

THERE WERE MULTIPLE OBJECTIVES for the using arts-based learning as a complimentary pedagogical approach. The first objective was to increase students' awareness of the perspectives of physicians and patients expressed through differing artistic mediums. Secondly, I wanted students to be able to reflect upon how they as future health care leaders can incorporate the aforementioned perspectives into their own decision-making processes. Third, as demonstrated in the management education literature, arts-based learning is used to strengthen leadership skills such as creativity and innovation. By integrating arts-based learning with artwork and narratives unique to the health care sector, students would ideally be able to develop more innovative approaches to problem solving and strategic thinking applied to the organization and delivery of health care services. Lastly, I wanted students to work toward developing a stronger bridge between management and direct patient care. A particular concept in health care service delivery that is receiving attention in health care management, and likewise in health care management courses, is patient-centered care. The Institute of Medicine (IOM) defines patient-centered care as:

> "Providing care that is respectful of and responsive to individual patient preferences, needs, and values, and ensuring that patient values guide all clinical decisions." (2001: 6).

Since one of the objectives for incorporating art-based leaning is to provide a deeper understanding of the patients' perspective on illness and care, it is well suited to teaching a managerial perspective that emphasizes patient-centeredness.

Instructional methods

{337}

Rather than focus on art and literature that depicted general leadership skills, I wanted students to concentrate on the application of leadership skills within a healthcare setting. To meet this objective, I chose an arts-based learning experience that enabled students to engage in reflection and analysis of how the patient and physician experiences as expressed through the arts influenced their own leadership styles and decision-making processes.

Students were asked to view patient artwork and to read essays by physicians that described the physicians' emotional experience with patients. The patient's artwork provided a window into how the patient views themselves in the context of their illness. The physicians' narratives chosen provided insight into how physicians interact with the patient on a person-to-person level.

The paintings students were asked to view were illuminations of a cancer patient's experience, in which the artist provided images of himself and of familiar landscapes that portrayed his life as he visualized it rather than as a cancer patient (Sullivan, 1998). Students were also asked to read two essays by physicians. The first was by Patch Adams (1998), which described his interaction with children in his self-described role as a "clown-shaman". Using symbolic objects and aromatherapy, the author recounted the healing power, emotionally and physically, that resulted from a doctor-patient relationship based on compassion, empathy and a mutual desire to "know each other". (p. 401).

The second story was by physician, Dr. Eric Ring, titled *Forgive Me I'm Bleeding*. In his writings he described his personal experiences with patients as a medical student (Ring, 1998). The narrative chronicled the author's reaction to medical errors that occurred to patients assigned to his care. The narrative provided, through a moving account of a medical error that resulted in a patient's death, a means of understanding the emotional response clinicians experience when medical errors occur.

Discussion Questions

After viewing the paintings and reading the physician narratives, students were asked to respond to a series of discussion questions. The questions were designed to encourage reflection both personally and professionally, as well as to utilize the insights acquired from the artwork and narratives to encourage innovative approaches to developing health care systems that support patient-centered care. The questions were presented sequentially, moving students from personal reflection, to considering how their reactions to the art and narratives would affect their decisions professionally and, finally, to translate the insights they gained from the art and narratives into potential actions to improve patient care.

The first two questions required students to be reflective and describe their reactions to the essays and artwork from different perspectives. The first question asked students how they would describe, on a personal level, the patient's and physician's experiences as expressed in the essays and artwork. The second question asked students to take the perspective of a hospital administrator and describe their reaction to these same experiences. The intent of both of these questions was for students to reflect on the emotional aspects of the patient and physician experiences and to elicit an empathy toward and understanding of their perspectives. How one reacts personally and professionally may differ but the underlying response and ability to understand the patient and caregiver's perspective connects one's personal and professional actions.

The third discussion question required that students apply their understanding of physicians' and patients' perspectives and asked how these perspectives could be used to support and enhance patient-centered care. By applying their understanding of physicians' and patients' perspectives into a situation that involved problem-solving and decision-making, students were able to strengthen their understanding of the importance of collaboration and communication, as well as enhance their abilities to develop innovative and creative responses to improving patient care (Fontaine, 2008).

REFLECTIONS AND RESPONSES: An important outcome of arts-based learning within this course was for students to establish a stronger connection and empathy for the patient who they will ultimately serve. An equally important outcome was for students to become more aware of the experiences of clinicians and the relationship that they have with patients.

Reflecting on their own personal reactions to the paintings and narratives, students referred to the expression of emotions from the patients and the physicians and of the emotional bond that can develop between physicians and patients. Students also noted how creative expression was used to provide not only as means of expression for patients but also as a temporary respite from their fears and concerns surrounding their illness. The discussions illustrated that students related to the artist not simply as a patient but as an individual whose thoughts and emotions depicted a life quite separate from the health care environment. Through a reflection on the artist's paintings, students became aware that art served as means for patients to cope with an illness. It was noted in our discussions that art, as exemplified in the paintings, offered a means for the artist to escape his illness temporarily. The discussions also led to a realization that paintings could provide a sense that one was not suffering through an illness alone. It was evident from our class discussions that students were able to relate to what the artist expressed through his paintings. Together we gained a deeper appreciation of the value of artistic expression for patients.

From an administrative perspective, a common observation throughout the discussion was the recognition of patient art as a powerful means of non-verbal communication. As administrators, the idea that patients may not always communicate their thoughts and feelings directly but may be able to more fully express them through artistic means; provided them with a deeper insight into the patients perspective and a greater empathy for the patient's experience. As such, the idea of including activities that involve patients in creating art and displays of patient artwork were suggested as a means to improve communication between patients and providers, and as an important part of the therapeutic process for patients.

The essays written by physicians, which revealed the emotions of physicians and how these emotions can shape the physician-patient relationship, provided an equally valuable perspective. The responses to the physician narratives allowed students to view physicians not only in terms of their medical proficiency, but also as the students noted, by their expressions of care and compassion when responding to patients. Citing the narrative by Adams (1998), students commented on how he embodied the concept of healing by not only concentrating on the medical condition of the patients but also by providing moments of joy and comfort to the children in his care . The narrative by Ring (1998) elicited concern regarding how medical errors can occur. In contrast to the preceding narrative, there was specific discussion regarding how insensitivity to patients, as described in Dr. Ring's narrative, can adversely affect the quality of care provided.

From an administrator's perspective, the narratives underscored the significance of the physician-patient relationships, in terms of both patient satisfaction and patient care. An interesting aspect of the responses to the physicians' narratives was recognition that not only patients need an outlet to express their emotions but medical staff may as well. In reading the narratives and thinking about their own responses as administrators, it was noted that as an administrator it is important to establish an environment in which physicians can convey their concerns and complaints to administrative staff.

In applying the insight gained from the observation of paintings and narratives, students offered innovative ideas for improving patient-centered care that involved both communication skills and collaborative efforts among providers and administrators. Improving communication among medical providers (physicians and allied health staff) and patients, as well as between administrators and patients was repeatedly noted. Suggestions to improve communications took a number of forms such as offering educational programs for medical providers that focused on communication skills, the importance of the dissemination of information to patients, listening to patients concerns and preferences regarding medical interventions and treatment plans, and revising internal policies and procedures to promote more patient and family involvement in decision-making. From a practical standpoint, the responses indicated the belief that improved communications between physicians and patients as well as among medical providers and administrators could reduce medical errors, improve patient safety, and could result in less medical malpractice suits.

An unexpected outcome of the discussion of the application of the differing perspectives acquired through arts-based learning centered on the acceptance of change. The majority of students in the MHL Program are working adults, many of whom are in clinical or managerial positions in health care organizations. While from an administrative and medical provider perspective, improving communications with the intent of empowering patient decision-making was a sought after outcome, most responses included the caveat that efforts to achieve this outcome should be introduced gradually. There appeared to be recognition that patient-centered care involves not only acknowledging patient experiences and expectations but acting upon them. The action required meant greater patient involvement in decisions regarding the course of their care. The thought of greater patient involvement raised the concern about the rapidity of change to surface. Would physicians and staff accept greater involvement in patient decision-making or will it be viewed as challenging the knowledge and training of healthcare professionals? Will patients along with their families have and be able to understand the medical information necessary to make critical decisions regarding their care? The questions noted exemplified the concerns of future healthcare leaders who are taking into account the perspectives of physicians and patients when considering administrative actions to improve patient-centered care.

{341}

Overall, the experiences of patients and physicians expressed through art and literature was seen as contributing in a practical way to administratively support efforts to achieve patient-centered care. Administrative efforts identified as contributing to patient-centered care included: communicating more openly with patients and providers, seeking greater input from all levels of staff, becoming more innovative in designing delivery approaches that emphasized patient's needs, and providing opportunities for utilizing the arts as a means of patient expression and healing. The learning experience also raised questions that challenged the conventional medical construct for decision-making authority and challenged their own ideas on how to introduce changes in the delivery of care that further promote the patient-centered approach.

Insights acquired from the paintings and narratives elevated the primacy of focusing on the patients needs and wants in the design and delivery of care. Referencing the paintings and narratives, discussions stressed the importance of empathy in patient relations, the need for physicians to take additional time and to exercise listening skills, and the value of educating patients so that they can take a more active role in determining their own course of care. All of the aforementioned factors are essential for achieving more patient-centered care. The use of arts-based learning also appeared to encourage students to offer innovative ideas that illustrated an awareness of patient and physician perspectives. Specific ideas included paying greater attention to creating a less stressful, more comfortable, and aesthetically pleasing physical environment; offering ideas ranging from the use of warm colors in exam rooms and patient rooms to providing plants and flowers in common areas. To enable medical providers to spend more time with patients, increasing the use and accessibility to information technology, particular the use of electronic records was frequently mentioned. A clear appreciation for the value of arts was also apparent in the discussions which noted the need for offering ancillary services to include art, music, and the creation and display of artwork, in order provide an increased focus on the treatment of the whole person not simply the illness.

New Directions for Arts-Based Learning and Health Care Leadership

THE HEALTH CARE SECTOR IS FACED with seemingly intractable health care challenges that have not been met by the application of new versions of past responses or through the safety of incremental change. Leadership skills strengthened through arts-based learning will ideally facilitate the discovery of creative and innovative solutions to some of the pressing concerns facing health care organizations. Greene and Burke (2007) offered potential outcomes for arts-based learning in the development of health care leaders that included accelerated development of insights, expanded alternatives for problem solution and strategic leadership, and encouraging critical thinking. Based on the concepts and ideas for applying arts-based learning to healthcare leadership education proposed by Greene and Burke, one can extend the application of arts-based learning in health care leadership education to specific problem-solving applications in the health care sector. As the MHL courses illustrated, arts-based learning can be successfully adapted to health care management courses that focus on the development and strengthening of leadership skills. Given the unique aspects of the health care sector, when integrating arts-based learning using the embedded approach, it is recommended that examples of artwork relevant to the health care sector are utilized. The use of health related artwork allows for a better understanding and applicability of the insights that are gained. The example for integrating arts-based learning also demonstrated that arts-based learning can be used to address a particular organizational and delivery concept; in this instance patient-centered care. The insights gained from arts-based learning and the application of new knowledge gained from a deeper understanding of differing perspectives and experiences is not limited to the education of future health care leaders. The continuing education of current leaders and manager in the health care filed can benefit from the leadership skills instilled from arts-based learning. Continuing education and training programs, not bound by curriculum requirements, are free to explore other methods of arts-based training that include non-embedded approaches, for example improvisational drama, poetry or sculpture classes, that can fundamentally shift the "way of knowing" and repertoire of skills of health care leaders.

Creative leadership demands creative-problem solving and there are many areas in health care operations in which arts-based learning can assist leaders in developing innovative solutions. As we continue to explore arts-based learning applications to healthcare management, future health care leaders should apply their learning experiences towards the development new approaches for improving patient care. These approaches could include creating a culture of safety, advocating for and enabling an environment that encourages greater consumerism and patient involvement in health-care decision-making, experimenting with practices that improve the patient experience, and innovative practices that balance cost-effectiveness and quality of care. The examples presented in this chapter begin to illustrate how art-based learning can be effectively applied to health care leadership education. Because the decisions made by healthcare leaders require the inclusion of multiple perspectives, exploring how arts-based learning can be applied in a cross-disciplinary process that involves a collaborative learning experience between learners in healthcare management and clinical practice is another area that merits further exploration. As educators continue to experiment with ways of integrating arts-based learning in health care leadership and management courses and programs, emphasis needs to be placed to how the skills acquired through arts-based learning are applied to finding creative and novel solutions to reforming the organization and delivery of health care services.

SHERRY FONTAINE, Ph.D. is Associate Professor and Director of Healthcare Leadership Programs at Park University. Prior to joining Park University she was Director of Doctoral Programs in Health Policy, Health Education, and Educational Leadership at D'Youville College in Buffalo, NY. Dr. Fontaine also served as a faculty member in graduate health management and policy programs at University of Memphis and University of South Carolina. She currently serves and has served on several nonprofit boards for the arts, health and community development organizations. She has also been a consultant for health and nonprofit organizations in the areas of strategic planning, marketing, executive development programs, and program evaluation. Her research has been published in *Health Marketing Quarterly, Journal of Health Care Marketing ,Health Care Strategic Management, Journal for Volunteer Administration, Ethics in Nonprofit Management, Cross-National Issues in Public Administration, Academic Exchange, Journal of Public Affairs Education, Journal of Higher Education and Outreach, Academic Exchange Extra and Academic Exchange Quarterly.*

{344}

References

ADAMS, P. (1998). When healing is more than simply clowning around. *Journal of the American Medical Association,* 279 (5): 401.

ADLER, N. (2006). The arts and leadership: Now that we can do anything, What will we do? *Academy of Management Learning and Education,* 5 (4): 486-499.

BARTELME, L. (2005). The view from the trenches: An interview with Harvey Seifter and Tim Stockil. *Journal of Business Strategy*, 26 (5): 7-13.

BARTUNEK, J. AND CARBONI, J. (2006). A time for hope: Response to Nancy Adler. *Academy of Management Learning And Education.* 5 (4): 500-504.

BOISAUBIN, E. AND WINKLER, M. (2000). Seeing patients and life contexts: The visual arts in medical education. *American Journal of Medical Science*, 319 (5): 292-296.

BOYLE, M. AND OTTENSMEYER, E. (2005). Solving businesses problems through the creative power of the arts: Catalyzing change at Univlever, *Journal of Business Strategy*, 26 (5): 14-21.

BUELL, J. (2008). Living the organization's mission, vision and values. *Healthcare Executive.* Nov/Dec :21- 24.

CORRIGAN,P. (1999). *Shakespeare on Management: Leadership Lessons for Today's Managers.* London: Kogan Page Ltd.

FONTAINE, S. (2008). Arts-based learning and healthcare leadership. *Academic Exchange Quarterly.* 12 (1) :183-187.

GOLD, M. AND HIRSHFELD, S. (2005). The behaviors of jazz as a catalyst for strategic renewal and growth. *Journal of Business Strategy.* 26 (5): 40-47.

GREENE, L. AND BURKE, G. (2007). Artful leadership in healthcare: Encouraging the possibilities. *The Journal of Health Administration Education.* 24 (4): 377-390.

INSTITUTE OF MEDICINE ,Committee on Quality Health Care in America (2006). *Crossing the Quality Chasm: A New Health System for the 21st Century.* Washington, DC: National Academy Press.

KOUZES, J. AND POSNER, B. (2002). *Leadership the challenge* (3rd ed.). San Francisco, CA: Jossey-Bass.

MACNAUGHTON,J. (2000). THE humanities in medical education: context, outcomes and structures. *Journal of Medical Ethics: Medical Humanities.* 26: 23-30.

MOCKLER, R. (2002). Using the arts to acquire and enhance management skills. *Journal of Management Education.* 26 (5): 574-585.

NORTHOUSE, P. (2004). *Leadership theory and practice.* (3rd ed.). Thousand Oaks: CA: Jossey-Bass.

PINK, D. (2004). Breakthrough Ideas for 2004. *Harvard Business Review.* February: 21-22.

PINK, D. (2006). *A whole new mind.* New York: Berkley Publishing Group.

PRESS GANEY ASSOCIATES. (2006, September). The growing importance of physician-hospital relations (CEO Update Archives). South Bend, IN: Melvin Hall.

PUCCIO,E., MURDOCK, M. and Mance, M. (2007). *Creative leadership: Skills that drive change.* Thousand Oaks, CA: Sage.

RING, E. (1998). Forgive me, I'm bleeding. *Journal of the American Medical Association,* 279 (5): 403.

SULLIVAN, E. (1998). Illuminations at the Massachusetts General Hospital Cancer Center. *Massachusetts General Hospital Cancer Center.* Retrieved on May 30, 2007, from HTTP://WWW2.MASSGENERAL.ORG/CANCER/ABOUT/ENVIRONMENT/ILLUM/INDEX.ASP .

TAYLOR, S. AND LADKIN, D. (2009). Understanding arts-based methods in management development. *Academy of Management and Learning.* 8 (1): 55-69.

WEAR, D. (2006). Viewpoint: trends and transitions in the medical humanities. *AAMC Reporter.* Retrieved August 3, 2009, from HTTP://WWW.AAMC.ORG/NEWSROOM/REPORTER/OCT06/VIEWPOINT.HTM .

WIENCKE, M. (2007). Connecting patients to patient care, Retrieved June 1, 2007. Web site: HTTP://WWW.DARTMED. DARTMOUTH.EDU/FALL06/PRINT/US_PAINTINGS.PHP.

YUKL, G. (2006). *Leadership in organizations* (6th ed.). Saddle River: NJ: Prentice-Hall.

Honouring the Patient's Voice in Health Professional Education

Seema Shah MD, MSPH

THERE IS INCREASING RECOGNITION that patients have a vital role to play in health professional education (HPE), helping to balance biomedical learning about illness with real world learning about the experience of illness (Morris & O'Neill, 2006). The University of British Columbia (UBC) undertook a participatory action project, bringing together community members (patients and organizations), students, and faculty to develop, evaluate, and refine patient-led interdisciplinary HPE workshops. Drawing on the effectiveness of the use of patient narratives in HPE, this article describes an innovative workshop activity combining the direct sharing of patient narratives with the use of a literary narrative of illness. Results suggest the following may be valuable approaches to teach students about the lived experience of illness: 1) the use of patient educators; 2) the combined use of in-person patient narratives and literary illness narratives; and 3) the involvement of patients who are also health professionals.

> *I don't actually know why I fell apart that year. There were a number of things that happened during the preceding couple of years, but not one obvious thing that I identified as* **the** *cause. When asked why I fell into a deep, dark depression. I explained that things just got progressively worse, spiraling out of control. I went from this incredible emotional volatility to a complete numbness. At peace with death, I experienced a suicidality (yes, I know suicidality is not actually a word, yet it's the only word that seems to fit) I tried to explain what was still unexplainable even to myself.*

In the summer of 2008, I responded to a UBC Division of Health Care Communication (DHCC) posting to become involved in an initiative entitled: "UBC Community Partnerships for Health Professional Education." The posting asked, "Would you like *your voice* to be heard in the education of Health Professionals?" And, more specifically, it offered the opportunity to become involved in a campus-community collaboration to "develop a workshop where students learn about chronic health problems from people who live with them every day."

I went through medical school, internship, and residency taking my health for granted. Illness first struck in 1998 in the form of chronic depression and struck again in 2001 in the form of chronic fatigue syndrome. Debilitated by illness, I permanently left general practice in 2004. Needless to say, illness has changed my life, my experience of the world, and my way of thinking about health and health care.

I became involved in this project because I saw it as an opportunity to share my voice and potentially contribute to change in the system. In addition to my personal experience with illness, I thought my background in health care had the potential to bring a unique perspective to this project. This includes my experience as a medical student, a family physician, and a physician with training in public health and preventive medicine. I also thought my more recent interest in the use of literature in medicine might lend itself well to this project.

Providing the Framework

HEALTH CARE IS EXPERIENCING a shift away from a paternalistic approach towards a more patient-centred model of care, which takes into account the individuality of each patient and views the patient as an active, informed partner, involved in all decisions regarding their care (Morris & O'Neill, 2006; Silow-Carroll, Alteras, & Stepnick, 2006). This model is based on concepts that were at the core of my training in public health and preventive medicine – "prevention, therapeutic alliances, and holism" (Basso, 2004, para.4).

In this paper, I use the term "patient" because it is the most commonly used and understood term to identify individuals who are receiving care from health professionals, within the context of that relationship. It is meant to include other terms that also connote this contextual identity and are preferred by some, including: client, consumer, service user, and survivor. Some people consider the term patient to be pejorative, implying a more passive and submissive role. However, I think it is not so much the term that is in need of changing, but rather the nature of the patient-provider relationship – which is really at the crux of the movement towards patient-centered care.

The concept of patient-centered care extends beyond the patient-provider encounter to health care in general. To date, most efforts to include patients in HPE have placed patients in a passive role, such as acting as "standardized patients" or serving as teaching examples on ward rounds. When I was a medical student, interpersonal skills were mainly taught through the use of standardized patients – actors *given* patient voices scripted by health professionals. Both in clinical and classroom settings, patients were present to be practiced "on" and preceptors were expecting "right" answers from students. I didn't question what or how I was being taught. It took becoming a patient myself to make me realize the lack of authentic patient voice and experience in HPE.

{350}

Fortunately, there is increasing recognition that patients have an active and vital role to play in the development and delivery of HPE due to their firsthand knowledge and experience of illness (Morris & O'Neill, 2006; PMETB, 2008). Not surprisingly, such recognition is not only from health professionals, but from patients as well. In his classic book, *The Wounded Storyteller*, medical sociologist Dr. Arthur Frank describes the (re)claiming of voice and active involvement of patients in the construction of medical knowledge and practice. Or, more simply, the desire of patients "to speak rather than being spoken for and to represent oneself rather than being represented" (1995, p.13).

Participatory action research

This initiative used a participatory action research (PAR) approach. PAR – also known as community based research – a grassroots approach to research that addresses issues important to marginalized populations (Merrifield, 1997; Reid, Brief, & LeDrew, 2009). In other words, PAR includes communities being studied in every step of the research process and values the firsthand, experience-based knowledge community members contribute. Not only is PAR participatory, inclusive, and knowledge-generating, it is also action-oriented (Merrifield, 1997; Reid, Brief, & LeDrew, 2009).

In this project, students, community members, and faculty worked together to develop, evaluate, and refine interdisciplinary patient-led educational workshops for health professional students. This took the form of a pilot workshop and a modified second workshop that were overseen by an advisory board for the project. The approach was intended to provide opportunities for the community to have a voice in the training of their future health care providers.

The planning team I joined included: a paid facilitator from the UBC DHCC, a UBC School of Nursing professor (one of the original investigators), two health professional students recruited from UBC (one from social work, one from occupational therapy), a representative from the Vancouver-Burnaby Branch of the Canadian Mental Health Association, and two other "patients" (community members living with chronic illness). A variety of health disciplines were involved because, in addition to better understanding the role students' specific disciplines could play in improving patient care, a desired goal of our workshops was to help students better understand the role of other health disciplines in order to promote collaboration and optimize patient care (Health Council of Canada, 2007).

Narrative methods in health professional education

AS A SUBCOMPONENT OF PAR, narrative methods were used in this project through the sharing of patients' stories as a means to teach students. The use of patient narratives is one of the most recent techniques utilized to bring the patient perspective into HPE (PMETB, 2008).

Health professionals are routinely taught to *take* a patient's history – that is, take whatever pieces of a patient's history they decide are relevant to create the "official story" of the patient's illness (Couser, 1997; Watson, 2007). They are usually taught to follow a standard format, with any information straying outside of this considered extraneous and beyond the time constraints of an encounter (Charon, 2006).

In his groundbreaking book, *The Illness Narratives: Suffering, Healing, and the Human Condition*, psychiatrist and medical anthropologist Arthur Kleinman notes that the typical health provider-patient interaction excludes consideration of the impact and meaning of illness in an individual's life. As a result, important opportunities to improve the subjective experience of illness and quality of life for patients are missed. Kleinman, therefore, emphasizes the need "to make the patient's and the family's narrative of the illness experience more central in the education process" (1988, p.255). He re-emphasized the need to incorporate the humanities into HPE in a recent Globe and Mail article (Kleinman, 2009). Understanding the patient's unadulterated experience of illness brings the patient's perspective squarely into HPE, thereby providing opportunities for students to adopt a more patient-centred approach (Kumagai, 2008) and to create change in the system.

Becoming a patient myself made me aware of how limiting the "standard format" approach to patient care is. Encountering health care providers who have truly listened and tried to understand the individuality of my experience of illness has been crucial to improving the quality of my life. This has made me realize how essential the understanding of patients' stories is to the provision of optimal care. Bringing patients' stories into HPE has taken many forms, including talking directly with students, as well as narratives told through video, visual art, music, and literature (Jotkowitz & Fadlon, 2004; Kumagai, 2008).

Oral (face-to-face) narratives of illness

PATIENTS CONVEYING THEIR NARRATIVES THROUGH talking directly with students can offer firsthand insight into the experience of illness and foster empathy in a way that can't be obtained through other means of teaching - one example of this is the formation of a very real interpersonal connection, a "personal attachment with someone previously viewed as very different from himself or herself" (Kumagai, 2008, p.655). Patient teachers and their narratives also tend to be particularly memorable for students (Farrell, Towle, & Godolphin, 2006).

Literary narratives of illness

THERE IS STRONG EVIDENCE THAT the arts and humanities can be effectively used in HPE to hone observational, reflective, and interpretive skills, as well as promote better provider-patient relationships by fostering compassion and empathy (Brett-MacLean, 2007; Staricoff, 2004). The arts can stimulate insight and understanding by portraying different perspectives and complex situations. The use of patient narratives from the literature is one way of including more of the "life world" of patients (Early, 2009).

Narrative Medicine (NM) provides an approach to the hands-on use of literature in medicine. Rita Charon, a physician and literary scholar who pioneered the NM movement, calls it a "clinical cousin" of literature-and-medicine. She describes NM as "a clinical practice informed by the theory and practice of reading, writing, telling, and receiving of stories" (Charon, 2006, p.viii). Close reading of and reflecting on literary works engages the reader more fully in a given scenario than clinical, sociological, or historical descriptions (Charon, 1995). This is often coupled with reflective writing, an established experiential method to teach health professional students empathy and one that often brings unrecognized feelings and attitudes to the surface (Alcaukas & Charon, 2008; DasGupta & Charon, 2004).

My interest in the combination of literature and medicine was sparked over a decade ago with the onset of illness. Ironically, prior to this, my passion for literature and creative writing had been put on the back burner *because of* medicine. But consistent with Arthur Frank's observation, illness became "a call for stories" (1995, p.53).

I began keeping a journal for the first time and this helped lay the foundation for crafted personal narratives of illness. I have to give credit to my psychiatrist at the time for suggesting I read William Styron's *Darkness Visible* (1990). Unlike my medical textbooks, reading this book was the first time I felt someone was describing depression in the debilitating way I was experiencing it. Subsequently, I sought out and was incredibly fortunate to find a therapist adept at using literature, journalling, and creative writing as part of the therapeutic process.

When I learned of the use of literature in HPE, I could see why this would be a very effective way to bring the patient's "voice" into HPE and teach students about the lived experience of illness. This came full-circle for me when I found out, very coincidentally, that a published illness narrative of mine had been used in a narrative medicine elective for medical students (Shah, 2004).

Narratives of patients who are also health professionals

PHYSICIANS WHO THEMSELVES have become patients occupy both roles, and thus potentially can provide critical perspectives on issues of communication and compassion. From their experiences as patients, they may gain insights for improving doctor-patient communication and relationships. These insights may then be applied to communication training in medical education. (Klitzman, 2006, p.447)

Thirteen years after the publication of *When Doctors Get Sick*, Mandell and Spiro followed up with all surviving physician-patient contributors and found that most felt that "illness had made them better physicians, particularly for the human side of care" (2000). Similarly, Klitzman found that physicians with a history of serious illness reported increased sensitivity to patients' experiences and empathy in doctor-patient relationships (Klitzman, 2006).

I believe my personal experience with illness drastically changed the way I practiced medicine in many ways. It led me to practice with more empathy and greater understanding of the importance of active listening, validating experience, and involving patients in decision-making, among other things.

Developing a workshop

OUR WORKSHOPS FOCUSED specifically on mental illness. We had four planning meetings to prepare for our first workshop. The patients on the committee were deemed "community educators" (CE), as they were responsible for workshop facilitation.

The planning team decided on the following workshop objectives: 1) recognizing the client's expertise in contributing to care; 2) appreciating the human-to-human experience (including the importance of active listening and recognizing the value of each interaction, even if a problem cannot be "fixed"); and 3) describing the factors contributing to, and the effects of, stigma on clients.

Initially our approach was for each CE to share their personal story with the students and then field questions. However, I expressed an interest in doing something experiential along with directly my sharing personal story, in order to give the students more of a "felt sense" of living with chronic illness. The other committee members supported my efforts to develop my own experiential activity, which incorporated the workshop objectives through the use of a literary illness narrative.

Use of an illness narrative

IN ADDITION TO THE MERITS of using literary narratives in HPE already described, I believe they possess unique characteristics that could complement the oral narratives shared in patient-led workshops.

Storytelling is an art and a skill, one that is particularly challenging when it comes to stories about difficult topics such as illness (Frank, n.d.; Neimi & Ellis, 2001). Illness narratives, be they written or oral, need to be carefully crafted in order to draw the reader/audience in and effectively convey experience. Expertly written stories are created with intention, relaying specific themes (e.g., workshop objectives) and complex scenarios in a way that is clear and engaging (Alcauskas & Charon, 2008; Neimi & Ellis, 2001; Raoul et al., 2007). Equally important is what these narratives *don't* do. As professional storytellers Ellis and Neimi point out, effective storytelling "is not about making the listener squirm, want to run away, or pity you" (2001).

Representing chaos

ARTHUR FRANK PROPOSES three types of illness narratives: the restitution narrative, the quest narrative, and the chaos narrative. The chaos narrative is written (or spoken) with a sense of immediacy while events are actually being lived and before the individual has had the time and distance needed to make sense of the experience. However, despite its name, Frank notes that the chaos narrative is not technically a "narrative"– a term implying coherence and plot (Frank, 1995). But where, then, does this leave the representation of chaos, a state of illness that is important for others – especially health care providers – to understand?

Kathlyn Conway, in her book *Illness and the Limits of Expression*, emphasizes the necessity of a skilled writer and distance from the experience in order to transform chaos into a coherent narrative. Without this transformation, she adds, "we are left, ironically, with a verbal chaos that fails to communicate the feeling of chaos" (2007, p.105).

Conway, thus, suggests that:

> the best storytellers are successfully able to hold in tension these two different and seemingly contradictory purposes at the heart of illness narration – to represent the devastation of the experience and to transform the raw and shattered experience into a story with shape and coherence (2007, p.101)

Creating distance

I BELIEVE ANOTHER POTENTIAL BENEFIT of incorporating literature into workshops developed and led by patients is the creation of some distance between the patient and the material. By this I mean that what is shared is not solely personal and the focus is not only on the individual patient. This can add a layer of safety for the patient by providing a less threatening approach and offering a way of sharing insight from personal experience, which may be of particular relevance to stigma-laden illnesses, such as mental illness.

{356}

The issue of personal motivation, be it conscious or not, is another consideration when patients choose to share their stories with an audience. Literary scholar Anne Hunsaker Hawkins addresses this issue with understanding and not judgment, pointing out how, when it comes to illness, the "therapeutic impulse to tell one's story can become narcissistic" or very narrowly focused on the feeling of having been wronged (2007, p.115). Neimi and Ellis stress that difficult stories should only be shared publicly if the teller has already worked through the material enough to avoid engaging in "personal therapy" (2001, p.31).

For the workshop I chose a short story ("Unwanted Companion" by Ruth Krahn) that is a fictional narrative told from the perspective of a depressed woman (1999). I selected this story in particular because I felt it addressed the workshop objectives, accurately reflected important aspects of my own experience with depression, and spoke to me at an emotional level.

Implementation

MY EXPERIENTIAL ACTIVITY was part of a two-and-a-half hour workshop held at a community mental health agency. All of the planning committee was present. Thirteen students attended from the following health professions: social work (5), nursing (4), occupational therapy (1), pharmacy (1), and dietetics (2). After a brief introduction to the workshop, including roundtable introductions, I facilitated my activity with a brief group discussion following. During this time, students could reflect on the activity and ask relevant questions about my personal experience. The workshop ended with a wrap-up, giving students the opportunity to share any thoughts about the session with the group.

Use of an illness narrative from the literature

THE STORY, "UNWANTED COMPANION," consists of a depressed woman carrying on three separate conversations: one with her adult daughter, one with 'depression' itself, and one with the reader/audience (Krahn, 1999). As the story is almost completely dialogue, it was possible to approach it like a script, without altering the original text. Students didn't have an opportunity to read the story prior to the workshop, therefore a role-play was an interactive way for them to absorb the story, as opposed to having each student read the story independently.

Four volunteers were recruited from the group to do the role-play, reading aloud the different "voices" in the story. Two volunteers sat across from each other on one side of the "stage," one playing the depressed woman and the other her daughter. Another student sat on the other side of the "stage," also playing the depressed woman, alternately in conversation with the audience and 'depression' (played by a fourth student, standing behind her and looming over her shoulder).

Given that social and emotional learning is most effective when combined with the development of insight (Cherniss et al., 1998), as well as reflective writing being an established method for teaching empathy (DasGupta & Charon, 2004), a brief reflective writing exercise was scheduled post-activity, followed by group discussion. During the discussion, I was able to share my personal experience. I believe the insight I shared from the perspective of a patient added to the interpretation of the story, while the story acted as a springboard for the sharing of my stories of illness.

Evaluation

AN 'EVALUATION FRAMEWORK' was used to determine the utility of the workshop; specific evaluation tools, criteria, and methods were developed by our planning group using a participatory action research design. All students were asked to complete a pre and post survey about the workshop to capture changes in their knowledge, skills and attitudes. They were also invited to complete an individual follow-up interview. Interviews were intended to assess students' reflections on their learning experiences. Finally, a focus group with the planning group (community educators, organization representative, students, and faculty) was conducted to understand the benefits, challenges, and supports needed to facilitate their teaching roles, and particularly to sustain their efforts beyond one workshop. For this paper, I will only report on students' evaluation of my experiential activity.

Transcripts, qualitative survey questions, and other data sources were read for reporting ideas and grouped into themes accordingly. Quantitative questions were compared on the pre and post surveys, looking for shifts in attitudes, knowledge, and behaviour.

Results

OF THE THIRTEEN STUDENTS who attended the first workshop, twelve returned a completed survey set (pre- and post-test). Eight students participated in individual follow-up interviews.

I repeated the short story role-play in another workshop, but final results for this workshop are still pending. However, some committee observations and participant comments from the second workshop are included below.

Results suggest that the use of the chosen fictional narrative and accompanying role-play was effective in conveying the workshop objectives to varying degrees. By bearing witness to the enacted scenario, students were able to see the power of their words and the importance of considering different perspectives. Many students related to the daughter, as they thought they might act similarly. This was revealing for many students who perhaps had never been able to see how their interactions affected the individual they were trying to help.

> I think what struck me most was the role-play in the beginning, as I found it very realistic, and it taught me more about how depression is both perceived by the family members and those who have it. – Social Work Student (workshop 1)

One student specifically stated that they thought literature was a great way of explaining the effects of mental illness to others and seeing the experience of illness through the patient's eyes.

I think that as health care providers it is important that we sympathize with patients and make an effort to understand their struggles, but if we ourselves have never experienced a mental illness it is impossible to truly appreciate all of the struggles. However I think that exercises that push us to imagine how our lives would be different are a useful technique. – Occupational Therapy Student (workshop 2)

The planning team noticed that the role-play seemed to have a larger emotional impact on students than we anticipated, visibly affecting some of the students. This highlighted the importance of preparing students for the potential impact of the upcoming material and discussing safety at the beginning and end of the workshop.

Impact of oral narratives

BASED ON GENERAL REVIEW OF STUDENT COMMENTS, the physical presence of patients and hearing their stories directly appeared to have a definite impact on conveying workshop material.

I felt like I could take it home with me because I could see that it was actually real rather than just theories and textbooks, it was actually someone who was right there. - Social Work Student (workshop 1)

My Perspective

INVOLVEMENT IN THIS INITIATIVE was a very positive experience for me. As a patient, it was empowering to have the opportunity to speak rather than being spoken for. My focus group feedback reflects this.

Overall, it was a wonderful and energizing experience. I felt that the committee . . . truly listened to and valued the input of the community educators, allowed them to be involved in every aspect of the process and were very supportive and encouraging.

Not only was I allowed to share *what* I thought was most important, I was also allowed me to share in *the way* I thought would be most powerful and effective.

> I really appreciated that the group was open to letting us think outside the box for the activities that we came up with . . . thinking about what kind of activity [we could use] that would be experiential, that would get across some of the things that I feel living with chronic illness.

As a physician unable to continue practicing due to chronic illness, this opportunity gave me the chance to put my medical training and experience to good use and make a meaningful contribution as a health professional. I was specifically able to draw upon: 1) my experience as a medical student; 2) my experience as a family physician providing direct care to patients; 3) my training and work in preventive medicine and public health, with a focus on the whole person and systemic change; and 4) my recent interest and learning related to the field of narrative medicine.

{360} Discussion

BASED ON FEEDBACK from the workshop development committee and positive results for the actual workshop, students gained a better understanding of the patient's lived experience of illness.

Consistent with previous research, both in-person sharing of patient stories and the use of literary narratives of illness appeared to be very effective methods of communicating important aspects of patients' subjective experience of illness.

Why add direct involvement of patients in the use of literary narratives of illness in HPE? In this approach an effort can be made to include patients who may not be represented in literary texts. Literary scholar G. Thomas Couser notes that, although published narratives of illness have served as a means for marginalized individuals to counter traditional medical discourse, the genre of life writing about illness is not diverse in terms of race and class (1997).

With respect to the selection of literature, patients can provide an important perspective, identifying works they feel most accurately represent their experience of illness and the world. They can also facilitate discussions about literary illness narratives in a way that is very different than those who are healthy, bringing their firsthand insight and experience into the interpretation.

I was able to share personal "patient" insights when discussing the mother-daughter conversation in the short story, helping students see how some of the daughter's comments may have come across as judgmental or condescending to the depressed woman and affected how she chose to respond. By shifting perspective, they realized there may be very understandable reasons why she was not always forthcoming.

Having community educators present helped to emphasize the individuality of the illness experience. For instance, putting ourselves within the scenario, we each had different ideas of how we felt the daughter could have been most helpful to us. This illustrated that there were no "right" answers, but rather skills and approaches that served to optimize provider-patient interactions, such as active listening and seeing the patient as the expert in their own life.

Commenting on "characters" allowed students to be honest in a way I don't think would have been possible if we were only focusing on my personal story. Similarly, I could respond honestly to their comments, from the perspective of a patient, *through the text* without putting students on the defensive.

I think the fact that I am also a health professional allowed the students to feel more comfortable expressing their thoughts. Drawing on the concept of peer education, facilitation of HPE workshops by patients who are also health professionals might strengthen facilitator-participant identification and act as a bridge between the patient and provider perspectives. Along these lines, Klitzman suggests that narratives of physician-patients' experiences may be "more poignant and compelling to fellow doctors than those of lay patients in encouraging health care providers to be more open and sensitive to problems in communication with patients" (2006, p.452). This may be an area worth exploring in future research.

{361}

The experiential activity described in this paper reflects an innovative approach to HPE, incorporating some novel ideas that appear to have promise, including: 1) the use of patient educators; 2) the combined use of in-person patient narratives and literary illness narratives; and 3) the involvement of patients who are also health professionals. It seemed to be an effective method of teaching students about the lived experience of illness to complement their biomedical textbook learning.

Everyone says ... that what I've lost will return once my depression is treated.

They don't understand ... that whatever I lost took the ability to have fun, the desire to live and the ability to live in this world away from me.

They [health professionals] think that if someone no longer actively feels the need to kill themselves, they have fixed the problem. It really doesn't matter that you still don't want to be here as long as you are here ...

Caren is the first health professional who has listened and tried to understand (and I think she does). And that has been *huge*.

– Seema Shah, Journal entry, 2000

It was important to me that this project wasn't just an academic exercise, but led to the creation of something tangible with the potential for ongoing real world application. Involvement in this project left me feeling that my voice was heard and that already I was helping lead to changes in the system in a very real way.

Seema Shah is a physician who has completed a residency in preventive medicine and a master's degree in public health. She left general practice in 2004 due to chronic illness. Since then she has facilitated workshops using literature and/or creative writing for people living with chronic illness and for health professional students. Creative writing about her experience with illness and health care has been published or is forthcoming in Portfolio milieu 2004 (an anthology of Canadian women's writing), Women Who Care: Women's Stories of Health Care and Caring, and Blood and Thunder: Musings on the Art of Medicine.

References

ALCAUSKAS, M & CHARON, R. (2008). Right brain: Reading, writing, and reflecting: Making a case for narrative medicine in neurology. *Neurology, 70*, 891-894

BASSO, M. JR. (2004). Preparing successful future physicians to meet emerging social needs in humanitarian ways. *The Yale Journal for the Humanities in Medicine.* Retrieved from HTTP://YJHM.YALE.EDU/ESSAYS/MBASSOIA. HTM

BRETT-MACLEAN, P. (2007). Use of the arts in medical and health professional education. *University of Alberta Health Sciences Journal, 4*(1), 26-29.

CHARON, R., BANKS, J. T., CONNELLY, J. E., HAWKINS, A. H., HUNTER, K. M., JONES, A. H., ET AL. (1995). Literature and medicine: Contributions to clinical practice. *Annals of Internal Medicine, 122*(8), 599-606.

CHARON, R. (2006). *Narrative medicine: Honoring the stories of illness.* New York: Oxford University Press

CHERNISS, C., GOLEMAN, D., EMMERLING, R., COWAN, K., & ADLER, M. (1998). *Bringing emotional intelligence to the workplace.* Piscataway, NJ: The Consortium for Research on Emotional Intelligence in Organizations.

CONWAY, K. (2007). *Illness and the limits of expression.* Ann Arbor, MI: The University of Michigan Press.

COUSER, G.T. (1997). *Recovering bodies: Illness, disability, and life writing.* Madison, WI: The University of Wisconsin Press.

DASGUPTA, S., CHARON, R. (2004). Personal illness narratives: Using reflective writing to teach empathy. *Academic Medicine, 79*(4), 351-356.

EARLY, J. S. (2009). Inviting in the life world: Illness narratives and personal and creative writing in medical education. *The Yale Journal for Humanities in Medicine.* Retrieved from HTTP://YJHM.YALE.EDU/ESSAYS/ JEARLY20090921.HTM

Shah

FARRELL, C., TOWLE, A., & Godolphin, W. (2006). *Where's the patient's voice in health professional education?*(Conference Report). Vancouver, B. C.: University of British Columbia, Division of Health Care Communication, College of Health Disciplines.

FRANK, A. W. (1995). *The wounded storyteller: Body, illness, and ethics.* Chicago: The University of Chicago Press.

FRANK, A. W. (n.d.). Stories and healing: Observations on the progress of my thoughts. Retrieved from HTTP:// LITSITE.ALASKA.EDU/HEALING/FRANK.HTML

HAWKINS, A. H. (2007). Writing about illness: Therapy? Or testimony? In Raoul, V., Canam, C., Henderson, A.D., & Paterson, C. (Eds.), *Unfitting stories: Narrative approaches to disease, disability, and trauma* (pp. 113-127). Waterloo, ON: Wilfred Laurier University Press.

HEALTH COUNCIL OF Canada. (2007). *Why health care renewal matters: Learning from Canadians with chronic health conditions.* Toronto: Health Council.

JOTKOWITZ, A., FADLON, J. (2004). Testimonials in medical education: the TIME project. *Medical Encounter, 18*(3), 5-7.

KLEINMAN, A. (1988). *The illness narratives: Suffering, healing, and the human condition.* New York: Basic Books.

KLEINMAN, A. (2009, July11). Health care's missing care. *The Globe and Mail,* p.A13.

KLITZMAN, R. (2006). Improving education on doctor-patient relationships and communication: Lessons from doctors who become patients. *Academic Medicine, 81*(5), 447-453.

KRAHN, R. (1999). Unwanted companion. In Edwards, W. M. & Serviss, S. A. (Eds.), *Study in grey: Women writing about depression.* Edmonton, AB: Rowan Books, Inc.

KUMAGAI, A. K. (2008). A conceptual framework for the use of illness narratives in medical education. *Academic Medicine, 83*(7), 653-658.

Mandell, H., Spiro, H. (2000). When doctors get sick: A reprise (introduction). *The Yale Journal for the Humanities in Medicine.* Retrieved from HTTP://YJHM.YALE.EDU/ARCHIVES/REPRISE/REPRISEINTRO.HTM

Merrifield, J. (1997). Knowing, learning, doing: Participatory action research. *Focus on Basics: Connecting Research and Practice, 1*(A). Retrieved from HTTP://WWW.NCSALL.NET/?ID=479

Morris, P. & O'Neill, F. (2006). Preparing for patient-centred practice: developing the patient voice in health professional learning. *Professional Lifelong Learning: beyond reflective practice.* Trinity and All Saints College, Leeds

Neimi, L. & Ellis, E. (2001). *Inviting the wolf in: Thinking about difficult stories.* Little Rock, AR: August House Publishers, Inc.

Postgraduate Medical Education and Training Board Report (PMETB). (2008). *Patient's role in healthcare – The future relationship between patient and doctor.*

Raoul, V., Canam, C., Henderson, A.D., & Paterson, C. (2007). Introduction: Aesthetics, authenticity, and audience. In Raoul, V., Canam, C., Henderson, A.D., & Paterson, C. (Eds.), *Unfitting stories: Narrative approaches to disease, disability, and trauma* (pp. 25-32). Waterloo, ON: Wilfred Laurier University Press.

Reid, C. E., Brief, E., & LeDrew, R. (2009). Our common ground: Cultivating Women's Health Through Community Based Research. Vancouver: Women's Health Research Network.

Shah, S. (2004). The life of a loser: A work-in-progress (so to speak). In Rose, I., Pare,

A., Leclerc, C., & Chojnacki, M. (Eds.), *Portfolio milieu 2004* (pp. 102-118). Toronto, ON: Sumach Press.

Silow-Carroll, S., Alteras, T., & Stepnick L. (2006). *Patient-centered care for underserved populations: Definition and best practices.* Washington, D. C.:Economic and Social Research Institute.

Staricoff, R. L. (2004). *Arts in health: a review of the medical literature.* Abingdon, UK: Arts Council of England.

STYRON, W. (1990). *Darkness visible: A memoir of madness.* New York: Random House.

WATSON, S. (2007). An extraordinary moment: The healing power of stories. *Canadian Family Physician, 53,* 1283-1287.

{367}

Shah

Author's Note

Seema Shah

This project was made possible through funding from the UBC Teaching and Learning Enhancement Fund.

I would like to thank the "UBC Community Partnerships for Health Professional Education" project Advisory Board for collaborating with me so that I was able to submit this article about my workshop experience for publication. I appreciate the Advisory Board and the workshop planning team supporting my efforts to develop my contribution. I specifically want to acknowledge the planning team: Ms. Cathy Barzo, Ms. Stacey Creak, Dr. Wendy Hall, Ms. Andrea Harstone, Ms. Sue Macdonald, Ms. Lisa Marie Sterr, and Mr. Justin Wallace for their contribution to workshop development. In addition, I want to thank the research team: Dr. Angela Towle (principal investigator) and Lesley Bainbridge, Grant Charles, Marion Clauson, David Fielding, William Godolphin, Wendy Hall, Sue Murphy, and Michael Lee (co-investigators) as well as the project's research coordinator, Ms. Cathy Kline and former project coordinator, Ms. Stacey Creak, for sharing the project-specific information required for me to write this paper. I'd like to express my appreciation to Ms. Creak and the following collaborators for reviewing the article and providing me with very valuable feedback: Dr. Wendy Hall from the UBC School of Nursing, Dr. Towle from the Division of Health Care Communication, and Ms. Sue Macdonald from the Vancouver-Burnaby Branch of the Canadian Mental Health Association. Thank you also to Dr. Kathryn Alexander from the Department of Arts and Humanities at the University of Western Ontario for her extremely helpful feedback. And, finally, I am so very grateful to my therapist, Ms. Caren Durante – for truly listening and for encouraging me to share my stories of illness through creative writing.

Correspondence regarding this article should be sent to:

CONTACTSEEMASHAH@GMAIL.COM.

Digital Storytelling in the Classroom: Promoting Engaged Learning

Christine Walsh

DIGITAL STORYTELLING HAS EMERGED as a creative process that provides opportunity for people to tell their stories through the use of modern digital technologies. Students in a graduate level social work course used the digital storytelling process to deeply engage with concepts of diversity, oppression and social justice on a personal level. In our courses, students identified that the digital storytelling process was useful in not only sharing personal stories of oppression but served to link all of the components of the class together in a immediate, powerful way. As one participant explained:

"Because this class allowed for students to invest in their own stories and their own experience, it allowed for a significant depth of self-reflection vis-à-vis the wide range of topics addressed. As the academic learning process often involves suppressing to a certain extent one's intuition, one's story, one's creativity and one's personal experience with the subject matter, the digital story telling opportunity provided a medium to move beyond those barriers and engage freely with the subject matter."

In feedback such as the quote below, students also reflected on the ways in which digital storytelling could promote a deeper understanding and connection between practitioners and clients in professional practice.

"I think that the whole process of digital storytelling helps us share our stories and become stronger not only as individuals, but as a group of people. It would be a valuable tool to use in practice, especially because there is a barrier between us and our clients due to a power differential, and digital storytelling gives clients the power to share their stories and be heard."

CHRISTINE WALSH, Ph.D., RSW is an Associate Professor in the Faculty of Social Work, University of Calgary, and teaches a course on oppression, social justice, and diversity that utilizes a mixed method of teaching practices – including the creation of digital stories by the students in small groups.

Digital Stories and Experiential Learning

Teaching Medical Students about Patients as Educators

Kim A. Bullock, Kathleen L. McNamara, Donna D. Cameron,

As we are made of water, bone, and biochemistry, we are made of stories. The students that share their stories in our circles recognize a metamorphosis of sorts, a changing, that makes them feel different about their lives, their identities.

– Joe Lambert, Director,
Center for Digital Storytelling, Berkeley, CA

Evolution of Teaching Methods in Medical Education

THE FOUNDATIONS OF MEDICAL EDUCATION include more than the narrow confines of didactic teaching in the classroom, with textbooks and tomes as the source of learning. Knowledge is increasingly linked with application, personal connection, intellectual curiosity and transformation. In order for transformative learning to take place, students must take their scientific knowledge and migrate from campus to the community. They must be willing to listen and learn through partnerships outside of the academic institution[1]. Under the guidance of instructors who seek to develop altruistic and effective physicians, experiential learning becomes a "text" that is no less important than the basic sciences in contribution to the complementary art and science of medical education. Engagement in experiential learning creates opportunity for both self-discovery and scholarship. In combination with innovations in teaching and learning, it can result in a heightened sensitivity towards patients, colleagues, and the healing practice.

The incorporation of experiential learning, and more specifically, service-learning, has grown as a formal pedagogy within medical education since its first implementation in pre-clinical curricula through pilot programs in the early 1990's[2 & 3]. It has gained momentum in its acceptance by educators, medical scholars and leaders in higher education across disciplines. With this development, university engagement in the community has initiated new modalities of learning in the 21st century, prompting many institutions to revise the terms of knowledge and scholarship. Communities willing to collaborate with institutions of higher education and foster co-learning experiences are a potent means of establishing new forms of teaching. Students are prompted to reflect on the contributions of community partners in their educational development and to see them as venues for exploring the inter-relationships between health, social factors and change. With the emergence of new technology and innovative uses, new methodologies have arisen to incorporate technology for learning both in- and outside the classroom. Communication through technology, as is achieved through digital storytelling, calls students to articulate both the stories of the patients they encounter and their own formative stories in relationship to those clients. The creation of digital stories promotes effective communication and emotional engagement while producing compelling narratives.

Digital stories are defined by two main components: a narrative and visual representation of that account[4]. Although primitive digital stories may convey the narrative through text, an audio element such as vocal or musical accompaniment may be included to accentuate the story. Although the novel incorporation of digital storytelling in medical education is far from the methodology's roots in documentary filmmaking, performing arts and oral history, the most fundamental element is retained: the effective and artistic transference of information. Digital storytelling is implemented in medical education as a tool to promote successful doctor-patient relationships, which requires clear communication. Effective communication is essential for involving patients in advancing their own health and wellness. This skill is cultivated through the process of collecting patient narratives with complementary audio-visual elements, and ultimately compiling and editing these elements into succinct and cohesive prose. In the following section we will further explore the background and process of developing digital stories.

Background of Digital Storytelling

WITH THE CONCURRENT DEVELOPMENT of new technologies and continually increasing access to digital media and the web, the *digital stories* methodology has evolved significantly over the past fifteen years since its inception in 1994 at the San Francisco Digital Media Center, now the Center for Digital Storytelling. From its roots in the performing and literary arts and the traditions of oral history, the Center's "Digital Storytelling" methodology has been adopted across the spectrum of business, academic and non-profit and institutions.[5]

This method of constructing and conveying a story through visuals and sound is now being implemented in a variety of arenas with diverse purposes, objectives and outcomes. According to *BusinessWeek* magazine, "Digital storytelling is the hot new trend in online marketing"[6]. Soft drink companies have now adopted similar style in ad campaigns, telling the "story" of their product that has traveled around the world to get into your hand. Similarly, it has also been used by small business owners to develop a relationship with widespread customers by conveying the story of how and why they came into business.

Anthropologists were another early employer of digital storytelling, having implemented this technique as a method for extracting and documenting the narratives of indigenous populations, immigrants, and many of the other often "unheard" voices in our world. With guidance from professionals and increasingly comprehensible tools, digital storytelling techniques have been used as a tool for teaching and empowering Hispanic youth who are learning English as non-native language[7].

In both medical practice and education, digital storytelling is used to maximize mutual physician-patient understanding, and convey the human element in complex medical realities. Two pediatric physicians at the University of Iowa have developed and maintained a *Virtual Pediatric Hospital* since 1992. This online tool offers comprehensive online support for medical students, residents, fellows, and attending physicians practicing pediatrics, as well as pediatric patients' parents and family members[8 & 9]. Complete with extensive photos, patient stories and medical histories, an integrated picture of each case is portrayed.

The purpose of incorporating digital storytelling in medical education at Georgetown University is to facilitate a reflective process among future physicians. This process is based on active listening, personal commitment, and building physician-patient trust, which is essential in providing quality care[10]. Through eliciting stories that relate to personal health, patients are engaged as educators who contribute to the students' comprehensive understanding of interrelated determinants of health. By promoting patients participation in their own health affairs, physicians are ultimately able to provide better and more lasting care.

The Center has defined seven key elements that contribute to the development of powerful digital stories: Point (of View), Dramatic Question, Emotional Content, Gift of your Voice, Power of the Soundtrack, Economy, and Pacing. In preparation for the project, students are trained to implement these seven elements, as well as hone any technical skills needed to record these interactions. The Point of View, which directs the editing process, is defined as the specific realization you are trying to communicate within your story. Whether the story is being told from the medical student's or the patient's point of view, the story may have a different trajectory. The Dramatic Question is what keeps the audience engaged from the opening of the story until the last line. In the home visiting program, it may be an outcome of what was revealed to the students over successive visits, a particular development in their health status, or the process by which the patient develops self-health management skills and plan of action.

The emotional content of the digital story is what personalizes the content. This will vary depending on whether the story's narrator is a commercial product, a young man coming of age, or an elderly matriarch with complex health needs. The fourth and fifth key elements, "The Gift of Your Voice" and "The Power of the Soundtrack" have expanded since the inception of digital storytelling some fifteen years ago. Audio can be captured and integrated in digital stories more fluidly than in the past. When integrated effectively, it adds a level of depth beyond what a text narrative and photos can convey, furthering the impact of the story. The sixth element, Economy, conveys the principle of "less is more." With fewer images and less text or narrative, the constructor of the digital story must seek and rely on the interplay between a distinct but concise narrative and corresponding visual images. The art is in defining the relationship between these components by intentionally pairing them to convey a larger context. Finally, students are encouraged to consider the pace at which the story unfolds and to use this as an additional formative element. The impact of a lingering silence, pause or quick succession of visuals can easily impact the overall tone of the digital story.

The rapidly increasing availability of the tools used in capturing digital representation of narrative exchange is a significant factor in the evolution of digital storytelling. There has been a resultant growth in the opportunity for the adoption of digital stories as a teaching tool across disciplines. In addition to the evolution of applicable tools, there are a growing number of learners who are prepared and open to the use of technology in learning experiences, as confirmed by Julie Coates in *Generational Learning Styles*.[11] Among the key tools in developing digital stories, digital cameras have seen significant progress in the congruent decrease in cost and increase in comparative quality since their emergence in 1991, according to product specification reports. Similarly, the steady increase in quality and portability of digital audio recording devices, in addition to advances in audio editing software on computers have contributed to wide-spread use and ease of incorporation in learning experiences.

The powerful medium of digital storytelling is easily combined with other learning modalities, and in diverse educational settings. This tool is being implemented in anthropological and environmental studies, history and English literature. There is a natural alliance between digital storytelling and the medical disciplines, in particular, mental, social and behavioral health. By extension, it is also gaining traction in both qualitative and quantitative research, including community action research, partnerships in participatory health improvement, and ethnography. Participatory digital media has also been used in international work as a means to disseminate information, exposing controversial subject matter, which are at risk for being diluted by popularized forms of communication, such as *YouTube* and *Vimeo*. This can create tension or challenges in clarifying the formalized constructs associated with the educational usage of digital storytelling, and the epistemology, theory and methodology required for scientific research and learning.

In moving from traditional research initiated by individual or co-principal investigators, digital stories requires the involvement of filmmakers, technology specialists, community justice advocates, narrators and individuals with expertise in building bridges with community residents. Through the increased access to these technologies amidst an increasingly tech-savvy population, digital storytelling is being implemented across disciplines that are not traditionally technology driven.

As a tool for facilitating the art of medical education, digital storytelling provides notable benefit to both the medical student and the patient. Through the reflective process detailed above, students meditate on the richness of information and are in fact inspired to dig deeper and uncover the full medical story of their patients' life. By necessity for production of the narrative, students must interact with the patient as active listeners, probing to uncover the full context of the medical story. As such, this method is used to stimulate inquiry and elicits reflection among medical students.

Although there is room for a process like this in medical education, it can be both time-consuming and challenging to coordinate. Practitioners must acknowledge the appropriate time and place for utilizing the full digital storytelling procedure. Within the context of service-learning the pace of the project, faculty support and involvement in the community through an established relationship contribute to the success of project implementation.

Service-Learning at Georgetown University School of Medicine

SERVICE-LEARNING AT GEORGETOWN UNIVERSITY SCHOOL OF MEDICINE began in 1995 as a three-year demonstration project funded by the Pew Charitable Trust. The primary objective of the original project was for university faculty to partner with respected community leaders to supplement students' clinical knowledge base with richness that stems from interaction and observation in community settings.[12]

Since its inception, our service-learning program has been part of *Introduction to Health Care*, a year-long required course for all first-year medical students. The course serves as an orientation for a student's entire career in medicine, providing a systematic way of organizing perspectives on health care. The course augments clinical coursework by framing the patient as part of the larger community and society. It also introduces students to the strengths, limitations, and flaws of our current health care system, encourages a spirit of altruism and concern for the individual patient as a person, and builds a foundation for social justice and health for the population as a whole.

Key stakeholders in the original program included representatives of the DC Commission on Public Health, Georgetown faculty from the Department of Family Medicine and the School of Nursing & Health Studies, and established community leaders in the northwest quadrant of the District of Columbia. Together they collaborated to develop the goals and objectives, specific student projects, and the curriculum.

The service-learning program began at eleven community sites, including local schools, churches, clinics with diverse outreach programs, residential sites for teen mothers and their children, and after-school programs for teens or targeted high-risk youth. The number of community partner organizations more than doubled in the first ten years of the program, providing thriving, collaborative experiential learning opportunities for our students.

Our program consists of the entire first-year class, community partners, faculty members and Service-Learning Program administrators. Teams of three to ten medical students, working with a faculty team leader and a community partner, identify and address community assets and health needs in six to eight community visits throughout their first year of medical school. They also develop their ability to understand and address the complex health challenges they will encounter in patient care throughout their professional careers. Community partners provide access to community members and contribute to the education and awareness of medical students about community priorities, goals and ways of thinking and acting. Faculty team leaders from over ten disciplines in the medical center attend the community visits, review students' plans for each session, guide students' reflections about the community-based learning experiences during the community visits, and collaborate with community partners to assess students' professionalism and teamwork. Finally, service-learning program administrators provide the support and resources necessary to ensure that students, faculty, and community partners obtain the greatest benefit from their experience.

The Service-Learning initiative has doubled since 1995, growing from 42% of the medical school class with eight faculty members and eleven community sites, to 100% of the class with over twenty-five faculty and community partner sites. For thirteen years, the Service-Learning Program has increased its skill-building component to include mapping community assets, surveys, assessments of health risks and implementing health promotion projects. Students' service projects include outreach activities that serve people with disabilities; a drop-in center for primarily Spanish-speaking parents and families; a national organization that addresses federal and state health priorities; shelters for homeless persons; and shelters for survivors of intimate partner abuse and their children.

Other collaborative health activities that service-learning teams have engaged in involve accompany faculty team leaders and lay health workers on home visits with patients. One particular team of students accompanied community health promoters from a local community health center to visit the homes of chronically ill and medically underserved residents in the District of Columbia. The goals of the students on this team were:

- To provide important service as they learned more about the living conditions and health needs of the homebound elderly;

- To increase understanding of the unique challenges of treating patients with multiple chronic conditions;

- To practice communicating with patients and teaching them about their medical conditions;

- To work effectively as a member of a healthcare team;

- To explore the influence of socioeconomic factors, culture, and religion on the health and wellbeing of the patients.

Another team of medical students, accompanied by a medical doctor and several graduate social work students, visited the homes of parents of young children. Before and after each visit, the team discussed characteristics of the community, the lifestyle of the community residents they visited, and the issues faced by the different families they visited. This discussion helped them to understand and approach families from an interdisciplinary perspective.

A home-visiting program embedded in the community-based learning experience ignited medical students' interest in the nexus between health, social justice, and the acute need for change. Incorporating the digital storytelling component to this project gives families a platform to express their multidimensional visions and goals. In addition to exposing students to the sociological, genealogical, ethnographical, political and economic perspectives of these community members, the project continues to enrich the lives of the families involved.

Development of Digital Stories in Medical Education at Georgetown University

A FUNDAMENTAL ASPECT OF DIGITAL STORYTELLING as part of the pre-clinical medical education at Georgetown University School of Medicine is the emphasis on product and the learning process, rather than the final product or compilation of facts and figures. Although the digital stories created by the medical students are valued and assessed on the quality and comprehensiveness of the product, the purpose of pursuing this methodology in the Service-Learning curriculum is the process by which the story is solicited, captured, and shaped. Given its place in medical education, this is a natural shift that acknowledges the purpose of this exercise in the larger context.

The inclusion of the digital storytelling component in the Service-Learning class was sparked by the storytelling and rich histories of African-American residents of the District of Columbia who interfaced with students at their community sites over the years. The students were very responsive as they listened to the vivid stories such challenged families were forced to face, many in silence in their neighborhoods. Certain sites allowed for profound personal exchanges between the students and the community members, leading the Director and Assistant Director to search for ways to digitally capture these powerful connections and mutually-satisfying learning experiences. The profound insights engendered from the home visits, battered women shelters, adolescent transient homes, etc, provided exemplary opportunities to document and memorialize these teachable moments and engagements.

The process of creating digital stories allows for multiple contributors to participate in the process of revelation, discovery and artistic expression. It was for this reason that the Assistant Director selected the digital storytelling methodology as a medium for conveying information through client-student exchanges. Through interactions with one particular African-American family, students learned about the powerful influence that decades and generations of racism, discrimination and poverty can have on health.[13] However the students also witnessed the power of faith, cultural pride, and ancestral memory on this family's determination to recover, survive and eventually thrive. This family also shared their personal treasures and memorabilia that served as a source of identity, hope and strength regardless of the current adversity. One particular patient in the home visiting program shared the oral history of her family's legacy from their roots in slavery, and its continued impact on their health.

For the past three years, students have brought digital cameras, documented the interviews, and captured the reflective wisdom of this family's matriarch, who has traced the family's lineage back to the slaves of George Washington's Mount Vernon plantation[14 & 15]. She rose from modest means as a sickly child with rheumatic fever to gain a college education and become a powerful community leader, resource to District Councilmen, and other political leaders.[16] Through her arduous work she was able to enact legislation to recognize and celebrate the work of Lincoln in emancipating slaves in the District of Columbia prior to the national emancipation of slaves.[17 & 18] She also exposed unjust environmental practices, leading to a DC Council bill named in her honor.[19] Finally, her family artifacts from slavery and other period pieces stunned the students and challenged their own views on the impact of this "peculiar institution," and its long reach down the centuries. The troubled past of this family has influenced the cultural and medical history of both their ancestral and current family health. Current family members have shared insights with students and introduced realities of health that challenge their personal understanding of illness and disease etiology.

With all of this rich information, students eagerly began the process of creating their own digital stories as representations of patient narratives. They recognized early on that process was just as important as form and function. Their goal was not simply to reproduce what they had heard, but to communicate the rich multidimensional experience they witnessed. What came forth was their own unrealized artistic talent and originality, an appreciation for the challenges that go into writing and rewriting the narrative and the sense of sheer joy in creating a lasting communication product.

The students recognized that the authentic voice comes through the crucible of shaping and re-shaping the words to sync with the images. This included taking the montage of text and pictures, and analyzing how they represent the perspective of the subject, her life experience and health history. Throughout the course, students were required to debrief and reflect on their evolving piece, critique their work as artists do with their emerging creations.

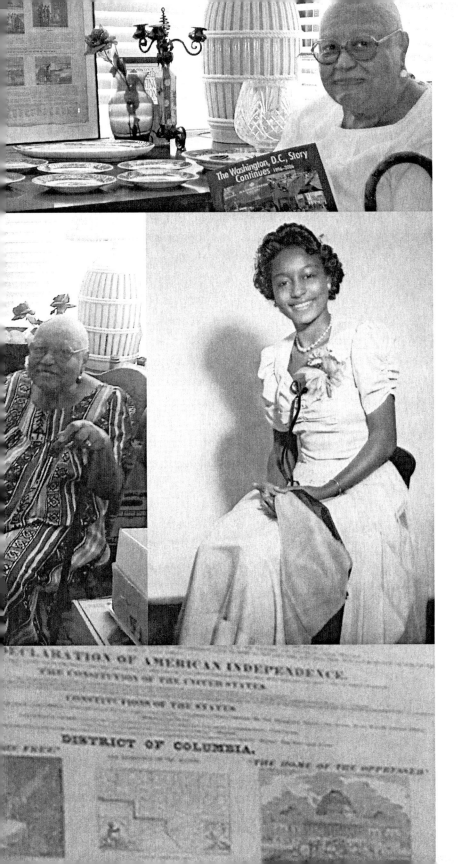

I see myself as a revivalist. I bring back to life what has been buried. I revive the old and make it new again. My whole life has been an opportunity to teach people about their history. You never forget your ancestry. Your roots grow deep and make a connection as to who you have been, who you are and will be. Your ancestors inspire, comfort and encourage you.

I'm a drumbeat for justice, and my work hopefully stirs the soul to follow the music of freedom.

– Loretta Carter Hanes

Following Lambert's Seven Elements of Digital Storytelling[20], students contemplated: Did the narrative or pictures reflect the personal meaning they were striving to convey? Did the digital pictures connect with the narrative to elicit impact from the audience? In creating the digital story, did students engage in self-reflection, exploration and meaning? How was the narrator, and by extension, their family, affected by the students during the home visits? Finally, were the students more sensitized, more humanized, more aware of the cultures, traditions, etc., that influence health, healing and wellness?

The incorporation of digital storytelling in the medical curriculum has the potential to not only give the students and the community an opportunity to engage in a mutually satisfying project, but to serve as an emotional bridge for students who appreciate the social challenges individuals and communities face. This can translate into a more sensitized physician or a reflective doctor who shares in the humanity of his/her patients, rather than serving as a disengaged clinician. The voices of patients can be heard: their pain, joy, liberation from sickness, or appreciation of the finality of death.

Although digital storytelling has been used by the university as a lens to focus outwardly on the community, it has also turned inward as well, providing community members insight into the institutional academic process and resources. This allows for capacity-building, empowerment, and structural change regarding traditional campus-community relationships. Community partners acquire a greater appreciation for the resources and assets within the institution, and thereby acquire new ways to increase their capital and strengths. This offers them a deeper understanding of the resources available, which can be leveraged as they seek to improve their environment and community's health.

Digital storytelling offers the opportunity for patients to serve as teachers, and for students to listen to their patients in their authentic voice, unchallenged or edited. Instead of focusing solely on patients' deficits or needs, students learn to identify their strengths and potential, and see them as partners in health promotion. The social elements of health then inform students' biological training, providing bi-directional understanding and appreciation, which can be included in health improvement strategies and further connections within the community. The crafting of digital stories offers a new approach to the life-long learning process, whereby creative expression is used to articulate well-being through the life-cycle, and provides a powerfully therapeutic mode of self-expression.

Among the many lessons learned from the initial implementation of the project was that students and instructors must be prepared for the complexities and challenges associated with creating digital stories. Students must view this work as not merely picture taking, data collection or cataloging assignment. Rather, students and instructors must recognize there is a methodology to production that includes various phases from pre-production through publication. The focus, however, must be on the process: the planning, formulation, writing, editing, and coordination of the palette of pictures in synthesis with narration. Each advancement in the process must be carefully reviewed and critiqued to make sure the content remains true to the experience, and input by the subject is paramount. The pictures should evoke interest in the viewer, and the narration should be precise yet reflective. Incorporating audio, particularly vocal recording, requires advanced preparation and additional time for implementation. Although the initial cohort of students in the project did not include audio elements in their digital stories, further training was provided for students in successive groups to apply this additional element.

Using digital storytelling to promote medical learning requires an integrative appreciation and clinical competency, which first year medical students can achieve. However, this requires a more substantial investment of time and involvement by the instructor along with a full appreciation of the nexus of patho-physiology, disease expression, influence on patient's perception of themselves and their world view. The inter-relationships between health, our perception of the world, and how we articulate our experiences find an expression in art, the humanities, and digital storytelling.

With increasing access to the internet and growing role of the patient in promoting and maintaining their personal health care, individuals are accessing online resources for questions about their health and disease. In this context, educators must adapt their teaching techniques to allow for new roles of both patients and communities to be active agents of health promotion[21]. Digital storytelling is one mechanism for engaging both students and patients to learn about each other, their interconnected roles within the health care system, and the importance of collaboration. It encourages participants to recognize and explore their authentic voice, and to use that voice to encourage dialogue about individual and community action that can lead to lasting change.

Conclusion

MEDICAL EDUCATION MUST EXPAND BEYOND the traditional paradigm of transmitting a body of technical and scientific knowledge from instructor to students. In the 21st century, with its complex health problems and new diseases, medical students must receive a wide body of information from a variety of sources including both community organizations and members at large. Service-Learning is a community-centered approach which provides a platform for integrating community voices in the education of future physicians through the utilization of digital storytelling in the learning process. Through service-learning, there is ample opportunity to incorporate digital storytelling in a platform to merge health, humanities and art resulting in the development of more holistic, collaborative and reflective physicians.

KIM BULLOCK, MD, is a family medicine and emergency room physician. She has infused social-learning theory, reflective patient- and community-centered practice into her classroom and clinical teaching. She has encouraged students to appreciate the interaction of health, humanities and the creative arts in relation to wellness, healing and recovery. Dr. Bullock nurtured her interests in the use of narrative as a personalized and empowering therapeutic method at Yale University as a History of Science and Medicine major. She continued her exploratory work through special community projects at the University of Michigan Medical School and the Georgetown University/Providence Hospital Family Medicine Residency Program. In the Department of Family Medicine at Georgetown University Medical Center, Dr. Bullock serves as Director of the Community Health Division and Assistant Director of Service Learning, where she has strengthened community partnerships within pre-clinical medical education and used digital stories to expand student participation and engagement in diverse local communities. Special areas of interest and publications include cultural and linguistic competency, ethnography and participatory action research.

KATHLEEN MCNAMARA is the Program Coordinator of the Community Health Division in the Department of Family Medicine at Georgetown University Medical Center. She coordinates service-learning in pre-clinical medical education, and the development of physician leaders in community health through the Department's fellowship programs. A graduate of Providence College in Public and Community Service Studies, she maintains her commitment to civic engagement, experiential education and campus-community partnerships through her current position and past year of service in the AmeriCorps*VISTA program. As a former preventative health coalition coordinator, she continues to pursue health promotion and outreach activities in both professional and personal capacities, particularly through the application of graphic arts and technology.

DONNA CAMERON, PhD, MPH. Since 1999, Dr. Cameron has served as a health educator and Director of Service-Learning in the Department of Family Medicine at Georgetown University Medical Center. She has coordinated health education, service and outreach projects with scores of faculty, first-year medical students, and community members and leaders. She is skilled in developing, maintaining and strengthening community partnerships and providing professional development for faculty while preparing students for community-based learning and research. Designing curricula, presenting workshops, facilitating small groups, playing inspirational piano music, and writing are among her interests.

Notes

1   Ramaley, J. (2007) Beyond the Ivory Towers. *Wingspread Journal.*

2   Seifer, S. (1998) Recent and Emerging Trends in Undergraduate Medical Education: Curricular Responses to a Rapidly Changing Health Care System. *Western Journal of Medicine,* 168, 400-441.

3   Magzoub, M., Schmidt, H. (2000) A Taxonomy of Community-based Medical Education. *Academic Medicine,* 75(7), 699-707.

4   Kajder, S., Bull, G., & Albaugh, S. (2005) Constructing digital stories. *Learning and. Leading with Technology,* 32(5), 40-42.

5   Atchley, D., Lambert, J. (2006) The Evolution of Digital Storytelling: An Abbreviated History of Key Moments During the First Sixteen Years (1993-2006). HTTP://WWW.STORYCENTER.ORG/TIMELINE.HTML.

6   Stepanek, M. (2000, May 15). Tell Me a (Digital) Story: The power of digital storytelling. *BusinessWeek Magazine.*

7   Vinogradova, P. (2009) Pedagogy of Multi-literacies and Digital Stories in ESL Instruction. Language, Literacy, and Cultural Doctoral Program (Doctoral Dissertation, University of Maryland, Baltimore, 2009).

8   D'Alessandro, D., D'Alessandro, M. (2004). A pediatric digital storytelling system for third year medical students: The Virtual Pediatric Patients. *BMC Medical Education,* 4:10

9   D'Alessandro, D., D'Alessandro, M. (2009) *Virtual Pediatric Hospital online:* HTTP://WWW. VIRTUALPEDIATRICHOSPITAL.ORG/MISC/ABOUTUS.SHTML, copyright 1992-2009, BioMed Central, Ltd.

10   Scott, J., Cohen, D., DiCicco-Bloom, B., Miller, W., Stange, K., and Crabtree, B. (2008) Understanding Healing Relationships in Primary Care. *Annals of Family Medicine,* 6(3), 15-322.

11   Coates, J. (2007) Generational Learning Styles. River Falls, WI: Learning Resource Network.

12   Cameron, DD and Bullock, KA. (2008) Service-Learning in Medical Education: A Catalyst for Community-based Research. In (Eds.) Stanton, B., Galbraith, J. and Kaljee, L. *The Uncharted Path from Clinic-based to Community-based Research.* (pp. 201-217). Hauppauge, New York: Nova Publishers

13   Connors, J. (Ed.). (2001). Growing up in Washington, D.C.: An Oral History. Charleston, SC: Arcadia.

14   Horton, L. (1997) A History of the African American People: The History, Traditions & Culture of African Americans. Detroit: Wayne State University Press.

15   Barakat, Matthew. (2001, January 17). Mount Vernon commemorates slave emancipation. *Washington Informer.* Provided by ProQuest LLC.

16   Milloy, C. (2006, April 16). Emancipation Day's Unsung Champion. *Washington Post.*

17   Smith, K. (2008) The Washington, DC Story Continues: 1996-2006. Washington, DC: Intac, Inc. 56.

18   Blair, W., Younger, K. (Eds.). (2009). Lincoln's Proclamation: Emancipation Reconsidered. Chapel Hill, NC: University of North Carolina Press.

19   Loretta Carter Hanes Pesticide Consumer Notification Amendment Act of 2008, Washington DC City Council Bill 17-0493. Bill became effective June 11, 2008.

20   Lambert, J. (2002) Digital Storytelling: Capturing Lives, Creating Community. Berkeley, CA: Digital Diner Press. HTTP://WWW.STORYCENTER.ORG/COOKBOOK.PDF.

21   Wyatt, T., Hauenstein, E. (2008) Enhancing Children's Health Through Digital Story. *Computers, Informatics, Nursing.* 26(3), 142-148.

References

BESSELL, A., DEESE, W., MEDINA, A. (2007) Photolanguage: How a picture can inspire a thousand words. *American Journal of Evaluation.* 28, 558-569.

CARISON, E., ENGEBRETSON, J., CHAMBERLAIN, R. (2006) Photovoice as a Social Process of Critical Consciousness. Qualitative Health Research. 16(6), 836-852.

CHIO, V., FANDT, P. (2007) Photovoice in the Diversity Classroom: Engagement, Voice, and the "Eye/I" of the Camera. Journal of Management Education. 31(4), 484-504.

FOSTER-FISHMAN, P., NOWELL, B., DEACON, A., NIEVAR, M., McCANN P. (2005) Using Methods That Matter: The impact of reflection, dialogue and voice. American Journal of Community Psychology. 36(3/4), 275-291.

GOODHART, F., HSU, J., BAEK, J., COLEMAN, A., MARESCA, F., MILLER, M. (2006) A view through a different Lens: Photovoice as a tool for student advocacy. Journal of American College Health. 55(1), 53-56.

JURKOWSKI, J., PAUL-WARD, A. (2007). Photovoice with Vulnerable Populations: Addressing disparities in health promotion among people with intellectual disabilities. *Health Promotion Practice*, 8(4), 358-365.

KAJDER, S. (2004, January) Enter Here: Personal Narrative and Digital Storytelling. *The English Journal*, 93(3), 64-68.

LOPEZ, E., ENG, E., ROBINSON, N., AND WANG, C. (2005). Photovoice as a Community-Based Participatory Research Method. In Israel, B., Eng, E., Schulz, A., Parker, E. (Eds.) Methods in community-based participatory research for health (326-348). San Francisco, CA. Jossey-Bass.

NOWELL, BL, BERKOWITZ, SL, DEACON, Z AND FOSTER-FIHMAN, P (2006). Revealing the Cues Within Community Places: Stories of identity, history, and possibility. American Journal of Community Psychology. 37(1/2) 29-46.

WANG, C, BURRIS, MA (1997). Photovoice: Concept, methodology, and use for participatory needs assessment. health Education and Behavior. 24(3), 369-387.

Sharing the Voices of Our Elders Through Digital Story

Patti Fraser

IT HAS BEEN ARGUED THE only way to know someone is through story.

As the participating artist and the 'story mentor' in the Silver Harbour Centre Digital Storytelling Group, I have for close to two decades worked with diverse communities to help them through the written word, or in digital media, to tell the stories from their lives. I have become attuned to resonances that reverberate through groups of people when an idea or theme is expressed that speaks energetically to what we may be engaged in uncovering or expressing collectively as a group.

Engaged in the practice of discovering our most authentic selves through the recording of our voices, in the images of ourselves and others, in the language of our making is more than the endorsement of the personal voice or an individual's statement. It is an engagement with the most human part of our selves. It is our need to seek meaning through the stories of our lived experience. This inquiry leads irrevocably to the web of human and worldly interaction. It creates a communically shared experience of the world. We need to be working with our elders to ensure their voices, images and the authentic stories are brought to 'life' for future generations. They are the stories of hope and change, of survival and endeavor, of places long gone and still here, of our deepest human need to make meaning in the world."

"If we don't tell our stories we disappear."

PATTI FRASER, MA, Resident artist in the Arts Health and Seniors Project
Doctoral Program, Centre Cross Faculty Inquiry In Education,
University of British Columbia

My mother's body:
A story of grieving, remembering, and touch

(an autoethnographical story)

John J. Guiney Yallop

As educators, as researchers, we are often taught to not pay attention to our emotions, except to control them and keep them out of our teaching and out of our research. I do the opposite. I invite the emotions into teaching and into research. I believe that we need to listen to our emotions, that we need to pay attention to what they are saying to us, what they are showing us, what they are teaching us. I said during the defence of my doctoral research that the emotions can guide our living and that I believe they can also guide our research as well. Rather than keep the emotions out, I want to invite them in.

–John J. Guiney Yallop
in Day & Guiney Yallop, 2009, p. 53.

This chapter first appeared as a Featured Artist piece (Guiney Yallop, 2009) in issue 7 of The Canadian Creative Arts in Health, Training and Education Journal.* I was grateful and honoured that this piece had found a home. That it is now finding another home, and hopefully another audience, in this publication also leaves me with feelings of gratitude and of being honoured. As a researcher whose writing is my research (Guiney, 2002; Guiney Yallop, 2005; Guiney Yallop, 2008), I write in order to better understand my experiences

---

* The Canadian Creative Arts in Health, Training and Education Journal. was the original journal of The International Journal of The Creative Arts in Interdisciplinary Practice, IJCAIP, HTTP://IJCAIP.COM

(Richardson, 2002). My writing is autobiographical (Bullough and Pinnegar, 2001) in that I draw on stories from my lived experiences. I draw on memory (Armstrong, 2006; Frank, 1995) understanding that memory has limitations but also has power. I write with the hope that the stories of those remembered lived experiences will be evocative for others (Bochner & Ellis, 1996; Ellis, 1997; Ellis & Bochner, 2008). I use arts-based research (Cole et al., 2004), specifically poetic inquiry (Cahnmann, 2003; Leggo, 2001, 2004, 2005; Luce-Kapler, 2004; Prendergast, Leggo, & Sameshima, 2009). While my work in this chapter is not poetic inquiry in that it does not contain any of my poems, although it could be argued that many of my daughter's words within it are poetry, I drew on my poetic voice, my emotional voice, to access the emotions as I wrote. I believe, as I stated in the piece from my writing with Liz Day (Day & Guiney Yallop, 2009) cited above, that we need to bring the emotions more fully into our work, into our learning, into our teaching, into our research (Boler, 1999). I believe that we need more research that has the power to move us (Cole & McIntyre (2006)

WHEN MY MOTHER WAS DYING, she went on a trip, unplanned and uncharted, time-travelling through her life, packing and unpacking parts of herself along the way, returning after each stage of the journey as a retouched postcard with a message scrambled for us, her children and grandchildren, to decipher. Eventually her body became the souvenir of how she loved us.

My mother died of Alzheimer's disease in the morning of April 23, 2005. She took her last breath with my youngest brother and his spouse by her side. It was as it should be. I was in a hotel room only minutes away from the nursing home where my mother lay dying, preparing breakfast for my daughter and two of her cousins – my youngest brother's daughters. When the call came that my mother's death was imminent, I tried to balance my desire to be by her side when she took her last breath with my respect for the three young girls who were finishing their breakfast. I did not want to give them the impression that death was a frenetic truncating of life, but a natural progression. It was as it should be. I told the girls that they could finish their breakfast, but that we had to leave soon. My mother died before I arrived at the nursing home. It was as it should be. At least, that is what I tell myself.

When I went up to the room which the staff at the nursing home had prepared for my mother to spend her last days in with her family members by her bedside, I looked at my mother's body laying there in the bed, life so soon having left it. This was the body through which I had entered the world, where my own life had begun. This was the body which had carried me, wrapped in a blanket, on my journey home from the hospital where I was born, sitting on a slide pulled by a horse through a Newfoundland snowstorm because the ploughs could not get down into our small outport community to clear the snow from the one road that ran down into it. This was the body that had held me before I learned to walk, the body that had tucked me in at night, the body that had put homemade poultices on my infected wounds, the body that had picked lice from my hair and had boiled my underwear and bed sheets to kill the fleas that had infested our beds, the body that had sometimes gone without food so that I could eat. This was the body I had seen grow smaller as I grew older. This was my mother's body. My mother was dead.

With my daughter, I went to the bed where my mother's body lay.

"Can we touch her?" my daughter asked.

"Yes," I replied.

"Is she dead?"

"Yes, she's dead."

"Can she hear us?"

"I don't know, but you can certainly say something to her if you wish."

Guiney-Yallop

"Good-bye, New Grandma. I love you," my daughter said as she put her hand on my mother's forehead and rubbed it across her cheek.

"New Grandma" was the name my daughter had given to my mother when my partner and I first travelled with her, shortly after the adoption and before her fifth birthday, to Newfoundland to meet my mother and other members of our daughter's new and forever family. At the time, my mother was in the late stages of Alzheimer's and living in the nursing home where she would spend her last days. She was confined to her bed or to a large wheelchair with a tray where her meals were served and from which she was fed. We visited New Grandma each day, sometimes two times a day. We tried to plan our visits around mealtimes. Our daughter, a child my partner and I were, ourselves, just beginning to get to know, moved us with her remarkable capacity for compassion. She wanted to help feed my mother. As she slowly lifted the spoonfuls of food to my mother's mouth, she also stroked my mother's arm and looked deeply into her eyes. My mother's eyes were fixed on my daughter and would only occasionally move to gaze at me or at my partner. As well as stroking my mother's arm as she spoke softly, my daughter put her hand to my mother's cheeks and she gently brushed back my mother's hair with her fingers. She even played with my mother's toes after performing a dance in front of the large wheelchair – a performance for her New Grandma.

{394}

Neither my partner nor I knew for sure what communication was taking place between my mother and our daughter, but we knew that touch, touching each other, was important to them both. My mother, through her body, seemed to be receiving the love my daughter was pouring over her. Our daughter was receiving the gift of giving. It was as it should be. Just over a year later, my daughter leaned in over the bed and kissed my mother's body, the body of her New Grandma. And then I followed her lead. I kissed my mother's body and said, "Good-bye, Mom. I love you." My daughter, not yet six years old, was teaching me how to grieve.

In fact, it was my daughter who had led me back to Newfoundland to be at my mother's side before she died. Caught in the vortex of trying to balance work demands and family responsibilities, I thought that I could wait until my mother died and then travel to Newfoundland for the funeral. I had, I told myself, already grieved my mother's absence from my life as Alzheimer's consumed more and more of her. But when I told my daughter that New Grandma was going to die soon, she immediately said, "We have to go and say 'Good-bye.'" And so we went. Although work initially continued to pull, I resisted and turned fully to my daughter's needs, which I was beginning to realize were also my own, and for two days before my mother's death, when we were not at the hotel room, my daughter and I were at the nursing home saying 'Good-bye.' It was as it should be.

Guiney-Yallop

That morning, after my mother's death, sitting outside the nursing home in the car I had rented we called my partner on our cell phone. Speaking first, our daughter said, "Papa, it's a very sad day. My New Grandma died." They cried together for awhile, and then my daughter passed the phone to me. My parents had loved my partner, and he had loved them. We had decided that he would stay in Ontario and take care of our home and our pets while our daughter and I flew to Newfoundland to say good-bye to Mom from all three of us. More than a decade earlier, he had also stayed home while I went to say good-bye to my father from both of us. Now, once again, in this moment, our love for each other allowed my partner and I to touch with words and with silence. Language, over distance, became our embrace. Later that night, back at our hotel room, my daughter put down the book she was reading and began to cry. "Daddy, I'm feeling sad," she said, "because my New Grandma died and now I don't have a New Grandma anymore." I held her in my arms. We held each other. In words and in tears we expressed to each other the loss we were both feeling. As I write this, the grief continues – my eyes fill with more tears, tears that will never really stop.

After my mother first moved into the nursing home, whenever I would visit from Ontario I would bring a bottle of red wine. This was a way of connecting with her, of connecting her with me, with her memories of me. In the past, whenever I travelled back to Newfoundland for a visit, my mother would have her rare glass of red wine, something she indulged in only with me. Eventually, as the Alzheimer's progressed, she could no longer hold a glass, and so I stopped bringing the red wine. When my partner and I visited her in the nursing home, we always brought strawberries. My mother, who was by then spoon-fed all of her meals, would reach for the fresh red fruit and, clasping it in her good hand, bring it to her lips. Food was the last pleasure that she seemed to consciously connect with in life – food, and the sights and sounds of young children, sights and sounds that also nourished her.

By the time my daughter met my mother for the first time, Mom's capacity to reach for a strawberry had disappeared, but her mouth opened to receive the soft food my daughter offered on a spoon. As I looked at my daughter, so uninhibited about touching my mother, I wondered about my own hesitancy to touch my mother's body over the years. The desire to touch was there and I had made small connections with my mother's hands and arms, and I would kiss her forehead or her cheek good-bye whenever we parted, but touching my mother's body with the intensity of a warm embrace had come to seem something like an intrusion, a demand for too much. I recalled that as I had grown older my mother had begun to shrink away from the affection I would show through touch. I had learned to respect her boundaries without, at least I hoped, withdrawing the affection I felt for her. Still, I wondered why a woman who lived through her body, who loved the smell and taste of food, who worked her hands into the dough she kneaded for bread and whose hands wrung clothes dry and stroked her cats and dogs, a woman who enjoyed the colour of flowers and the feel of a breeze on her face or cool water on her feet, who listened to music with a smile—why did she seem so wary of affection expressed through the body in touch or in words?

I reflected back to the beginning of my life. My birth made Mom the mother of six children, all under the age of ten years. Perhaps the demands on her body, demands from meeting the needs of six young children, and then of another one a few years later, children who depended on her for their survival, made her cautious about how her body's energy was used. Physical affection was not considered a necessity, at least not after a certain age.

Looking at my daughter touching my mother's body I also recalled the progression of my mother's Alzheimer's, and how I had dealt with it. As my mother was invaded by this disease, I tried, through my writing, to come to grips with her illness, and the effects it was having on me and on our family. I wrote about my mother, and about my father who had died of lung cancer several years before my mother's Alzheimer's became evident. I wrote about how my parents had shown their love for me throughout the time I had with them, a love shown often through actions and almost never in words. My writing led me to understanding, to acceptance, and to healing. In writing about my mother I would compare her body to the landscape that had surrounded me in my childhood, the landscape of the island of my birth, the island that held me like my mother held me, the island whose shores were entered, formed, and transformed by the Atlantic Ocean, an ocean that moves in me, that forms and transforms me every time I write. The shoreline of Newfoundland is where I return, in body whenever I can, or at other times at least in spirit, to reflect, to write, to write my life – its present, its past, and its future. My mother's body gave me life, remembered my past, and could foretell my future. Both Newfoundland and my mother's body held me, both nourished me (and continue to nourish me), and yet both were (and still are) mysteries to me. But both also invite me to know them, to try to understand what they can tell me about myself and, more importantly, about how to relate that self to others. Newfoundland and my mother's body taught me about the depths and the boundaries of self and of relating, and about how to explore those depths and how, respectfully and with dignity, to cross those boundaries; they also taught me about grieving, about remembering, and about what touch would come to mean to me – lessons I am still learning.

The last time I touched my mother's body we were at the funeral home. My daughter, wondering about my family's conversations with each other and with her, again with her comfort and curiosity, invited me to examine and articulate my own beliefs and my own choices.

"What did they mean when they said that New Grandma is in heaven with your dad?" my daughter asked me.

"That's their belief," I explained. "It was also New Grandma's belief. It isn't my belief. I believe that New Grandma is in my heart. I also believe that she's with my dad because I believe he's in my heart, too."

Wanting to ensure that she felt free to construct her own beliefs and make her own choices, I added, "You can choose to believe whatever you want."

Looking away for a moment, my daughter then looked back at me and said, "I believe that she's in heaven and she's in my heart."

The last time I saw my mother's body it was wrapped in a box and suspended over the open arms of the earth. Since then, whether sitting at my mother's grave, or crouched beside the blue spruce tree my partner planted in our backyard in Brampton, Ontario, in memory of my mother, or swimming in the salty waters on the west coast of Newfoundland for a holiday visit to Gros Morne, or walking along the edge of the tide that now comes in and out of my new home in Wolfville, Nova Scotia, I touch again my mother's body. The metaphor is my reality.

And one day she will take me back, back into her arms, back into body. One day, perhaps, I will learn what Newfoundland and my mother's body were, and still are, trying to teach me. {397} One day, perhaps, I will learn what my daughter, at the age of five years, seemed to already know. It is as it should be. At least, that is what I am telling myself.

DR. JOHN J. GUINEY YALLOP is a parent, a partner, and a poet. Dr. Guiney Yallop's research includes poetic inquiry, narrative inquiry, autoethnography, and performative social science. He uses these methodologies to explore identities, communities, and emotional landscapes. His writing has appeared in literary and scholarly journals. He has presented his work at national and international conferences. Dr. Guiney Yallop is an Assistant Professor in the School of Education at Acadia University. He lives in Wolfville, Nova Scotia, with his partner, Gary, their daughter, Brittany, and their pets.

References

ARMSTRONG, L. A. (2006). *The ecology of identity: Memoir and the construction of narrative*. Unpublished doctoral dissertation, University of British Columbia, Vancouver, BC.

BOCHNER, A. P., & ELLIS, C. (1996). Talking over ethnography. In C. Ellis & A. P. Bochner (Eds.), *Composing ethnography: Alternative forms of qualitative writing* (pp. 13-45). Walnut Creek, CA: AltaMira.

BOLER, M. (1999). *Feeling power: Emotions and education*. New York: Routledge.

BULLOUGH, R. V., JR., & PINNEGAR, S. (2001). Guidelines for quality in autobiographical forms of self-study research. *Educational Researcher*, 30(3), 13-21.

CAHNMANN, M. (2003). The craft, practice, and possibility of poetry in educational research. *Educational Researcher* (April), 29-36.

COLE, A., & MCINTYRE, M. (2006). *Living and dying with dignity: The Alzheimer's project*. Halifax, NS: Backalong Books.

COLE, A. L., NEILSEN, L., KNOWLES, J. G., & LUCIANI, T. T. C. (Eds.). (2004). *Provoked by art: Theorizing arts-informed research*. Halifax, NS: Backalong Books.

DAY, L. & GUINEY YALLOP, J. J. (2009) Learning, Teaching, and Researching through Poetry: A Shared Journey. *Creative Approaches to Research [Online]*, 2(2), 46-57, Available at http://search.informit.com.au/fullText; dn=300407430428855;res=IELHSS

ELLIS, C. (1997). Evocative autoethnography: Writing emotionally about our lives. In W. G. Tierney & Y. S. Lincoln (Eds.), *Representation and the text: Re-framing the narrative voice* (pp. 115-139). Albany: State University of New York Press.

ELLIS, C., & BOCHNER, A. P. (2000). Autoethnography, Personal Narrative, Reflexivity: Researcher as Subject. In N. K. Denzin & Y. S. Lincoln (Ed.), *Handbook of Qualitative Research* (pp. 733-768). Thousand Oaks, CA: Sage Publications.

FRANK, A. W. (1995). *The wounded storyteller: Body, illness, and ethics.* Chicago: University of Chicago Press.

GUINEY, J. J. (2002). *School life for gays: A critical study through story.* Unpublished Master of Education, Brock University, St. Catharines.

GUINEY YALLOP, J. J. (2009). My mother's body: A story of grieving, remembering and touch. Featured Artist. *The Canadian Creative Arts in Health, Training and Education Journal [Online], (7),* 29-35.

GUINEY YALLOP, J. J. (2008). *OUT of place: A poetic journey through the emotional landscape of a gay person's identities within/without communities.* Unpublished doctoral dissertation. The University of Western Ontario. London, ON.

GUINEY YALLOP, J. J. (2005). Exploring an emotional landscape: Becoming a researcher by awakening the poet. *Brock Education,* 14(2), 132-144.

LEGGO, C. (2005). Pedagogy of the heart: Ruminations on living poetically. *Journal of Educational Thought,* 39(2), 175-195.

LEGGO, C. (2004). Living poetry: Five ruminations. *language & literacy: A Canadian Educational E-Journal [On-line],* 6(2), [unpaginated] Available at HTTP://WWW.LANGANDLIT.UALBERTA.CA.

LEGGO, C. (2001). Research as poetic rumination: Twenty-six ways of listening to light. In L. Neilsen, A. L. Cole, & J. G. Knowles (Eds.), *The art of writing inquiry.* Halifax, NS: Backalong Books.

LUCE-KAPLER, R. (2004). *Writing with, through, and beyond the text: An ecology of language.* Mahwah, NJ: Lawrence Erlbaum Associates.

PRENDERGAST, M., LEGGO, C. & SAMESHIMA, P. (Eds.). (2009). *Poetic Inquiry: Vibrant voices in the social sciences.* Rotterdam, The Netherlands: SensePublishers.

RICHARDSON, L. (2000). Writing: A method of inquiry. In N. K. Denzin & Y. S. Lincoln (Eds.), *Handbook of qualitative research* (pp. 923-948). Thousand Oaks: CA: Sage Publications.

{400}

Paying Tribute to Caregivers through Arts-informed Research as a Path to Hope and Change

Ardra Cole and Maura McIntyre

Accoring to the Alzheimer Society of Canada (2008) it is estimated that 450 000 Canadians over sixty-five are living with a form of dementia and this figure will likely reach three-quarters of a million by 2031. With the continued provincial and national decline in health care support for seniors at home and in long term care facilities and the inverse incidence of Alzheimer's disease in an aging population, the need for non-professional (family) caregivers has become a necessity. And yet, little attention is paid to these "hidden victims" of the illness (Given, Collins & Given, 1988; Winter & Gitlin, 2007). Beyond the practical difficulties of coping with the multiple challenges of caregiving, family members often find themselves dealing with the social stigma attached to the disease (Cole & McIntyre, 2008a; McIntyre & Cole, 2008a, 2008b; Post, 2000; Westergard, 1985). David Shenk (2001, p. 87) maintains that "the unique curse of Alzheimer's is that it ravages several victims for every brain it infects." The emotional well-being of family caregivers has significant implications for the quality of care provided those with Alzheimer's disease (McKee, Smyth & Neundorfer, 2004). Social stigma is a serious obstacle to the emotional well-being of caregivers (Neugaard et al., 2008; Post, 2000).

Against this backdrop and guided by Post's (2000, p. 128) assertion that: "For dementia care to improve, we must struggle to overcome the stigma associated with this condition" we have developed a decade-long program of research focused on understanding and representing the emotional complexities of what it means to care for a loved one with Alzheimer's disease. One overarching purpose of our work is to promote and increase national pride about care and caregiving practices (Cole & McIntyre, 2008a). At its heart, our research is about paying tribute as a path to hope and change. For us, paying tribute in/through research is tied to moral responsibility. Our hope is that by celebrating the efforts of Canadians to give care and paying tribute to caregivers across Canada (McIntyre & Cole, 2008a, 2008b) we can help to advance a broad ethic of care (Post, 2000).

In this chapter we explore: a) what a research agenda with paying tribute at its heart might look like; b) what it means to pay tribute in/through research; and c) why it is important for researchers to assume responsibility to pave a path to hope and change.

A Methodological Note

CONVENTIONAL FORMS OF RESEARCH are primarily results-oriented, focus on advancing propositional knowledge, and reach limited audiences. In the service of our lofty goal of putting care on the map we are informed in our research approach by principles, processes, and forms related to the arts. The main purposes of arts-informed research (Cole & Knowles, 2008) are: to enhance understanding of the human condition through alternative (to conventional) processes and representational forms of inquiry; and to reach multiple audiences by making scholarship more accessible. The methodology infuses the languages, processes, and forms of literary, visual and performing arts with the expansive possibilities of scholarly inquiry for purposes of advancing knowledge. Arts-informed research is part of a broader commitment to connect the work of researchers with the life and lives of communities through research that is accessible, evocative, embodied, empathic, and provocative. Tied to moral purpose, arts-informed research is an explicit attempt to make a difference through research not only in the lives of ordinary citizens but also in the thinking and decisions of policy makers, politicians, legislators, and other key decision makers. For us, drawing on various art forms and processes and principles of art making and representation such as: installation and textile art, photography, narrative, performance, and new media shifts research toward a process- (rather than product-) orientation that creates spaces for engagement, sites for learning, and opportunities for comfort, connection, and support. In so doing, our aspirations for our research are focused more on what takes place in the conduct of the inquiry and in the engagement with representations of the research than in the creation of propositional knowledge and research results.

What a Research Agenda with Paying Tribute at its Heart Might Look Like

IN SUBSTANCE AND FORM OUR WORK AS RESEARCHERS is an act of love and a tribute to our mothers who both lost their lives to Alzheimer's disease. Our program of research began with our autobiographical explorations of our experiences of caring for our mothers through their illness. Over a decade later, while our explorations into experiences of care and caregiving has taken us back and forth across Canada many times and into the communities, homes, and lives of hundreds of family caregivers in diverse locations and care circumstances, our commitment to research as an act of love and tribute has sustained and been sustaining.

Informed by the work of installation artists and contemporary art museum curators, over the past decade, we created and exhibited, in numerous public venues, three large-scale multimedia installations to represent our research on caregiving and Alzheimer's disease. *Living and Dying with Dignity: The Alzheimer's Project*, a seven piece installation depicting themes and issues associated with caring for a loved one with Alzheimer's disease, was displayed in prominent, public venues in Toronto, Sudbury, Halifax, and Victoria. *Putting Care on the Map: Portraits of Care and Caregiving across Canada*, an eleven-piece installation created from data gathered in a cross-Canada study of what care looks like for family caregivers in diverse care circumstances and locations, was recently launched at Toronto City Hall. *Gray Matters: A Collective Remembering of Care* has been exhibited as part of *Putting Care on the Map* as well as on its own in three public venues in Ontario. From stories gathered in conversation with family caregivers we created *Love Stories about Caregiving and Alzheimer's Disease*–a forty-five-minute spoken word performance in three acts–that we performed to audiences of family caregivers, health professionals, high school students, academics, and members of the general public.

After our final community performance we worked with an international filmmaker and the technical crew at Mount St. Vincent University in Halifax to produce a video and DVD of *Love Stories about Caregiving and Alzheimer's Disease* (Cole & McIntyre, 2006b) now in circulation. Subsequently we completed work with playwright Martin Julien and a group of professional actors on the production of an audio CD version of *Love Stories about Caregiving and Alzheimer's Disease* (McIntyre & Cole, 2007). HTTP://WWW.OISE.UTORONTO.CA/RESEARCH/MAPPINGCARE/LOVE_VIDEO.SHTML

Both of these projects are intended for wide distribution of the research to diverse audiences. And, while this project is "completed", we continue to perform our research findings especially to Alzheimer Society chapters across the country. In our current work, *The Care Café: Understanding Caregiving and Alzheimer's Disease across Canada*, we specifically address the need for caregiver community development and support as we continue our focus on understanding the emotional complexities of caregivers' experience. In informal group and café-like settings we invite family caregivers to participate in a 'show and tell' sessions organized around an artifact of care that they have brought to the session.

{403}

What it Means to Pay Tribute in/through Research

OUR COMMITMENT TO PAYING TRIBUTE through research is consistent with the perspective of Sarah Lawrence Lightfoot (1997, p. 142) who advocates "a shift of research stance–from focus on weakness to pursuit of strength, from preoccupation with disease to concern for health, from inquiry into dysfunction to examination of productivity." When called to the caregiving role, so-called ordinary people go to extraordinary lengths to provide creative and imaginative care to their loved ones. They find themselves needing to learn new skills, become strong advocates, even political and community activists—all while trying just to carry on. Against considerable odds and challenges and often with little systemic support, family caregivers assume and carry out myriad roles and responsibilities in efforts to provide loving care and preserve the dignity of their loved ones. It behooves us, as researchers, to find ways to access and gain deeper insights into caregivers' experiences and to support and pay tribute to their work and to caregiving in general. To do so requires thinking differently about how research is designed and undertaken. In this section we set out a list of qualities or features that continue to inform and shape our research agenda and provide examples from our program of work that illustrate the various ways in which paying tribute paves our research path.

Research that pays tribute:

- Invites open and broad participation
- Respects differences
- Appreciates similarities and differences of people's experiences
- Honours stories as a way of knowing and the process of storytelling as a way of connecting
- Involves deep listening
- Elevates the choice to give care
- Emphasizes the everyday
- Dignifies the 'domestic'
- Pays attention to "ordinary" routines of caregiving relationships
- Forefronts relationship in all aspects of the research process
- Respects privacy and intimacy
- Acknowledges diversity and complexity of relationships
- Normalizes challenges of caregiving
- Promotes empathy and understanding across difference

Research that pays tribute:
- Invites open and broad participation.

Our recruitment and outreach strategies are both logical and systematic, and intuitive and responsive. Our goal is to be inclusive rather than representative; conventional notions about sampling do not inform our work. The relationships with the personnel in many local Alzheimer Societies across the country that we have maintained over the course of our Canadian-centred decade long program of work has kept us in close touch with the communities that our research is for and about. We attribute the success of our outreach and participant recruitment strategies to the large number of caregivers who wish to tell their stories of experience and caregiving in personally meaningful ways that cannot be accessed or contained by conventional data collection approaches. We have designed recruitment and information gathering strategies that create more and different opportunities for people – some who have been unwilling to participate in conventional research approaches like interviews and focus groups – to contribute what they know about caregiving and that enable us to access different kinds of information. We have travelled to remote places to learn about the complex support system designed by a woman in her mid-seventies who takes two ferries and drives for four hours to visit her same-sex partner in long-term care. We have learned about extended family and community from a woman, living on a Native reserve in northern B.C., who travels fourteen hours and stays overnight in a hotel once a month to take her husband to the doctor in Vancouver; and, we have marvelled at the emotional and psychological {405} endurance of a man in his late eighties who is caring at home for his bedridden wife who has not been able to speak for two years.

For a Care Café in Miramichi, New Brunswick, the local Alzheimer Society (part-time) staff person took seriously our suggestion that the occasion of the Care Café might be a good opportunity to do outreach to family caregivers in the community who are not accessing existing services. Joanne did word-of-mouth outreach; drove to Native reserves in the area to invite people to attend; and she did print, leaflet and T.V. advertising. When we arrived to facilitate the Care Café, she had already made it a festive occasion by providing refreshments, decorating the room and setting up a raffle (complete with prizes)! It was no wonder that twice as many people attended than we anticipated – and that the group was a spectacular, heartening site of community development.

We also have learned much from members of the public who visited our exhibits and ended up sharing their own stories with us through the various means we provide such as voice-activated recorders, journals and writing spaces, and invitations to leave artifacts. The methods we have used to facilitate a unique quality of contact with caregivers have resulted in extensive, rich, and multi-dimensional data that we have worked hard to render in authentic and meaningful ways.

Cole · McIntyre

Research that pays tribute:

- ☞ Respects differences.
- ☞ Appreciates similarities and differences of people's experiences.

One significant way in which we pay tribute to caregiving is through an ongoing collection and display of photographic portraits of family caregivers to people with Alzheimer's disease in Canada. *Who Cares?* shows the faces of ordinary Canadians who live in small and big cities, towns and communities, and remote rural locations across the country. Some care for their loved one at home, some provide care in an institution. Many caregivers are alone in the care they provide; many others provide support as part of a care team. We took the pictures in the course of our conversations with people about their experiences of care and caregiving. The images reflect (often invisible) differences in age, socio-economic status, culture, sexual orientation, geography, education and life experience. What is most visible in these portraits is that most caregivers are older women. In *Who Cares?*, we pay tribute to the family caregivers across Canada who participated in our research and more generally to all people who give care. In our efforts to raise the profile of care and caregiving we hope to encourage the choice to give care in individuals who previously did not see themselves as caregivers.

{406}

In gatherings of family caregivers we are mindful of the commonality of shared experience and the solidarity that this engenders, but also careful about the differences of people's experiences. For example, in one of our focus group discussions, when the "Alzheimer's Wives" of Halifax, Nova Scotia, a self-proclaimed group of similarly aged older women, met a young urban lesbian woman caring for her father we encouraged the reciprocal learning process that the encounter engendered. Proceeding with the moral assumption that all family caregivers do the very best that they can according to their care circumstances, judgement can be dismissed and respect for different choices and experiences can be embraced as a guiding principle.

Research that pays tribute:

- ☞ Honours stories as a way of knowing and story telling as a way of connecting
- ☞ Involves deep listening.

In our Care Cafés, when we invite family caregivers to tell stories of experience 'through' an object that means 'care' to them, the power of this process is immediately evident as they freely talk about their experiences within the context of relationship and tied to both their own and their loved one's personal history. Through this alternative group process that emphasizes peer support we make connections with, between and among individuals and communities not normally accessing existing services. People bring objects and artifacts that speak to them of the caregiving experience and, through these objects, tell stories about what it means to care for their loved one. For example, in one Care Café one woman brought a fresh piece of strawberry shortcake and, with tears rolling down her cheeks, told the group that this was the first spring in her life, the first spring in forty-two years, that her mother hadn't made her strawberry shortcake on her birthday. Alzheimer's disease had gotten in the way. Marcel, a man in his early fifties brought a blade for a table saw. He talked about taking early retirement so that he could learn woodworking from his father who was a cabinetmaker. With the sudden onset of Alzheimer's disease, however, the tools have been set aside and Marcel and his brother take turns providing support to their father in his home. As each person spoke the quality of attentive listening only increased as the room filled up with stories of patience and sorrow and frustration. In an atmosphere filled with humour, respect and dignity what had been story turned to testimonial as each individual was heard and honoured in their efforts to give care. One woman left the meeting and told us that she had never attended a support group before, but planned never to miss one again.

Research that pays tribute: {407}
- ☞ Elevates the choice to give care.

Research that goes beyond a consideration of the "burden" that is caregiving and that explores caregiving as a positive (Butcher, Holkup, & Buckwalter, 2001) and even "growth-enhancing" (Sherrell, Buckwalter & Morhardt, 2001) experience for the caregiver is beginning to be recognized as an important focus of inquiry. *What Care Looks Like* is one part of an eleven-piece mixed media exhibit entitled *Putting Care on the Map.* It clearly illustrates our choice to portray caregiving in a positive light. We created the exhibit *What Care Looks Like* from information and material gathered in 2006 and 2007 through in-depth contact with family caregivers in three regions of the country – Halifax and rural Nova Scotia; Sudbury and the "near north" of central Ontario; Vancouver Island, the northern Gulf Islands and mainland British Columbia. With the help of local Alzheimer Society chapters, community outreach, and word-of-mouth contact we travelled to small towns and cities, rural communities, and out of the way places to visit and talk with family members caring for their loved ones at home and in long-term care facilities. The diversity of individuals, care circumstances and care relationships that we encountered was remarkable. We were honoured to be welcomed into people's lives and to be invited into intimate worlds of care.

For one of our data collection methods we offered participants a disposable camera and invited them to take pictures of what care looks like to them. When we spent time immersed in analysis of hundreds of photographs and accompanying explanatory notes we saw care portrayed as creative and imaginative acts. We chose to present the photographs of what care looks like in a series of large scale montages that depict the many diverse ways that people choose to provide care that moves beyond coping to reflect qualities consistent with theories of person-centred care with love at the centre (Kitwood, 1997).

Research that pays tribute:
- ☞ Emphasizes the 'everyday' and dignifies the 'domestic'
- ☞ Pays attention to the ordinary routines of caregiving relationships.

As daughters of women who lived with and died with Alzheimer's disease, we remember and use the practical and emotional realities that were our own experience of caregiving to guide our work. Rooted as we are in the everyday routines of caregiving, we found ourselves drawn to three dimensional installation art with its assemblage quality of found materials. Using the "everyday" and "ordinary" as guides we chose universal, domestic symbols and forms in order to keep "the academy and the kitchen table" together (Neilsen, 1998) and make our work broadly accessible. Kitchen table inquiry, says Neilsen, "aims to make visible in research what has not been made visible, and hence not valued; the material work in the parentheses of our lives, the stuff of daily living that makes it all hang together or fall apart" (pp. 143-144). In *The Alzheimer's Project* this meant mounting a free standing thirty-foot clothes line hung with overwashed white female undergarments in several prominent, busy public venues. It meant portraying the narrative of care in the mother-daughter relationship through photographs affixed to the fronts of three refrigerator doors – and then mounting these in a public space. By foregrounding these symbols of the ordinary routines of caregiving we dignify the domestic, and pay tribute to the people who persevere in these daily acts of care. Our overarching purpose is to find ways to use various metaphorical frames to remember and represent elements of our mothers' lives and, more generally, to interrogate the constructs of illness and health as they relate to the presence and preservation of human dignity.

Research that pays tribute:
- ☞ Forefronts relationships in all aspects of the research process.

Over the years of our program of research and across the diversity of projects that we have developed, we have enjoyed longstanding relationships with family caregivers. We are honoured that people remain in touch with us and feel connected to our work long after their role as "participants" in our research has ended. Individuals go to lengths to follow up and remain connected with us long after "formal" research meetings have ended: they call us with additional thoughts, mail us packages of information and artifacts and email us with ideas and updates. We were surprised and deeply touched when several family caregivers who had participated in our research attended the opening reception of our public exhibit of *Putting Care on the Map* at Toronto City Hall in September 2008. One woman, who had recently lost her loved one and who had travelled a long distance from northern Ontario to attend, explained that the process of participating in the exhibit helped her to bring closure to the experience of caring for her mother.

Research that pays tribute:
- Respects privacy and intimacy.

In the course of our interactions and conversations with family caregivers we have heard about the everyday routines of caregiving and we have also been told some very dramatic, hair-raising stories. The 'material' or data that we have collected is rich with the stuff of human intrigue: love, loss, abandonment, betrayal and forgiveness. When faced with the question of how to represent the intimacies of other people's lives, for example an older man's learning about the fasteners on his wife's undergarments, we are vigilant about considering each and every representational decision we make. Guided by the imagined presence of the participants themselves, we ask ourselves: "Would Thomas be comfortable with this rendering of the material? Would it make sense to him? Would he feel too exposed?" Respecting privacy and honouring the intimacy we have engendered with participants preserves the dignity of individuals, their loved ones and decisions about care.

{409}

Research that pays tribute:
- Acknowledges diversity and complexity of relationships.
- Normalizes challenges of caregiving relationships.

Daughters caring for mothers; wives caring for husbands; husbands caring for their wives, at home and in long-term care facilities. A woman cares for her big sister; one woman is seventy-seven, the other, eighty-six. A woman cares for her mother-in-law; she has been divorced from that woman's son for eighteen years. A teenager cares for her grandmother while her parents work nights. A retired woman returns to her hometown to care for her alcoholic father, who neglected her throughout her childhood. Two sons provide round the clock care to their father; another won't say the name "Alzheimer's disease".

Our program of work arose from our own experiences. As daughters caring for our mothers and well aware of our own unique challenges, we were inspired to connect with other caregivers and to know more about what care looks like for those in different care relationships and circumstances. Over the years we have been guided by this pursuit and celebrate the many diverse and complex relationships that we have been privy to.

In listening to the stories of family caregivers we consistently are struck by the strength of caregivers' commitment to preserve the self and dignity of their loved ones, often in the face of considerable challenge and further complicated by the dynamic complexities of love—as tender, kind and affectionate as well as grounded in responsibility, commitment and duty. This focus on the complexities of loving care is the overarching theme of our spoken word performance, *Love Stories: About Caregiving and Alzheimer's Disease*.

Research that pays tribute:
☞ Promotes empathy and understanding across difference.

{410} One important way that we evaluate the success of our work is through its ability to facilitate connections between and among diverse individuals. People gather through our work in a variety of ways: in organized conversation circles or focus groups, at public talks and at the opening receptions of our exhibits, and in informal chance meetings. We intentionally provide spaces for community development in and around the work, believing that these encounters are rich with learning and promote empathy and understanding across difference. For example, we organized one part of *The Alzheimer's Project* installation specifically to encourage people to meet and connect through a social activity. "Loving Care", with its three card tables, twelve chairs, bowls of candy and games, is a site within the exhibit where people gather. With heads bowed and fingers busy with puzzle pieces, conversation between people of very different ages and life circumstances can occur, information about incontinence can be exchanged, community resources critiqued, and stories shared.

We are also committed to countering the stigma associated with Alzheimer's disease and actively promote opportunities for connection among caregivers living in geographic proximity who might not otherwise cross paths. Our current research project, *The Care Café* consists of a gathering of family caregivers hosted by the local Alzheimer Society chapter as part of their caregiver support program. People are invited to bring an object/artifact that symbolizes care for them to an informal gathering at the Society office. Each person in the group then speaks about the significance of that object and is invited to tell stories of their experiences of caregiving. The "show and tell" format is evocative and engaging; people who do not typically participate in support groups come forward with objects and stories of experience. Our experience is consistent with the group work done by Hunter (1993) who used "props as a check-in" and a mechanism for community development (p. 137). Through discussion of an object, "insight into the challenges faced by others is gained, and it starts to become apparent that members can offer each other solutions to each other for specific problems" (p.137).

Why It Is Important for Researchers to Assume Responsibility to Pave a Path to Hope and Change?

AS RESEARCHERS IN PUBLICLY FUNDED INSTITUTIONS we acknowledge the privileged status of our positions. We also acknowledge that with privilege comes responsibility. For us, this responsibility extends far beyond the 'knowledge production' communities of scholars and researchers of which we are part. We strive to make a difference in the lives of those who give care and those who support and promote caregivers in their work, to create spaces for engagement and sites for learning. Opportunities for comfort, connection, and support—are steps forward on a moral path toward advancing a broad ethic of care.

We imagine a world where those who are aging, ill, and with diminishing capacity for self-care continue to be valued members of society. We look forward to a time when people helping their aging and ill loved ones to live with dignity are acknowledged for and supported in their labours of love. And the place to begin, says Post (2000, p. 13), "is not in moral abstraction but in listening attentively to caregivers and affected persons … Much can be learned by observing the remarkable solicitude and loyalty that many caregivers feel, despite insufficient support systems."

{412}

ARDRA L. COLE, Ed.D, is a Professor and Co-director of the Centre for Arts-informed Research (CAIR) in the Department of Adult Education and Counselling Psychology, Ontario Institute for Studies in Education, University of Toronto. She has published extensively in conventional and non-conventional academic prose and in alternative, scholarly, non-print media throughout her career as a teacher educator and qualitative research methodologist. She is co-editor of The Arts-informed Inquiry Series which includes: *The Art of Writing Inquiry* (2001); *Provoked by Art* (2004); *The Art of Visual Inquiry* (2007); and *Creating Scholartistry* (2008) (Backalong Books and CAIR). Her most recent book is *Handbook of the Arts in Qualitative Research: Perspectives, Methodologies, Examples, and Issues* (2008) published by Sage. Ardra's ongoing research (with Maura McIntyre) on care and caregiving and Alzheimer's disease involves multimedia installation and performance. WWW.OISE.UTORONTO.CA/RESEARCH/MAPPINGCARE

MAURA MCINTYRE, Ed.D., is an adjunct professor at the Ontario Institute for Studies in Education of the University of Toronto. She is a founding member of the Centre for Arts-Informed Research at OISE/UT, and has published and presented in a variety of alternative representative forms. Maura and Ardra have been working on a program of research in the area of care and caregiving and Alzheimer's disease for the past decade. Community development, public education and knowledge translation to diverse audiences guide their research agenda. Information about the current project, *The Care Café: Understanding Caregiving and Alzheimer's Disease Across Canada* can be found at WWW.OISE.UTORONTO.CA/RESEARCH/MAPPINGCARE.

{413}

References

BUTCHER, H., HOLKUP, P., & BUCKWALTER, K. (2001). The experience of caring for a family member with Alzheimer's disease. *Western Journal of Nursing Research, 23,* 33-55.

COLE, A. L., & KNOWLES, J. G. (2008) Arts-informed research. In J. G. Knowles & A. L. Cole (Eds.). *Handbook of the arts in qualitative research: Perspectives, methodologies, examples and issues* (pp. 55-70). Thousand Oaks, CA: Sage.

COLE, A. & MCINTYRE, M. (2006). Love stories about caregiving and Alzheimer's disease [DVD]. [Directed by A. Bromley, edited by Chris Beckett]. Mount Saint Vincent University Studio, Halifax, NS.

COLE, A., & MCINTYRE, M. (2008, September 22-27). *Putting care on the map: Portraits of care and caregiving.* A 12-piece research exhibit about caregiving and Alzheimer's disease. Toronto City Hall Rotunda.

GIVEN, C. E., COLLINS, C. E., &, GIVEN, B. A. (1988). Sources of stress among families caring for relatives with Alzheimer's disease. *Nursing Clinics of North America, 23,* 253-259.

HUNTER, B. (2003). Simplify your life. In Capuzzi, D. *Approaches to group work: A handbook for practitioners* (pp.135-139). Columbus, Ohio: Merrill Prentice Hall.

KITWOOD, T. (1997). *Dementia reconsidered: The person comes first.* Buckingham, UK: Open University Press.

LAWRENCE-LIGHTFOOT, S. & HOFFMAN DAVIS, J. (1997) *The art and science of portraiture.* San Francisco, CA: Jossey-Bass.

MCINTYRE, M., & COLE. A. (2007). Love stories about caregiving and Alzheimer's disease [CD]. [Directed by M. Julien, sound editing by Dale Morningstar]. The Gas Station Recording Studio, Toronto, Ontario. HTTP://WWW.OISE.UTORONTO.CA/RESEARCH/MAPPINGCARE/LOVE_VIDEO.SHTML

McIntyre, M, & Cole, A. (2008a). *Love stories about caregiving and Alzheimer's disease*. Audio CD created and produced by A. Cole & M. McIntyre, directed by M. Julien. Toronto, Ontario: Centre for Arts-informed Research.

McIntyre, M., & Cole, A. (2008b). Love stories about caregiving and Alzheimer's disease: A performative methodology. *Journal of Health Psychology, 13*(2), 213-225.

McKee, J. Smyth, K. & Neundorfer, M. (2004). Survival of persons with Alzheimer's disease: Caregiver coping matters. *The Gerontologist, 44*, 508-519.

Neilsen, L. (1998). *Knowing her place: Research literacies and feminist occasions*. Halifax, NS & San Francisco, CA: Backalong Books & Caddo Gap Press.

Neugaard, B., Andersen, E., McKune, S. L., & Jamoom, E. W. (2008). Health-related quality of life in a national sample of caregivers: Findings from the behavioural risk surveillance system. *Journal of Happiness Studies, 9*(4), 559-575.

Post, S. (2000). *The moral challenge of Alzheimer disease*. Baltimore, MD: John Hopkins University Press.

Shenk, D. (2001). *The forgetting. Alzheimer's: portrait of an epidemic*. New York: Doubleday.

Sherrell, K., Buckwalter, K., & Morhardt, D. (2001). Negotiating family relationships: Dementia care as a midlife developmental task. *Families in Society, 82*, 383-392.

Westergard, M. P. (1985, April). *A younger Alzheimer's spouse speaks out*. Paper presented at a Symposium on Adult Education and Aging, Brigham Young University, Provo, Utah.

Winter, L., & Gitlin, L. N. (2007). Evaluation of a telephone-based support group intervention for female caregivers of community-dwelling individuals with dementia. *American Journal of Alzheimer's Disease and Other Dementias, 21*(6), 391-397.

PART 5

Interdisciplinary
Art Practice for
Personal and
Community Healing

Performing Beauty, Practicing Home

Collaborative Live Art and the Transformation of Displacement

Devora Neumark

BORN IN SHADOW OF THE *SHOAH*, the stories about home that were repeatedly told within the culture of my youth emphasized the six million Jews who were systematically murdered under the Nazi regime; the stories also included references to the familial losses incurred during the Polish pogroms and forced exiles of the Soviet Gulag era. These narratives were not just passed down orally or taught in the texts; the history was haptically felt and daily remembered over the first fifteen years of my life as internalized oppression passed on through the generations resulted in severe physical and psychological abuse. Unfortunately, my personal history is not all that different from many people's history around the world impacted by the destruction of home through acts of individual aggression or domicide – the politically motivated willful destruction of houses and homes that has been and continues to function as a major weapon in the arsenal of cultural oppression.[1]

Felix Guattari draws connections between the ecological crisis and "a more general crisis of the social, political and existential" (1992: 119) in the final chapter of *Chaosmosis: An Ethico-Aesthetic Paradigm*. He asks: "[. . .] how do we change mentalities, how do we reinvent social practices that would give back to humanity – if it ever had it – a sense of responsibility, not only for its own survival, but equally for the future of all life on the planet, for animal and vegetable species, likewise for incorporeal species such as music, the arts, cinema, the relation with time, love and compassion for others, the feeling of fusion at the heart of cosmos?" (1992: 120). Guattari's sense of urgency seems prescient now with forty-two million people currently displaced involuntarily

{419}

1. In the opening paragraphs of the Preface to *Domicide: The Global Destruction of Home*, J. Douglas Porteous and Sandra E. Smith write: "Currently, no word exists for the action of destroying peoples' homes and/or expelling them from their homeland. We suggest the neologism 'domicide,' the deliberate destruction of home that causes suffering to its inhabitants. A second term, "memoricide," concerns deliberate attempts to expunge human memory, chiefly though the destruction of memory's physical prop, the cultural landscape (e.g., in Muslim Bosnia, 1990s)."

(according to the UN Refugee Agency) and climate change "considered by many scientists to be the most serious threat facing the world today" according to the Canadian environmental activist David Suzuki (http://www.davidsuzuki.org/climate change/).

Adjoining my own troubled history with home – that includes the 1995 destruction of the loft I was renting then at the hand of an arsonist – my creative practice has emerged from a persistent investigation of how art can address and help shift perceptions about victimhood and agency through dialogue and the imaginative enactment of self-authored *what if* scenarios. Informed by the oral history tradition and ritual practices that are so wholly integrated within the Jewish life cycle, my live art interventions and community collaborations have explored the curative power of storytelling and the salutary repetition of quotidian gestures transposed from ordinary domestic contexts. Performing the autobiographical and enacting simple recurrent motions-as-communication have provided me with the means to make sense of my life experience and connect with others concerning the deleterious impact of coercive force relative to dislocation while examining the association between trauma and memory.

At the center of this inquiry into ethics, aesthetics, the power of public mourning, and connection to place, is a series of questions about home's properties, associations, and manifestations (or lack-there-of) in the political, cultural, emotional, and embodied realms. How do the stories we tell *about* home, influence our experiences *of* home? Once displaced, what are the conditions necessary for making home anew? What role does beauty play in this complex process? Working with two of my most recent collaborative live art projects as case studies – *Why Should We Cry? Lamentations in a Winter Garden* and *homeBody* – I will examine the ways in which performative encounters in the public sphere can contribute to creating favorable conditions for individual and collective healing while offering the possibility for imagining new experiences of home in the aftermath of forced displacement.

I believe that relational symbolic experimentations in the public sphere emergent from profoundly personal experiences can have tangible effect in the corporeal world because they nurture creative risk-taking and the emergence of new schemas for co-existence while expanding the range of political dissent and activism. As Deirdre Heddon asserts while writing about the history of feminism, autobiography and performance: "The radical feminist act was not only the publicizing of the personal but also the insistence that the person was never only personal since it was always structural and relational. This was precisely the point about the politics of the personal. The politics of the personal is that the personal is *not* singularly about me" (2008: 161). (Italics in the original text.) Live art's performativity inevitably invites an awareness of interdependence and reinforces the mutuality of identities.

Why Should We Cry? Lamentations in Winter Garden

BEGINNING WITH THE FALL EQUINOX and ending on the winter solstice 2008, Ottawa-based artist Deborah Margo and I invited individuals with experience of displacement to publicly share their culturally-specific mourning songs and personal contemplations about migration, home, and beauty. Hosted by DARE-DARE Centre de diffusion d'art multidisciplinaire de Montréal, these gatherings (held in Cabot Square Park at the corner of Atwater and Sainte-Catherine Streets) explored the processes of coping with the loss that often accompanies the disruption of home (Altman & Werner, 1985; Porteous & Smith, 2001) emphasizing the power of collective public singing and shared storytelling to influence psychological wellbeing and social reconstruction (Stein, 2004; Unwin, Kenny, & Davis, 2002; Urbain, 2008; Zelizer, 2003).

Over the past twenty-five years I have been exploring how artistic practice – because of its formal demands, repetitive nature, symbolic force, and relational aspects – encourages and supports my own healing process. I have come to identify ways to intentionally invite others to probe the potential for wellness in their own lives without presuming that what works for me would be applicable to anyone else.

Similarly, Deborah and I did not enter into this project assuming an a priori or unchanging definition of beauty and home, nor did we assume a homogenous potential for beauty in the personal and communal healing process. While affirming a central role for lamentation songs, vocal explorations of mourning, and the sharing of narratives related to the (un)making of home, our intention was to leave open the possibility for people to explore and name for themselves how the terms *beauty* and *home* makes sense given their own experiences of displacement (lived personally or handed down from previous generations). Even so, Deborah – the daughter of Holocaust survivors – and I did come to this project with our own experiences of familial deracination and as such our relationship to the subject, and by extension to each of the other participants in the project, was proximate. Our familiarity with the Jewish chronicles of displacement including *The Book of Lamentations* was a common starting point between us and positioned us as insiders familiar with the dynamics of dislocation and cognizant of the ways in which the construction of narratives matter personally and politically.

Although the question of beauty has been central to certain Judaic texts – such Isaiah's prophecy: "To appoint unto them that mourn in Zion, to give them beauty instead of ashes, the oil of joy for mourning" (61:3) and Solomon's Song of Songs – when it comes to the issue of home, Judaism has tended to focus more significantly on the experience of alienation. Arnold M. Eisen is clear to point this out in his introduction to *Galut: Modern Jewish reflection on*

{421}

homelessness and homecoming: "The loss and leaving of home stamp all the narratives of Genesis – from Cain the perpetual wanderer, through Abraham's departures for Canaan and beyond, to the final descent into Egypt. [...] Even the marvelous promise of home conveyed by Deuteronomy is overwhelmed at the book's conclusion by the threat of renewed homelessness" (p. xi). This is but one culturally specific example of the power of narrative to shape history. There are many others including the predictions about cataclysmic or transformative events to occur in the year 2012 linked to the end of the Mayan calendar and the Hopi prophecies about imminent great change. Can a concentration on sharing beauty's ethical and aesthetic potential contribute to how things evolve from here on?

During each *Lamentations* event, Deborah and I invited four different communication procedures aimed at establishing the conditions within which people could bear witness to their own and others' experiences. Improvisational vowel toning warm-up exercises and the more formally structured teaching/learning and listening/singing of songs in Creole, Spanish, Latvian, Mandarin, Anishnabai, and Inuktitut, were complemented by stories shared in the talking circle and informal conversation over hot drinks, fruit, and sweet snacks. In addition to accounts of the impacts from colonial occupation of Turtle Island, the Acadian deportation, the Shoah, and the partition of India, people referred to their forced migrations from Haiti, Palestine, Mexico, Lebanon, Latvia, China, Chile, Peru, Poland, and Algeria.

The group dynamic changed each time a new person joined or someone left – in many ways echoing the social dynamics within the communities of origin and the communities displaced individuals attempt to become part of. The difficulty to find teachers and the uncertainty of their showing up speak volumes about the precarity of recent refugees and immigrants. And yet, once they attended one session, many returned and spoke of how vital an experience it was for them to have such a recurrent group encounter focused on such pressing issues in a manner that was convivial, creative, and caring.

Although we had determined certain parameters for the project, Deborah and I deliberately {423} left the structure flexible and loose trusting that other participants would take ownership of the process if they felt comfortable to do so. While we initially shared the facilitation between us, it didn't take long before others offered to lead the warm-up sessions, distribute food, videotape the proceedings, and play instruments to accompany the teachers/learners in song, etc. People assumed these responsibilities spontaneously and autonomously, extending and altering the process – and even the structure – of the *Lamentations* project. It became apparent that the emergence of this voluntary responsibility shared amongst the group members served to make the group more cohesive and coherent. For some, this participation was not incidental to the process of exercising self-determination relative to grieving the loss of home as they assumed a place for themselves within the group equal to that of Deborah's and my own and felt that their contributions were useful and appreciated.

The dynamic involvement rather than passive spectatorship of each of the individuals involved created a sense of affirmation and commonality reinforced the singularity of each person's contribution. Gradually it became obvious how important these relational dynamics were to the mourning process on the one hand and coming to a new sense of belonging and being at home on the other.

Over time, a sense of compassionate, non-judgmental responsiveness developed amongst the participating individuals as we each gave voice in speech and song about the challenges related to moving from place to place. "Music is often seen to unite us, and also to promote our self-awareness and self-esteem, mutual tolerance, sense of spirituality, intercultural understanding, ability to cooperate, healing – to name but a few. Above all, there is a recurrent conjecture that music can enable people, somehow, to 'get inside' each other's minds, feel each other's suffering and recognize each other's shared humanity – that is, in common understanding, to have *empathy* for each other" (Laurence, 2008: 14). As we shifted from one communication process to another, what became apparent was that however much the music (both the wordless harmonics that resulted from the vowel warm-up explorations and the lamentation songs themselves) was integral to the experience of empathy and consolation shared amongst the participants, the process of teaching/learning, the sharing of personal narratives and the casual exchanges provided a diversity of potential spaces for exchange, each one serving to reinforce the positive causatums of what was shared and explored in the other. As such, while music was what ostensibly brought people together, what seems to have strengthened the bonds between individuals of such differing ages, cultural, and linguistic heritages, educational backgrounds and experiences with migration was the combination of song and the public articulations of intimate recollections of traumatic experiences.

Although at times awkward and even disjointed, the transitions between the warm-up exercises, talking circle, formal singing lessons and informal conversations, could be understood as mirroring the halting and less than fluid process involved in the passage between different stages of the journey to dwelling cycle (Seamon, 1989). In his (February 17, 2008) CBC radio interview with *Writers and Company* host Eleanor Wachtel renowned neurologist

Oliver Sacks, author of *Musicophilia: Tales of Music and the Brain* (2007), suggested that people can borrow from the flow of music to bring flow into their own experience when they are otherwise incapable of doing so.

The rhythms of music can liberate movement physically and emotionally especially as music is associated with parts of the brain that are responsible for activating procedural and emotional memory as distinct from knowledge or event memory that so often is disrupted as a result of traumatic experience. Further, as Sacks has found through the use of magnetic resonance imaging of brain activity, music has a wider distribution than verbal language (Hargreaves & North, 1999; Konecni, Brown, & Wanic 2007). With the music opening the flow of emotion, it can help us move past the numbness to bring mourning into an active state so that the grief can first be recognized for what it is and subsequently be processed and integrated to allow for a renewed connection with and celebration of life.

A certain solace was possible because of the strength in numbers, especially as destabilizing current local and world affairs impacted many of the participants directly. Events at Barriere Lake, Quebec (located four hours north of Montreal and home to members of the Algonquin First Nations), and in Gaza for example, led us to discuss the ongoing colonial oppression of the people's indigenous to Turtle Island and Palestine, while a denied immigration application for the wife of one of the *Lamentations* participants raised questions about Canadian Federal immigration policies.

Conversations with individuals who have taken part in the *Lamentations* project have included affirmations that deliberate acts of beauty matter to people who are ready and able to make sense of their hardships in relation to home and develop new associative connections. Pakuluk, for example, one of the Inuit park dwellers who became a regular contributor to the project after observing from a distance for the first several sessions, made a point of asking to go on record declaring how hearing the sounds of the hand drum and the songs of Native cultures sung by indigenous people and individuals of varying other origins in the Atwater metro station meant that for once he and his friends no longer had to feel ashamed of being who they are.

homeBody

IN THE DAYS AND WEEKS following the final *Why Should We Cry? Lamentations in a Winter Garden* event on December 21, 2008, I felt a strong urge to continue exploring beauty, home, and the power of participatory public art. I was therefore pleased to accept the invitation to contribute to Concordia University's Faculty of Fine Arts launch of two art research spaces at Concordia

University in February 2009.² Within the framework of the inaugural activities, Reena Almoneda Chang, Meena Murugesan, Émilie Monnet and I endeavored to create the conditions within which a self-selecting group of mostly strangers could open up the possibility to co-investigate the notions of home and beauty as relational practice and as context-emergent, ephemeral affirmations of life and civic engagement. Having worked with Reena, Meena and Émilie individually on other projects and knowing of their interest in both home and body, I invited them to join me in this research/creation process. *homeBody* and the accompanying open seminar were the first creative collaborations between the four of us.

Reena Almoneda Chang is a movement artist and educator who draws from her performance and community work on the transformation of grief due to forced displacement through dance and the creation of contemporary ritual. Meena Murugesan self-identifies as an Indo-contemporary dancer, documentary filmmaker and community arts educator committed to working towards personal and social transformation. Émilie Monnet is a performance artist and community activist of Anishnaabe First Nation and French descent. Having lived in different parts of the world, she now is settling home in the traditional lands of Mohawk people (Montreal).

2. The two research labs are: 1) (Canada Research Chair in Inter-X Art Practice & Theory) Sandeep Bhagwati's *matralab* and 2) (Canada Research Chair in New Media Arts) Sha Xin Wei's *Topological Media Lab*.

We sent out word inviting others to share choreographed and improvised movements, storytelling and song in the *matralab* and critical reflection during the open seminar which I titled *Radical Beauty for Troubled Times: a conversation about the (un)making of home in an age of domicide* hosted by the *Topological Media Lab*. As with the *Lamentations* project, the importance of bearing public witness in *homeBody* was crucial to the healing process. "History cannot be held privately. No one person 'owns' a story. Any one story is embedded in layers of remembering and storytelling. Remembering is necessarily a public act whose politics are bound up with the refusal to be isolated, insulated, inoculated against both complicity with and contest over claims to ownership" (Pollock, 2005: 5).

> In the collective story, there are so many layers to home and by sharing, they all resonated with me. I felt the suffering and pain from everyone's story about where one is at home in the body, in the land, etc. There is baggage from everyone, suffering within each person and that made the story collective. I could relate to this and felt that it connected us: I felt a kinship with everyone.

> Émilie Monnet: April 7, 2009 in conversation with Devora Neumark. {427}

> This type of inquiry more accurately reflects the 'real' world, which is not a controlled environment. The inquiry is not only the domain of the researcher, but of others participating in the experience – inquiry becomes a group process, and therefore more multi-dimensional, drawing from a larger pool of experience and perspective. That it is performative or live means that the inquiry benefits from the heightening of creative tension/flow and energy that comes with performance, therefore opening more windows in the senses through which we can understand and process information & different multiple realities.

> Reena Almoneda Chang: April 15, 2009 email addressed to Devora Neumark.

On the first evening we had oriented the room so that much of the activity took place against the far wall of the *matralab*'s black-box theatre space. People mostly sat facing the wall as if it were a stage. During the second and third *homeBody* sessions we rearranged the setting and worked entirely within a circle format switching between one large inclusive and two concentric circles.

Writing about performance, Erika Fischer-Lichte affirms: "Aesthetic experience and liminal experience ultimately coincide due to the workings and effects of the autopoietic feedback loop. The liminal situation is not only a result of the experience of elusiveness, generated by the permanent, reciprocal transitions between subject and object positions. Rather, every turn the feedback loop takes must also be seen as a transition and hence as a liminal situation" (2008: 177). As is evident in the following excerpt from the verbatim of my April 7, 2009 conversation with Émilie, there is a strong correlation between interactivity and precarity:

> For me the participative aspect was new: it felt like I was stepping out of my comfort zone. Although in the *Why Should We Cry? Lamentations in the Winter Garden* project that I took part in on two occasions there was that aspect, I felt in *homeBody* this component was more present. The wall was safe, the wall was strong, something that I could take my strength from. I was also aware of the impact that the wall had on people. The experience became more communal more accessible and collective when we stepped away from the wall and changed the format to a circle. I felt more vulnerable and I think that is good.

Moving from the wall to the circle was a provocative shift for Meena as well as can be inferred from her email dated April 14, 2009: "I think it's really the sharing aspect that I found the most challenging and altering." In response to a question about what new learning had occurred during the *homeBody* events that I posed to all three women in the weeks after the event, Reena wrote: "Doing this project I discovered another way of sharing my dance with the public that is not 'performance' based in the Western concert tradition, but rather in which movement and the way of being in the body is less formal, less focused on projecting outwards towards an audience and also less insular because of the desire to interact with others in a spontaneous manner." This more fluid exchange process led Reena to learn new things about other cultures and the seemingly generalized acceptance of ghosts in her own Filipina/Chinese culture (as she mentioned during *homeBody* and confirmed in an email exchange dated April 15, 2009).

Likewise, the following exchange between *homeBody* participants and myself points to the importance of bearing witness and being witnessed by others:

It was so dangerous to be home in that body that I had to pull myself out of myself, dislodge myself from my body, or at least my mind as I usually know it, and in that state I could live in my body in a completely different way that was about being there, really being there with the fish. That was the biggest struggle because it was so unfamiliar and in no time I would swallow more water and they had to pull me out. But I was very happy because I had a glimpse of what it was like to step outside of one frame of consciousness. It was then that I realized that I didn't have only one state of consciousness or one frame of reference but that I could actually embody more than myself: that I could step out of my way and get into the fish.

Marilou Esguerra (*homeBody* participant): February 17, 2009 verbatim

Dear Reena, Meena and Émilie, just wanted to thank you for a wonderful experience. I left quickly with my friend and she left because her back was hurting but she loved it. I feel like all of the people in the room are my closest of friends now after this encounter. My thanks to Devora and to you all for the exploration and the chance to be so intimate so quickly with people who were initially strangers. I ran into Carmen, the Colombian woman. We met each other by chance elsewhere today and she and I hugged hello and goodbye and briefly spoke about our first close encounter. I would like to know the name and have the contact of the Asian woman who was at one with the fish.

Janet Lumb (*homeBody* participant): February 20, 2009 email to D. Neumark.

Hello Janet and thank you for your enthusiastic email (that Meena forwarded to me)! I am greatly appreciating your participation - your presence and the stories you shared have continued to inhabit me. Taking note of your interest in getting in touch with the woman who was at one with the fish, I sent off an email to her indicating that you would be happy to be in contact with her and provided her with your email address so that she could get in touch with you directly.

Devora Neumark: February 21, 2009 email to J. Lumb.

Hello Devora, Thank you for your lovely letter. *Indeed, it was in the telling of the story that I recognized my oneness with the fish. Back in the ocean, it was both happenstance and my survival. But now, I take great delight in knowing that I can be remembered as "the woman who was (at) one with the fish".* Thank you for giving me the opportunity to share, and for your sharing too. (Italics added.)

M. Esguerra: February 22, 2009 email to D. Neumark.

The Stranger as Witness

As I HAVE OFTEN NOTED in previous live art events that I've convened in public space[3] and has been affirmed in other instances of arts-based healing processes (Laurence, 2008; Schutz, 1964; Stein, 2004) the risk to share one's sorrow can seem somewhat easier in the company of others who are also willing to disclose personal information and reveal themselves emotionally. "When group members validate each other's stories and songs of past sorrow, it resembles the witness's role in a testimony" affirms Kimberly Wedeven Segall (2005: 138). In part the possibility to open one's heart within the context of art projects such as *Why Should We Cry? Lamentations in a Winter Garden* and *homeBody* is because the people who bear witness to the sorrow and the hope are mostly strangers.

As far as I can tell the stranger factor worked in the following two ways: 1) Knowing that one's story was carried by others who would not ordinarily be present in one's quotidian life alleviated, or at least mitigated, the burden of disclosure while simultaneously alleviating, or at least mitigating, the burden of the witness and the vulnerability that often accompanied both processes of disclosure and witnessing; 2) Sharing one's experience in public amongst a circle of strangers provided participants with the sense of being part of something larger than ourselves and thus lent legitimacy to one's experience within a greater socio-cultural and even political process of meaning-making. I think that the risk to share one's life experience in public is possible also because the memories, feelings, and thoughts that arise during such a project are able to be given

{430}

---

3. Note especially: *s(us)taining* (1996), *présence* (1997), *the art of conversation* (2000), *she loves me not, she loves me* (2001), and *the kindest thing* (2002), *holding ground* (2003), *and how shall our hands meet?* (2006), *Uprooted* (2007), and *Bearing Witness: Stories of Survival, Loss, and (not) Belonging* (2008).

attention in symbolic form, easing the risk of disclosure (even towards oneself) when in real life such awareness may be too hard to bear.

Writing of the need to release strong feelings related to cycles of violence through the practices of rituals, songs, public storytelling, and funeral laments in Africa and the Middle East, Segall states: "Cultural performances incorporate these emotions into a larger narrative in an artistically-bound controlled form, which can work toward social healing" (139). Not all of the *Lamentations* and *homeBody* participants had as immediate and intense experiences of violence than what Segall recounts. Nevertheless the fact that these projects were framed as artistic events, seemed to have provided a sense of safety that contained and channelled the oft-times strong emotions arising as we shared songs and difficult stories. The co-creative process functioned much in the same way as Winnicott's *potential space* – the creative possibility located between external and internal realities. Here, in addition to the activation of individual potential creativity, what emerged from the temporary collective served for some as a new schema of healthy co-existence.

Beauty and Political Agency

RECENT EXPLORATIONS OF THE GENERATIVE POSSIBILITIES for living in balance with the rest of nature points to a shift in political, cultural, environmental, economic, social, and academic priorities (Charlton, 2008; Hester, 2006; Ndejuru, Neumark, Ngirumpatse & Wesley, 2008; Shiva, 2004). Beauty too is going through a theoretical revision after decades of being dismissed as irrelevant, at least within the Western art canon. Dr. Richard F. Mollica, Harvard Medical School Professor and Director of the Harvard Program in Refugee Trauma, who frequently writes on issues pertaining to global mental health, social and personal healing, human rights, and the obstacles and pathways to peace, posted the following to his blog on June 28, 2007: "Except in beauty there is no healing. Beauty is the salve and ointment that creates our healing space and healing relationships. Beauty is the pre-eminent healing medium" (http://healinginvisiblewounds.typepad.com). Furthermore, Kathleen Marie Higgins author of the critical essay: *Whatever happened to beauty? A response to Danto* argues that rather than consider beauty "at odds with political activism because it is not a directly practical response to the world," politically motivated movements have "much to gain from beauty. [. . .] It may be insensitive, at times, to luxuriate in aesthetic comfort while human misery abounds. But the mesmerizing impact of beauty may, even in miserable conditions, rekindle our sensitivity. [. . .] [T]he condition of contemplating beauty is essential to the total economy of political 'engagement'" (Higgins, 1996: 283). Higgins goes on to identify core concepts relative to beauty and political engagement to do with the how beauty impacts our human capacity to recognize and develop moral insight; teaches us to be mindful of nuance; and plays on our willingness to confront our own worst fears.

In articulating her second concept Higgins states: "our political commitments are suspect if they cannot survive confrontation with beauty" (1996: 283). Furthermore she claims that: "If one's political commitments are not themselves submitted to reflective reconsideration, they may come to function as fixed ideas, guiding action, but unresponsive to changing circumstances" (1996: 283). Here Higgins points to, but stops short of, asserting what I think may be beauty's greatest potential, that is the lesson about ephemerality and indeterminacy that beauty offers especially at this particular threshold of ecological crisis and multiple populations transposition (i.e. mammalian, fish, and flora) being experienced around the globe (Altman & Werner, 1985; Blunt, 2005; Porteous & Smith, 2001).

Weighing in about the need to re-define the notion of beauty, Janet Wolff proposes: "If aesthetics can be re-thought as the debate about value after the loss of certainty – a 'groundless aesthetic' – then the return to beauty has a different look" (2006: 154). Not only does what Mollica has to say resonate strongly with me; since my involvement with *Why Should We Cry? Lamentations in a Winter Garden* and *homeBody* I am even more convinced that exploring the concepts and experience of beauty and home as conditional, contingent and context-determined can lead to a greater sense of possibility for survival and harmonious cohabitation of our home, planet Earth. Our stories matter – they can remind us that everything everywhere is interdependent. Perpetuating what Higgins has claimed as "the modern avoidance of beauty" (1996: 283) will certainly not provide us the necessary context within which to develop the skills we now need to choose life and celebrate it (Ingold, 2000). Our stories matter – if only to get us to act *as if*.

Devora Neumark Interdisciplinary artist Devora Neumark is a faculty member in the MFA-Interdisciplinary Art program at Goddard College (Vermont) and co-director of Engrenage Noir / LEVIER, a Montreal-based non-profit community and activist arts advocacy and funding organization whose most recent initiatives are intended to stimulate dialogue about healthy interdependence and ethical responsiveness while encouraging artistic creation addressing the systemic causes of poverty. Neumark is also currently a Humanities PhD Candidate at Concordia University's Centre for Interdisciplinary Studies in Society and Culture. Her research project "Radical Beauty for Troubled Times: The (un)making of Home" examines how a deliberate engagement with beauty and home can, on the one hand, strengthen intracultural alliances and, on the other, perpetuate cycles of violence: in other words, how very often the affirmation of beauty and the settling at home of one population sets into motion homelessness for others.

{433}

Neumark

References

ALTMAN, I. & WERNER, C. M. (Ed.), (1985). *Home Environments: Human Behavior & Environment Advances in Theory & Research*, New York and London: Plenum Press.

BLUNT, A. (2005), Cultural Geography: Cultural Geographies of Home, *Progress in Human Geography*, 29:4, 505-515.

CHARLTON, N. G. (2008). *Understanding Gregory Bateson: Mind, beauty, and the sacred earth*. Albany: The State University of New York Press, Albany.

EISEN, A. M. (1986). *Galut: Modern Jewish reflection on homelessness and homecoming*. Bloomington & Indianapolis: Indiana University Press.

FISCHER-LICHTE, E. (2008). *The transformative power of performance: A new aesthetics* (S. I. Jain, Trans.). London and New York: Routledge. (Original work published 2004).

GUATTARI, F. (1995). *Chaosmosis: An ethico-aesthetic paradigm*. (P. Bains & J. Pefanis, Trans.). Bloomington & Indianapolis: Indiana University Press. Original published in 1992.)

HARGREAVES, D. J. & NORTH, A. C. (1999). The functions of music in everyday life: Redefining the social in music psychology, *Psychology of Music*, 27(1), 78-83.

HEDDON, D. (2008). *Autobiography and Performance*. New York: Palgrave Macmillan.

HESTER, R. T. (2006). *Design for ecological democracy*. Cambridge, MA: MIT Press.

HIGGINS, K. M. (1996). Whatever happened to beauty? A response to Danto. *The Journal of Aesthetics and Art Criticism*, 54(3), 281-284.

INGOLD, T. (2000). *The perception of the environment: Essays in livelihood, dwelling and skill*. London and New York: Routledge.

Konecni, V. J., Brown, A. & Wanic, R. A. (2007). Comparative effects of music and recalled life-events on emotional state. *Psychology of Music*, 36(3), 289-308.

Laurence, F. (2008). Music and empathy. In O. Urbain, O. (Ed.), *Music and Conflict Transformation: Harmonies and Dissonances in Geopolitics* (13-25). London & New York: I.B. Tauris.

Mollica, R. F. (2006). *Healing invisible wounds: Paths to hope and recovery in a violent world*. Nashville: Vanderbilt University Press.

Ndejuru, L., Neumark, D., Ngirumpatse, P. & Wesley, S. (2008). The Scent of Home Beautiful. In A. Bertrand, H. Roelants, & S. Wright (Eds.), *Livraison n⁰ 9*: As *If All Were Well* (62-79). Strasbourg & Montreal: Rhinocéros & Centre des arts actuels Skol.

Pollock, D. (Ed.). (2005). *Remembering: Oral history performance*. New York: Pallgrave Macmillan.

Porteous, D. J. & Smith, S. E. (2001). *Domicide: The Global Destruction of Home*. Montreal: McGill-Queen's Press.

Sacks, O. (2007). *Musicophilia: Tales of music and the brain*. New York: Alfred A. Knopf, Inc.

Schutz, A. (1964). Making music together. In S. Frith, (Ed.), *Popular music: Critical concepts in media and cultural studies* (197-212). London: Routledge.

Seamon, D. (1989). Reconciling old and new worlds: The dwelling – journey relationship as portrayed in Vilhelm Moberg's "Emigrant" novels'. In D. Seamon & R. Mugerauer, (Eds.), *Dwelling, Place and Environment* (227-245). New York & Oxford: Columbia University Press.

Segall, K. W. (2005). Stories and songs in Iraq and South Africa: From individual trauma to collective mourning performances. *Comparative Studies of South Asia, Africa and the Middle East,* 25(1), 138-151.

Shiva, V. (Ed.). (1994). *Close to home: Women reconnect ecology, health and development worldwide*. Philadelphia and Gabriola Island: New Society Publishers.

STEIN, A. (2004). Music, Mourning, and Consolation. *Journal of the American Psychoanalytical Association,* 52(3), 783-811.

UNWIN, M. M., KENNY, D. T. & DAVIS, P. J. (2002). The effects of group singing on mood. *Psychology of Music,* 30(2), 175-185.

URBAIN, O. (ED.). (2008). *Music and conflict transformation: Harmonies and dissonances in geopolitics.* London and New York: I.B. Tauris.

WINNICOTT, D. W. (2005). *Playing and Reality.* New York: Routledge. First published in 1971.

WOLFF, J. (2006). Groundless beauty: Feminism and the aesthetics of uncertainty. *Feminist Theory,* 7(2), 143-158.

ZELIZER, C. (2003). The role of artistic processes in peacebuilding in Bosnia-Herzegovina. *Peace and Conflict Studies,* 10(2), 62-75.

{436}

About the editors

CHERYL MCLEAN, MA, has published research about the creative arts in interdisciplinary practice for four years in her role as editor and publisher of *The International Journal of The Creative Arts in Interdisciplinary Practice*, IJCAIP. She is also editor of the CAIP, Creative Arts in Interdisciplinary Practice, research series which includes three volumes, "*Creative Arts in Interdisciplinary Practice, Inquiries for Hope and Change, Creative Arts in Research for Community and Cultural Change, and Story, Technology and Transformation.* In addition to her background in the Social Sciences (University of Western Ontario) and ongoing work in publishing and adult education, she is also experienced as an artist and researcher creating *ethnodrama* for social change.

She completed graduate studies in Creative Arts Therapies at Concordia University in Montréal with special interests in drama approaches in mental health and gerontology. Cheryl McLean also studied in projects for two years as an actor (realism, Stanislavski influenced approaches) working under the mentorship of Dr. Muriel Gold, formerly the Artistic Director of the Saidye Bronfman Theatre, Montreal. Her research with Maimonides Jewish Geriatric Hospital and The Rene Cassin Institute for Social Gerontology involved group therapy with older persons in an Over 60 mental health program, writing a performance script based on client stories and fieldwork and solo acting in multiple roles in the original ethnodrama "*Remember Me for Birds.*" This performance about aging, mental health and autonomy was presented in its final form as an hour long solo ethnodrama with multi-media elements at universities, medical schools, and national conferences in Canada and the U.S. The research was influenced in field work by drama and therapeutic approaches (*Current Approaches in Drama Therapy*, 2000), realism and Stanislavski acting approaches and qualitative (narrative and performative) approaches, (writings by Norman K. Denzin, *Performance Ethnography, Critical Pedagogy and the Politics of Culture*, 2003) and developments in the emerging playwriting and research performance genre, *ethnodrama*, Johnny Saldana, (*Ethnodrama An Anthology of Reality Theatre*, 2005).

She has taught the course "Creative Responses in Death and Bereavement" at the University of Western Ontario, London, and presented and facilitated group story workshops for interdisciplinary audiences at universities, health organizations, and national conferences in Canada and the US.

In her current keynote presentation, *Living Stories of Hope and Change*[*], audiences are introduced to *The Creative Arts in Interdisciplinary Practice* through topical research as well as personal narratives, stories, and performed monologues from the ethnodrama and film "Remember Me for the Birds"[†] (a research based performance about aging, mental health, and autonomy). This presentation is followed by an experiential creative arts practice story/performance workshop in which participants access and perform their own narratives and personal stories in a step-by-step developmental group process.

CherylMcLean@ijcaip.com

Denzin, N.K., *Performance Ethnography, Critical Pedagogy and the Politics of Culture,* Sage Publications, Thousand Oaks, London, 2003.

Gold, M., *Therapy Through Drama: The Fictional Family*, Charles C. Thomas Publisher, Ltd., Springfield, Illinois, 2000.

Lewis, P., Johnson, D.R. (eds), *Current Approaches in Drama Therapy*, Charles C. Thomas, Publisher, Ltd., Springfield, Illinois, 2000.

Saldana, J. (Ed.), *Ethnodrama: An Anthology of Reality Theatre*, Walnut Creek, CA: AltaMira Press., 2005.

* "Living Stories of Hope and Change" Presentation Summary
http://creativeartpractice.blogspot.com/2010/06/it-is-well-known-that-creative-arts-can.html

† "Remember Me for the Birds" (YouTube video clip)
http://www.youtube.com/watch?v=pQv23vYDh0M

† "Remember Me for the Birds" brief background and description
http://ccahtecrossingborders.blogspot.com/2007/10/blog-post.html

CAIP Research series BLOG: http://www.creativeartpractice.blogspot.com
International Journal of The Creative Arts in Interdisciplinary Practice IJCAIP http://www.ijcaip.com

ROBERT KELLY, Ph.D. is an artist/educator who is an associate professor in the Faculty of Arts and an adjunct associate professor in the Faculty of Education at the University of Calgary. He is also an Advisory Board member for The International Journal of the Creative Arts in Interdisciplinary Practice.

His recent book *Creative Expression, Creative Education* (co-edited with Carl Leggo, University of British Columbia) presents the case for creativity as a primary rationale for education. He is currently

researching and developing two new volumes on creativity and educational practice. *Volume 2: The Creative Disposition* focuses on developing personal and professional creativity among educators. *Volume 3*, entitled *Educating for Creativity* explores the methodology of teaching in an educational culture of creativity.

Robert's research is focused on the concept of creativity and its applications for educational practice. He is currently researching and developing a triadic model for transforming school culture through the strands of professional development, methodology and organizational structure. He has originated a matrix for the development and assessment of creative maturity that is central to transformational strategies.

As an artist, Robert currently has two major touring bodies of work, *Minutia* and *The Concept of Raven*. *Minutia* is an interactive installation made up of eleven books of concrete poetry each based on a word from the sentence fragment "the first time I heard the sound of a page turning." *The Concept of Raven* is a series of large painted low-relief works that uses the raven to explore human behavior. His newest work in progress, a large outdoor installation entitled *White Noise*, explores the hypocrisy of the hyper-consumption of Western culture.

HTTP://WWW.ROBERTKELLY.CA

Photo from installation collage for ethnodrama
"Remember Me for Birds,"a performance about
aging, mental health and autonomy.

These are stories from people housed in an area of Montreal that
is home to one of the highest density aged populations in North
America. But theycould be stories from people you know anywhere
across this country.These are stories about freedom and survival."

–from introduction, script, "Remember Me for Birds", C. McLean

POMMES
DE TERRE

© 2003 Maxi-Livres pour l'édition française.

© 2002 Rebo Productions Ltd.

Photographies originales : © R&R Publishing Pty. Ltd.

POUR L'ÉDITION FRANÇAISE

Sous la direction de la Centrale d'achats Maxi-Livres

Direction éditoriale : Alexandre Falco.

Responsable des publications : Françoise Orlando-Trouvé.

Responsable de l'ouvrage : Bénédicte Sacko.

Réalisation : Atelier Gérard Finel, Paris.

Traduction / adaptation : Cécile Giroldi.

Révision : Martine Pfeiffer, Béatrice Lecomte.

Mise en pages : Hélène Ladégaillerie.

Malgré le soin apporté à sa réalisation, cet ouvrage peut comporter
des erreurs ou omissions. Nous remercions le lecteur de bien vouloir
nous faire part de toute remarque à ce sujet.

ISBN 2-7434-4551-3

Imprimé en Slovénie

POMMES DE TERRE

De délicieuses recettes parfumées et originales pour
une cuisine créative

Succès du Livre

Avant-propos

Tout comme la tomate, l'aubergine et le piment doux, la pomme de terre fait partie des solanacées. Cultivée depuis toujours par les peuples de la cordillère des Andes, elle fut importée en Europe par les conquistadors au XVIe siècle. Une cinquantaine d'années plus tard, les Anglais devaient faire la même découverte en Virginie, sur le continent nord-américain. En France, longtemps méprisée, réservée au bétail et aux indigents, c'est au XVIIIe siècle seulement qu'Antoine Augustin Parmentier, pharmacien et agronome français, parviendra à populariser sa consommation. La pomme de terre a aujourd'hui conquis tous les continents et toutes les tables ! Mets sain et délicieux, la pomme de terre est l'un des aliments qui se prêtent au plus grand nombre de préparations culinaires, des plus simples aux plus sophistiquées. Soupe de pommes de terre aux pois, rösti au fromage, crêpes aux pommes de terre garnies de saumon fumé, gratin de poisson au citron… Classiques ou originales, les savoureuses recettes contenues dans cet ouvrage vous invitent à la gourmandise !

Correspondances

200 g de pommes de terre :

Eau : 158 g

Protéines : 4,6 g

Glucides : 33,6 g

Énergie : 152 kcal (640 kJ)

Potassium : 868 mg

Magnésium : 38 mg

Fer : 1,2 mg

Calcium : 18 mg

Vitamine B1 : 0,18 mg

Vitamine B2 : 0,10 mg

Vitamine C : 28 mg

Recette

Placez les pommes de terre dans une passoire et rincez-les à l'eau froide.

Essuyez-les avec un torchon ou du papier absorbant.

Mélangez-les dans un bol avec les œufs, les oignons, la farine, la coriandre, le fromage et le poivre noir.

Faites chauffer l'huile dans une grande poêle antiadhésive (au manche amovible) à feu moyen. Versez le mélange et laissez cuire 15 minutes.

Placez la poêle sous le gril du four préchauffé à feu moyen et laissez cuire 10 minutes jusqu'à ce que le dessus soit doré et la crêpe bien cuite.

Coupez en plusieurs parts, et servez celles-ci nappées de yaourt.

Ingrédients

1 kg de pommes de terre râpées

2 œufs légèrement battus

2 oignons émincés

2 cuillerées à soupe de farine

1 cuillerée à café de coriandre fraîche, finement ciselée

60 g de cheddar râpé

poivre noir du moulin

2 cuillerées à soupe d'huile d'olive

6 cuillerées à soupe de yaourt nature

Crêpe de pommes de terre **au fromage**

Recette

Placez les pommes de terre et le bouillon dans une grande marmite et portez à ébullition.
Ajoutez la feuille de laurier et laissez mijoter à feu moyen 15 minutes, jusqu'à ce que les
pommes de terre soient tendres.

Ajoutez les pois et le basilic, puis laissez mijoter encore 5 minutes, jusqu'à ce que les pois
soient tendres. Ne les laissez pas trop cuire sinon ils risquent de perdre leur belle couleur. Ôtez
la feuille de laurier et le basilic.

Mixez la soupe progressivement jusqu'à ce qu'elle soit homogène, puis transvasez-la à
nouveau dans la marmite et réchauffez-la à feu doux.

Avec une louche, versez la soupe dans des bols et couronnez d'1 cuillerée de crème. Remuez
doucement avec une fourchette pour créer un effet de volute à la surface,
puis saupoudrez de poivre noir.

Soupe aux pois à la menthe
& aux pommes de terre

Ingrédients

4 pommes de terre (environ 500 g) pelées
et finement coupées

1 l de bouillon de volaille peu salé

1 feuille de laurier

450 g de petits pois congelés

2 tiges de basilic

4 cuillerées à soupe de crème allégée

poivre noir concassé

8

Pommes de terre

Recette

Chauffez le beurre, puis ajoutez le curcuma, l'ail, le curry en poudre, le garam masala, le gingembre et le piment. Faites-les revenir jusqu'à ce que le parfum des épices s'exhale.

Pendant ce temps, épluchez et hachez tous les légumes sauf les courgettes, que vous détaillerez en rondelles, et les pois.

Ajoutez les légumes hachés au mélange épicé, et versez le bouillon. Portez le tout à ébullition. Laissez mijoter 45 minutes jusqu'à ce que les légumes soient bien tendres. Ajoutez le lait de coco, les courgettes et les pois. Laissez mijoter encore 15 minutes. Salez et poivrez selon votre goût. Décorez cette soupe épaisse avec la coriandre et servez-la accompagnée de naan (pain indien) passé au four et de concombre au yaourt.

Ingrédients

30 g de beurre, ordinaire ou clarifié

1 cuillerée à soupe de curcuma

4 gousses d'ail finement hachées

1 cuillerée à soupe de curry doux en poudre

1 cuillerée à soupe de garam masala

1 cuillerée à soupe de gingembre finement râpé

1 cuillerée à café de copeaux de piment

4 pommes de terre moyennes

2 patates douces

2 navets

Soupe indienne
aux légumes & au curry

1 panais

4 carottes de taille moyenne

1 courge butternut de taille moyenne,

ou 1 belle part de potiron

4 courgettes de taille moyenne

400 g de pois écossés

1 l de bouillon de légumes

40 cl de lait de coco

sel et poivre

feuilles de coriandre ciselées, pour servir

Recette

Pour la marinade, mélangez l'huile, le jus de citron, le piment et l'ail dans un récipient. Coupez les poulpes en deux dans le sens de la longueur. S'ils sont très petits, laissez-les entiers. Placez-les dans le récipient et laissez mariner toute une nuit au réfrigérateur, ou au moins deux heures.

Faites cuire les pommes de terre à l'eau ou au four à micro-ondes jusqu'à ce qu'elles soient tendres. Égouttez-les, puis laissez-les légèrement refroidir. Découpez-les en petits morceaux.

Pour la concassée de tomates, mélangez dans un récipient les tomates, la coriandre, l'oignon, le vinaigre, l'huile, le jus de citron et le poivre noir.

Préchauffez le gril ou le barbecue.

Tapissez un plat de service de feuilles de roquette. Garnissez ensuite de pommes de terre, de concombres et d'oignons. Égouttez les poulpes. Faites-les cuire au barbecue ou au gril en les tournant fréquemment, toutes les 3 à 5 minutes, jusqu'à ce que les tentacules se tordent. Veillez à ne pas les laisser cuire trop longtemps, sinon leur chair risque d'être trop ferme.

Disposez les poulpes sur la salade. Servez avec la concassée de tomates et du pain croustillant.

Poulpes au barbecue
& salade de pommes de terre

Ingrédients

500 g de petits poulpes nettoyés

500 g de pommes de terre rosevals

roquette ou salade mélangée

2 concombres finement coupés

2 oignons verts émincés

Pour la marinade :

2 cuillerées à soupe d'huile d'olive

le jus d'1 citron vert

1 piment rouge coupé en dés

1 gousse d'ail pilée

Pour la concassée de tomates :

4 olivettes coupées en dés

25 g de coriandre fraîche, finement ciselée

½ oignon rouge coupé en dés

10 cl de vinaigre balsamique, ou de vinaigre de xérès

1 cuillerée à soupe d'huile d'olive

1 cuillerée à soupe de jus de citron

poivre noir du moulin

Recette

Préchauffez le barbecue. Badigeonnez d'huile les rondelles de patates douces. Faites-en cuire quelques-unes à la fois, 4 minutes de chaque côté, jusqu'à ce qu'elles soient dorées et croustillantes. Égouttez-les sur du papier absorbant.

Placez les épinards et les feuilles de roquette, les tomates, les oignons, les olives et le parmesan dans un saladier et remuez délicatement. Couvrez et placez au frais.

Dans un bol, préparez la sauce en mélangeant les feuilles d'origan, le sucre, le vinaigre et le poivre noir.

Dressez la salade sur un plat de service, ajoutez les patates douces, et nappez de sauce avant de servir.

Ingrédients

1 kg de patates douces coupées en fines rondelles

3 à 4 cuillerées à soupe d'huile d'olive

185 g de pousses d'épinard

185 g de roquette

3 tomates finement coupées

2 oignons rouges émincés

4 cuillerées à soupe d'olives noires dénoyautées

60 g de parmesan, en copeaux

Salade de patates douces

Pour la sauce :

2 cuillerées à soupe de feuilles d'origan fraîches

1 ½ cuillerée à soupe de sucre roux

9 cl de vinaigre balsamique

poivre noir du moulin

Pommes de terre

Recette

Placez les lardons dans une grande casserole à fond épais, et laissez-les dorer 5 minutes à feu moyen jusqu'à ce qu'ils soient croustillants. Égouttez-les sur du papier absorbant.

Faites fondre le beurre dans la casserole, et laissez cuire les oignons, le céleri et le thym à feu doux 4 à 5 minutes jusqu'à ce que les oignons soient tendres.

Incorporez les lardons de nouveau dans la casserole, puis ajoutez progressivement la farine, sans cesser de remuer. Laissez cuire 1 minute. Ôtez la casserole du feu et ajoutez le bouillon petit à petit, en remuant toujours. Portez à ébullition, puis baissez le feu. Ajoutez les pommes de terre et laissez cuire 10 minutes, jusqu'à ce qu'elles soient tendres.

Hors du feu, ajoutez la crème et le persil. Replacez la casserole de nouveau sur le feu et laissez cuire 1 à 2 minutes, en remuant constamment, sans porter à ébullition. Servez la soupe dans les assiettes, puis parsemez de ciboulette et servez immédiatement.

Ingrédients

250 g de lardons fumés hachés menu
30 g de beurre
2 gros oignons hachés
4 branches de céleri hachées
2 pincées de thym séché
2 cuillerées à soupe de farine

Soupe de pommes de terre **au bacon**

1,5 l de bouillon de volaille

2 grosses pommes de terre coupées en petits dés

60 cl de crème fraîche

3 cuillerées à soupe de persil finement ciselé

2 cuillerées à soupe de ciboulette finement ciselée

Recette

Faites revenir l'oignon et le gingembre 5 minutes dans une grande casserole, avec l'huile, jusqu'à ce qu'ils soient tendres. Ajoutez les pommes de terre, et laissez frire 1 minute en remuant fréquemment.

Mélangez le cumin, la coriandre, le curcuma et la cannelle avec deux cuillerées à soupe d'eau froide pour obtenir une pâte. Incorporez au mélange de pommes de terre et d'oignon, en remuant bien, et laissez cuire pendant 1 minute jusqu'à ce que le parfum des épices se dégage.

Ajoutez le bouillon et assaisonnez à votre goût. Portez à ébullition, puis baissez le feu, couvrez et laissez mijoter 30 minutes jusqu'à ce que les pommes de terre soient tendres. Mixez pour obtenir un mélange homogène ou filtrez à l'aide d'une passoire métallique. Versez à nouveau la soupe dans la casserole et réchauffez-la un peu. Décorez avec le yaourt et le poivre noir.

Soupe indienne épicée
aux pommes de terre & à l'oignon

Ingrédients

1 cuillerée à soupe d'huile
1 oignon haché
1 morceau de gingembre frais de 1 cm, râpé
2 grosses pommes de terre coupées
en dés de 1 cm
2 cuillerées à café de cumin en poudre
2 cuillerées à café de coriandre en poudre

1 cuillerée à café de curcuma
1 cuillerée à café de cannelle en poudre
1 l de bouillon de volaille
sel et poivre noir
4 cuillerées à soupe de yaourt nature
pour la décoration

Recette

Coupez les extrémités de chaque ciboule en ôtant 5 cm à partir de la base. À l'aide d'un couteau bien aiguisé, tranchez-les en fines lamelles en veillant à ce que celles-ci restent attachées à un bout. Plongez-les ensuite dans un récipient rempli d'eau glacée, puis laissez tremper environ 1 heure jusqu'à ce qu'elles se courbent.

Faites revenir le reste des ciboules, coupées en diagonale, dans une grande casserole avec un peu d'huile d'olive. Ajoutez le chou-fleur et les pommes de terre, ainsi que les graines de carvi. Faites rissoler 10 minutes jusqu'à ce que les légumes soient dorés.

Versez le bouillon, et portez à ébullition. Laissez mijoter 45 minutes, puis mixez jusqu'à ce que la soupe soit homogène.

Ajoutez les petits morceaux de chou-fleur réservés et laissez mijoter encore 10 minutes.

Garnissez de yaourt, de graines de carvi et de lamelles de ciboules, puis servez.

Ingrédients

1 botte de ciboules émincées
2 cuillerées à soupe d'huile d'olive
1 chou-fleur de taille moyenne coupé en morceaux
(réservez quelques petits bouquets)
600 g de pommes de terre coupées en dés
1 cuillerée à café de graines de carvi
1 l de bouillon de légumes
6 cuillerées à soupe de yaourt nature
graines de carvi pour décorer

Soupe de pommes de terre allemande
au chou-fleur & au carvi

Recette

Faites chauffer l'huile dans une cocotte, puis faites revenir les poireaux à feu moyen 5 minutes, jusqu'à ce qu'ils soient tendres et dorés. Ajoutez le safran et les patates douces, puis laissez cuire 5 minutes jusqu'à ce que les patates commencent à se ramollir, tout en remuant.

Versez le bouillon sans cesser de remuer. Ajoutez le bâton de cannelle et le bouquet garni. Portez à ébullition, puis baissez le feu et laissez mijoter 30 minutes jusqu'à ce que les patates douces soient tendres. Ôtez le bâton de cannelle et le bouquet garni.

Faites cuire les pâtes *al dente* dans une grande casserole d'eau. Égouttez-les bien.

Mixez progressivement la soupe jusqu'à ce qu'elle soit homogène. Versez-la à nouveau dans la cocotte, ajoutez les pâtes et réchauffez le tout à feu doux. Si la soupe est trop épaisse, ajoutez un peu d'eau.

Pour confectionner les croûtons, découpez les feuilles de brick avec un moule à biscuits en forme d'étoile. Badigeonnez les morceaux avec un peu d'huile, saupoudrez de parmesan, puis placez une autre étoile au-dessus. Faites-les dorer au four, jusqu'à ce qu'ils soient croustillants.

Versez la soupe dans des bols, faites-y flotter les croûtons, et parsemez de ciboulette.

Ingrédients

2 cuillerées à café d'huile de colza

2 poireaux finement tranchés

1 pincée de safran

1 kg de patates douces à chair jaune orangé, finement coupées

1 l de bouillon de volaille peu salé

1 bâton de cannelle

Soupe aux pommes de terre,
aux pâtes & aux poireaux

1 bouquet garni

100 g de ditalini (petites pâtes pour potage)

2 cuillerées à soupe de ciboulette fraîche,
finement ciselée

croûtons

2 feuilles de brick

1 cuillerée à soupe d'huile d'olive

2 cuillerées à soupe de parmesan râpé

Recette

Pelez, puis hachez finement l'ail. Épluchez, puis coupez en dés les oignons, les carottes et les pommes de terre. Coupez le poivron et les tomates en dés. Placez tous les ingrédients dans une grande marmite remplie d'eau et portez à ébullition. Puis baissez le feu et couvrez partiellement.

Laissez mijoter 2 heures, en remuant de temps à autre. Salez, poivrez et servez la soupe brûlante après l'avoir parsemée de persil.

Ingrédients

4 gousses d'ail
2 oignons
2 carottes
4 pommes de terre
1 poivron vert
440 g de tomates en conserve, concassées
½ chou vert de taille moyenne finement tranché

Soupe portugaise aux haricots rouges

440 g de haricots rouges en conserve,
égouttés et rincés
500 g de saucisse fumée coupée en dés
1,5 l de bouillon de volaille
sel et poivre
2 cuillerées à soupe de persil finement ciselé

Recette

Préchauffez le four à 200 °C/Th. 7.

Coupez les pommes de terre en deux. Placez-les dans un grand saladier avec l'huile. Salez, poivrez, puis mélangez bien avant de les placer sur une plaque huilée, côté chair au-dessous. Faites cuire environ 20 minutes jusqu'à ce qu'elles soient tendres. Laissez refroidir.

Pendant ce temps, mélangez dans un petit récipient le saumon coupé en petits morceaux, la crème, l'oignon d'Espagne, le raifort, la ciboulette. Salez et poivrez.

Creusez légèrement les moitiés de pommes de terre, et coupez-les un peu à la base pour qu'elles tiennent droit. Farcissez-les d'une cuillerée à café de préparation au saumon, puis disposez-les sur un plat.

Garnissez chaque pomme de terre avec un carré de saumon fumé, des œufs de saumon et de la ciboulette.

Laissez reposer 2 heures au réfrigérateur avant de servir.

Pommes de terre nouvelles
au saumon fumé

Ingrédients

12 pommes de terre nouvelles à chair rose
12 pommes de terre nouvelles à chair blanche
sel
poivre
1 cuillerée à soupe d'huile d'olive
150 g de saumon fumé finement haché
3 cuillerées à soupe de crème fraîche

2 cuillerées à soupe d'oignon d'Espagne finement haché
2 cuillerées à café de raifort en pot
½ botte de ciboulette finement ciselée
50 g de saumon fumé, coupé en 24 petits carrés
câpres égouttées, œufs de saumon et quelques brins de ciboulette pour décorer

Recette

Faites bouillir 15 à 20 minutes les pommes de terre dans de l'eau salée jusqu'à ce qu'elles soient tendres. Égouttez-les.

Pendant ce temps, laissez fondre 25 g de beurre dans une grande casserole, et faites revenir l'oignon et le céleri 2 à 3 minutes jusqu'à ce qu'ils soient tendres. Ajoutez la farine et laissez cuire 1 minute tout en remuant, puis versez doucement le bouillon de poisson. Laissez cuire en continuant de remuer jusqu'à ce que le mélange épaississe. Ajoutez ensuite le jus et le zeste de citron. Poivrez.

Préchauffez le four à 200 °C/Th. 7. Retirez la casserole du feu, ajoutez le cabillaud, les moules et le persil tout en remuant. Transvasez le tout dans un plat de cuisson. Réduisez les pommes de terre en purée avec le reste de beurre et le lait. Assaisonnez puis, avec une fourchette, étalez la purée régulièrement sur le poisson. Laissez cuire 30 à 40 minutes jusqu'à ce que le dessus soit doré.

Gratin de poisson au citron

Ingrédients

1 kg de pommes de terre coupées en morceaux

sel et poivre noir

50 g de beurre

1 oignon haché

2 branches de céleri coupées en rondelles

2 cuillerées à soupe de farine

25 cl de bouillon de poisson

le jus d'1 gros citron et le zeste finement râpé

450 g de filets de cabillaud coupés en petits dés

175 g de moules cuites (sans leurs coquilles)

2 cuillerées à soupe de persil frais, finement ciselé

4 cuillerées à soupe de lait

Recette

Préchauffez le four à 200 °C/Th. 7. Placez les pommes de terre et les deux tiers des ciboules dans un saladier. Ajoutez le beurre, assaisonnez et mélangez bien le tout.

Faites chauffer l'huile dans une poêle allant au four, puis ajoutez le mélange de pommes de terre, pressez avec le dos d'une cuillère pour bien l'aplatir. Faites frire 5 à 6 minutes jusqu'à ce que les bords commencent à brunir, puis placez la poêle au four, et laissez cuire 10 minutes jusqu'à ce que le dessus soit bien doré.

Réglez la température du four à 230 °C/Th. 8. Mélangez le fromage et le reste de ciboules puis, hors du four, parsemez-en le mélange de pommes de terre. Replacez la poêle au four, et laissez cuire encore 6 à 8 minutes jusqu'à ce que le fromage forme des bulles et soit doré.

Ingrédients

500 g de pommes de terre râpées et pressées
1 botte de ciboules hachées
25 g de beurre fondu
sel et poivre noir
1 cuillerée à café d'huile d'arachide
100 g de gruyère râpé

Rösti au fromage

Recette

Placez les pommes de terre râpées dans un torchon propre et pressez pour en extraire le maximum de jus. Faites revenir l'oignon et le lard 5 à 8 minutes dans une poêle antiadhésive, avec le beurre et 1 cuillerée à soupe d'huile, jusqu'à ce que l'oignon soit tendre.

Disposez les pommes de terre dans un grand récipient. Ajoutez le mélange d'oignon et de lard, l'œuf, la farine, le persil et l'assaisonnement, tout en remuant. Faites chauffer la moitié de l'huile restante dans la poêle, ajoutez le mélange à base de pommes de terre, et aplatissez-le avec une spatule en bois. Faites chauffer 10 minutes à feu doux jusqu'à ce que la base soit dorée.

Faites glisser le gâteau sur un grand plat. Placez ensuite un autre plat par-dessus, et retournez. Faites chauffer le reste de l'huile dans une poêle, puis glissez-y doucement le gâteau, sur le côté non cuit. Laissez cuire à feu doux 10 minutes jusqu'à ce qu'il soit doré et croustillant.

Gâteau de pommes de terre
au lard & à l'oignon

Ingrédients

750 g de pommes de terre grossièrement râpées

15 g de beurre

2 cuillerées à soupe d'huile

1 oignon haché

6 tranches de lard fumé sans couenne,

coupées en lanières de 1 cm

1 œuf moyen, battu

1 cuillerée à soupe de farine

2 cuillerées à soupe de persil frais,

finement ciselé

poivre noir

Pommes de terre

Recette

Faites cuire les pommes de terre 1 heure au four, jusqu'à ce qu'elles soient tendres. Retirez-les et laissez-les refroidir un peu pour pouvoir les prendre en main. Coupez-les en deux et creusez-les de façon à ne laisser que 5 mm de chair. Coupez les peaux des pommes de terre en gros morceaux et badigeonnez-les d'huile.

Préchauffez le barbecue, ou le gril.

Disposez les peaux sur la grille légèrement huilée, et faites cuire 5 à 8 minutes sur chaque côté jusqu'à ce qu'elles soient dorées et croustillantes.

Elles seront délicieuses agrémentées d'une sauce de votre choix

Peaux de pommes de terre
cuites au barbecue

Ingrédients

6 grosses pommes de terre

huile d'olive

Pommes de terre

Pommes de terre

Recette

Placez les pommes de terre dans une grande casserole d'eau bouillante. Couvrez et laissez cuire 5 minutes, jusqu'à ce qu'elles soient tendres. Égouttez-les bien.

Pendant ce temps, faites chauffer l'huile dans une grande poêle à fond épais. Faites-y revenir l'oignon et le lard 5 minutes, en remuant de temps à autre, jusqu'à ce que l'oignon soit tendre. Ajoutez les rondelles de saucisse et laissez cuire 5 minutes, en remuant de temps à autre, puis ajoutez les pommes de terre, les champignons et le romarin. Laissez cuire 5 minutes de plus jusqu'à ce que les pommes de terre commencent à dorer.

Ajoutez les tomates, la sauce Worcestershire et assaisonnez. Laissez cuire 5 minutes encore jusqu'à ce que le mélange commence à bouillonner et que tous les ingrédients soient cuits.

Chipolatas aux pommes de terre

Ingrédients

500 g de pommes de terre, coupées en petits dés de 1 cm

1 cuillerée à soupe d'huile

1 oignon haché

4 tranches de lard sans couenne et non fumé, coupées en lanières de 1 cm

450 g de chipolatas coupées en fines rondelles

125 g de champignons de Paris coupés en 4

1 pincée de romarin en poudre

400 g de tomates en conserve, concassées

1 cuillerée à soupe de sauce Worcestershire

poivre noir

... Pommes de terre

Pommes de terre

Recette

Placez les pommes de terre, la féta, l'œuf, la ciboule, l'aneth, le poivre, le jus et le zeste de citron dans un récipient de taille moyenne. Mélangez bien. Couvrez et placez au frais 1 à 2 heures jusqu'à ce que le mélange durcisse. Façonnez des boulettes de la taille d'une balle de golf, à la main. Aplatissez-les légèrement et farinez-les.

Faites chauffer un peu d'huile dans une poêle. Faites cuire plusieurs beignets à la fois jusqu'à ce qu'ils soient dorés sur les deux côtés. Égouttez-les sur du papier absorbant et servez immédiatement. Décorez avec de l'aneth et du citron.

Ingrédients

400 g de purée de pommes de terre

120 g de féta émiettée

1 œuf battu

3 ciboules finement hachées

3 cuillerées à soupe d'aneth finement coupée

1 cuillerée à soupe de jus de citron

zeste d'1 citron finement râpé

poivre noir du moulin

farine

huile d'olive

aneth et quartiers de citron pour décorer

Beignets de pommes de terre
à la féta

Recette

Faites cuire les pommes de terre 15 à 20 minutes dans de l'eau bouillante salée, jusqu'à ce qu'elles soient tendres. Égouttez-les bien. Réduisez-les en purée, puis laissez-les refroidir 15 minutes. Mélangez la purée froide avec la moitié de la chapelure, le fromage, le poireau, la sauge et le persil. Salez et poivrez. Liez avec les jaunes d'œufs. Avec vos mains, façonnez 12 saucisses. Couvrez et laissez reposer 1 heure au réfrigérateur.

Assaisonnez la farine. Battez l'œuf. Trempez les saucisses dans la farine, puis dans l'œuf battu, avant de les rouler dans le reste de chapelure. Faites chauffer un fond d'huile dans une grande poêle, et faites frire les saucisses 10 minutes en les tournant jusqu'à ce qu'elles soient dorées. Égouttez-les sur du papier absorbant, et gardez-les au chaud pendant que vous préparez la salade.

Dans un saladier, mélangez l'huile, le vinaigre et le sucre. Ajoutez les tomates coupées en deux, avec l'oignon, le concombre et le basilic.

Assaisonnez et servez avec les saucisses.

Saucisses du pays de Galles

Ingrédients

100 g de pommes de terre

sel et poivre noir

100 g de chapelure de pain blanc

150 g de cheddar râpé

1 petit poireau haché

1 pincée de sauge en poudre

1 cuillerée à soupe de persil frais, finement ciselé

1 pincée de poivre de Cayenne

1 œuf de taille moyenne

2 jaunes d'œufs

3 cuillerées à soupe de farine

huile

Pour la salade :

3 cuillerées à soupe d'huile d'olive

2 cuillerées à café de vinaigre balsamique

1 pincée de sucre brun

150 g de tomates cerises

1 oignon rouge émincé

1 concombre émincé

feuilles de basilic fraîches

Recette

Tapissez six plats de cuisson individuels, préalablement graissés, de pommes de terre, d'oignons, de ciboulette et de poivre noir.

Mélangez le yaourt et la crème dans un récipient. Nappez-en les pommes de terre, puis parsemez de parmesan. Laissez cuire 45 minutes à four chaud, 180 °C/Th. 6, jusqu'à ce que les pommes de terre soient tendres et gratinées.

Ingrédients

1 kg de pommes de terre coupées en fines rondelles

2 gros oignons émincés

2 cuillerées à soupe de ciboulette fraîche, finement ciselée

poivre noir du moulin

250 g de yaourt nature

25 cl de crème fraîche épaisse

60 g de parmesan râpé

Gratin de pommes de terre

Recette

Tapissez un moule à gâteau de 24 cm de diamètre de papier d'aluminium préalablement beurré. Préchauffez le four à 210 °C/Th. 7.

Faites revenir les poireaux, les échalotes et le thym à l'huile d'olive, jusqu'à ce que le mélange soit doré et tendre, environ 15 minutes. Ajoutez le persil. Salez et poivrez. Puis réservez.

Pelez les patates douces et les pommes de terre. Coupez-les en fines rondelles de 2 mm d'épaisseur. Pour cela, utilisez de préférence un coupe-légumes ou une mandoline.

Tapissez le fond du moule avec la moitié des pommes de terre, puis nappez celles-ci d'un peu de pesto. Recouvrez avec un tiers du mélange aux poireaux, étalé régulièrement. Ajoutez une couche de patates douces, nappez de pesto, et recouvrez d'un autre tiers de mélange aux poireaux. Continuez ainsi jusqu'à ce que tous les ingrédients aient été utilisés. Terminez par une couche de patates douces.

Nappez de crème fraîche et saupoudrez de parmesan et de paprika mélangés. Faites cuire 50 minutes au four à 210 °C/Th. 7, jusqu'à ce que les pommes de terre soient tendres. Laissez reposer 5 minutes et servez chaud.

N.B. : Pour une présentation élégante, confectionnez des gâteaux individuels en beurrant 12 petits moules à soufflé, et procédez de la même façon en divisant les ingrédients proportionnellement au nombre de moules.

Gâteau aux pommes de terre

Ingrédients

2 cuillerées à soupe d'huile d'olive	700 g de patates douces
3 gros poireaux finement coupés	700 g de pommes de terre à chair blanche
6 échalotes hachées	200 g de pesto
1 cuillerée à soupe de thym frais	200 g de crème fraîche
200 g de persil frais, ciselé	2 cuillerées à soupe de parmesan râpé
sel et poivre	1 pincée de paprika

Pommes de terre

Recette

Placez les pommes de terre dans une casserole, recouvrez d'eau froide, et portez à ébullition. Baissez le feu et laissez mijoter 10 à 15 minutes jusqu'à ce que les pommes de terre soient tendres. Égouttez et laissez refroidir.

Placez les œufs dans une casserole, recouvrez-les d'eau froide et portez à ébullition à feu moyen, puis laissez-les cuire 10 minutes. Égouttez-les, puis passez-les sous l'eau froide. Ôtez ensuite les coquilles, et coupez-les en quatre.

Faites rissoler le lard 10 minutes à feu moyen dans une poêle antiadhésive, en remuant de temps à autre, jusqu'à ce qu'il soit grillé. Égouttez-le sur du papier absorbant.

Dans un saladier, mélangez délicatement les pommes de terre, les œufs, le bacon, l'oignon, les ciboules, l'aneth et la menthe.

Pour l'assaisonnement, mélangez la mayonnaise, le yaourt, la moutarde et le poivre noir dans un bol. Avec une cuillère, nappez-en la salade et remuez.

Ingrédients

1 kg de pommes de terre coupées en petits dés

3 œufs

4 tranches de lard sans couenne, coupées en fines tranches

1 oignon haché

2 ciboules hachées

2 cuillerées à soupe d'aneth frais, finement ciselé

1 cuillerée à soupe de menthe fraîche, finement ciselée

Salade de pommes de terre

Pour la sauce à la moutarde :

25 cl de mayonnaise

3 cuillerées à soupe de yaourt nature

1 cuillerée à soupe de moutarde de Dijon

poivre noir du moulin

Recette

Faites cuire les pommes de terre 15 à 20 minutes dans de l'eau bouillante salée, jusqu'à ce qu'elles soient tendres. Égouttez-les. Laissez-les refroidir quelques minutes, puis pelez-les. Ajoutez le lait, et réduisez-les en purée. Assaisonnez, puis incorporez l'œuf, la farine et les ciboules, en battant bien afin d'obtenir une pâte à crêpes.

Faites chauffer une poêle antiadhésive à fond épais, puis ajoutez un peu d'huile. En utilisant 2 cuillerées à soupe de pâte à chaque fois, confectionnez quatre crêpes. Laissez-les cuire 2 à 3 minutes sur chaque côté, jusqu'à ce qu'elles soient dorées. Égouttez-les sur du papier absorbant, et gardez-les au chaud pendant que vous préparez deux autres fournées.

Mélangez la crème fraîche et l'aneth. Servez les crêpes surmontées d'une tranche de saumon et d'un peu de crème à l'aneth. Poivrez, et décorez de brins d'aneth et de quartiers de citron.

Crêpes aux pommes de terre
garnies de saumon fumé

Ingrédients

300 g de pommes de terre à purée

sel et poivre noir

15 cl de lait entier

1 gros œuf

25 g de farine

4 ciboules finement coupées

1 cuillerée à soupe d'huile

10 cl de crème fraîche

2 cuillerées à soupe d'aneth frais, finement ciselé

150 g de saumon fumé en tranches

1 citron coupé en quartiers

et brins d'aneth pour décorer

Recette

Pour préparer la purée, effeuillez le brin de romarin, puis faites chauffer les feuilles avec l'huile, à feu doux, dans une petite casserole. Retirez la casserole du feu. Laissez reposer pour que les saveurs se dégagent, si possible plusieurs heures. Plus les feuilles auront mariné dans l'huile, plus leur parfum sera prononcé. Faites bouillir ou cuire au four à micro-ondes les pommes de terre jusqu'à ce qu'elles soient tendres. Égouttez-les bien. Ajoutez le lait et l'huile au romarin et réduisez-les en purée. Assaisonnez de poivre et de jus de citron. Gardez la purée au chaud, ou réchauffez-la juste avant de servir.

Faites chauffer l'huile à feu moyen dans une grande poêle antiadhésive à fond épais. Faites revenir le poireau et l'ail 1 à 2 minutes, tout en remuant, jusqu'à ce qu'ils soient tendres. Ajoutez l'origan, les champignons et le céleri. Laissez cuire 2 à 3 minutes toujours en remuant. Incorporez la purée de tomates en continuant de tourner. Laissez cuire 3 à 4 minutes, jusqu'à ce que le mélange devienne rouge foncé et dégage un fort parfum.

Toujours en remuant, ajoutez les courgettes, les tomates et le vin. Portez le tout à ébullition. Réduisez le feu, puis laissez mijoter 5 minutes en remuant de temps à autre, jusqu'à ce que le mélange commence à épaissir.

Ajoutez le poisson. Laissez cuire 6 minutes jusqu'à ce qu'il soit à point. Veillez à ne pas le laisser cuire longtemps, sinon il risque de s'émietter. Ajoutez le basilic et le persil en remuant. Disposez un peu de purée sur chaque assiette, nappez de ragoût au poisson et servez avec une salade verte ou des légumes verts cuits à la vapeur.

Ingrédients

2 cuillerées à café d'huile d'olive

1 poireau haché

1 gousse d'ail pilée

1 cuillerée à café d'origan en poudre

4 champignons plats tranchés

1 branche de céleri finement coupée

1 cuillerée à soupe de purée de tomates

2 courgettes émincées

400 g de tomates en conserve, concassées

12 cl de vin blanc sec

Ragoût de poisson
à la purée au romarin

500 g de filets de poisson fermes (lotte, bar ou moruette)

1 cuillerée à soupe de basilic frais, finement ciselé

1 cuillerée à soupe de persil frais, finement ciselé

Pour la purée au romarin :

1 brin de romarin frais

2 cuillerées à café d'huile d'olive

2 grosses pommes de terre finement coupées

6 cl de lait écrémé, tiède

poivre blanc du moulin

jus de citron, facultatif

Pommes de terre

51

Recette

Mélangez les pommes de terre, les patates douces, l'oignon, la farine, le persil, le parmesan, les œufs et le poivre noir.

Badigeonnez légèrement une poêle antiadhésive d'huile d'olive. Faites chauffer à feu vif, puis versez 2 à 3 cuillerées à soupe du mélange précédent. Pressez légèrement pour obtenir des galettes. Laissez cuire celles-ci sur chaque côté 4 à 5 minutes jusqu'à ce qu'elles soient dorées. Transvasez-les dans un plat de cuisson tapissé de papier absorbant. Gardez-les au chaud en les plaçant au four à feu doux. Répétez l'opération avec le reste du mélange. Faites cuire 3 à 4 galettes à chaque fois ou autant que la poêle peut en contenir.

Servez-les avec le hachis d'agneau, de la sauce tomate et une salade verte.

Pour le hachis d'agneau : faites chauffer l'huile à feu moyen dans une casserole. Faites revenir l'oignon et le céleri 2 à 3 minutes, jusqu'à ce qu'ils soient tendres. Toujours en remuant, versez la purée de tomates, et laissez cuire 3 à 4 minutes jusqu'à ce que le mélange devienne rouge foncé et dégage un parfum prononcé. Ajoutez l'agneau, les tomates, le persil et le poivre noir. Laissez cuire en remuant de temps à autre, 5 à 10 minutes, jusqu'à ce que la viande soit chaude et la sauce épaisse. Servez sur les galettes de pommes de terre.

Hachis d'agneau rôti
& galettes de pommes de terre

Ingrédients

Pour les galettes aux trois pommes de terre :

200 g de pommes de terre, râpées
200 g de patates douces à chair blanche, râpées
200 g de patates douces à chair jaune, râpées
1 oignon rouge finement haché
2 cuillerées à soupe de farine
2 cuillerées à soupe de persil frais, finement ciselé
1 cuillerée à soupe de parmesan râpé
2 œufs légèrement battus
poivre noir du moulin

Pour le hachis d'agneau rôti :

1 cuillerée à café d'huile
1 petit oignon coupé en dés
1 branche de céleri hachée
2 cuillerées à soupe de purée de tomates
400 g de rôti d'agneau coupé en dés
425 g de tomates en conserve, concassées
2 cuillerées à soupe de persil frais, ou de basilic finement ciselé
poivre noir du moulin

Recette

Épluchez les pommes de terre, tranchez-les et placez-les dans un saladier.
Mélangez bien les ingrédients de l'assaisonnement et nappez-en les pommes
de terre.

Égouttez les artichauts et les champignons. Mélangez délicatement les
artichauts et les champignons avec les pommes de terre. Garnissez le tout de
noix et de persil.

Ingrédients

8 pommes de terre cuites

400 g de cœurs d'artichauts en conserve

400 g de champignons de Paris en conserve

Salade de pommes de terre
aux artichauts

Pour l'assaisonnement :

4 cuillerées à soupe de vinaigre blanc

le jus d'1 demi-citron

1 bonne pincée d'aneth en poudre

sel et poivre noir du moulin

brins de persil et noix coupées en 4 pour décorer

Recette

Pour confectionner les galettes, mélangez bien les pommes de terre, les panais, l'oignon, la sauge, l'œuf, la chapelure et l'assaisonnement dans un grand récipient. Couvrez et laissez reposer 20 minutes au réfrigérateur.

Pendant ce temps, préchauffez le four à 180 °C/Th. 6. Mélangez les pommes, le zeste et le jus de citron, le sucre et le miel dans une petite casserole à fond épais avec deux cuillerées à soupe d'eau. Portez à ébullition, couvrez, puis baissez le feu et laissez cuire 8 à 10 minutes jusqu'à ce que le mélange forme une purée grumeleuse. Retirez du feu et remuez bien pendant 1 minute. Ajoutez la sauge, et, si vous le souhaitez, la crème fraîche. Réservez. Badigeonnez six petits moules d'1 cuillerée à soupe d'huile. Répartissez ensuite le mélange de pommes de terre, badigeonnez le dessus avec la moitié de l'huile restante et laissez cuire 15 minutes. Retirez les galettes du four, badigeonnez-les avec l'autre moitié de l'huile et laissez-les cuire 5 minutes de plus jusqu'à ce qu'ils brunissent.

Servez avec la sauce aux pommes.

Galettes aux pommes de terre
& aux panais

Ingrédients

350 g de pommes de terre grossièrement râpées

150 g de panais grossièrement râpés

1 oignon finement râpé

1 cuillerée à soupe de sauge fraîche, finement ciselée, ou 1 cuillerée à café de sauge en poudre

1 œuf de taille moyenne, légèrement battu

4 cuillerées à soupe de chapelure

sel et poivre noir

2 cuillerées à soupe d'huile d'olive

Pour la sauce aux pommes :

300 g de pommes pelées, évidées et hachées

le zeste et le jus d'1 demi-citron

2 cuillerées à soupe de sucre et de miel liquide

1 cuillerée à soupe de sauge fraîche, finement ciselée, ou 1 cuillerée à café de sauge en poudre

3 cuillerées à soupe de crème fraîche (facultatif)

Recette

Découpez la chair de roussette en six parts égales. Réservez.

Faites chauffer le barbecue. Avec un couteau, tranchez la peau des poivrons et placez ces derniers sur la partie la plus chaude du gril. Au bout de 12 minutes, leur peau doit se couvrir de cloques et être légèrement noircie. Placez les poivrons dans un sac en plastique hermétique. Laissez-les fumer et refroidir, puis pelez-les.

Placez les pommes de terre au-dessus de la partie la plus chaude du barbecue (si vous le souhaitez, vous pouvez les enfiler auparavant sur des brochettes de métal). Laissez-les griller 25 à 30 minutes, en les tournant de temps à autre, et en les badigeonnant de vinaigrette à l'orange.

Ajoutez les courgettes sur le barbecue. Laissez-les cuire jusqu'à ce qu'elles soient légèrement grillées, mais tendres. Badigeonnez-les de temps à autre avec de la vinaigrette. Elles doivent cuire en tout 8 à 10 minutes.

Ajoutez les morceaux de roussette, et faites-les cuire 6 minutes sur chaque côté. Badigeonnez-les de temps à autre de vinaigrette. Coupez le cœur de la trévise en deux dans le sens de la longueur et faites-le griller. Badigeonnez-le de vinaigrette. Laissez-le cuire 4 à 5 minutes jusqu'à ce que ses feuilles soient flétries et légèrement carbonisées. Retirez du gril tous les légumes et le poisson. Réservez au chaud.

Transvasez la vinaigrette dans un bol allant au four à micro-ondes. Faites-la chauffer 2 minutes à température élevée en remuant de temps à autre jusqu'à ce qu'elle frémisse. Versez-la ensuite sur les légumes et le poisson, et servez aussitôt.

Pour la vinaigrette à l'orange : mélangez bien tous les ingrédients. Transvasez dans un bocal fermé par un couvercle hermétique et secouez vigoureusement avant de servir.

La vinaigrette peut être préparée une semaine à l'avance.

Ingrédients

1 kg de chair de roussette, coupée en morceaux de 2,5 cm

2 poivrons rouges, ou jaunes

12 petites pommes de terre à peau rouge

vinaigrette à l'orange

3 courgettes, coupées en tranches dans la longueur

1 cœur de trévise (chicorée rouge)

Roussette au barbecue
& légumes à l'orange

Pour la vinaigrette à l'orange :

2 cuillerées à soupe d'huile d'olive

1 cuillerée à café de gingembre haché

1 cuillerée à soupe de sauce soja

le zeste d'1 citron

25 cl de jus d'orange

2 cuillerées à soupe de vinaigre balsamique

1 pincée de poivre de Cayenne

1 cuillerée à café de moutarde en poudre

Pommes de terre

Recette

Préparez d'abord la purée. Faites cuire les pommes de terre 15 minutes dans de l'eau bouillante salée, jusqu'à ce qu'elles soient tendres. Placez le lait, le beurre, l'assaisonnement et la ciboule hachée (réservez-en 2 cuillerées à soupe) dans une casserole et faites chauffer le tout. Retirez du feu avant ébullition. Égouttez et réduisez les pommes de terre en purée ; tout en remuant, versez celle-ci dans le mélange à base de lait. Assaisonnez et gardez au chaud.

Pendant ce temps, préchauffez le four à 180 °C/Th. 6. Mélangez la chapelure avec la moitié du basilic et la moitié de la ciboulette. Ajoutez 3 cuillerées à soupe d'huile, le zeste de citron et l'assaisonnement. Placez le saumon sur une plaque de cuisson et enrobez-le de chapelure. Faites-le cuire 15 minutes au four jusqu'à ce que le dessus soit doré, et la chair bien cuite. Pendant ce temps, battez avec un fouet la cuillerée à soupe d'huile restante et le jus de citron dans un récipient. Ajoutez les tomates, les 2 cuillerées à soupe de ciboule mises de côté et le reste de basilic et de ciboulette. Assaisonnez-le tout. Servez le saumon avec la salade et la purée, parsemez de feuilles de basilic.

Saumon pané & salade de tomates

Ingrédients

50 g de chapelure de pain blanc

6 cuillerées à soupe de basilic frais, finement ciselé

2 cuillerées à soupe de ciboulette ciselée

4 cuillerées à soupe d'huile d'olive

le zeste et le jus d'1 demi-citron vert

4 filets de saumon d'environ 175 g chacun

200 g de tomates cerises coupées en 2

feuilles de basilic pour décorer

Pour la purée :

750 g de pommes de terre coupées en morceaux

sel et poivre noir

20 cl de lait demi-écrémé

40 g de beurre

1 botte de ciboules hachées

Recette

Mélangez les pommes de terre, l'oignon, le saumon, la moutarde, la mayonnaise et l'œuf. Assaisonnez à votre goût. Façonnez des croquettes avec le mélange, puis roulez-les dans les miettes de biscuits au fromage. Faites chauffer l'huile dans une poêle. Laissez cuire les croquettes à feu moyen, jusqu'à ce qu'elles brunissent. Égouttez-les sur du papier absorbant.

Ingrédients

3 grosses pommes de terre cuites et réduites en purée

1 oignon râpé

440 g de saumon rose en conserve, égoutté et émietté

1 cuillerée à café de moutarde de Dijon

2 cuillerées à soupe de mayonnaise

1 œuf battu

220 g de biscuits salés au fromage, pilés

huile pour friture

Croquettes **au saumon**

Pommes de terre

Recette

Préchauffez le four à 180 °C/Th. 6. Placez le haddock dans une cocottte. Ajoutez 40 cl de lait, le bouillon de poisson, la feuille de laurier et l'oignon piqué de clous de girofle. Portez lentement à ébullition. Baissez ensuite le feu, couvrez et laissez mijoter 5 minutes jusqu'à ce que le poisson soit tendre. Retirez ce dernier avec une écumoire et laissez-le refroidir.

Passez le jus de cuisson et réservez. Faites fondre la margarine dans une petite casserole, ajoutez la farine et remuez pendant 1 minute. Ajoutez le jus réservé, et laissez cuire en remuant constamment jusqu'à ce que la sauce bouillonne et épaississe. Laissez mijoter à feu très doux pendant que vous préparez le poisson.

Ôtez la peau du haddock, et séparez sa chair en gros morceaux. Mélangez ceux-ci avec le saumon et les pois, puis disposez-le tout au fond d'un plat de cuisson en céramique rectangulaire. Mélangez le persil, les câpres, le zeste et le jus de citron à la sauce, et poivrez. Nappez-en le mélange de poissons, puis réservez au frais.

Placez les pommes de terre dans une casserole, recouvrez d'eau et laissez mijoter 20 à 25 minutes jusqu'à ce qu'elles soient tendres. Égouttez-les bien. Faites chauffer les 10 cl de lait restants. Mixez les pommes de terre en ajoutant progressivement le lait tiède jusqu'à ce que le mélange soit onctueux et homogène. Poivrez. Couvrez le mélange de poissons entièrement de purée. À l'aide d'une fourchette, cannelez la surface, puis parsemez de fromage. Laissez cuire au four 30 minutes. Servez avec une salade verte croquante ou des haricots verts cuits à la vapeur.

Gratin au haddock
& au saumon fumé

Ingrédients

800 g de haddock	225 g de pois frais ou congelés
50 cl de lait demi-écrémé	3 cuillerées à soupe de persil frais ciselé
20 cl de bouillon de poisson peu salé	1 cuillerée à soupe de petites câpres égouttées
1 feuille de laurier	1 cuillerée à soupe de zeste de citron
1 oignon piqué de 3 clous de girofle	1 cuillerée à soupe de jus de citron
50 g de margarine	poivre noir, concassé
50 g de farine	900 g de pommes de terre finement coupées
100 g de saumon fumé, coupé en fines lanières	30 g de cheddar râpé

Pommes de terre

Recette

Préchauffez le four à 180 °C/Th. 6. Beurrez un grand plat de cuisson. Détaillez les pommes de terre en fines rondelles. Mélangez le sel, le poivre, la noix de muscade et le fromage. Tapissez le fond de la cocotte d'une couche de pommes de terre, et parsemez d'1 cuillerée à soupe de mélange au fromage. Répétez l'opération.

Placez ensuite une couche de pêches sur les pommes de terre et continuez ainsi en alternant deux couches de pommes de terre et de fromage et une couche de pêches jusqu'à ce qu'il ne reste plus d'ingrédients. Terminez par une couche de pommes de terre et de fromage.

Incorporez la crème fraîche. Couvrez (avec un couvercle ou du papier aluminium), enfournez et laissez cuire environ 1 heure jusqu'à ce que les pommes de terre soient tendres. Ôtez le couvercle durant les dernières 15 minutes de cuisson pour que le dessus soit bien doré. Servez avec du poulet ou du poisson.

Ingrédients

4 pommes de terre de taille moyenne pelées

sel et poivre

1 pincée de noix de muscade

225 g de fromage râpé

200 g de pêches séchées

17,5 cl de crème fraîche, ou d'un mélange

de crème et de lait

Gratin de pommes de terre **aux pêches**

Recette

Placez le lait, les feuilles de laurier, les 2 moitiés de poireau et le haddock dans une casserole. Portez à ébullition, puis laissez mijoter 2 à 3 minutes. Couvrez et laissez reposer 10 minutes. Ôtez le haddock, jetez la peau et les arêtes. Séparez la chair en plusieurs morceaux, et réservez. Jetez les poireaux, mais réservez le lait et les feuilles de laurier.

Faites chauffer le beurre dans une grande poêle à fond épais, et faites fondre le lard 2 à 3 minutes. Ajoutez les rondelles de poireaux, et laissez cuire 5 minutes jusqu'à ce qu'elles soient tendres. Ajoutez les pommes de terre, et laissez cuire encore 3 à 4 minutes jusqu'à ce qu'elles soient légèrement tendres.

Ajoutez le lait réservé, les feuilles de laurier et 15 cl d'eau. Assaisonnez. Portez à ébullition, puis couvrez et laissez mijoter 15 minutes. Jetez le laurier. Mélangez la moitié de la préparation aux pommes de terre avec la moitié du haddock, à l'aide d'un mixer ou d'un presse-purée. Puis replacez le tout dans la poêle. Incorporez le mélange et le haddock restants, puis ajoutez la crème tout en remuant. Réchauffez doucement.

Assaisonnez, et versez un trait de jus de citron si vous le souhaitez.

Ajoutez le persil tout en remuant, et parsemez de ciboulette.

Haddock aux poireaux & au lard

Ingrédients

75 cl de lait entier	500 g de pommes de terre
2 feuilles de laurier	coupées en morceaux de 3 cm
3 poireaux (1 coupé en 2 dans le sens de la	15 cl de crème fraîche liquide
longueur et 2 coupés en rondelles épaisses)	jus de citron (facultatif)
500 g de filets de haddock	2 cuillerées à soupe de persil frais,
25 g de beurre	finement ciselé
125 g de lard fumé sans couenne	2 cuillerées à soupe de ciboulette fraîche,
sel et poivre noir	ciselée, pour la garniture

Recette

Préchauffez votre four à 200 °C/Th. 7.

Faites cuire les pommes de terre à l'eau bouillante. Une fois cuites, ajoutez le beurre et le lait, et réduisez le tout en purée. Versez celle-ci dans un grand plat de cuisson préalablement graissé.

Versez un tiers de la crème sur les pommes de terre, et parsemez d'oignon à l'aide d'une cuillère.

Disposez les filets de poisson au-dessus. Saupoudrez de chapelure et de fromage. Nappez avec le reste de crème et saupoudrez de paprika.

Enfournez, et laissez cuire 30 minutes.

Ingrédients

6 pommes de terre de taille moyenne

30 g de beurre

5 ou 6 cuillerées à soupe de lait chaud

30 cl de crème

1 petit oignon finement haché

6 filets de maquereau

65 g de chapelure

2 cuillerées à soupe de fromage râpé

paprika en poudre

Filets de maquereau
sur lit de purée

Recette

Confectionnez d'abord la pâte. Mixez la levure, la farine, le sel et le beurre jusqu'à ce que le mélange ressemble à une fine chapelure. Battez les jaunes d'œufs, la crème et l'eau froide dans un petit bol. Puis ajoutez ce mélange à la farine, en actionnant le mixer jusqu'à ce que la pâte forme une boule. Divisez-la pour former quatre disques. Enveloppez-les de film alimentaire, et laissez reposer 24 heures si possible, ou au moins 30 minutes.

Pour préparer la farce, faites revenir le poireau dans l'huile et le beurre. Ajoutez le chou, et laissez cuire jusqu'à ce que les légumes soient tendres. Pendant ce temps, coupez les pommes de terre en dés, faites-les bouillir, puis réduisez-les en purée ; versez celle-ci dans le mélange au poireau, tout en remuant. Salez et poivrez. Ajoutez la noix de muscade et l'aneth. Mélangez intimement.

Pour confectionner les pirojki, abaissez chaque disque de pâte sur 3 mm d'épaisseur, puis découpez des cercles d'environ 8 cm de diamètre. Avec une cuillère à dessert, placez un peu de farce au centre, puis mouillez légèrement les bords. Repliez pour recouvrir complètement la farce, et appuyez pour bien souder. Badigeonnez ensuite les pirojki d'un peu d'œuf battu, ou de lait. Disposez-les sur une plaque huilée ou beurrée, et laissez-les cuire environ 20 à 25 minutes à 190 °C/Th. 6, jusqu'à ce qu'ils soient croustillants et dorés. Vous pouvez aussi les faire frire. Dans ce cas, égouttez-les bien ensuite.

Servez immédiatement avec un peu de crème ou de la sauce aux herbes ou au piment doux (ce n'est pas l'usage en Russie, mais c'est excellent).

Pirojki à la russe

Ingrédients

Pour la pâte :

600 g de farine

4 cuillerées à café de levure

1 pincée de sel

125 g de beurre coupé en dés

2 gros jaunes d'œufs

20 à 40 cl de crème fraîche

1 à 2 cuillerées à soupe d'eau froide

Pour la farce :

1 cuillerée à soupe d'huile d'olive

1 cuillerée à soupe de beurre

1 gros poireau finement haché

3 feuilles de chou finement hachées

2 grosses pommes de terre

sel et poivre, 1 pincée de noix de muscade

1 à 2 cuillerées à soupe d'aneth frais

1 œuf battu ou un peu de lait

crème et sauce aux herbes, ou au piment doux

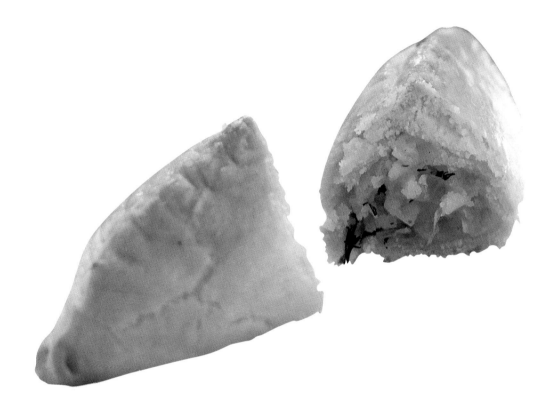

Conseil

Il est possible de congeler les pirojki crus : disposez-les sur une plaque, puis, une fois congelés, glissez-les dans un sac à congélation. Pour les faire cuire, posez-les sur une plaque du four sans les décongeler, et laissez cuire 30 à 35 minutes.

Pour **8 personnes**, en accompagnement

Recette

Pelez et coupez les patates douces en gros morceaux. Arrosez-les avec 2 cuillerées à soupe d'huile d'olive, mélangez bien, puis disposez-les dans un grand plat de cuisson avec les gousses d'ail. Salez et poivrez. Laissez cuire environ 1 heure jusqu'à ce que les patates soient tendres et dorées sur les bords. Retirez-les du four, et gardez-les au chaud.

Mélangez l'oignon et le piment aux herbes fraîches. Ajoutez les patates douces et mélangez intimement.

Battez les 4 cuillerées d'huile d'olive restantes et le vinaigre, puis mélangez le tout avec les patates. Ajoutez les cacahuètes, remuez encore et servez. Assaisonnez à votre goût et décorez avec des brins d'herbes aromatiques.

Ingrédients

2 kg de patates douces pelées
6 cuillerées à soupe d'huile d'olive
20 gousses d'ail en chemise
sel et poivre
1 oignon d'Espagne haché menu

Salade de patates douces
aux cacahuètes

1 à 2 petits piments rouges finement hachés
125 g d'herbes aromatiques fraîches de votre
choix (coriandre, persil, aneth, ciboulette…)
2 cuillerées à soupe de vinaigre balsamique
500 g de cacahuètes grillées
sel et poivre du moulin

Recette

Préchauffez le four à 200 °C/Th. 7. Faites chauffer la moitié de l'huile dans un wok ou une grande poêle à fond épais. Ajoutez les oignons et laissez-les frire 8 à 10 minutes jusqu'à ce qu'ils soient bien dorés.

Disposez un tiers des patates douces dans un plat de cuisson et recouvrez-les avec la moitié des oignons frits. Assaisonnez, puis ajoutez une seconde couche de patates. Couvrez avec le reste d'oignons, assaisonnez, puis ajoutez une dernière couche de patates.

Versez le bouillon. Couvrez le plat avec du papier d'aluminium et laissez cuire 40 à 45 minutes, jusqu'à ce que les patates soient tendres. Ôtez le papier d'aluminium, versez l'huile restante. Augmentez la température du four (230 °C/Th. 8) et laissez cuire encore 8 à 10 minutes jusqu'à ce que le jus se soit en grande partie évaporé, et que les patates soient gratinées.

Patates douces & **oignons au four**

Ingrédients

3 cuillerées à soupe d'huile d'olive

3 oignons coupés en fines rondelles

750 g de patates douces coupées en fines rondelles

sel et poivre noir

15 cl de bouillon de volaille ou de légumes

Recette

Préchauffez le four à 180 °C/Th. 6. Faites cuire les pommes de terre 45 à 60 minutes jusqu'à ce qu'elles soient tendres. Retirez-les du four et laissez-les un peu refroidir.

Coupez leur sommet et creusez-les profondément. Placez leur chair, la purée de tomates et la sauce au piment dans un récipient, et réduisez le tout en purée. Incorporez les haricots tout en remuant, et poivrez à votre goût.

Avec une cuillère, déposez la purée de haricots dans les pommes de terre creusées. Saupoudrez de paprika, et laissez cuire 10 à 15 minutes jusqu'à ce que la purée soit bien cuite et légèrement brune.

Ingrédients

4 pommes de terre

1 cuillerée à soupe de purée de tomates

1 à 2 cuillerées à café de sauce au piment

315 g de haricots rouges en conserve, rincés et égouttés

poivre noir du moulin

paprika

Pommes de terre
aux haricots rouges & au piment

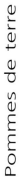

Recette

Faites cuire les patates douces 10 à 15 minutes dans une casserole d'eau bouillante, jusqu'à ce qu'elles soient tendres. Égouttez-les bien, puis réduisez-les en purée.

Faites chauffer le lait dans une casserole. Incorporez-le aux pommes de terre, avec l'ail, le cheddar, le persil, la ciboulette et le poivre noir. Battez la purée jusqu'à ce qu'elle soit bien homogène, puis servez-la chaude, parsemée de ciboulette fraîche.

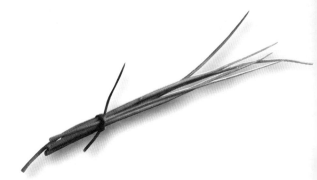

Purée de patates douces

Ingrédients

750 g de patates douces coupées en gros morceaux
3 cuillerées à soupe de lait entier
1 gousse d'ail pilée
40 g de cheddar finement râpé
1 cuillerée à soupe de persil frais, finement ciselé
1 cuillerée à soupe de ciboulette fraîche, ciselée,
et quelques brins pour décorer
poivre noir

Recette

Faites chauffer l'huile dans une grande poêle avant d'y incorporer l'ail, les poireaux et les carottes. Laissez cuire 5 minutes tout en remuant, jusqu'à ce que les poireaux soient tendres. Ajoutez les tomates. Portez à ébullition, puis baissez le feu et laissez mijoter 10 minutes jusqu'à ce que le mélange réduise et épaississe. Incorporez les haricots, sans cesser de remuer, et laissez cuire encore 3 à 4 minutes. Poivrez.

Transvasez ce mélange dans un plat de cuisson préalablement graissé. Nappez, à l'aide d'une douille, de purée de pommes de terre, et parsemez de fromage. Laissez cuire 20 minutes, jusqu'à ce que le dessus soit bien doré.

Ingrédients

1 cuillerée à soupe d'huile
2 gousses d'ail pilées
le blanc de 2 poireaux coupés en fines rondelles
2 grosses carottes coupées en rondelles
440 g de tomates en conserve,
égouttées et réduites en purée

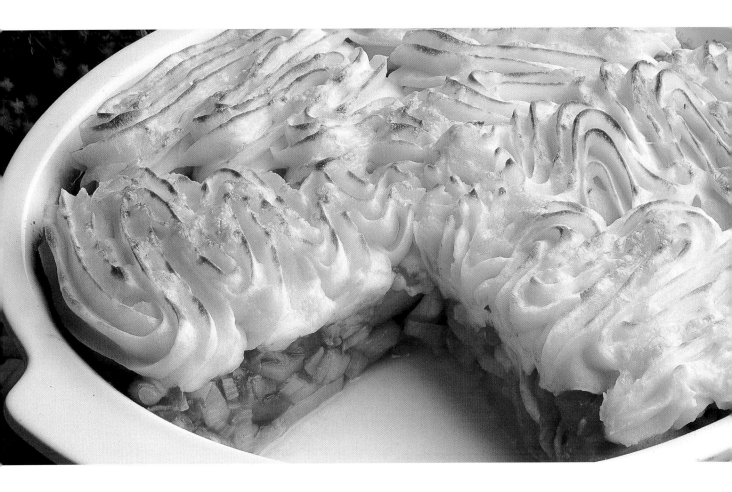

Hachis de haricots

440 g de haricots de Lima
ou de haricots blancs, égouttés
poivre noir du moulin
750 g de pommes de terre,
cuites et réduites en purée
60 g de cheddar râpé

Recette

Préchauffez le four à température modérée. Placez le pain sur une plaque, et laissez-le cuire dans la partie inférieure du four 20 à 30 minutes jusqu'à ce qu'il soit croustillant. Laissez-le refroidir, écrasez-le avec un rouleau à pâtisserie et réservez.

Pendant ce temps, faites cuire les pommes de terre 15 minutes dans une grande casserole d'eau bouillante salée, jusqu'à ce qu'elles soient tendres. Égouttez-les, puis réduisez-les en purée et ajoutez la mayonnaise. Laissez refroidir 30 minutes.

Incorporez ensuite le thon, le persil, la ciboule et le zeste de citron à la purée, en écrasant bien le tout. Farinez vos mains et façonnez huit galettes. Saupoudrez-les de farine, trempez-les dans l'œuf, puis dans la chapelure.

Versez un fond d'huile dans une grande poêle, faites-la chauffer, puis faites cuire les galettes 3 à 4 minutes sur chaque côté, jusqu'à ce qu'elles soient croustillantes et dorées. Égouttez-les sur du papier absorbant, puis servez avec des quartiers de citron, si vous le souhaitez.

Galettes au thon,
aux pommes de terre & aux ciboules

Ingrédients

4 tranches de mie de pain	2 ciboules finement hachées
700 g de pommes de terre coupées en 2 ou en 4, suivant leur taille	le zeste finement râpé d'1 demi-citron
3 cuillerées à soupe de mayonnaise	3 cuillerées à soupe de farine
400 g de thon à l'huile en boîte, égoutté	1 œuf moyen, battu
1 cuillerée à soupe de persil frais, finement ciselé	huile pour friture
	1 citron coupé en quartiers pour décorer

Pommes de terre

Recette

Râpez les pommes de terre à la main, ou à l'aide d'un robot ménager. Placez-les ensuite dans une passoire, salez, puis mélangez bien le tout. Laissez reposer 20 minutes. Pressez pour extraire le maximum de liquide, et mélangez les pommes de terre avec la Maïzena, dans un bol.

Battez légèrement l'œuf. Ajoutez-le aux pommes de terre avec le reste des ingrédients (sauf l'huile). Mélangez intimement. Faites chauffer l'huile dans une grande poêle à fond épais. Prélevez l'équivalent d'1 cuillerée à soupe du mélange aux pommes de terre, versez-la dans la poêle. Faites frire ainsi plusieurs beignets à la fois. Ils doivent faire environ 6 cm de diamètre.

Laissez-les frire environ 4 minutes jusqu'à ce qu'ils soient dorés, puis retournez-les. Une fois qu'ils sont bien croustillants, égouttez-les sur du papier absorbant. Servez-les chauds avec de la sauce au poisson, ou en guise d'accompagnement.

Ingrédients

2 grosses pommes de terre
1 pincée de sel
50 g de Maïzena
1 gros œuf
3 ciboules hachées
1 petit oignon finement haché

Beignets **vietnamiens**

Conseil

Vous pouvez aussi utiliser des patates douces,

ou du taro.

3 gousses d'ail finement hachées

2 cuillerées à café de sauce au poisson

2 cuillerées à café de curry en poudre

poivre noir moulu

15 cl d'huile

Recette

Coupez les pommes de terre non pelées en gros morceaux. Faites-les bouillir 10 minutes dans de l'eau salée jusqu'à ce qu'elles soient tendres, mais fermes. Égouttez-les, puis replacez-les au chaud dans la casserole.

Dans une poêle, faites chauffer l'huile d'olive, et faites revenir les oignons environ 8 minutes, jusqu'à ce qu'ils soient bien dorés. Baissez le feu, couvrez, puis laissez cuire 20 minutes. Dans un bol, battez l'huile d'olive, le vinaigre, le jus de citron et l'ail jusqu'à ce que la vinaigrette épaississe. Nappez-en les pommes de terre, et remuez, en ajoutant toutes les herbes aromatiques, le zeste de citron, du sel et du poivre noir selon votre goût.

Ajoutez enfin les oignons et mélangez délicatement le tout.

Salade de pommes de terre chaudes
aux herbes

Ingrédients

1,5 kg de pommes de terre

2 cuillerées à soupe d'huile d'olive

4 oignons blancs pelés et émincés

50 g d'aneth frais finement ciselé

50 g de cerfeuil frais finement ciselé

50 g de persil frais finement ciselé

le zeste d'1 citron

sel et poivre du moulin

Pour la vinaigrette :

15 cl d'huile d'olive

3 cuillerées à soupe de vinaigre de vin blanc

le jus d'1 citron

3 gousses d'ail

Pommes de terre

Recette

Épluchez les patates douces et la courge. Réservez 200 g de chaque et tranchez-les. Hachez le reste et placez-le dans une casserole et couvrez d'eau. Portez à ébullition, puis laissez mijoter 30 minutes jusqu'à ce que les légumes soient tendres.

Égouttez-les, réduisez-les en purée, et réservez. Dans une cocotte, faites chauffer l'huile d'olive, puis ajoutez l'oignon, la carotte, le céleri, l'ail, la pâte de curry, ainsi que les tranches de potiron et de patates douces et de courge. Faites sauter environ 10 minutes jusqu'à ce que l'oignon soit tendre.

Ajoutez le riz et mélangez afin qu'il soit bien imprégné. Ajoutez le vin. Laissez cuire jusqu'à ce que le jus de cuisson soit complètement absorbé. Ajoutez les feuilles de laurier, la purée de patates et de courge réservée, et une partie du bouillon. Remuez énergiquement jusqu'à ce que tout le liquide soit absorbé, puis ajoutez à nouveau un peu de bouillon. Continuez ainsi jusqu'à ce que tout le bouillon ait été utilisé, puis retirez la casserole du feu.

Battez la crème et les épices au fouet, dans un petit bol. Ôtez les feuilles de laurier de la préparation au riz, et servez le risotto dans des bols. Garnissez d'une bonne cuillerée de crème aux épices, et d'un peu de ciboulette.

Ingrédients

1 kg de patates douces

500 g de courge butternut, ou 1 belle part de potiron

2 cuillerées à soupe d'huile d'olive

2 oignons hachés

1 carotte hachée

2 côtes de céleri hachées

2 gousses d'ail pilées

1 cuillerée à café de pâte de curry verte

400 g de riz sauvage

Riz créole aux patates douces
& à la crème épicée

20 cl de vin blanc

80 cl de bouillon de volaille

2 feuilles de laurier

150 g de crème épaisse

1 pincée de cannelle

1 pincée de coriandre en poudre

1 pincée de cumin en poudre

½ botte de ciboulette finement ciselée

Pommes de terre

Recette

Disposez les pommes de terre dans une grande casserole d'eau bouillante, puis couvrez et laissez mijoter 5 minutes jusqu'à ce qu'elles soient tendres. Égouttez-les et réservez.

Pendant ce temps, placez le poulet dans un saladier avec l'oignon, le curry en poudre et 1 cuillerée à soupe d'huile d'olive. Mélangez bien et réservez. Répartissez les feuilles de salade sur quatre assiettes et couvrez-les de lanières de poivron et de concombre.

Mélangez la mayonnaise, le jus de citron et le piment. Assaisonnez et réservez. Faites chauffer le reste d'huile dans une grande poêle, et faites revenir le poulet 10 minutes, en remuant de temps à autre jusqu'à ce qu'il soit tendre et bien cuit.

Ajoutez les pommes de terre et laissez cuire 5 minutes, en remuant fréquemment, jusqu'à ce que les deux ingrédients soient légèrement dorés. Disposez le tout sur les assiettes de salade au poivron et au concombre, et nappez d'assaisonnement à la mayonnaise.

Poulet au curry
& salade de pommes de terre

Ingrédients

450 g de pommes de terre
coupées en petits morceaux de 1 cm
3 blancs de poulet coupés en lanières de 1 cm
1 oignon rouge finement haché
2 cuillerées à soupe de curry doux en poudre
2 cuillerées à soupe d'huile
400 g de salade mélangée
1 poivron jaune épépiné, coupé en lanières
1 concombre, coupé en lanières

Pour l'assaisonnement :
6 cuillerées à soupe de mayonnaise
le jus d'1 demi-citron
1 petit piment vert épépiné, finement haché
poivre noir

Recette

Placez la purée dans un récipient. Ajoutez les œufs, le lait, la crème et le beurre, et mélangez intimement.

Incorporez la farine et la ciboule à la purée, et mélangez bien le tout. À l'aide d'une cuillère, versez le mélange dans des moules à muffins, et laissez cuire 25 à 30 minutes à 180 °C/Th. 6. En les piquant avec un couteau, vérifiez que les muffins sont cuits : la lame doit ressortir bien propre.

Servez tiède ou froid.

Muffins aux pommes de terre
& à la crème

Ingrédients

250 g de pommes de terre en purée

2 œufs légèrement battus

25 cl de lait

20 cl de crème fraîche

60 g de beurre fondu

320 g de farine tamisée

3 cuillerées à soupe de ciboule fraîche, ciselée

Pommes de terre

95

Index